The Challenges of Modernity to the Orthodox Church
in Estonia and Latvia (1917-1940)

ERFURTER STUDIEN ZUR KULTURGESCHICHTE DES ORTHODOXEN CHRISTENTUMS

Herausgegeben von Vasilios N. Makrides

Band 6

PETER LANG

Frankfurt am Main · Berlin · Bern · Bruxelles · New York · Oxford · Wien

Sebastian Rimestad

The Challenges of Modernity to the Orthodox Church in Estonia and Latvia (1917-1940)

PETER LANG
Internationaler Verlag der Wissenschaften

Bibliographic Information published by the Deutsche Nationalbibliothek
The Deutsche Nationalbibliothek lists this publication in the Deutsche Nationalbibliografie; detailed bibliographic data is available in the internet at http://dnb.d-nb.de.

Zugl.: Erfurt, Univ., Diss., 2011

Cover Design:
© Olaf Gloeckler, Atelier Platen, Friedberg

Cover Illustration:
Fiftieth Anniversary of the Ascension
Parish of Riga, 1929. Sitting in the middle
is Archbishop Jānis (Pommers),
left of him, Archpriest Kirils Zaics,
and on the far right, Archpriest Jānis Jansons.
© Jānis Kalniņš, private archive

547
ISSN 1612-152X
ISBN 978-3-631-62437-1
© Peter Lang GmbH
Internationaler Verlag der Wissenschaften
Frankfurt am Main 2012
All rights reserved.

www.peterlang.de

Table of Contents

Preface

This book, which is a slightly modified version of my PhD dissertation at the University of Erfurt, came about as a result of the attempt to combine three of my main interests. Ever since adolescence, I have had a vivid interest in the Baltic states, languages, and societies. During my undergraduate studies, I developed an interest in the Christian tradition of Eastern Europe; the Orthodox Church. My third interest encompasses various theories and conceptions of modernity and the modern condition. The present work thus attempts to assess the impact of the modern condition on the Orthodox Church in Estonia and Latvia.

My master's thesis considered Orthodox Christianity as a factor in the rise of Estonian national consciousness. My thesis ended at the beginning of Estonian independence after the First World War, because the entire context of Estonian society changed. Instead of acting as the local part of the state-sanctioned Orthodox Church, the Estonian Orthodox leadership had to readjust to a minority status in a secular state. The present study scrutinises the subsequent period. It begins with the Russian revolution in 1917, which opened up the possibility of independent existence for the local Orthodox Church, and ends with the first Soviet occupation of the Baltic States in 1940, when the Moscow Patriarchate forcefully reintegrated the 'schismatics.' I extended the scope beyond Estonia to include its southern neighbour Latvia, since there were similar developments and struggles in these two Baltic States.

I would like to thank all those who have helped me over the last five years to the completion of my dissertation. Firstly, the *Interdisziplinäres Forum Religion* of the University of Erfurt deserves great thanks for its funding over most of this time period. Also the *Graduiertenschule "Religion in Modernisierungsprozessen"* (University of Erfurt) and the *SOCRATES Teacher Mobility programme* of the European Union have helped fund several of my research stays in the Baltic States. However, funding without supervision is not really enough, and I would like to thank my supervisor, Prof. Dr. Vasilios Makrides, as well as all the other academic staff at the University of Erfurt, with whom I have had the pleasure of discussing aspects of my dissertation. Furthermore, the staff of the numerous libraries I have visited in Erfurt, Jena, Göttingen, Würzburg, Erlangen, Marburg, Lüneburg, Riga, Tartu, Tallinn, and Helsinki have also greatly helped me arrive at this point. Individual scholars, such as Archimandrite Grigorios Papathomas, Dr. Andrei Sõtsov, Dr. Inese Runce, Prof. Dr. Aleksandr Gavrilin, Prof. Dr. Karsten Brüggemann, Dr. Bradley Woodworth, Toomas Schvak, and a host of others, equally deserve thanks not only for their guidance and nice company, but also for the opportunities they have given me to improve my language skills. Special thanks go to Archpriest Jānis Kalniņš, who kindly provided an illustration for the front cover from his private archive and Demetria Worley, who thoroughly proofread the manuscript of the book. It would not have had the same clarity and style without her. The errors, omissions, and stylistic discrepancies that remain are entirely mine. Last but not least, my lovely wife Claudia and our two sons, Christian and Simon, both of which were born while I was working on this dissertation are responsible for innumerable unforgettable moments and for pushing me to finish this text in the end.

Notes on Terminology

In the northern Baltic Region, numerous languages were in use over the twentieth century. While most of the nobility were Baltic Germans, who communicated predominantly in German, the political leadership of the region until 1917, and then again from 1940/1944, was Russian-speaking. The local population consisted of Estonians and Latvians, who preferred to speak and write in Estonian and Latvian. When the Soviet Union occupied the two states in 1940, many Estonians and Latvians emigrated, predominantly to Finland, Sweden, Germany, and the Anglophone World, where they published partly in the local languages. Finally, many sources pertaining to diplomatic affairs and to the affairs of the Ecumenical Patriarchate of Constantinople are written in French.

In this study, all these languages are cited only in English translation for the sake of convenience. All the translations are my own, except where otherwise stated. In some cases, where translations between different languages give room for interpretation, this is noted. This is especially the case with the different forms of the designation 'Orthodox' in the various languages. The Estonian 'õigeusk' and the Latvian 'pareizticība' are direct translations from the German 'rechtgläubig' – 'of the correct faith.' To what extent the use of other synonyms, such as 'Orthodox' or 'Greek Catholic'[1] reflects a conscious decision on the part of the authors is often difficult to ascertain. Therefore, I am certain that a number of ambiguous formulations have escaped my attention and could have been mentioned. However, it is not my aim to do a linguistic analysis, but to analyse the discourse surrounding Orthodoxy in the two countries. For example, I call the administrative entity of a bishop an *Eparchy*, regardless of the distinct terms that exist in the various languages.

Both Estonian and Latvian underwent creeping orthographic reforms in the 1920s and 1930s. Although this has no impact on the citations in this book, it means that the place names in the region as well as personal names are differently written in different sources. Moreover, the place names in the region usually have at least three names – a German one, a Russian one, and a local Estonian or Latvian one. This plethora of names is sometimes important in the course of the dissertation, but usually I use the place names current today, occasionally noting the varieties of that name. Moreover, I use the modern Estonian or Latvian spelling of personal names, except for ethnic Russians who never published in these languages. Thus, what in English would be Bishop John appears in five forms in this thesis: the Latvian *Jānis* is the same as the Estonian

---

1 'Ortodoksne' and 'kreeka-katolik' in Estonian and 'ortodoksu' and 'grieķu-katoļi' in Latvian.

Joann and the Russian *Ioann*, transliterated using the standard German system. One article about Bishop Joann, moreover, used the German form *Johannes* and another one the Polish form *Iwan*. A similar problem occurs with some names with inconsistent spelling. I have tried to remain consistent in the text. I have moreover tried to keep ethnic Latvian names orthographically Latvian (with an -s at the end) and ethnic Russian ones transliterated.

Several words remain in the original languages throughout the thesis. These include the Estonian *täiskogu* and *Riigikogu* and the Latvian *saeima*. The *Riigikogu* and the *Saeima* (with a capital S) are the Estonian and Latvian parliaments, respectively. A *täiskogu* or an ecclesiastic *saeima* is a delegates' meeting, the highest administrative structure in the two Orthodox Churches, as is the *sobor* of the Russian Orthodox Church, which will also remain in the original.

Introduction

This work analyses the struggle of a specific section of the Estonian and Latvian nations, Orthodox Christians, to come to grips with modernity in the early twentieth century. After the end of the Russian Empire in 1917, the newly independent nation states were exposed to a very different kind of nationalisation than before. Instead of the imperial attempts to bind all citizens to the Russian State and its autocratic ruler, each of the new governments had to devise a way of channelling national sentiment to a new entity. Moreover, while the Russian Empire had kept strict regulations on confessional affiliation, independent Estonia and Latvia held a secular outlook and left faith to the churches and religious groups. The former Orthodox Church of the Russian Empire could not neatly fit into the new nation-state ideologies. The new national elite wanted to retain as few links as possible to the former 'oppressors,' as the Russians were henceforth officially called, and Orthodox Christianity was often considered a sign of Russianness.

Thus, the Orthodox faithful were doubly challenged. They could no longer count on the support of a powerful state church but had to construct an identity as a minority group. At the same time, they had to defend this new identity in a hostile political and social environment. This was not easy, since the canonical head of the Orthodox Church in Latvia and Estonia remained the Patriarch of Moscow, and most of the Russian minority in both countries was part of the local Orthodox community. The national movements, which had begun in the middle of the nineteenth century, could only take full effect in an independent state, with an institutionalised national history, language, and political culture. For most Latvians and Estonians, Orthodox Christianity was not, and could not be, an integral part of these efforts. In short, this work analyses the discourse on Orthodox Christianity as it related to the Estonian and Latvian nation building processes in the 1920s and 1930s. The analysis is based on published opinions or works on Latvian and Estonian Orthodoxy of the period from 1917 to 1940 and thus provides a variegated array of voices, which all contribute to a picture of the situation of Orthodox Estonians and Latvians between the World Wars.

The study forms part of the relatively recent research field of 'Orthodox Studies.' Similar to the various 'Area Studies' that have arisen as interdisciplinary research fields enjoying increasing popularity in academic institutions, also 'Orthodox Studies' pursue an interdisciplinary approach, endeavouring to analyse Orthodox Christian societies and issues from multiple angles. For the purpose of this particular study, insights from religious studies, political science, sociology, history, communications studies, and theology are combined to paint a comprehensive picture of the situation of Orthodox Estonians and Latvians in the interwar period. The entire study is informed by the assumption that the published word conveys an accurate depiction of the social and political context in which it appeared. Therefore, its main sources are the various Orthodox journals published in Estonia and Latvia, together with a number of other published references to the Orthodox Church in the Estonian and Latvian press. On the basis of this source material, the empirical parts analyse the way Orthodox Christianity was perceived in Estonian and Latvian society and how Orthodox Estonians and Latvians reconciled conflicting identities. Various theoretical approaches from different disciplines each form the backbone of a particular section in the empirical study and are, therefore, more thoroughly introduced as they become relevant.

A study on the Orthodox Church in interwar Estonia and Latvia is necessary, for there are, in my opinion, no unbiased and historically sound treatments of the developments in either Estonia or Latvia available.[1] All existing studies lack important developments and/or include clear errors. Interestingly, the interwar years of the other Orthodox Churches in the Baltic region have received extensive academic treatment. In the case of the Orthodox Church in Lithuania, two academically ambitious publications have recently appeared, covering the inner and outer life of this church.[2] Also the case of Poland has been extensively researched and covered in academic literature.[3] Numerous academic treatments concerning the Orthodox Church in the northern neighbour, Finland, have been published over the years.[4] Only the Latvian and Estonian cases have not been well researched. What research exists on these two cases, moreover, is not very objective.

The first comprehensive treatments of the Orthodox Church in the Baltic States appeared during the interwar period. In Latvia, the historian Antonijs Pommers, the brother of the first Latvian Bishop Jānis (Pommers), published a 'History of Latvian Orthodoxy' in 1931.[5] This historical sketch of 88 pages starts with the first (not very well documented) beginnings of the Church in the Middle Ages and only the last ten pages are devoted to the interwar period. Moreover, these last pages are heavily tainted by the author's personal involvement in the Latvian Orthodox Church. No similar monograph appeared in Estonia, although at least two Estonian historians devoted much attention to

---

1   Toomas Schvak is currently working on a PhD on the Estonian Interwar Orthodox Church, which might bridge this gap in the Estonian case.
2   Laukaitytė, 2003; Marcinkevicius and Kaubrys, 2005.
3   Papierzyńska-Turek, 1989; Mironowicz, 2005; Mironowicz et al., 2005.
4   Heyer, 1958; Setälä, U.V.J., 1966; Pispala, 1978; Hotz, 1979; Koukkunen, 1982; Purmonen, 1984; John, 1988; Frilander, 1995; Frilander, 1997; Raivo, 1997; Riikonen, 2007; Nokelainen, 2010.
5   Pommers, 1931a. See also chapter 4.1.3.

the conversion movements of the nineteenth century.[6] The Estonians, however, invited European scholars to the Petseri Monastery in 1937 to become acquainted with the Estonian Orthodox Church. One of these scholars was Helmut Risch, who later published a comprehensive 30-page overview in a German journal of church history.[7] This article provides surprisingly unbiased and detailed insights into the inner workings of the Estonian Orthodox Church from a perspective informed by political science. A similar article on the Latvian Orthodox Church from 1940 was much shorter and not the result of field research.[8] It mainly repeats the developments mentioned by Pommers in the afore-mentioned historical overview and brings no new information.

After the Second World War, there was no significant publication concerning the Baltic Orthodox Churches until the 1950s, when the Latvian and Estonian emigrant communities began publishing. Here, the Estonians were clearly more active, publishing three books and one article on the Estonian Orthodox Church before 1966.[9] These works consist mainly of memories from a peaceful past and injustices suffered during the Soviet occupation. On the Latvian side, only one article concerning the Latvian Orthodox Church appeared in 1954,[10] until the administrator of the Latvian Orthodox Church in Exile, Alexander Cherney, published an overview book in London in 1985.[11] This work is written with the injustices suffered by the Orthodox Church in the Baltic Region clearly in mind and brings historical details only in order to justify its argument. The other treatments from the émigré community were apologetic in nature. Their authors glorified the independence period and condemned the Soviet takeover.

The Baltic German community in exile also started to publish in the 1950s. Its output included an edited volume on Baltic church history.[12] There are passing references to the Orthodox Churches in the volume, and it relishes memories of a glorious past, when the Baltic Germans and the Lutheran Church were the unchallenged masters of the Baltic Provinces. Only three contributions were devoted to the interwar period and they cover mostly developments within the German minority.

Next to such self-interested treatises, several academics in the West showed an interest in the Orthodox Church of the Baltic Region. The German Wilhelm

---

6   Kruus, 1930; Rebane, 1932; Rebane, 1933. See also chapters 2.1.2. and 4.1.4.
7   Risch, 1937; "Igaunijas Pečoru klosterī Eiropas zinatnieki izdara pētīšanas darbus" [European researchers carried out research work in the Estonian Petseri Monastery] in *TuD*, 13/16, 1937, p. 256. See also chapter 4.2.1.
8   Schubart, 1940.
9   *Apostlik õigeusk*, 1951; Fridolin, 1953; Juhkam, 1961; Laatsi, 1966.
10 Starcs, 1954.
11 Cherney, 1985. In the 1990s, this book was translated and published in Latvian.
12 Wittram, Reinhard, 1956.

Kahle, after having spent a year in Estonia in 1938, wrote a monumental work on the relationship between Orthodoxy and Lutheranism in the Baltic Area, which was published in 1959.[13] However, his focus on *Russian* Orthodoxy and *Baltic German* Lutheranism disregarded the developments of national churches. After noting that the interaction suddenly dwindled following the First World War, he concludes that "the direct relationship between Russian Orthodoxy and Baltic Protestantism ended with the *Umsiedlung* of 1939."[14] A second Western scholar, the Finnish political scientist U.V.J. Setälä wrote his doctoral dissertation on the Finnish State's relations with the Orthodox Church 1917-1923. It contains numerous references to developments in Estonia, which are further elaborated in separate articles by the same scholar.[15] In the USA, Wassilij Alexeev wrote his doctoral thesis and several articles on the Baltic Orthodox Church under German occupation during the Second World War.[16] In Germany, there appeared an article on the so-called 'mission of Pskov' during the occupation.[17] However, since the developments before and after 1940 differ so immensely, these works on the German occupation hardly provide any new insights into the interwar period. The treatment of '*Religion in the Soviet Union*' by Walter Kolarz deserves mention, because it includes short historical sketches of almost all religious communities in the entire Soviet Union, including the Orthodox Churches in the Baltic region.[18]

Within the Soviet Union, there were no significant academic works concerning the Estonian Orthodox Church.[19] In Latvia, on the other hand, the Marxist historian Zigmunds Balevics devoted much attention to church issues in the interwar period. However, his Soviet schooling and communist theory makes his works difficult to use as unbiased sources. His 1962 book on '*The Orthodox Clergy in Bourgeois Latvia*' was written in order to "help the believers judge the falseness and two-sidedness of religious morality for themselves."[20] His 1964 assessment of the relationship between church and state in bourgeois Latvia is interspersed with references to communist theory and refers to the churches as

---

13 Kahle, 1959.
14 Kahle, 1959, p. 279. For the *Umsiedlung*, see also von Hehn, 1984; chapter 2.3.4.
15 Setälä, U.V.J., 1962; Setälä, U.V.J., 1966; Setälä, U.V.J., 1972.
16 Alexeev, 1957; Alexeev, 1974; Alexeev and Stavrou, 1976..
17 Treulieb, 1965. This mission, organised by Moscow-subordinate Metropolitan Sergej Voskresenskij of Vilnius, consisted in sending missionaries from the Baltic area to the Soviet regions occupied by German forces to re-Christianise the Russians. It was very successful. See Oboznyj, 2008.
18 Kolarz, 1962, p. 118-123.
19 Excepting the doctoral dissertation of the Metropolitan of Tallinn, later Patriarch of Moscow Aleksij II (Ridiger), which he completed in 1984. It was, however, published only in 1999, after serious revision. Aleksij, 1999, p. 6-7.
20 Balevics and Kadiķis, 1962, p. 3.

nothing but puppets in the hands of the fascists in government.[21] His small 1987 overview book on the history of the Latvian Orthodox Church is less ideologically tainted, but remains less than credible at times. Its designated task was "to gather existing research and provide the reader with an overview of the history of the Orthodox Church in Latvia."[22] However, this work does not represent a change of style, as significant parts are taken directly from the 1964 book. Nonetheless, Balevics had access to the original sources and his treatments are historically valuable.

Meanwhile, in a little volume from 1984, dedicated to Latvian Agrarian History, two other Soviet Latvian historians showed interest in the Orthodox Church. Heinrihs Strods and Aleksandr Gavrilin both contributed articles on the Orthodox Church in the nineteenth century.[23] In the years leading up to the collapse of the Soviet Union, Aleksandr Gavrilin published several articles on Latvian Orthodox Church in the nineteenth century, and he has continued his publishing activity in the post-Soviet period.[24] The work of Gavrilin cannot be overrated, especially when it comes to extrapolating the original sources of the nineteenth century history of Baltic Orthodoxy. However, he remains somewhat caught within the traditional discourse of Orthodox Church history, which is mostly concerned with the number of faithful, of churches and monasteries, and who heads what Eparchy when. This becomes obvious in a contribution to a recent French volume on the Orthodox Church in Eastern Europe during the twentieth century.[25] The section on the interwar period is lacking in analytical detail. It seems more important to mention numbers and names than to put them in historical context. Gavrilin's most recent monograph, dedicated to the life and work of the Latvian Bishop Jānis Garklāvs moves slightly away from this tendency, turning more to the discourses of and long-term developments within Latvian Orthodoxy.[26] The nine volumes of 'Orthodoxy in Latvia' edited by Gavrilin between 1993 and 2010 contain a number of interesting contributions. The largely statistical treatment of the 1920s by K. Ozoliņš and the analysis of the autocephaly discussions of the 1930s by Andris Kūla merit special mention.[27] The latter has also published an extensive article on the situation of the Latvian Orthodox Church during the Second World War.[28]

---

21 Balevics, 1964.
22 Balevics, 1987, p. 3-4.
23 Strods, 1984; Gavrilin, 1984.
24 See all his works in the bibliography.
25 Gavrilin and Pazāne, 2009.
26 Garklāvs was consecrated Bishop of Riga under the jurisdiction of the Moscow Patriarchate during the German occupation in 1943. Gavrilin, 2009, p. 176.
27 Kulis, 1993; Ozoliņš, 1997.
28 Kūla, 2007.

Other post-Soviet Latvian academic treatments include the works of Arch-priest Jānis Kalniņš, who has published a source compendium on Archbishop Jānis (Pommers),[29] a biography of the Archbishop,[30] and a historical commentary on the Orthodox Church of Latvia.[31] While the source compendium is very useful and the biography of Bishop Jānis contains much important information, the historical commentary does not stand up to scrutiny. It is clearly written as a polemic against some particular interpretation of history, although it is not entirely clear which interpretation.[32] As an appendix to the second edition of Kalniņš' autobiography from 2005, several archival documents and parish histories also exist in published form.[33]

Another biography of Bishop Jānis from 2004 does not contain any new information and the way it exalts Jānis' achievements beyond measure reminds the reader of medieval hagiographies.[34] Heinrihs Strods has published an important biographical volume on Metropolitan Augustīns (Pētersons), who headed the Latvian Orthodox Church from 1936 to his death in 1955.[35] This work is detailed and analytical; however, critics claim that since it was paid for by the family of Metropolitan Augustīns, it lacks some critical distance and independence.[36] Jurij Sidjakov has published numerous letters and documents from Archbishop Jānis' archive, which have proved very useful for this study.[37] The official view of history – as presented in a recent volume on Post-Soviet developments in the Latvian Orthodox Church – is less useful, with sweeping generalisations and a pro-Russian bias.[38] Finally, the 2008 dissertation of Inese Runce on the Latvian church-state relationship 1906-1940 must be mentioned.[39] This work has given me a thorough understanding of the legal and political framework in which religions operated in interwar Latvia.

The Estonian Orthodox Church has received much attention in the academic world, especially since the clash between the Patriarchates of Moscow and Constantinople over the jurisdiction of Estonian territory.[40] However, most of this attention has been very biased and one-sided. As the most comprehensive vol-

---

29   Kalniņš I, 1993; Kalniņš II, 1993.
30   Kalniņš, Jānis, 2001.
31   Kalniņš, Jānis, 2007.
32   See the review by Strods, 2008.
33   Kalniņš, Jānis, 2005a.
34   Požidaev, 2004. See also Žitie, 2008.
35   Strods, 2005.
36   See the review by Kalniņš, Jānis, 2005b.
37   Sidjakov I, 2008; Sidjakov II, 2009; Sidjakov III, 2011. Much of Sidjakov's work is also published on the internet.
38   *Latvijas Pareizticīgā Baznīca*, 2009.
39   Runce, 2008.
40   See Rimestad, *forthcoming*, 2013a; Rimestad, *forthcoming*, 2013b.

ume of this genre, the monumental monograph on '*The Orthodox in Estonia*' by late Moscow Patriarch Aleksij II, himself born and raised in interwar Estonia, should be mentioned.[41] However, it remains more concerned with names and numbers than with context and analysis. On the other side, there are the works written under the auspices of Archimandrite Grigorios Papathomas, an Orthodox canon law specialist, who has taken an interest in the fate of Estonian Orthodoxy.[42] These works are clearly apologetic; they do everything possible in order to exclude certain interpretations of the history of the Estonian Orthodox Church. Corresponding works from the side of the Moscow Patriarchate display similar flaws.[43]

At the same time, a number of more neutral young academics have written on the Estonian Orthodox Church, including Andrei Sõtšov, who wrote his BA thesis on the Church during the Second World War, continued with its history under Stalin (1945-1953) in his MA thesis, and dedicated his PhD dissertation to the Khrushchev era (1954-1964).[44] Anu Raudsepp wrote a useful MA thesis on the influence of the Riga Orthodox Seminary on Estonian society, and Urmas Klaas wrote on the structure of the Orthodox Church in South Estonia until 1917, both in 1998.[45] Toomas Schvak is currently writing his PhD dissertation on the Estonian Orthodox Church history of the interwar period. The Lutheran church historian Riho Saard has devoted some effort to the Orthodox Church. In 2008, for example, he published an historical sketch of the first years of the Estonian Orthodox Church after the First World War.[46]

With only a few exceptions, most of the above-mentioned works were written in Estonian, Latvian, or Russian. Moreover, they are either concerned only with historical data or are trying to justify a certain view of history. In addition, many are written in a traditional church history style, detailing which bishop collected how much money for the construction of which church. Very few concern the inner life of the Estonian and Latvian Orthodox Churches beyond the legal, canonical, and statistical frameworks. Notable exceptions are the numerous treatments of the Second World War as well as the works of individual authors.[47] The most important exception is Jeffers Engelhardt, an American who

---

41 Aleksij, 1999. A shortened version of the thesis, extended until the present, was published in 2010 together with over 200 reproduced documents. However, this book is not for sale on the free market. *Pravoslavie,* 2010.
42 Papathomas and Palli, 2002; *Istina,* 2004; Kala, 2007.
43 Prekup, 1998.
44 See all his works in the bibliography.
45 Raudsepp, 1998a; Klaas, 1998. Raudsepp also published a short version of her thesis in German as Raudsepp, 1998b.
46 Saard, 2008.
47 Especially Riho Saard and Mikko Ketola. See their works in the bibliography.

became interested in Estonian Orthodoxy and wrote a dissertation at the University of Chicago in 2005 on the musical practices of the Estonian Orthodox Church.[48]

I conceptualise my book as a contribution at three different levels to these largely divergent strains of research on the Orthodox Church in Estonia and Latvia. On the descriptive level, I attempt to provide a comprehensive treatment of the development of this little known part of the Orthodox Church in a Western language. Second, I evaluate the various existing, seemingly incompatible, narratives of this development. Third, I attempt a genuine analysis of the discourse surrounding Orthodox Christianity in interwar Estonia and Latvia, something that is completely missing from the existing treatments.

This is accomplished in four main parts. The first part considers general questions concerning the notoriously elusive concept of modernity and, more specifically, Orthodox Christianity coming to terms with modern changes. The three remaining parts each look into a specific challenge of modernity, as defined in the beginning of the first part. The second, and most substantial, part analyses the way the Orthodox Churches of Estonia and Latvia severed the link to the Russian Empire that made them inferior in the eyes of many national activists and the opposition they faced in doing so. It consists of a concise historical outline of the development of the Orthodox Church in Estonia and Latvia from 1917 to 1940 in conjunction with an analysis of the discussions within each of the communities concerning the inner and outer structure of the Church, following a largely chronological order. It asks how the modernising political setting of the new nation states of Estonia and Latvia challenged the organisation of the Orthodox Church. Which power struggles concerning church structures and organisation occurred within the Orthodox Church or between the Church and the secular authorities? How did Orthodox elites try to mobilise their constituencies to adjust to the new context?

This last question connects parts two and three. However, part three does not address organisational adjustment but rather concerns all kinds of non-structural issues. Once the structures of the Church had been reformed to emancipate the local Orthodox Church from Russian leadership, Orthodox Estonians and Latvians began to adapt the activities and service of the Church. They widely discussed issues such as congregational singing and the Church calendar and argued that the language and liturgy of the Church should become more 'indigenous.' At the same time as Orthodox Latvians and Estonians worked to create a more modern Orthodox Church, they were often perceived by the predominantly Lutheran society as remainders of the Russian Empire, as less developed, as less devoted Estonians and Latvians. Of importance here is how the Orthodox press

---

48 Engelhardt, 2005.

reacted to such accusations and attempted to change the conception of normality.

Part four analyses the accusation that the dominant national historiography did not adequately distance itself from the biased historical accounts of previous periods when it came to the Orthodox Church. Baltic German platitudes concerning the arrival of Orthodox Christianity to the Baltic shores were perpetuated in history schoolbooks and professional historiography. The part answers the question of which arguments Orthodox spokesmen used to justify their views and how they attempted to transform the historical conception of the overall population.

A final section sums up the findings and arrives at a general conclusion. There are four appendixes (chapter 6.), including maps of Estonia and Latvia, both before and after 1917 (chapter 6.1.) and a timeline listing the most important developments in the two churches (chapter 6.2.). A paradigmatic speech, held by Archbishop Jānis (Pommers) of Riga in 1923 is reproduced as chapter 6.3., and chapter 6.4. lists the most important actors with brief biographies.

1. Modernity and Orthodox Christianity

This first part considers general issues that ought to be clarified before turning to the discourse on Orthodox Christianity in the specific cases of interwar Estonia and Latvia. It will do so in three main steps. First, a chapter is devoted to my understanding of the concept of modernity and the challenges it poses, especially to the Orthodox Church in interwar Estonia and Latvia. The second chapter then considers the way Orthodox Christianity in general and the Russian Orthodox Church in particular have been perceived to encounter modernity. Finally, the third chapter involves a closer look at discourse analysis and the mass media, which form the source basis of the study. This chapter also includes an historical sketch of the Orthodox press history in Latvia and Estonia, a history full of mudslinging and intrigues.

1.1. Modernity

Since the height of the post-modernity-debate in the social sciences of the late 1980s, the characterisations of the term 'modernity' abound in an amazing number. To attempt an overview is a dead end. This chapter, therefore, only sketches out my understanding of the concept of modernity without going into details of the history of the concept. My understanding is based on the assumption that modernity should not be understood as a historical epoch but rather, as "a complex set of interpretive practices."[1] The concept does not refer to any objectively identifiable type of society or social construct, but rather to internalised and abstract interpretive practices, in other words, the way one relates to the world.[2] Instead of conceptualising modernisation as a process with a teleological endpoint, as has often been the case, especially in Anglo-Saxon social theory,[3] modernisation implies coming to terms with the mental configurations of modernity.

These mental configurations are threefold. First, there is the exclusive emphasis on rationality as the way to knowledge. Max Weber famously defined the modern mind as displaying "the knowledge, or rather the belief, that, if one *desires* to understand something, one *can*. In other words, no mysterious unpredictable powers influencing the world exist as such; rather, everything is – in

---

1 George, 1994, p. 42.
2 This understanding of modernity has been shaped by the lecture of political scientists and social theorists such as Max Weber, Michel Foucault, Zygmunt Bauman, Richard Ashley and Jim George. A good introduction to this kind of modernity conceptualisation can be found in George, 1994.
3 See Knöbl, 2001 for a critical assessment of the modernisation theories of the 1950s and 1960s.

principle – *controllable* through *calculation*."[4] The second characteristic of modernity is an emphasis on opposites and dualisms. For every modern concept, there exists a counter-concept, filled with everything the former concept is not. Conceptual pairs such as modern – traditional, Western – Oriental, liberal – oppressive and individual – collective are very important to the modern mind, and one half of the pair is always much more positively connoted than the other one.

Finally, the third mental configuration of modernity is an emphasis on progress. This progress is always conceptualised as moving towards the more positive half of a conceptual pair. A society may be modernising, Westernising, liberalising, or individualising, and this would be progress. If it was traditionalising, Orientalising, becoming more oppressive, or collectivising, then this would imply that it was hopelessly trapped in regression. At this point, I ought to mention the two major alternative conceptions of modernity that arose in the nineteenth century, communism and fascism. Both of these political ideologies were thoroughly modern, in all three respects, but they emphasised some dualisms differently from the dominant Western modernity. In the case of communism, it was the dualism individual – collective that was reversed. Fascism reversed the dualism universal – particular.

These three aspects of the modern mental condition are obviously highly simplified, and no phenomenon or society anywhere has ever been completely modern. In fact, following the poststructuralist school of thought, modernity cannot be substantially defined; its characteristics can only be identified in various discourses. For the remainder of this study, I am not interested in enumerating the elements of some specific modernity, but simply in analysing the reaction of a particular social and religious community to the propagation of the discourse of modernity. I am not aiming to assess the modernity of the Orthodox Church in the Baltic States as such, but rather its reaction to the modernising context which confronted it in the interwar years.

1.1.1. The Challenges of Modernity

In this understanding, the challenges of modernity pertain more to the need to discursively reposition oneself than to substantial threats. In the particular case of the Orthodox Church in Estonia and Latvia, these challenges arose primarily from the political upheavals of 1917, when both nation-states gained independence for the first time in their history. This is not to say that these challenges were completely non-existent before then, nor is it an attempt to construe the

---

4   Weber, Max, 1919, p. 594 (Emphasis in original).

previous periods as pre-modern. However, there are several aspects of the Baltic context which make the demarcation of 1917 tenable.

First, the discourse of modernity was not prevalent in the Russian Empire of the nineteenth century. Primarily, the continued existence of a strict separation between the estates hindered the rise of universal discourse. Moreover, the political system had not embraced nationalism, either as the criteria for adherence to the polity or as a construct to encompass all current citizens. When the discourse participation grew towards the end of the century, one can see the challenges of modernity pressing the tsars to modernise the polity, especially following the 1905 revolution.[5] Certain fundamentally non-modern traits remained, however, such as privileged classes and religious confessions[6] and very uneven levels of integration. Reactions to the challenges posed by modernity, although already long present in the Russian Empire, were in no way exhausted at the time of the 1917 revolution.

A second aspect is the special context of emerging nation states. Whereas ethnic Estonians and Latvians had been the unprivileged population of the Empire's three 'German' provinces until 1917, the revolutions entailed, on the one hand, a restructuring of the administrative boundaries along roughly ethnic lines and, on the other, a complete shift in political power constellations, with ethnic Germans being forced out of power positions.[7] The new political elites were in a very different position than their predecessors and were intent on making the newly proclaimed states more modern than the Russian Empire, exposing its citizens (and churches) more directly to modernity. Third, the newly established Estonian and Latvian polities both insisted on the secular nature of the state. The Orthodox Church, which had heretofore been a part of the powerful state church of the Russian Empire, was now thrown into a secular environment where it had to completely redefine its identity and role. Moreover, not only was the political environment secular, but what religious culture remained was majority Lutheran. This required the Orthodox Church to rethink its former disdainful official view of Lutheranism.

These challenges arose on different levels and with different contents. First, there was the challenge of coming to terms with a changing political, social, and legal context. This challenge has been aptly described by Zygmunt Bauman, who characterised the modern condition as "conscious of its own historicity."[8] One consequence of this historicity is the insight that the modern state "had to impose a unified order on vast territories heretofore regulated by a variety of local traditions, [...] make the creation and maintenance of social order a matter

---

5 For the modernisation of the Russian Empire, see Hildermeier 2000; Baberowski, 2007, p. 60-66.
6 See Tuchtenhagen, 1995.
7 See also chapter 2.1.3.
8 Bauman, 1993, p. 164.

of deliberation, conscious design, monitoring, and daily management, rather than limit itself to the observance of traditional customs and privileges."[9] Bauman's likening of the pre-modern state to a gamekeeper and the modern one to a gardener highlights these aspects. While the gamekeeper only has to see to it that there is food in the food trough and a fence to guard the game from outside danger, the gardener has to fertilise the soil, plant seeds, water the sprouts, and weed the garden. It is relatively straight-forward to analyse this change in the Baltic States, since they were exposed to the discourse of modernity quite suddenly after 1917.

The shift in the design and role of the political structures pose a challenge to religious organisations in three ways. First, the former take over some of the functions that the latter traditionally attended to, such as social and political organisation and education. Second, the interaction between churches and political structures multiplies with the modern omnipresence of the state. Religious organisations are forced to rethink their relationship with a state that no longer defines and legitimates itself religiously.[10] A third aspect of the political challenge of modernity is the advent of modern secular ideologies, in the present case, mainly nationalism and socialism. These ideologies, which are no longer grounded in a religious understanding of the world, challenge the monopoly of religion on the construction of meaning. They will be elaborated in the next section.

A second challenge of modernity lies in the birth of the subject and its individual identity as a result of the emphasis on rationality. This challenge is most clearly described by the poststructuralist school, especially Michel Foucault. In Foucault's 'Discipline and Punish' from 1975, the emergence of the modern prison in France around the turn of the nineteenth century is taken as a marker of the more fundamental shift from the 'representative regime' to the 'disciplinary society.'[11] The former, where the ruler punished by demonstrating his powers, was slowly replaced by the latter, where punishment served to discipline delinquents and make them conform to the norm. According to Foucault, this notion of rationally forcing normalisation of the individual subject did not only apply to prisons; in all social institutions – schools, hospitals, military – a new emphasis on making the individual conform to societal norms, regardless of his or her social standing and powers, took hold.

This idea that 'subjects' were self-governing entities in need of institutional control, on the one hand, made knowledge about society possible and, on the other, made individual identity something to be shaped, moulded, and formed in

---

9   Bauman, 1993, p. 165.
10   For this aspect, see Crone, 2003, p. 123-143, 188-197.
11   Foucault, 1975.

the course of one's lifetime.[12] The second challenge is thus characterised by a novel emphasis on identity issues and identity politics. It was no longer enough for religious organisations to refer to their many centuries of tradition. The need arose to justify their identities and facilitate their reproduction through reforms and adaptations.

The third challenge of modernity is the recasting of the role of history. According to the sociologist Gerard Delanty, modernity is "a particular kind of time consciousness which defines the present in relation to the past, which must be continuously recreated."[13] For the discourse of modernity, history is not written for the sake of providing practical examples from the past, but rather in order to legitimise the present in relation to a projected future.[14] Generally, this *telos* often references the frame of nationalism or socialism. Socialism projects a perfect society at the end of history. In the case of nationalism, "history became a weapon against inner and outer enemies, intended to legitimise the actions carried out for the national identity."[15] This modern conception of history poses a challenge to religious organisations first because their versions of history and their *telos*, salvation of the soul, is accorded only secondary importance. Second, church historians were not immune to the 'modern regime of historicity' dominating secular history and occasionally sought to introduce the nationalist, or even socialist, *telos* into theology.[16]

1.1.2. Modernity, Ideology, and Identity

Among the main challenges of modernity are those posed by modern ideologies. These ideologies – the '-isms' – each emphasise a particular modern dualism, where most usually the positively connotated half is the name of the ideology. Liberalism emphasises the liberal as opposed to the oppressive, secularism emphasises the secular over the religious, and nationalism stresses the national over the cosmopolitan. These challenges can at times amount to concrete threats, especially for minority groups. This especially happens when the ideology becomes dominant in national political culture, such as nationalism in most of

---

12 See Foucault, 1975, p. 262; Reckwitz, 2008, p. 236.
13 Delanty, 2007, p. 3070.
14 See Berger and Lorenz, 2008, p. 13.
15 Krzoska and Maner, 2005, p. 7.
16 For the case of nationalism, see e.g. Suttner, 1997, passim; Lehmann, 2002, p. 25. The most well-known case of the socialist *telos* introduced into theology is the liberation theology of South America, but also the 'Living Church' movement in the 1920s in Russia displayed these features. See Pospielovsky, 1984, p. 43-92 or the two contributions to the movement in Emhardt, 1929, p. 70-88.

interwar Europe. In the course of this study, two of these ideologies – socialism and nationalism – are repeatedly mentioned, and as such deserve a closer look.

Socialism, the idea that the world is moving towards a globally egalitarian society, is closely linked to anti-individualist theories of the early nineteenth century and especially to their re-appropriation later in the century by Karl Marx and Friedrich Engels.[17] Socialist ideas became prevalent in continental Europe at the end of the nineteenth century, trickling into the Russian Empire, and leading to the failed revolution of 1905 and the successful October Revolution of 1917. Radical Marxism-Leninism was successful only in the Soviet Union, whereas the rest of Europe embraced, to a greater or lesser extent, a more moderate social democracy. This included the Baltic States, where the Social Democrats remained an important political force throughout the interwar period.[18] While socialism was not a direct challenge to the Baltic Orthodox Church(es), as it was for the Orthodox Church in the Soviet Union, the developments in the Soviet Union were observed with deep anxiety by Orthodox circles, who were eager to oppose socialism *in toto*.

Nationalism more directly impacted the political culture of interwar Estonia and Latvia. The idea of nationalism is, however, almost as elusive as that of modernity. Ernest Gellner provides a classical definition: nationalism is primarily "a political principle, which holds that the political and the national unit should be congruent."[19] Secondarily, Gellner maintains that nationalism is the *sentiment* aroused by the violation of this principle and finally the *movement* accentuated by this principle. It is difficult to disagree with this formal definition, but it is not as easy to define its elements. The contested meaning of *national unit* is at the core of many theories of nationalism. For Anthony D. Smith, the champion of the *ethno-symbolist* approach, the national unit is the modern articulation of an existing ethnic community.[20] In other words, a group of human beings sharing some fundamental linguistic, historical, and/or cultural characteristics 'enters' modernity and demands political rights for the group as a group.

In Eastern Europe, this process occurred over the course of the nineteenth century, when various nationalist movements petitioned the multi-national Russian, Austro-Hungarian, and Ottoman Empires for more political rights as particular nations. When these empires crumbled during and after the First World War, a number of new nation-states emerged all over Eastern Europe, taking nationalism to the next stage, so to speak. The national elites, who previously

---

17   See Cox, 2007.
18   See chapter 2.1.3. for the political situation in the interwar Baltic States.
19   Gellner, 1983, p. 1.
20   See Smith, Anthony D., 1998 for a good introduction to his theory.

asserted their rights in the face of imperial governance, could now engage in nation- and state-building.[21]

This project, unlike the earlier nationalist one, not only posited the rights of 'the nation' as the highest goal, but also strove to achieve complete political and social integration within a given national territory.[22] No one should be excluded from the government of the nation-state, except possibly non-nationals. As 'the nation' was unlikely to be entirely integrated by the nationalist project, dissenting opinions continued to be voiced. To speak in Bauman's gardener metaphor, the attempt by the nation-state gardener to turn all vegetables in the garden into turnips is unlikely to succeed easily. As a result, in many European states, national dictatorships emerged, the best known in Italy and Germany, but equally present in Estonia and Latvia.[23]

An important element of the discourse of modernity is the impact it has on individual identity. Many theories on identity, which appear under the assumptions of the modern discourse conceive of it in essentialist terms as the *real* person *behind* the appearance. I am interested, instead, in a 'social constructionist' approach, which "examines people's own understandings of identity and how the notion of inner/outer selves is used rhetorically, to accomplish social action."[24] From this perspective, individual identities are not unitary but must be constructed anew in different social and institutional contexts. In the following, I analyse some ways of framing modern identities. The discussion focuses on three types of collective identity: religious identity, national identity and historical identity.

The German sociologist Bernhard Giesen distinguishes between three different types of collective identities: primordial ones, where boundaries are natural and unchangeable, traditional ones, where boundaries are implicit and bound to group dynamics, and finally, universalist identities, which in principle are available to all human beings who understand and accept their foundations.[25] Religious identities are prime examples of the last type. They often imply that non-members are of less value until they have been converted. However, it is important to keep in mind that such universalist identities are thoroughly modern. The average medieval European was "religious in a taken-for-granted manner now difficult to imagine."[26] His entire life was structured by the church through its calendar, the importance accorded to its dignitaries, and the way most art, music, and literature as well as education was religious.[27]

---

21   Kitromilides, 1989; Timmermann, 1998, p. 13-15.
22   See Crone, 2003, p. 188.
23   Timmermann, 1998, p. 14. See also chapters 2.1.3. and 2.3.3.
24   Benwell and Stokoe, 2006, p. 4.
25   Giesen, 1999, p. 13-43.
26   Bruce, 2002, p. 140.
27   Bruce, 2002, p. 56.

Secularisation changed this picture. According to Steve Bruce, "the basic proposition [of the secularisation thesis] is that modernization creates problems for religion."[28] Avoiding the pitfalls of many other secularisation theorists, Bruce defines secularisation as the process whereby "religion diminishes in social significance, becomes increasingly privatized, and loses personal salience *except where it finds work to do other than relating individuals to the supernatural.*"[29] By 'other work,' Bruce means cultural defence or cultural transition, i.e. when religion provides a bulwark in hostile or rapidly changing contexts. Europeans are no longer religious in the way that characterised medieval Europe. Modernity thus changed notions of religious identity, as adherence to a religious organisation no longer was an integral part of human life but became one of several avenues of identity affirmation.[30] The main thrust of secularisation did not arrive in the Russian Empire until the end of the nineteenth century, when socialist ideology appeared alongside traditional religious offers for the construction of meaning. According to the socialists, class identity had much greater potential to provide meaning and a more progressive outlook than the Orthodox Christian identity, propagated by the Slavophiles throughout the nineteenth century.[31]

In continental Europe, Protestant denominations since the Reformation had demanded of their adherents a much stricter observance of individual piety than had been the case in the medieval Catholic Church. The counter-Reformation introduced a similar requirement of adherence into the Roman Catholic Church. This hardening of fronts between denominations has been called confessionalisation, defined as the "formation of state, society, and culture as a result of the formation of a denomination in the sense of the construction of a dogmatic system of doctrine."[32] In other words, differences of confession were construed as more fundamental differences. Although this concept was worked out with special reference to Germany in the sixteenth and seventeenth centuries, it is possible to extend it, not only geographically, but temporally, into the nineteenth century. Olaf Blaschke has called the long nineteenth century (1830s-1960s) the 'second age of confessionalism.' According to Blaschke, this period was characterised by improved education of the clergy, centralisation of power, institutionalisation of denominational differences, and clerical attempts at social control.[33] Moreover, denominational distinction became an important marker of social antagonism. The Lutheran and Roman Catholic Churches were increasingly perceived as two monolithic entities or two poles of radical difference, and these

---

28   Bruce, 2002, p. 2.
29   Bruce, 2002, p. 30.
30   Bruce, 2002, p. 14.
31   Buss, 2003, p. 172-173.
32   Klueting, 2007, p. 391.
33   Blaschke, 2000, p. 61-63.

differences were reproduced and emphasised in political and academic discourse. Ernst Christoph Suttner has demonstrated how confessionalisation also governed relations between the Roman Catholic and Orthodox Churches from the early eighteenth century onwards.[34] The emphasis on finding common ground for reconciliation between the two churches gave way to an accentuation of their irreconcilable differences. Union was henceforth only considered possible through renouncing former allegiances and starting from scratch.[35]

However, the modernisation of religious identity, which we can grasp with the concepts of secularisation and confessionalisation, is only one side of the coin. The American philosopher and theologian Adam Seligman has proposed an entirely different way of framing modernity, namely as 'the wager of authority.'[36] He distinguishes between the traditionally dominant idea of radically externalised moral authority and the modern insistence on internalised morality. For Seligman, externalised authority is something that has been completely lost in modernity. The ideals propagated by the discourse of modernity are for Seligman a wager, "that an internalized authority in the form of morality governed by [...] reasonable rules is sufficient to constitute the self and sacrality."[37] According to Seligman, what I have called 'religious identity' above is only a 'civil identity'; it posits an 'instrumental self' that maximises utility founded on internalised moral authority. Truly religious identities, those that externalise moral authority and thereby make it nonnegotiable have, however, not disappeared, and provide a complex additional dimension to any analysis of religious phenomena. It is not enough to analyse religious communities as interacting communities, but the heteronomous moral authority, the 'complete other' needs to be taken into account. Membership in a church is often more than a mere choice of preference; it touches core concepts of selfhood.[38]

Nationalism has already been mentioned as an ideology of modernity. This ideology provided a novel framework for the constitution of modern identity. Over the course of the nineteenth century, national identity became an increasingly important part of individual identity, especially in Eastern Europe. In Ernest Gellner's theory of nationalism, emphasis is placed on the parallel existence of vertically differentiated territories, each one of which is, or at least aspires to be, educationally self-sufficient. Where previously, a relatively homogeneous international *high culture* had existed *above* the unorganised agricultural masses, which were deemed *low culture*, the principle of nationalism reevaluates the latter at the expense of the universality of the former. Unwittingly,

---

34 Suttner, 1999, p. 186-202.
35 Suttner, 1999, p. 199. This situation endured until the Second Vatican Council of 1962-1965, which is outside the scope of this study.
36 Seligman, 1999.
37 Seligman, 1999, p. 66.
38 Seligman, 1999, p. 76.

nationalism thereby universalises a new *high culture* within the putative nation, while rhetorically claiming to stand for traditional *folk culture*.[39] In other words, the previous distinction between a 'high' and a 'low' culture, i.e. horizontal stratification, is replaced by a parallel re-evaluation of various national *high cultures* within homogeneous, clearly defined national territories.

According to Gellner, thus, national identity is based on the re-evaluation of folk culture as the paramount identity. In Giesen's typology, such national identities would belong to primordial or traditional collective identities: They are either ethnic (unchangeable) or based on traditions, specific language use, and religious affiliation. Benedict Anderson has famously called this the 'imagined community.'[40] National identities must be propagated by influential individuals before they can gain hold within a population. They are not given and eternal, although their propagators often purport them to be. Thus, national identities are thoroughly modern constructs, although they are most often based on primordial and traditional characteristics.

Seligman also notes the almost necessary connection of primordially defined selves to modernity's own project.[41] Through rejecting transcendent moral authority in favour of rational morality, modernity caused many people to turn to a third spring of moral authority, the primordial, the ascribed, and the tribal. Thus, for Seligman national identities are the result of the failure of rationality. From the state perspective, we can recall Zygmunt Bauman's view that the impetus of rationally ordering a territory made the state embrace and propagate national identities. By taking Seligman together with Bauman we can conclude that the state, unable to sufficiently legitimise the desired order rationally and unable to use transcendent arguments, had to turn to the 'nation.'

National identities are thus at once modern and primordial. They are modern in their evolution and exploitation but primordial in their constitution and foundation. This tension makes national identification exceedingly complex and elusive. On the one hand, most differences between nationalities are straightforward for an outsider or analyst to recognise. On the other hand, however, novel differences can easily be fabricated, or differences can be politicised to take on a significance they did not have in the first place. National identity, therefore, has a fundamentally political and constructed nature while its adherents often perceive it as a natural characteristic. This politically absolutised tension is important to keep in mind when analysing discourses of national identification.

Finally, historical identity is closely connected with the third challenge of modernity. If modernity defines the present in relation to the past, then obviously identity is not exempted. Historical identity is the idea that one's identity

---

39   Gellner, 1983, p. 57
40   Anderson, 1998.
41   Seligman, 1999, p. 53.

is shaped by the historical development of the entity of which one is part. This is thus a wrapping up of the discussion of identity, for history is "the store room for understanding one's proper identity."[42] National historiography, especially for the smaller nations of Eastern Europe, which had heretofore not had much experience of political power, was of paramount importance for the shaping of a national identity. This historiography was meant to infuse the nation with pride in its origin and accomplishments, usually starting from nothing and ending a fully-fledged nation. It is difficult to over-estimate the role played by historians in the "great nineteenth-century process of the nationalisation of the European mental landscape."[43]

However, historical identity is a double-edged sword in many cases. The hegemonic national historiography, embodied in the "general historical knowledge of a society that is repeatedly echoed in the work of historians, political scientists and journalists" often de-legitimises differing narratives.[44] The 'master narrative' perpetuated by these multiple historical practices helps shape a desirable historical identity and exclude certain groups from participating in that identity, stressing the incompatibility of their version of history. Importantly, the 'official' historical identity is perpetuated through diverse historical practices, including the curricula of educational establishments.[45] This is a highly effective way of ensuring that the young members of the nation receive the 'correct' historical identity.

The relationship between historical and religious identity has been analysed by James Kennedy, who distinguishes between three types of relations in European historiographies: supersession, sacralisation, and conflict.[46] The first type, national history attempting to supersede religious affiliations, was most common in Protestant regions, where the dominant church could smoothly be subordinated to the nation state. In this reading, religion might have played its part in the past, but only as part of the national narrative. At the turn of the twentieth century, with the professionalisation of historical studies, religiously-minded historians were increasingly regarded as second class and religious history was relegated to an unimportant sub-field of the discipline.[47] Moreover, the profession of history increasingly left national and religious narratives to non-professionals.[48]

---

42 Lorenz, 1997, p. 400.
43 Leerssen, 2008, p. 85.
44 Thijs, 2008, p. 72.
45 Leerssen, 2008, p. 86. See also chapter 4. for the Baltic case.
46 Kennedy, 2008, p. 104-108.
47 Kennedy, 2008, p. 114.
48 Kennedy, 2008, p. 117.

The sacralisation strategy implied a magnification of the importance of religious identity as substantive of national identity. This strategy was pursued particularly where "a dominant confessional identity became nearly co-extensive with a single confession, itself effectuating the ethnicisation of religion."[49] This was the case in most of early twentieth-century Orthodox Europe, as the following chapter explains. Where no one confession was dominant enough to take on the role of a national church, some attempts were carried out to create a new 'national' religion. However, in many cases, neither strategy managed to establish hegemony, and historiography was characterised by conflict – between denominations, within them, or between religious and anti-clerical historians. These conflicts over the place religion should be accorded in the national historical identity – if any at all – show how "confessions did not constitute monoliths from which a nation's past was constructed, though the parameters of belief clearly delimited what vision of the national past were available."[50]

1.2. Orthodox Christianity Encounters Modernity

The perception of Orthodox Christianity in the West was historically often a gloomy one. The Baltic German church historian Adolf von Harnack, whose characterisation of 'the Greek church' started with the call to step back several centuries, represents the rule rather than an exception.[51] In the second half of the nineteenth century, while interest in the Orthodox Church grew markedly, especially among Protestant theologians, this interest was influenced by the 'modern regime of historicity': "the foreign confession was no longer regarded exclusively as having a dogmatically different theology but as an entity, historically shaped by the elements of the Gospels and the church of the first centuries."[52] In consequence, the nineteenth century preoccupation with Orthodox Christianity was often more of a projection of the Early Church into the present than the analysis of a contemporary entity.

This fallacy was present in von Harnack's overly negative characterisation of the Orthodox Church from around the turn of the twentieth century. Precisely this inaccurate conception had an immense impact on the opinions of "the entirety of European and Anglo-Saxon Christianity and even found its way with adequate modifications, into the Roman Catholic public to an extent that it is still dominating the public opinion."[53] The above statement from 1952 is some-

---

49   Kennedy, 2008, p. 123.
50   Kennedy, 2008, p. 132. See also chapter 4. for the Baltic case.
51   von Harnack, 1901, p. 135-136.
52   Benz, 1952, p. 193.
53   Benz, 1952, p. 230.

what outdated today, but the perception of the Orthodox Church as lagging behind in modernisation is still a strong prejudice among many Catholics and Protestants.[54]

Before analysing how the Orthodox Church(es) have reacted to the challenges of modernity, we need to distinguish between several viewpoints from which the church may be considered. First, as described above, the view from outside tended to deny that the Orthodox Church and its theology had evolved at all since the church Fathers of the first Christian centuries. Thus, the reaction to modernity was perceived as non-existent or, at least, characterised by extremely conservative attitudes. This view was especially potent among Baltic German Lutheran theologians, who had experienced the Russification drive of the second half of the nineteenth century and projected everything backward to the 'Russian soul.'[55] Therefore, this negative portrayal also became an important current of thought among Estonian and Latvian Protestant theologians throughout the interwar period, albeit in a less radical fashion. A general change in attitude did not really occur until after the Second World War, which is outside the scope of this study.

Another viewpoint from which to consider Orthodox Christianity and modernity is from within: How did Orthodox theologians react to the challenges of modernity? This question has been researched differently by various scholarly communities. First, the information contained in the historiography of the young East European nation states of the nineteenth and early twentieth century is not very objective, as will be described below.[56] Analyses of the question of Orthodox Christianity and modernity by émigré Russian Orthodox theologians since the interwar period are a second category of sources. Titles such as *Ways of Russian Theology*,[57] *The Orthodox Church – Its Past and Its Role in the World Today*,[58] and *Historical Road of Eastern Orthodoxy*[59] have immensely impacted the way the English-speaking world looks at the Orthodox Church. Each of these works, however, was written with the clear aim to settle the relationship between Eastern Orthodoxy and the West and purify the former of the influences of the latter.[60] They are somewhat polemic and the situation of their authors, in exile, must be kept in mind.

During the time of the Iron Curtain, there was little unbiased scholarship on the Orthodox Church and modernity, although some contributions by Western

---

54 See also Makrides, 2005, p. 182-185; Makrides 2011.
55 Benz, 1952, p. 249. For Russification, see Thaden, 1981; chapters 2.1.2 and 4.1.2.
56 See also Turda, 2008.
57 Florovsky, 1979 [1937].
58 Meyendorff, 1996 [1960].
59 Schmemann, 1992.
60 Especially Florovsky, 1979, "Translator's Note", p. xi-xv. See also Makrides, 2005, p. 185-186, 193.

historians touch upon the question.[61] In the post-Communist era, scholarship is flourishing, especially in the Greek case, where military rule ended in 1974. Unfortunately, the legacy of earlier nationalist historiography remains strong and hinders objective treatment of history.[62] However, two Greek scholars – Paschalis Kitromilides[63] and Demetrios Stamatopoulos[64] – have published less biased analyses in English, which will be used in the following discussion. For the Russian case, a number of detailed studies on the history of the Russian Orthodox Church have appeared in the last two decades,[65] which have proved useful.

As this short bibliographical sketch has made clear, it is impossible to speak about the Orthodox Church as a monolithic entity. Unlike the Catholic Church, which stressed hierarchical and organisational unity,[66] the Orthodox Church has accommodated various fragmentations of the political order with a correspond-ing fragmentation of church structures. The seven Ecumenical Councils of the first millennium established the Christian *Pentarchy* system, which is the foun-dation of the structures of the Orthodox Church. In this system, next to the Bishop of Rome (the successor of the Apostle Peter) and the Bishop of Jerusa-lem (the Holy City), the three Bishops of Constantinople, Alexandria and Antioch were accorded special importance, as their sees were administrative centres of the Eastern Roman Empire.[67] These five bishops were called Patri-archs to underline their importance, and they were declared the highest ecclesi-astic authorities within their clearly defined and independent jurisdictions.

Over the course of the centuries, other such *autocephalous* units – independ-ent churches who elect their own leader – appeared and sometimes disappeared in Cyprus, Mount Sinai, Georgia, Bulgaria, Serbia, and elsewhere.[68] The Ortho-dox Church in Russia became *de facto* autocephalous in 1448, when Iona was elected Metropolitan of Moscow without waiting for Constantinople's approval.[69] Official recognition was achieved in 1589/1593, when the Ecumeni-cal Patriarch granted Metropolitan Job the title *Patriarch of Moscow and All Rus'*. In the following sections, I describe each of the three challenges of mod-

---

61   Runciman, 1968; Adler, 1979; Stokes, 1979; Nyssen et al. , 1984; Ramet, 1988. The contributions to the debate by the so-called Orthodox Rigorists (such as Cavarnos, 1992 [1971]) have a very negative perspective and constitute the extreme fringes of Orthodoxy and therefore need not interest us further here. See also Kitsikis, 1994 for more on this movement.

62   Turda, 2008, p. 489; Millas, 2008, p. 508-509.

63   Kitromilides, 1989; Kitromilides, 2006.

64   Stamatopoulos, 2004; Stamatopoulos, 2006.

65   Rimskij, 1998; Firsov, 2002; Fedorov, 2003. See also Buss, 2003; Kostjuk, 2005.

66   Kehl, 2006, c. 571-572.

67   Maximos, 1980; de Vries, 1980; Kraft, 2003, p. 393.

68   See Heiler, 1971, p. 43-58 for a good introduction to the early autocephalies.

69   Heiler, 1971, p. 59-60; Schmemann, 1992, p. 310-313; Meyendroff, 1996, p. 96-99.

ernity as they relate to the Orthodox Church, first in the Balkans and then in the Russian Empire, before turning to the changes occurring with the First World War.

1.2.1. The Orthodox Church in the Balkans and Modernity

The concept of a *symphonia* between worldly and ecclesiastical powers has dominated the way Orthodox theology defines the ideal relationship between church and state. Unlike the Western notion of separate spheres for religious and secular authorities, the Eastern ideal emphasises the reciprocity of the two spheres.[70] The theological foundations of this model were worked out following the rise of the Eastern Roman Empire, and as long as the Empire existed, reality seemed to conform to the ideal. Imperial administration was dependent on the church for the moral authority, and the church depended on the Empire for earthly security and maintenance. Even after Constantinople was taken by the Ottomans in 1453, mainstream Orthodox theology clung to the symphonic ideal.

The reciprocal model, however, became less and less consistent with the reality of the church's existence. The Ottoman Empire introduced the *millet* system of political organisation: the Sultan delegated some of his authority as special privileges granted to laic or clerical officials who exercised them on behalf of the Ottoman state.[71] The Ecumenical Patriarch of Constantinople was accorded both secular and religious jurisdiction over all Orthodox Christians of the Empire. Thus, the Orthodox Church was, on the one hand, completely dependent on the Sultan's goodwill but, on the other, had much more power over the lives of its adherents than under the Roman Empire. According to Alexander Schmemann, a Russian émigré theologian, this confounded under-standing of authority led the Greek-dominated Patriarchate of Constantinople to forget its universal mission and replace it with Greek chauvinism.[72] Steven Runciman, noting a similar development, links it with the secular Greek elite, who influenced the Patriarchate in their favour and laicised its administration. Over the course of the eighteenth century, this lay administration attempted to increase its influence by appointing Greek-speaking Metropolitans in Romanian, Serbian, and Bulgarian lands.[73]

---

70 Schmemann, 1992, p. 214-216.
71 Sugar, 1996, p. 8; Stamatopoulos, 2006, p. 253-254.; Kraft, 2003, p. 394.
72 Schmemann, 1992, p. 279-281.
73 Runciman, 1968, p. 360-384. See also Sugar, 1996, p. 9-10. While this trend is replic-able, its reasons must be sought at a much deeper level than crude nationalism. See also below for more on this development..

The dominant Orthodox historiographies view the spread of nationalism in the nineteenth century as a corruption of the true Christian Orthodox spirit by Western ideas.[74] Nationalist ideas came chiefly from Western-educated lay persons, who were often less favourably inclined towards the church. When Greece declared its independence in 1830, the Patriarchate of Constantinople remained in the Ottoman Empire. Many political leaders in the new nation-state, therefore, no longer regarded it as responsible for the church in Greece, since the Patriarch was a citizen of an enemy state.[75] One of the earliest actions of the first Greek regent, King Otto of Bavaria, was a unilateral declaration of autocephaly for the Orthodox Church of Greece in 1833. In its place, he installed a church regime that was heavily influenced by the church-state regulations of European Protestant regions and the synodal structure of the Russian Orthodox Church.[76] At first, the Patriarchate of Constantinople refused to acknowledge the secession of the Greek Church, but it gave in seventeen years later and officially granted the Orthodox Church of the Greek independent state autocephaly.[77]

In the other states that emerged from the crumbling of the Ottoman Empire in the Balkans, similar processes were at work; the lay leaders of the national uprisings and fledgling states did their utmost to bring the local Orthodox Church under their aegis, declaring it independent from Constantinople in the process.[78] Often the church was the institution with the most knowledge of the population and the one which enjoyed the highest trust; therefore, it was a very useful ally for the new national elites.[79] Thus, in most cases, the church could not freely react to modern political institutions. Rather, the church was instrumentalised by these institutions to perform state-building functions, such as bringing the population in line with the authorities and collecting information.

There were a few cases where this did not happen. The Patriarchate of Constantinople continued to hold an ecumenical vision of a single, united Orthodox World. It was, however, pressured by influential Greeks in Istanbul and the administration in independent Greece to become a bastion of Greek nationalism in the dying Ottoman Empire.[80] The Orthodox in the Habsburg Empire were another special case. At the close of the seventeenth century, 450,000 Serbs voluntarily resettled on the Austro-Hungarian side of the border with the Ottoman Empire. As a reward for their changed allegiance, the Habsburgs granted them special privileges in 1690, "guaranteeing the migrants and their descendants an

---

74 Schmemann, 1992, p. 289-290; Meyendorff, 1996, p. 81; Kitromilides, 2006.
75 Kitromilides, 2006, p. 234.
76 Kitromilides, 2006, p. 234-235.
77 Kraft, 2003, p. 398-399; Kitromilides, 2006, p. 236.
78 Kitromilides, 1989, p. 180-182; Suttner, 1997, p. 235-245. For the exceptional, peaceful Serbian experience, see Kraft, 2003, p. 406-407; Kitromilides, 2006, p. 237-238.
79 Suttner, 1997, p. 245-246; Kitromilides, 2006, p. 247-248.
80 Kitromilides, 1989, p. 183-184; Kraft, 2003, p. 404-405; Kitromilides, 2006, p. 246-247.

extra-ordinary religious, cultural, and political autonomy."[81] The Metropolitan of Sremski Karlovci was recognised as the political and religious head of all Orthodox Christians throughout the Austro-Hungarian Empire. These privileges were initially confirmed by subsequent emperors but were gradually abolished from the 1770s onwards. Nevertheless, due to the lack of powerful secular elites among the Austro-Hungarian Serbs, the Metropolitan successfully resisted any attempts to challenge his power base and maintained belief in a re-establishment of the privileges of 1690 until well into the nineteenth century. Thus, in the Balkans, there were no real attempts by the Orthodox Church to come to grips with political modernity. This task was left to secular elites, who were extensively influenced by the modernised states of Western Europe.[82]

The second challenge of modernity, the reframing of individual identity, was more readily answered by the Orthodox Church of Southeast Europe. The oft-cited Hellenising efforts of the Greek-speaking Phanariot elite can be rejected as superficial characterisations of Western observers, all too readily adopted by the incipient historiographies of the Balkan nation states.[83] However, it clearly illustrates a response to the second challenge; the idea that identity was not given but could be shaped with the help of institutions led the secular elites to define a desirable identity. This ideal identity was obviously near to the identity of those who defined it – in the case of the Phanariots, a Greek-speaking bourgeoisie. In order to create this new type of Christian, the Phanariots founded schools and academies of Greek learning in non-Greek lands and used their influence in the Patriarchate to ensure that the bishops of these areas had such education.[84]

When, in the course of the nineteenth century, the *millets* of the Ottoman Empire became 'national minorities' (as Stamatopoulos has titled his article), this did not please the Patriarchate of Constantinople. First, as noted, the newly independent Greeks rejected their former Patriarch in Constantinople, creating institutions of their own, with a new ideal identity.[85] The Patriarchate, which was severely punished by the Sultan for not having openly objected to the Greek revolt, was torn between the traditional accommodation policy *vis-à-vis* the Ottoman State and the nationalism propagated by several influential lay people.[86] In 1850, it set a precedent by accepting the declaration of autocephaly from the Orthodox Church of independent Greece after seventeen years of not acknowledging this body. Although the Patriarchate expressively argued that it

---

81 Adler, 1979, p. 272. See also Kraft, 2003, p. 395.
82 Kitromilides, 1989, p. 184-185; Aleksov, 2006, p. 167-178.
83 Kraft, 2003, p. 395-396; Kitromilides, 2006, p. 238; Stamatopoulos, 2006, p. 255.
84 Runciman, 1968, p. 376-378, 383; Kitromilides, 1989, p. 156-157; Kraft, 2003, p. 399-40; Stamatopoulos, 2006, p. 255.
85 Kitromilides, 1989, p. 159-177; Kraft, 2003, p. 295-298.
86 Kitromilides, 1989, p. 181-184; Kitromilides, 2006, p. 230, 246-247; Stamatopoulos, 2006, p. 266.

did not accede to Greek demands but granted autocephaly only due to the new territorial borders, it was obvious that this was only rhetoric.[87]

Now that the Patriarchate had granted autocephaly to one church, it was possible for every new political entity to demand its own independent church, so-called 'autocephalism.' Autocephaly was granted to Serbia in 1879 and Romania in 1881/1885, before the First World War reorganised the map of Eastern Europe completely. In the 1920s, the national churches of Czechoslovakia, Albania, Poland, Finland, and Estonia all turned to the Patriarchate and demanded autocephaly. For Grigorios Papathomas, a canon law specialist, the problem was not so much secular nationalism as the procedural errors such nationalism was prone to make. Autocephaly and autonomy are to be granted, not proclaimed, according to canon law. Most national churches, emerging in the nineteenth century in the Balkan lands, did not follow the procedural steps canon law prescribes and simply proclaimed autocephaly. The schism initiated with the Ecumenical Patriarchate did not worry the secular nationalists, and eventually, the Patriarchate had to develop a 'system of autocephaly,' in order to avoid alienating the bulk of Orthodox adherents from the true Church.[88]

The one case where a proclamation of autocephaly was not acknowledged by Constantinople was the Bulgarian Exarchate.[89] This is a case of the Patriarchate of Constantinople resisting the redefinition of its identity. When the Bulgarian Eparchies tried to detach themselves from the Patriarchate of Constantinople, the latter refused to accept a parallel Orthodox Church structure for Bulgarians within the Ottoman Empire. The Bulgarians appealed to the Sultan, who established a Bulgarian *millet* in 1870, headed by an Exarch seated in Constantinople. This move prompted a strong reaction from the Patriarchate, which in 1872 condemned the Bulgarian Bishops of 'phyletism,' i.e. limiting oneself to a distinct ethnic community in contrast to the ecumenicity of the church, because the establishment of a Bulgarian Exarchate "brings discrimination on the basis of ancestry, conflicts and jealousy on the basis of nationality into the Christian Church, and it contradicts the teachings of the Holy Gospels and the Holy Canon Law on which the church is founded."[90] The ensuing schism with the Bulgarian Church was not resolved until 1945, when the Patriarchate of Constantinople granted the Church of Bulgaria autocephaly.

---

87 Wittig, 1987, p. 87-88.
88 Papathomas, 2004. See also chapter 1.2.4. for more on issues of canon law and modernity.
89 See Kraft, 2003, p. 403-404; Kitromilides, 2006, p. 240-244; Stamatopoulos, 2006, p. 261-262.
90 From the German translation of the original synodal protocol, as quoted in Maximos, 1980, p. 408. An English 'semi-official' translation is quoted in Kitromilides, 1989, p. 181. This version calls the object of condemnation 'racism' and is therefore, in my opinion, somewhat misleading.

An important thing to note, is that the secular elites emphasised national identities above the universal Orthodox Christian identity, while the Patriarchate of Constantinople frantically tried to hold on to its traditional principles. For Orthodox canon law, the fundamental structure of the church is "not 'autocephaly,' but the principle of a unitary territory in which one single Bishop represents one single Church."[91] In the modern nation state, where territorial consolidation is linked with national identity, this principle runs into difficulties, especially when the population of a territory is not ethnically homogenous. The Patriarchate of Constantinople, whose core constituency dwindled with every new autocephalous church, had to turn more and more to its role as first among equals in the Orthodox World, without many believers of its own, whereas the new autocephalous churches quickly became state building instruments of the secular elites, fusing religious identity with the national one.[92]

The third challenge of modernity – the new role of history – did not really confront the Orthodox Church in the Balkans. In each of the new nation states that emerged from within the Ottoman Empire, national historiographies portrayed the Orthodox faith as the keeper of national identity in the face of Muslim political rule.[93] Not only had the church fostered Christian solidarity within the Orthodox *millet*, but it had also supposedly preserved the different national characteristics of each eventually independent nation. This mythology is especially clear in Romanian historiography, where 'Orthodoxism' dominated. The Orthodox Christian roots of Romanian national consciousness are excessively praised, and all Western European institutions are strictly repudiated as "artificial creations based on purely 'juridical' relationships between groups and individual."[94]

The rejection of the West was not unique to the Romanian context. Ion Dragoumis, a Greek nationalist, wrote in 1904 that "the Russians, the Bulgarians, the Romanians, the Austrians, the Italians, and the Turks do not really bother us. Their invasions and raids are nothing to us. We are concerned about the *idées modernes*, modern civilisation with its freemasonry, philanthropy, and solidarity. [...] The invasion of modern civilisation, and not of Bulgarians or Italians, corrupts us, infects us, and is about to eliminate us."[95] In reaction to the Western ideas, Southeast Europeans turned to the unique traditions and features of their nations, including Orthodox Christianity, when writing their own history. However, while anti-Westernism was fashionable among nationalists and

---

91   Maximos, 1980, p. 410. See also Kitromilides, 1989, p. 157-159, 177-178.
92   Suttner, 1997.
93   Kitromilides, 1989, p. 178-180; Kraft, 2003, p. 399-401; Sundhaussen, 2003, p. 619; Kitromilides, 2006, p. 240; Staab, 2011, p. 159-164.
94   Hitchins, 1992, p. 1075. See also Kitromilides, 1989, p. 182-183; Staab, 2011, p. 19-24, 159-170.
95   Quoted in Sundhaussen, 2003, p. 617.

historians, there were equally strong pro-Western currents among political leaders and other elites. Among this pro-Western party, there were quite a few who
aspired to modernise and rationalise the Orthodox Church itself. These mod-
ernisers often "were in clear opposition to the ecclesiastical tradition and [...]
accentuated the whole conflict and rendered the aversion of the Orthodox
Church towards modernization even stronger."[96]

Secular elites, not theologians, shaped the historiography of Southeast
Europe. Although lip service was paid to the Orthodox Church, religion often
played a marginal role even in the anti-Western discourses.[97] While individual
clerics certainly participated in nationalist discourses, these discourses were
always downplayed by the official church, especially the Patriarchate of Constantinople, as the Ottoman Sultan, until the First World War, saw to it that the
Patriarch did not act contrary to Imperial interests.[98] Outside of the Ottoman
Empire, the church was used as an instrument by the modernising secular elites,
rather than being able to shape its own response to the challenges of modernity.

1.2.2. The Orthodox Church in the Russian Empire and Modernity

The relationship between the Russian Tsar and the Patriarch of Moscow was
very different from the situation in the Ottoman Empire, where the Patriarch was
a mere functionary of the Sultan. In Russia, the power of the Patriarch surpassed
that of the Tsar at times. In the mid-seventeenth century, the very powerful
Patriarch Nikon attempted to carry out far-reaching reforms in the Russian
Orthodox Church. This caused a revolt from inside the church, resulting in the
schism of the so-called Old Believers (*Starovery*).[99] Nikon was deposed in 1666,
but the conflicts in the church did not stop, and when Patriarch Adrian died in
1700, Tsar Peter the Great did not allow a successor to be elected.

Instead, Peter reformed the entire Russian Orthodox Church, effectively
making it a department of the state. In 1721, he established the Most Holy
Synod, the new governing body of the church, consisting of several bishops and
appointed laymen and headed by a lay functionary, the *Oberprokuror*. Many of
the reforms Peter introduced in Russia resulted from his obsession with German
Lutheran order, and his church reforms were no exception. They were modelled
on the organisation of Lutheran Churches in the Baltic areas, headed by a
Konsistorium composed of clerical and lay members.[100] This way, modernity

---

96   Makrides, 2005, p. 194.
97   Sundhaussen, 2005, p. 26-27.
98   Stamatopoulos, 2006, p. 260-262.
99   Scheidegger, 1999. See also Florovsky, 1979, p. 86-113.
100 See Smolitsch, 1964, p. 118-120; Florovsky, 1979, p. 114-130.

arrived in the Russian Orthodox Church from outside, without having been invited in. As a state department, the church followed the tsars' line of policy and was completely bereft of institutional initiative.

Two initiatives during the first Russian Revolution of 1905 changed the picture somewhat. In April, Tsar Nikolai II issued a manifesto of freedom of religion (the Manifesto of Tolerance). Citizens were now free (within certain limits) to choose the church to which they belonged.[101] The following year, he introduced the *Duma* – a parliamentary assembly. However, it only possessed advisory powers vis-à-vis the still autocratic Tsar.[102] Among the important discussions of the *Duma* were the relationship between the Orthodox Church and the state and the reform of the former to better cope with the modern world. While the first two *Dumas* were too radical for Nikolai II and quickly dissolved, the third *Duma* (from 1907) counted among its members forty-five clergymen and two bishops, who made sure that the interests of the church were accounted for.[103] However, no large-scale reform of the church, as the church-goers and simple clergymen increasingly demanded, was undertaken.

Turning to the second challenge, we see that without the need to exercise worldly power or counter a hostile political environment, the Orthodox Church in Russia could focus on constructing an Orthodox Christian identity. After a period of decline in the eighteenth century, particularly in monastic life, the nineteenth century showed that the Orthodox Church remained vibrant even under state tutelage.[104] This is particularly well illustrated by the area of missionary activity. Russian Orthodox missionaries were sent to the native peoples of Siberia, to regions as far as Alaska, to the Muslim regions of Tatarstan and Central Asia, and to Japan and China.[105] Just like the Missions to the Slavs of the first millennium, primarily associated with St. Cyril and St. Methodius, these missions, usually lacking political motives, were based on three principles: vernacularisation, indigenisation, and education.[106]

The first of these principles denotes the effort to bring the faith to the heathen in their native language, creating – if necessary – a Christian vocabulary and an alphabet for the language. The prime example of this principle remains Cyril and Methodius's systematisation of Slavic language, including the Cyrillic alphabet, but the nineteenth century Russian missions also worked in native languages – occasionally devising scripts and orthography for them. The second principle indicates the wish that converts should be involved in the church as

---

101 Werth, 2007.
102 Hildermeier; 2000; Firsov, 2002, p. 343-345; Waldron, 2005.
103 Firsov, 2002, p. 360-361.
104 Meyendorff, 1996, p. 103-109. See also chapter 2.1 for more details on the development in the Baltic provinces.
105 Smirnoff, 1908.
106 Stamoolis, 1986, p. 67-70.

fully as possible, not only as lay members, but from an early stage entering the lower ranks of the clergy. With only higher clergy remaining foreign, the perception of the church as a foreign imposition was minimised. An example of this principle was the Russian mission to Japan, which was started 'accidentally' by Nikolai Kassatkin in 1861, and then spread independently, almost without the help of further missionaries.[107] Finally, the principle of education was most important in the inner mission to the native peoples of the more remote regions of the Russian Empire. James J. Stamoolis recounts how a Russian missionary monk, Makarius Gloukharev, went to a native tribe in the Altai Mountains of Central Asia and lived there many years as a servant, teaching basic medicine and hygiene before starting to baptise the first Christians.[108] Over fourteen years, he baptised only 675 adults into Christianity. These principles, although not modern in themselves, had to involve some kind of modernisation in the nineteenth century. In the remote regions of Russia, analphabetism and tribal lifestyles were widespread, and the Orthodox missions helped expose their inhabitants to the discourse of modernity. Nikolai Ilminskij, for example, developed a highly successful system of teaching uneducated converts reading and writing in addition to the Russian language.[109]

Another development related to the second challenge of modernity was the identification of Russianness with Orthodox Christianity. Just as in the Balkans, where the Orthodox faith was an important aspect of the national identity of Greeks, Romanians, Serbs, and Bulgarians, so too in the Russian Empire. However, since the latter was a multinational empire, the equation of Orthodoxy and Russianness ran into difficulties in the Imperial periphery. This was felt most clearly in the Western borderlands of the Empire, where there were important non-Russian Catholic and Lutheran minorities. The so-called Uniate Church, Orthodox in liturgical form and origin but in communion with the Pope in Rome, was the most important disturbing entity.[110] While Tsar Aleksander I (1801-1825) expected all churches in the Empire to help shape public morality, his successor, Nikolai I (1825-1855), directed his attention primarily to the Orthodox Church, which served as the cornerstone of official Russian nationalism.[111] With the help of a Uniate bishop, Iosif Semaško, the 'return' of the Uniate Church to its Orthodox 'home' was carried out in 1839.[112] Schemes to emancipate the Catholic Church from the influence of the Pope were even

---

107 Stamoolis, 1986, p. 35-40.
108 Stamoolis, 1986, p. 29-30.
109 Stamoolis, 1986, p. 31-33.
110 For more on this church, see Weeks, 2001. See also Florovsky, 1979, p. 61-63.
111 Fedorov, 2003, p. 172-208.
112 See Weeks, 1996; Suttner, 1999, p. 231-234. See also chapter 3.2.1.

worked out.[113] At the same time, a number of reforms within the Orthodox Church were developed and implemented by the Tsarist government.

Importantly, all the initiatives came from the secular administration and the church had to comply. Since the Patriarchate had been abolished, the church had no 'will of its own,' so to speak, and was a mere instrument of the state. There were not many voices within the church pleading for another policy. In fact, only lay theologians, somewhat distanced from the church, embraced the idea that the Orthodox faith destined the Russians to a saving role in the nineteenth century. These active lay persons were divided among the so-called Westernisers, who saw Western institutions as worthy to imitate, and the Slavophiles, who praised the Russian spirit and the Orthodox faith as something unique.[114] Both currents were characterised by a certain conservatism, which distinguished them from the radical, revolutionary, and irreligious currents of communism and anarchism, as well as from positivism, liberalism, etc. According to Konstantin Kostjuk, a political scientist, it was this religious conservatism which enabled the Russian Empire to keep revolution at bay through the nineteenth century.[115]

A third response to the challenge of individual subjectivity is the development of the concept of *sobornost'*, which appeared as the fundamental characteristic of the Orthodox Church in contrast with the Western Christian Churches in the philosophy of the Slavophile Aleksej Khomjakov.[116] *Sobornost'* is the Russian translation of the Greek *katholikos* and denotes the unity and universality of the church. In principle all decisions in the Orthodox Church are made by the entire church. For Khomjakov, the *sobornost'* of the Russian Orthodox Church stood in stark contrast to the authoritarianism of the Roman Catholic Church and the individualism of the Protestant Churches, both inferior ecclesiologies. According to Kostjuk, Khomjakov was the first to infuse the concept with a socio-political connotation, which guided many of the Slavophile ideas over the course of the nineteenth century.[117]

The development of civil society in Russia therefore took on a special character. In the West, the Enlightenment concept of civil society denoted a sphere of civilised interaction among citizens distinct from the liberal state, on the one hand, and the private or family, on the other.[118] Since a liberal government only existed in Russia for a few months between the two revolutions of 1917, no full-fledged civil society had a chance to develop, but a sphere between the state and

---

113 See Dolbilov and Staliūnas, 2005.
114 Buss, 2003, p. 168-170; Kostjuk, 2005, p. 90-107.
115 Kostjuk, 2005, p. 107.
116 Kostjuk, 2005, p. 247. See also chapter 1.3.4.
117 Kostjuk, 2005, p. 247.
118 Kocka, 2007, p. 87.

the private was growing from the second half of the nineteenth century.[119] Among other areas, this sphere developed from within the church, where modern subjectivity increasingly emancipated itself from state tutelage and family constraints.[120]

The third challenge of modernity did not occur in the Russian case. Historiography in the late Russian Empire, according to the historian Thomas Sanders, "remained incapable of generating a binding national vision that transcended class, ethnicity, and locality."[121] Drawing on the insights of the art critic Wladimir Weidle, Sanders claims that the wide Russian plains impeded the establishment of a coherent linkage between the horizontally conceptualised high culture of the intelligentsia in Moscow and St. Petersburg and the vertically limited cultures of common Russians. Not that there were no attempts to do so, but they were obstructed by both the autocratic government and the growing influence of the socialist groups. The latter, once they had established a universally binding lens for historical interpretation after the Bolshevik revolution, had an easier task to 'nationalise' Russian history, although in this case, it might be more appropriate to call the process 'internationalisation.'

1.2.3. The Orthodox Church in the Aftermath of the First World War

In general, the Orthodox Church did not experience much exposure to modern forms of political organisation before the rise of the nation state in the nineteenth century. In the two cases where this was not the case, a modern organisation was forced upon the church (as in Russia), or it naively believed it could keep its former privileged role (as in Austro-Hungarian Serbia). In the Balkans, there were no real attempts to come to grips with political modernity. This task was left to secular elites, who were extensively influenced by the modernised states of Western Europe, although rhetorically they often claimed to be anti-Western. In fact, the Orthodox Church response was not much different from the Roman Catholic Church's reaction to modernity. The latter also vehemently resisted modernising reforms and, in the political sphere, was surprisingly successful at doing so. The Vatican is still the same supranational entity as it was in the medieval era, although it arguably had an easier task with the Augustinian notion of the complete separation of divine and secular powers at its backbone.

In relation to the second challenge, it is clear that the Orthodox cultural elites were not happy about the Western individualism and nationalism. In Rus-

---

119 Hildermeier, 2000; Badcock, 2005.
120 See Freeze, 1983; Weber, Renate, 1993; Polunov, 1996, p. 72-96; Stamatopoulos, 2004; Manchester, 2008; Engelstein, 2009. See also chapter 3.1.
121 Sanders, 1999, p. 7. See also Baberowski, 2007, p. 61-62.

sia an entire anti-Western philosophy was devised, and the Patriarchate of Constantinople only grudgingly accepted the various 'national' churches that sprang up in newly independent states while making it clear that canon law did not accept national churches, only territorial ones.[122] The secular elite of Orthodox lands, however, clearly embraced the Western idea of the autonomous individual. The leaders of the new nation states from Greece to Romania emphasised the individuality of the respective nation and the importance of a church that would support the national government. In Russia, the church was completely controlled by the secular rulers. The national historiography of the new states did not pose a great challenge to the Orthodox Church in Russia and the Balkans, as these states were mostly majority Orthodox. It is interesting to note that the recasting of history in all the new nation states on the Balkan Peninsula emphasised the role of the church as important in the past, but only in Romania was there a clear reference to its importance in the present.

Very important changes to these arrangements of power happened during the First World War. In Russia, the February Revolution of 1917 brought about a quasi-democratic parliamentary system, of which the church took advantage, calling a local council (*sobor*) to discuss long needed church reforms. The idea of church reform had been on the agenda since the failed revolution of 1905, but it never came to more than plans.[123] The lively discussions at this *sobor* starting in August 1917 focused on re-establishing the canonical structure of which the Russian Orthodox Church had been deprived since the Petrine Reforms in the eighteenth century. The very first and most important decision of the *sobor* was the reinstatement of the Patriarchate of Moscow and All Russia, and Archbishop Tikhon (Bellavin) was elected Patriarch. The *sobor* officially continued its sessions through September 1918, primarily making decisions that affected the inner life of the church. However, in view of the Bolshevik seizure of power during the October Revolution, it was not able to put any of these decisions into effect.[124] Moreover, church life in the Soviet Union was extremely difficult from the beginning, as the militantly atheist regime did all in its power to discourage religious activity, from horrendous tax rates for clergy and anti-religious propaganda to physical persecution and punishment.[125] Among the more sophisticated measures taken against the church was the support of schismatic groups, such as the 'Living Church' movement, which argued for a radicalisation of the reform measures of the *sobor*.[126]

---

122 Makrides, 2005, p. 187-188.
123 Firsov, 2002; Tuchtenhagen, 1995.
124 For this council, see Schulz et al., 2005; Destivelle, 2006. See also chapter 3.1.
125 Kolarz, 1962, p. 36-94; Pospielovsky, 1984, p. 93-112.
126 See Pospielovsky, 1984, p. 43-92 and the two contributions on the movement in Emhardt, 1929, p. 70-88.

In the case of Constantinople, the War freed the Patriarchate from dependence on the Sultan, but put it at the mercy of the radically secular Kemalist Turkish regime. At the same time the Patriarchate's jurisdiction dwindled, and after the forcible population transfer between Turkey and Greece in 1923, only about 100,000 Orthodox Christians remained within Turkey.[127] Some dioceses of the Patriarchate within the borders of Greece remained, but the Orthodox Church of Greece exercised *de facto* jurisdiction over these dioceses. However, these changes prompted the Patriarch of Constantinople to pursue other, more outwardly directed activities, such as ecumenical endeavours and Pan-Orthodox reforms. An important impetus to this change was the election of the openly modernist Patriarch Meletios IV (Metaxakis) of Constantinople in the end of 1921.[128] The elections were boycotted by an important section of the Orthodox hierarchy and did not exactly follow the prescribed procedure, but were nevertheless recognised by the other autocephalous Orthodox Churches. Although Meletios IV remained Patriarch for only 18 months, he managed to completely turn around the character and scope of the Ecumenical Patriarchate with his inventiveness and organisational talent. According to Peter Plank, Meletios IV was the most important factor in assuring the survival of the institution of the Ecumenical Patriarchate and its prestige.[129]

A primary topic of interest to Patriarch Meletios IV of Constantinople was the Orthodox Diaspora, which was growing in Western Europe and the Americas. He was equally interested in good relations with other denominations and among the autocephalous Orthodox Churches. In relation to the first topic, he installed titular Metropolitans of the Ecumenical Patriarchate to shepherd and assist the Diaspora, including Metropolitan Germanos (Strenopoulos) of Thyateira, based in London.[130] Ecumenical relations, especially between the Anglican and Orthodox Churches were invigorated under Meletios IV – even belief in full ecclesiastical union was expressed on both sides.[131] Intra-Orthodox unity was furthered by Meletios IV by inviting representatives from all the important autocephalous Orthodox Churches to a Pan-Orthodox Conference in

---

127 Bryner, 1996, p. 25-26. See also Ohme, 2007.
128 Kitromilides, 2006, p. 247; Viscuso, 2006, p. xxi-xxii; Plank, 2007, p. 258-260.
129 Plank, 2007, p. 268.
130 Metropolitan Germanos later played an important role in the Latvian Orthodox Church. See chapter 2.3.3.
131 Katerelos, 2003, p. 215-216; Viscuso, 2006, p. lii-lv. The endeavours for union were especially intensive with Bishop Charles Gore as chairman of the Archbishop's Eastern Churches Committee. They were also closely monitored in Estonia, especially by Vassili Martinson, professor of Orthodox Theology at the University of Tartu (1923-1940). See his "Hommikumaa-õigeusu ja Inglise (anglikaani) kiriku vahekorrast." [On the relation between the Eastern Orthodox and English (Anglican) Churches] in *UE*, 5/1, 1925, p. 6-8; 5/2, 1925, p. 1-4. See also chapter 3.2.1.

May 1923.[132] The Conference was attended by delegates from the Church of Greece, the Church of Cyprus, the Church of Serbia, and the Church of Romania, as well as two representatives from the Church of Russia – Archbishop Aleksandr (Nemolovskij) of the Aleut Islands and Northern America and Archbishop Anastasij (Gribanovskij) of Chisinau and Khotyn. The two latter were not delegates from the official Russian Church but part of the exile church forming outside the Soviet Union.

During the eleven sessions of the Conference, many issues concerning Orthodox unity were discussed, most importantly the calendar issue. The Ottoman Empire, Russian Empire, and the Orthodox Churches followed the Julian calendar, which, by that time, lagged thirteen days behind the Gregorian calendar used in the West. However, simply adopting the Gregorian calendar, as the governments of Orthodox states had done, would not be accepted as a solution in the church, because it would appear defeating to follow Rome in the calendar question.[133] Professor Milutin Milanković of the Serbian delegation proposed an adjusted calendar, even closer to the sun year than the Gregorian one, and this calendar was unanimously adopted. That many Orthodox Churches, including the Church of Serbia and the Russian Church, later failed to ratify this decision is a separate issue. Other issues at the Conference, concerning re-marriage of widowed priests, married bishops, organisation of the Diaspora, and other issues of canon law remained discussions. Although decisions were reached on many of them, individual churches did not follow up on them and only the calendar issue remained as a visible result.[134]

Both Patriarchates experienced very significant changes, which in both cases involved losing former powers while regaining others and turning to previously unchartered territory. In relation to the challenges of modernity, one can say that the churches met these challenges on their own initiative for the first time. In both cases, the challenges were much more powerful than before, and the initial rush quickly turned into defensiveness. It is, thus, difficult to assess the progress of the Orthodox Church into modernity in the 1920s and 1930s because of the multiple facets of the historical context. The various local churches possibly would have fully adjusted to modernity, but the political contexts in which they operated did not allow them the freedom to make this adjustment. In Soviet Russia and Turkey, this limitation was due to the anti-religious views of the respective regimes. In the Balkan states, the close connection between national consciousness and Orthodox Christianity coated the church in an anti-Western rhetoric of Orthodox traditionalism. The aim of this study is to present two very

---

132 On this conference, see Katerelos, 2003; Viscuso, 2006.
133 Katerelos, 2003, p. 204, 236.
134 See chapter 3.1.3. for the calendar issue in the Estonian and Latvian case.

specific cases where the Orthodox Church was forced to embrace modernity, and successfully did so, at least for the interwar period.

1.2.4. The Orthodox Church and Modernity: the Legal Dimension

A final aspect of Orthodox Christianity's relation to modernity is the legal dimension. Christian churches all have their own legal codes that govern church life and, to some extent, the lives of the faithful. Once the modern state takes interest in the entirety of social life, treading on territory previously governed by churches, the secular legal code and its enforcement changes, potentially bringing civil law into conflict with the canon law of churches.

Peter Edge, a law scholar, distinguishes between six functions of law.[135] First, it is a way of ordering the social world: defining social order, mantaining that order, institutionalising difference, and prescribing moral behaviour. Second, law is seen as the last resort for resolution of disputes. Third, politicians may use law to respond to social problem areas, and fourth, law provides rules regulating the affairs between individuals. Fifth, law provides mechanisms for state control over society, and finally, law is a mechanism which empowers the individual. All these characteristics apply firmly to modern civil law. The application of civil law to religious communities emerged as a reaction to the problem of ordering a multi-religious society.[136] Whereas legal systems until the seventeenth century tended to see themselves as defenders of a particular religious institution, the new legal codes, emerging in modern states, renounced authority over religious issues. The courts no longer saw it as their task to judge the truth of religious contents. The legal reforms of the Russian Tsar Peter the Great were based firmly on Western legalistic foundations, but the Russian legal professionals only partly accepted the juridical worldview prevalent in the West.[137] For example, in the late nineteenth century, the Russian intelligentsia regarded legal indifference to religious issues a sign of Western moral decay. Adherence to Orthodox Christianity remained a legal advantage until the end of the Empire in 1917.[138]

Canon law, while fulfilling the six functions of law listed above, contains an additional dimension. Canon law is more than a way of ordering the church community. The foundation of canon law is found in "the will of God to establish His Church on earth. Consequently, the source of its authority stems from

---

135 Edge, 2006, p. 3-5.
136 Edge, 2006, p. 8-11.
137 Walicki, 1992, p. 21.
138 See Tuchtenhagen, 1995.

the will of God."[139] Especially in the case of the Orthodox Church, "the juridical element [...] should not be exaggerated, because that would mean a transformation of the church in a Theocracy."[140] Canon law is not simply a set of rules, but it is the church's ministry, guiding its members towards salvation.[141]

The Early Church developed canon law as a response to challenges from outside the church. Although the very first Christian communities expressed prodigious faith in the leadership of the Holy Spirit, this soon gave way to a worldly ordering of their institutions and social interactions. In the Roman Catholic Church, a specific type of legal discourse developed, leaning on Imperial Roman law. According to critics, such as Rudolph Sohm, a Protestant law historian writing in 1892, the legalistic thinking of the Roman Church falsified the Christian faith.[142] Instead of seeing canon law as an instrument to be used only in utmost need, the Catholic Church considered it as a divinely instituted legal system, in which the church, in the name of God, was the ultimate arbiter of salvation. The infallibility of the Pope – declared during the First Vatican Council, shortly before Sohm wrote his criticism – is seen as the apogee of this mode of thinking.[143] While Sohm's criticism is exaggerated, the same idea is expressed in many Orthodox critiques of the Roman Catholic Church; it acts as a legalistic entity instead of a community of love.[144] During the twentieth century, Roman Catholic canon law was systematised and codified in a single codex, in order to make its administration easier.

In the Orthodox Church, canon law never acquired the same status as in the Roman Catholic Church. Canonical regulations were never codified but are still found in disparate collections and individual sources. Moreover, the nature of Orthodox canon law is not prescriptive but rather corrective, "responding to a situation once it has occurred."[145] This can be attributed to the lack of a central legislating authority within Orthodoxy. Therefore, in addition to the formal legislation of various councils and patristic writings, canonical authority is attributed "to a host of other sources: civil legislation, rulings of patriarchs, acts of synods, canonical commentaries [...], canonical responses, and others."[146] The multiplicity of sources for canon law makes it difficult to discuss concisely. An Orthodox canon lawyer always refers to as many supporting canonical regulations as possible, starting with the canons of the Ecumenical Councils and

---

139 Patsavos, 1975.
140 Gherasim, 2007, p. 21.
141 This aspect is most clearly put forward by Coriden, 2000.
142 Sohm, 1892, p. 456.
143 Sohm, 1892, p. 458.
144 E.g. Bicilli, 1923; Meyendorff, 1984. See also Coriden, 2000, for an assessment of the developments within Roman Catholicism in the twentieth century.
145 Patsavos, 1975.
146 Viscuso, 2006, p. 5.

ending with local statutes.[147] The insistence by Orthodox canon lawyers on the importance of the historical and social context of each canon further complicates the issue.[148]

Two important characteristics of Orthodox canon law deserve to be singled out. The principle of *oikonomia*, the idea that a canonical regulation can be set aside for the general welfare of all, is emphasised in almost all treatments on Orthodox canon law.[149] According to this principle, human nature is imperfect and, therefore, cannot always follow all prescribed rules. It is possible for a bishop to make exceptions to canonical provisions when necessary for the salvation of those concerned. The second important principle is that of conciliarity, often cited in Russian as *sobornost'*. This principle, which maintains that important decisions of ecclesiastic life can only be taken by the church in its entirety, was a very important foundational principle at the *sobor* in Moscow 1917-1918.[150] While discussing the reinstallation of the Patriarchate, various Russian theologians expressed their understandings of *sobornost'*. Finally, it was agreed that the local council, the regularly convening *sobor*, was the highest authority in the Orthodox Church of Russia. The new Patriarch was to preside over the daily administration of the church. His position should be the first among equals of the bishops, and he would be responsible to the *sobor*.[151] As first among equals, the Patriarch was to be the visible head of the church and the natural arbitrator for any questions of wider scope than the Eparchy, but without the ability to take the initiative and 'rule' over the other bishops.

1.3. Discourse Analysis and Mass Media

Discourse analysis consists of two parts in need of an explanation. That is the discourse and its analysis. Briefly, a discourse is constituted by all texts and utterances concerning a specific topic that exist in a certain temporal, geographical, and communicational context.[152] Following the poststructuralist school of thought, its analysis uncovers "the symbolical and structural dimensions of discourses, the practice of discourse production and discursive power struggles, which by no means aim at social integration or a consensus, but rather mobilisation of collective action, defining normality and deviation as well as trans-

---

147 Gherasim, 2007, p. 27-28.
148 Patsavos, 1975. See also Afanasiev, 1967 [1936].
149 Patsavos, 1975; Viscuso, 2006, p. 21, 98; Gherasim, 2007, p. 26.
150 Destivelle, 2006, esp. p. 125-138.
151 Destivelle, 2006, p. 137-138.
152 See Jung, 2006, p. 34.

forming existing systems of knowledge and morality."[153] The Orthodox Church in the Baltic region is a good example to which to apply such an analysis, as it was considered a deviation from the norm by the Lutheran majority. Throughout the interwar period, the Orthodox actors tried, arguably in vain, to mobilise collective action in order to overturn their negative perception by the majority.

A discourse encompasses all expressions within a given context and, therefore, is impossible to capture and analyse as a whole, leaving the scholar to analyse only a section deemed especially representative and/or accessible. In my case, all utterances which refer to Orthodox Christianity in Estonia and Latvia between 1917 and 1940 are potentially relevant. However, almost no vocal utterances are recoverable and even written sources are preserved haphazardly. Therefore, I have limited my core source corpus to publications composed by Orthodox Christians in Estonia and Latvia during the given time period. These include, first and foremost, the Orthodox journals which existed in both countries throughout the period. Using press digests, cross-references, and event searches, I have also included many articles which reference Orthodox Christianity in the secular and Lutheran ecclesiastical presses. Occasionally, I have referred to archive materials or secondary sources in order to clarify a point.

Using the published press for discourse analysis, especially in relation to the challenges of modernity, is justified. Mass media represent the most convenient way of spreading and reacting to the discourse of modernity. It is widely assumed that mass media is paramount to the constitution of a public discourse within a public sphere. However, as Jörg Requate, a German historian, has argued, too little attention has been paid to the interplay between differing kinds of public spheres and mass media.[154] Requate combines various theoretical approaches to argue for a complex system of public spheres that are horizontally and vertically differentiated. Different public spheres (academic, ecclesiastical, political, cultural etc.) – more or less autonomous, partly overlapping – consist of internal structures of communication happening at three levels. At the 'encounter'-level, the communication occurs haphazardly in everyday situations, such as shopping, dining or having a drink. The 'gathering'-level is more direct and intentional, including meetings of associations and mass gatherings. Finally, at the level of 'mass media,' communication becomes more unidirectional and controllable. All three levels are important for the functioning of a public sphere, but the highest level has most relevance in relation to modernity.

The opinions published by the Orthodox press might not have always reflected the opinion of the Orthodox faithful as a whole, but they were by and large the ones the leadership of the church wanted to spread among the members and society at large. The distinction between the ecclesiastical and secular press

---

153 Keller et al., 2006, p. 12-13.
154 Requate, 1999, p. 12-15.

becomes important here, since the former was oriented to internal communication, whereas the secular press reached the general public. In both the Estonian and Latvian cases, moreover, the secular press appeared in three guises: a national one, a Russian one, and a German one. The interaction between the mass medias of several public spheres in the Baltic States has not, to my knowledge, been analysed.[155] Without pretending to carry out such an analysis, I indicate the cases where such interaction is noticeable.

In order to correctly assess these sources, a brief historical outline of the Orthodox periodical press in interwar Estonia and Latvia is necessary. The first official Orthodox journal in the Eparchy of Riga was *Rižskie Eparkhial'nye Vedomosti* (The Rigan Eparchy Messages), published in Russian from 1888.[156] It remained the official organ of the Orthodox Church in the Baltic lands until 1917, when it stopped publishing due to the First World War. In addition to this official Russian-language journal, the Estonians and Latvians began publishing journals in their own languages in the beginning of the twentieth century.[157]

The Estonian Othodox journal emerged in 1904 and was called *Usk ja Elu* (Faith and Life, *UjE₁*). It was published by Aleksander Värat, an ethnic Estonian archpriest, until November 1917, the last few months from exile in St. Petersburg.[158] Värat was not very positively regarded by Estonian nationalist circles, and by April 1917, it was decided that his journal was no longer the official voice of Estonian Orthodoxy.[159] Archpriest Anton Laar, a nationalist, tried to convince Värat to hand the journal over to him. He failed and established a new journal, *Uus Elu* (New Life, *UE*). This journal, which ran only four issues between 1918 and 1920, published as a monthly from 1921 until Laar's death in February 1933. Archpriest Konstantin Kokla, who had been a major contributor to Värat's journal until 1917, re-established *Usk ja Elu* (Faith and Life, *UjE₂*) in 1933, claiming that Laar's journal had not been commercially viable and that the Orthodox believers in Estonia longed for the return of the former journal.[160] The leadership of the Estonian Orthodox Church disagreed, and Kokla's journal was the official one only until 1936, when the chairman of the synod of the Estonian

---

155 Andreas Fülberth has also carried out a discourse analysis of the published discourse in the interwar Baltic States, focusing on the architectural and conservational debates surrounding the capitals. His topic is a very different one, but his approach is similar to mine. Fülberth, 2005.

156 There had been short-lived more or less official periodicals also previously, but they need not interest us here.

157 Gavrilin, 2006, p. 125. See also chapter 2.1.2.

158 Konstantin Kokla, "'Usk ja Elu' kõneleb seekord iseenesest" ['Faith and Life' speaks this once about itself] in *UjE₂*, 4/13, 1936, p. 199-200.

159 See chapter 2.2.1. See also chapter 6.4. for short biographies of the main actors.

160 Konstantin Kokla, "'Usk ja Elu' kõneleb seekord iseenesest" ['Faith and Life' speaks this once about itself] in *UjE₂*, 4/13, 1936, p. 199-200.

Orthodox Church, Archpriest Nikolai Päts, started publishing *Elutõde* (Truth of Life, *ET*). Thus, two Estonian Orthodox journals existed between 1936 and 1940, which occasionally referenced each other but seldom in positive terms. Both journals ceased publishing in 1940 due to the war.

A Russian-language journal for the ethnic Russian Orthodox in Estonia existed from 1931. This journal, called *Pravoslavnyj Sobesednik* (Orthodox Messenger, *PS*), was published by Archpriest Ioann Bogojavlenskij and was explicitly welcomed by Metropolitan Aleksander of the Estonian Orthodox Church. This journal, while publishing official notices from the Estonian Orthodox Synod, retained a more universal scope, focussing on the struggle with atheism and the situation in the Soviet Union.[161] Just as the other Estonian journals, *Pravoslavnyj Sobesednik* halted publication in 1940.

The first Latvian Orthodox journal appeared in 1906 with the name *Pareizticiīgo Latviešu Vēstnesis* (Latvian Orthodox Messenger, *PLV*), published by Archpriest Jānis Jansons in the provincial town of Tukums. It continued publication until the German occupation in April 1917. Two issues of a short-lived journal called *Krusta Ēna* (The Shadow of the Cross) appeared in 1920, before Archpriest Kirils Zaics and Teodors Būcens began publication in Riga of the journals *Ticība un Dzīve* (Faith and Life, *TuD*) in Latvian and *Vera i Žizn'* (Faith and Life, *ViŽ*) in Russian in 1923. Although the two journals shared a name and were published by the same people, they remained two separate journals, with only an occasional article appearing in both.

At end of 1931, Zaics claimed that the journals were no longer financially viable and asked for more money from the Synod of the Latvian Orthodox Church. When the Synod was not willing to provide more funding, the Latvian-language journal ceased publication, and Zaics transformed the Russian-language one into an international journal for Orthodox missionary theology and 'sect science,' which he funded privately.[162] This continued until November 1933, when Zaics was accused of taking money from the cash box of the Riga Cathedral and stripped of his clerical ranks.[163] The Latvian Synod appointed Archpriest Nikolai Perechval'skij of Riga as the new editor of the Russian-language journal and tasked Archpriest Pēteris Gredzens from the provincial

---

161 Interestingly, the first four issues were delivered together with an issue of the *Голос Литовской Православной Епархии* [Voice of the Lithuanian Orthodox Eparchy]. The relationship of Archbishop Elevferij of Lithuania to Ioann Bogojavlenskij, brothers, explains this. However, the Lithuanian Eparchy remained subordinated to the Patriarch of Moscow. In other words, the Russian-language journal obviously maintained a different stance towards the Patriarchate of Moscow than the rest of the Orthodox Church of Estonia, which wanted as little contact as possible. See also chapter 2.2.2.

162 Кирилл Зайц, "Указ Синода" [Synod Decision] in *ViŽ*, 10/1, 1932, p. 14-15; Кирилл Зайц, "Просьба" [Plea] in *ViŽ*, 10/1, 1932, p. 15-16.

163 Golikov and Škarovskij, 2002. See also chapter 2.3.2.

town of Talsi with reviving the Latvian journal. Both journals continued publication under these editors until 1940, when the Second World War made further publishing impossible.

The empirical sections which follow first juxtapose as many sources as possible in order to arrive at a historically sound account of the developments in the Estonian and Latvian Orthodox Church. This historical context then enables the analysis of the various strands of discourse. As the sources are seldom archival, but rather discursive in nature, it has not always been possible to separate contextualisation and analysis; thus, they often proceed simultaneously. However, there is a methodical order that I repeat in each of the following sections. Each begins with a general contextualisation, in which sources of a general nature, primarily from outside the scope of the analysed discourse, are used. Thereafter, the Orthodox discourse is analysed, to the extent in which it can be identified within the sources.

2. Orthodox Church Structures

The debates regarding structure in the Orthodox Churches of Estonia and Latvia during the interwar period centred on issues such as the canonical status of the churches, the relationship between ethnic Russians and the other nations, as well as the relationship of the churches with the respective states and their involvement in secular politics. This is the most substantial part of the book. It traces these debates from the year of the revolutions (1917) until the advent of the Second World War in 1940. The first chapter elaborates on the historical and institutional context in which the two Orthodox Churches operated. The second chapter traces the developments of the 1920s, when the two young churches euphorically savoured their independence. The third chapter then analyses the effects of this independence in the changed mental, institutional, and political circumstances from the 1930s through the end of the liberal order in 1940.

2.1. Orthodoxy and the Baltic Region

In order to understand the structural debates in the Orthodox Church in Estonia and Latvia, it is necessary to grasp the complex historical and socio-political context in which they occurred. This chapter is a thematic introduction to the Orthodox Church in the Baltic region, which I define as the territory of the interwar Estonian and Latvian nation-states. Since the history of the Orthodox Church in this region begins with the establishment of a vicar bishop's seat in Riga in 1836, this chapter starts with a section contextualising this event. The following section then tries to navigate between competing historiographic accounts of the history of the Orthodox Church in the region until 1917.[1] Third, a section briefly characterises the political developments in interwar Estonia and Latvia, before a fourth section details the demographics of the two states.

2.1.1. The Baltic Provinces in the Mid-Nineteenth Century

The Baltic Provinces of the Russian Empire were Estland, Livland and Kurland, annexed by Peter the Great after the Great Nordic War in the early eighteenth century.[2] These provinces had been controlled by German nobility and German

---

1   See chapter 4. for more on this historiography.
2   I will refer to their German names throughout to avoid ambiguities. See chapter 6.1. for a map. Estland and Livland came under the Russian crown in 1710/1721, while Kurland was annexed only in 1795.

bourgeoisie (the Baltic Germans) since the Baltic crusades in the thirteenth century. Although the Orthodox Church had sent the first Christian missions to the Baltic tribes at the beginning of the second Millennium AD, these efforts were not very successful. Catholic missionaries, who arrived on the Baltic shores beginning at the end of the twelfth century, had much more success, partly because they relied as much on the sword as on the Word. By the time of the annexation by the Russian Empire, there were practically no Orthodox believers in the Baltic areas beyond a few Russian craftsmen and merchants in the towns. Although the Baltic provinces became part of the Russian Empire, the Orthodox Church did not grow markedly, for Peter the Great granted the Baltic Germans a number of privileges, including the right of the Baltic German Lutheran Church to retain its monopoly among the Estonian and Latvian peasants.

The cultural and administrative hold on the provinces by the Baltic Germans can be illustrated by the total absence of the Russian language at all levels of the local administration. The few Estonians and Latvians, who managed to leave the peasant class, only did so by becoming Germans. The Russian Tsars went to great lengths to accommodate the privileges of the Baltic Germans. They were seen as progressive and diligent and were, therefore, often recruited to the Imperial administration and esteemed by Russian high society. In the Baltic provinces, they were the undisputed masters, controlling the Lutheran Church and most of the agricultural land.

The Estonian and Latvian peasants occupied the other end of the social ladder. At the height of feudalism in the late eighteenth century, they were considered a commodity without any legal or property rights of their own. When serfdom was abolished in the three provinces in 1816/1819, the feudal lords retained ownership of all the land, but the peasants were accorded personal freedom and became full subjects of civil law. The economic relation between the two groups was to be regulated by lease contracts.[3] While these new regulations improved the legal rights and status of the peasantry, they did pave the way for an improvement of their actual condition. Lease agreements with untenable conditions and demands were common, and although the peasants had legal rights on paper, they were unable to assert them in the face of the powerful landowners. This state of affairs led to a deterioration of the day-to-day situation for most peasants in the Baltic Provinces.

An unconnected development in the Baltic region was initiated by the policies of Tsar Nikolai I, who was more determined to consolidate the entire Empire than his predecessors. In 1832, he introduced new, consistent statutes for the Lutheran Church in the entire Russian Empire.[4] The new statutes had several

---

3   Wittram, Reinhard, 1973, p. 156-159; Plakans, 1995, p. 81-83; Raun, 2001, p. 47-48.
4   von Schrenck, 1933, p. 39-44; Tschoerner, 2005, p. 13-23.

far-reaching consequences for the Lutheran Church in the Baltic Provinces. Most significantly, it had lost its privileged position as the rights of the Orthodox State Church were extended throughout the Empire. However, it is more correct to view this as a side-effect of the new regulations, rather than their intention. There is no reason to believe that Tsar Nikolai meant to restrict the privileges of the Baltic Germans who remained among his most loyal subjects.

Unfortunately, the many positive consequences of the new church statutes were often forgotten in the polemic debates of the second half of the nineteenth century.[5] These benefits were most apparent in the increasing contact among Lutherans from Tallinn to Tashkent, who for the first time were united by a singular organisation. Also the requirement to hold yearly synods in each church province had positive results. The pastors of the countryside and those of the cities were, for the first time, given a common forum in which to discuss church politics and solve theological disputes. The three Baltic provinces of the Lutheran Church gained political weight through the synods, as they were able to channel their efforts and act in a more unified manner.[6]

Another result of Tsar Nikolai I's wish, in the memory of the Napoleonic invasion and the Decembrist uprising, to strengthen the borders of the Empire was the establishment of an Orthodox vicar bishop's seat in Riga in 1836. Since the end of the seventeenth century, when the liturgical reforms of Patriarch Nikon of Moscow led to schism in the Russian Orthodox Church, there had been an influx of Old Believers, fleeing persecution inside Russia, into the Baltic areas. In the course of consolidating the fringe groups of the Empire, efforts were increased to bring the Old Believers back to the Orthodox Church. Since the administrative structures of the Baltic Provinces differed from the other parts of the Empire, it was difficult for the Orthodox Bishop of Pskov, whose jurisdiction extended over Livland, to undertake much work there.[7] Therefore, Irinarch (Popov) was installed as Bishop of Riga. Irinarch had extensive experience outside Russia, as a priest in Italy and in Athens, but was completely ignorant of the specific situation in the Baltic Provinces. However, he was an energetic and productive man, who very soon made progress in reuniting some Riga Old Believers with the official church.[8]

A third important development was the failure of the harvest in 1840 and the famine in the following year. Since the peasants were no longer their property, the landlords felt less responsible for them, and they lost hope in securing any help from their masters. Although most of the peasants had never had any direct contact with representatives of the Russian authorities, they had heard about the

---

5   See chapter 4.1.
6   von Schrenck, 1933, p. 44-56.
7   Pommers, 1940; Gavrilin, 1999, p. 49-55; Aleksij, 1999, p. 159.
8   Gavrilin, 1999, p. 49-55; Aleksij, 1999, p. 162.

'benevolent' Emperor, who came to be seen as their only hope. Groups of peasants began travelling to the provincial capital Riga and rumours spread that the Emperor was distributing cheap land in the south of Russia to the starving Livland peasants.[9]

The unrest was suppressed with the help of the military by September 1841, but the peasants had already made the acquaintance of Bishop Irinarch, who treated them with respect and even promised to see what he could do to address their complaints. On the insistence of the Baltic German authorities, Bishop Irinarch was removed from his post in October and replaced by the more diplomatical Filaret (Gumilevskij).[10] Together with the rigorous use of military force, this resulted in hopelessness and pessimism among the peasants, who felt they had lost the only authority 'on their side.' Their dashed hopes contributed to their suppression for the next four years. When another famine occurred in 1845, the peasants again became unruly. This time, they turned immediately to the Orthodox bishop and asked to convert to Orthodoxy. The movement developed an internal dynamicism and by 1848, more than 100,000 peasants, 17% of the Estonian and 10% of the Latvian population of Livland had become Orthodox Christians, before the conversions suddenly stopped.[11]

The conversion movement was strictly confined to the province of Livland, and the number of conversions varied considerably from parish to parish. To serve all these new Orthodox believers, thirty-nine new Orthodox congregations were founded in the Estonian part of Livland and thirty-three in the Latvian part. Many of these congregations were temporarily accommodated in rather unpleasant premises such as stables, near-derelict buildings, or loud tavern lofts.[12] By 1848, only ten new churches had been built and a mere three more were under construction. Each of these was much smaller and plainer than the neighbouring Lutheran parish church. Nevertheless, each time a new congregation was founded, the conversion movement tended to intensify in its immediate vicinity, if only for a short while. In addition to the church buildings, it was also difficult to find priests that were able to work under the extreme conditions for these new

---

9   Raun, 2001, p. 45. According to Daniel Ryan, "peasant belief in the rumors has become virtually axiomatic in the literature on the subject." Instead of accepting this view, Ryan suggests seeing the rumours instead as a means to reconfigure social hierarchies. Ryan, 2008, p. 144-145. See also chapter 4.2.

10 Kruus, 1930, p. 128-130; Gavrilin, 1999, p. 99-101, Aleksij, 1999, p. 171-180.

11 The literature on the movement is extremely polemic in nature. Due to the political context and the historical distance, it is hardly ever possible to treat it without a bias. There are three source-based studies, each of which draw rather different conclusions from the events: Kruus, 1930; Gavrilin, 1999, p. 73-182; Ryan, 2008, p. 144-227. See also chapter 4.2.

12 Kruus, 1930, p. 298. Gavrilin notes the same even in the 1860s: Gavrilin, 1999, p. 221-222.

congregations. They had to minister to members who spoke a foreign language and lacked the most elementary knowledge of Orthodox Christianity in an entirely Lutheran environment.

Finally, a fourth development that began in the mid-nineteenth century should be mentioned; the nascent Estonian and Latvian nationalist movements, invariably termed the 'national awakening' by later historiographies.[13] Until the 1860s, only a handful of indigenous intellectuals, although fully Germanised externally, continued to call themselves Estonians or Latvians. After the agrarian reforms of 1849-1860, this group grew and soon began acting on behalf of the national movement, establishing newspapers and societies, writing poetry, and collecting folklore. The relationship between the rising national consciousness and Orthodox Christianity was very ambiguous.[14]

2.1.2. The Orthodox Church in the Baltic Provinces until 1917

Leaving aside judgement of the reasons and consequences of the conversion movement, it is obvious that the sudden increase in the number of Orthodox Latvians and Estonians profoundly impacted the social structure of the Livland province.[15] First, neither the existing social hierarchy nor the Orthodox Church were sufficiently prepared to cope with the sudden change. The Baltic German Lutheran pastors and landowners were at a loss concerning treatment of the converts. Their first reflex was to ridicule the conversions, blaming Orthodox agitators, rumours, and Russification measures. They simply could not understand why the Orthodox Church was needed in Livland at all. Then, they started to discriminate against the peasants who had converted, using confessional affiliation as a justification.[16]

The Orthodox Church, on the other hand, was compelled to form new parishes from scratch, as it were, since the few city parishes that existed could not accommodate the peasants in the countryside. The financial resources needed for this construction were not available. Many of the converts belonged to the

---

13 Raun and Plakans, 1990; Plakans, 1995, p. 89-100; Raun, 2001, p. 57-80.
14 This relationship in the Estonian case was the topic of my Master's Thesis. See Rimestad, 2007. See also chapter 4.2.
15 The conversions of the 1840s were strictly limited to the province of Livland, some authors even maintaining that conversion wishes in Estland and Kurland had been punished. von Harleß, 1887, p. 25; Aleksij, 1999, p. 197. See also chapter 4.
16 The actual extent of this discrimination is difficult to ascertain. Daniel Ryan argues, on the basis of primary sources, that many of these complaints, instead of showing religious discrimination, highlighted the long existing arbitrariness of the landlords by using "religious affiliation as a means of contesting status, rights, and obligations and of attacking local authority." Ryan, 2008, p. 191.

poorest strata of peasant society and could not contribute to founding a parish. Also the Most Holy Synod in St. Petersburg simply did not react to the sudden growth in membership in this previously unchartered territory. The Livland conversions, although numbering more than 100,000, only amounted to 5.3% of all conversions to Orthodoxy between 1825 and 1850.[17] The Orthodox Church was occupied re-integrating the Uniate Church and converting Muslims, and as such, there were no special funds allocated to the Baltic Provinces. The construction of new parishes and congregations was further hampered by the lack of knowledge of the local languages on the part of Orthodox clergy. The need for clergy resulted in numerous sudden ordinations of underprepared individuals.[18]

Lutheran antagonism, on the one hand, and the perceived inactivity of the Orthodox Church, on the other, led some converts to regret their decision, and a debate concerning the possibility to re-convert resulted. According to Imperial law, conversion away from the Orthodox Church was prohibited. However, numerous complaints from the Baltic German community and a revision report by the German-friendly Count Bobrinskij prompted Tsar Aleksander II to sign a secret concession in 1864, which suspended the rule that children of Orthodox parents must be baptised in the Orthodox faith.[19] Thus, formal affiliation with the Orthodox Church could be overcome by the following generation.

Structurally, one should mention that the vicariate of Riga had been elevated to a full Eparchy which encompassed Livland and Kurland in 1850 and was extended in 1865 to include Estland.[20] Thus, the Bishop of Riga could act independently. In the second half of the nineteenth century, the Orthodox Church constituted a parallel community to the Baltic German one. This included parallel education establishments. The parish schools of the Lutheran Church were not open to Orthodox pupils, and the Orthodox Church had to build a parallel parish school system. This led to a moderate 'education race,' in which the Baltic Germans were almost always ahead due to a large pool of intellectual resources.[21] Moreover, since secondary education was relatively closed to Orthodox believers, the Orthodox Church opened a School and Seminary in Riga. In contrast to other such seminaries in the Russian Empire, the Riga Seminary accepted peasants' sons in addition to the offspring of clergy and offered a

---

17 Freeze, 2004, p. 310. See also Rimestad, 2011, p. 75-76.
18 There were at least two Latvians (Dāvis Balodis and Jakobs Mihailovs) consecrated priests without graduating from a seminary and numerous local sacristans suddenly named priests in order to meet the need. Purviņš, 1929, p. 19-20; Gavrilin, 1999, p. 142-146; Ryan, 2008, p. 201-205.
19 von Harleß, 1887, p.192; Kahle, 1959, p. 151; Garve, 1978, p. 170; Gavrilin, 1999, p. 222; Aleksij, 1999, p. 257.
20 Gavrilin, 1999, p. 189; Aleksij, 1999, p. 231-232, 267.
21 Gavrilin, 1999, p. 199; Aleksij, 1999, 244; Kiverik, 2005, p. 54.

number of scholarships to poor pupils.[22] Throughout the nineteenth century, the classes consisted roughly of one third ethnic Russians, one third ethnic Latvians, and one third ethnic Estonians. Latvian and Estonian was taught at all levels, not only the first years as in the Lutheran schools. Another element of the parallel Orthodox Baltic community was the press, which emphasised the use of local languages more than the Baltic German press. Also brotherhoods were established, which collected funds for the construction of new churches and additional payment for the clergy.[23]

The Lutheran Church achieved a kind of *modus vivendi* with the Orthodox Church by 1874, when Tsar Aleksander II terminated all 'pastoral lawsuits' against Lutheran pastors having performed religious acts on members of the Orthodox Church.[24] This relative peace lasted less than ten years, as the ascent of Tsar Aleksander III to the throne in 1881 marked a change in the Imperial policy towards the Baltic provinces. The period initiated by Aleksander III is usually referred to in Estonian and Latvian historiography as the period of 'Russification.'[25] This included making the use of Russian language compulsory in schools, universities, courts, and administration. Moreover, it meant abolition of many of the Baltic German privileges and the special administrative, legal, judicial, and educational structures of the Baltic Provinces.

In the course of this process, a number of Orthodox churches were built, including the large representative Cathedrals of Riga (1884) and Tallinn (1900). An education from an Orthodox parish school was increasingly perceived as beneficial for later careers. As a result, numerous Lutheran parents sent their children to Orthodox schools.[26] After the judicial reforms, Tsar Aleksander III invalidated the secret concession of his predecessor, suddenly annulling many Lutheran baptisms over the last twenty years. However, attempts to use the Orthodox Church as a means to consolidate the Estonians and Latvians into the Russian Empire failed.[27] The national movements had already gained a strong enough foothold in society that re-nationalisation along imperial lines did not occur large scale. Nevertheless, a second conversion movement started in Estland in 1883 and spread over the Baltic Provinces before suddenly stopping in 1887, after more than 15,000 Estonian and Latvian peasants had converted to Orthodoxy.[28] This movement was not necessarily compliance with the

---

22 Gavrilin, 1999, p. 189-190; Raudsepp, 1998a, p. 25-46; Aleksij, 1999, p. 232-236.
23 Brandt, 1959, p. 250; Aleksij, 1999, p. 237-250, 351-355.
24 Garve, 1978, p. 191; Tschoerner, 2005, p. 92.
25 Thaden, 1981; Plakans, 1995, p. 100-101; Karjahärm, 1997; Raun, 2001, p. 57-80; Brüggemann, 2005, p. 135-136; Brüggemann, 2006, p. 405-406. See also chapter 4.2.
26 Brandt, 1959, p. 106-108; Gavrilin, 1999, p. 30; Kiverik, 2005, p. 57.
27 This had been especially the aim of Governor S. Šakhovskoj of Estland (1885-1897). Rebane, 1933, p. 204-206; Brandt, 1959, p. 196; Gavrilin, 1999, p. 282.
28 Rebane, 1933; Gavrilin, 1999, p. 288; Plaat, 2001, p. 127-138.

Russification policies, but rather a consequence of the Baltic German reactions, attempting to turn the Lutheran Church into a bastion of Germanness.[29] The Orthodox Church was perceived as closer to the peasants rather than the Lutheran master's church.

The Russification period, along with industrialisation and urbanisation paved the way for increased secularisation and de-churching among Latvians and Estonians. The growing influence of socialism also caught hold among the inhabitants of the Baltic Provinces. The failed Russian revolution of 1905-1907 marked a watershed in the social history of these provinces. They saw more of the bloodshed and political conflict than many other regions because their specific history had made the inhabitants more politically and socially aware. The literacy rate among adults was higher than 75% and the national movements had taken impressively modern forms. In regard to the religious question, the most important event during the Revolution was the Manifesto of Tolerance of April 1905, officially legalising the free choice of confession. For the first time in Russian history, conversion away from Orthodox Christianity was legally sanctioned. However, mass reconversions did not occur to the extent the Lutheran Church expected. Different sources give disparate figures, but only about 15% of the Orthodox population converted back to the Lutheran Church in the following four years.[30]

This relatively low percentage reflects how the confessional turmoil of the last twenty years had alienated many of the Estonians and Latvians from religion. Erich von Schrenck, a Baltic German church historian, notes many cases of blasphemous acts committed in both Lutheran and Orthodox churches and of pastors and priests abused and even murdered by revolutionary locals.[31] The churches were, even after the Revolution had calmed down in 1907, described by the local press as institutions of retardation. This negative language was only possible due to the relative freedom of the press promulgated by the October Manifesto. Moreover, the press used its newly won freedom to denounce Orthodox Latvians and Estonians of being Russified and unworthy of the Estonian and Latvian nations, thus confessionalising Baltic society.[32] From inside Russia, equally powerful voices laid the entire blame of the current Baltic 'mess' on the Lutheran Church and Baltic German, Latvian, and Estonian nationalism.[33] The influence of these pressures on the government can be seen in several unpub-

---

29 Garve, 1978, p. 193-208. See also chapter 4.1.1.
30 Karjahärm, 1998b, p. 536; Gavrilin, 1999, p. 328. In actual terms, the Lutheran reconverts only constituted 4.5% of all conversion away from the Orthodox Church in the years following the 1905 manifesto, with those returning to Catholicism and Islam being far more numerous. Freeze, 2004, p. 315.
31 von Schrenck, 1933, p. 159-163.
32 See chapter 3.2.3. for more on this.
33 See for example *Pravoslavie*, 1911.

lished plans to Russify the Baltic Provinces between 1905 and 1914 in which the Orthodox Church was to play a key role. However, none of these strategies survived past the planning stage.[34]

Several plans to reform the Orthodox Church in the Baltic Provinces to make it more successful were developed locally by Archbishop Agafangel (Preobraženskij) and centrally by the Most Holy Synod in St. Petersburg.[35] These plans for reform included improving the operation of the Orthodox parish schools and furthering the penetration of positively connoted Orthodoxy into all layers of Baltic society. Other than more publications in Estonian and Latvian, including the founding of Orthodox periodicals in the two languages, few concrete measures came of these efforts.[36] However, there were already attempts to make Orthodox Christianity more Estonian and Latvian in place. Jeffers Engelhardt has shown how the process of 'Estonianising' Orthodox Christianity took place in numerous Orthodox Estonian-language publications from 1905 onwards.[37]

2.1.3. Institutional Context in the Interwar Years

When the First World War erupted, the Estonians and Latvians regarded it primarily as a clash between the imperial ambitions of Russia and Germany.[38] The Russian Imperial administration was obviously wary of the Baltic Germans, who experienced some difficulty in deciding where to place their loyalty – with the Russian Empire, to whom they had committed themselves, or with their ethnic compatriots in the German *Reich*. In the autumn of 1917, the Baltic German Estates of all three Baltic Provinces voted to place themselves under the protection of the *Reich*.[39] The German troops had already entered the Lithuanian territories and Kurland in 1915, and continued north to occupy Livland and Estland after calls from the Baltic Germans there in 1917/1918.[40]

In the meantime, the February revolution of 1917 had installed the quasi-liberal democratic Provisional Government in Russia. The news was received with great euphoria, especially by the Estonians and Latvians, who saw this as an opportunity to restructure the outdated form of Baltic Provinces.[41] Instead of

---

34 Karjahärm, 1998a, p. 261-268.
35 Karjahärm, 1998b, p. 538-540; Gavrilin, 2006.
36 Karjahärm, 1998a, p. 266; Gavrilin, 2006, p. 125. See also chapter 1.4.1.
37 Engelhardt, 2005, p. 139-147. See also chapter 3.1.
38 von Rauch, 1977, p. 35.
39 Hiden and Salmon, 1994, p. 28.
40 von Rauch, 1977, p. 52-54; Plakans, 1995, p. 116-117.
41 von Rauch, 1977, p. 38; Plakans, 1995, p. 115; Raun, 2001, p. 99-102.

three provinces – Kurland, Livland, and Estland – they argued the Baltic lands should be divided according to ethnicity into an Estonian province and a Latvian province. Although the Provisional Government was reluctant to grant too many concessions to the Balts, a united Estonian province was created. This was facilitated by the choice of provincial commissars: the mayors of the provincial capitals. The city governments had been the first administrative structures to be nationalised, so both Tallinn and Riga had indigenous mayors: Jaan Poska in Tallinn and Andrejs Krastkalns in Riga.[42] However, the demands of the Latvians to annex Kurland and the district of Latgale in the Vitebsk *Gubernija* into the new Latvian province were not answered.[43]

All attempts to find new ways to administer the Baltic provinces were brought to a halt by the Bolshevik October Revolution, which turned the demands for autonomy within the Empire into ambitions for total independence. The looming German troops further strengthened these ambitions. A last-minute declaration of Estonian independence was proclaimed in Tallinn on 24 February 1918, shortly before German troops occupied the city.[44] This declaration was never recognised by the German occupants, but Britain, France, and Italy, alerted to the northward expansion of the German occupation, recognised the independence *de facto* in May 1918. The Latvians had to wait until the end of the war in November 1918 to proclaim their independence, which was quickly recognised *de facto*.[45]

Although the war was officially over and the independence of the Baltic States proclaimed, the violent struggle for nationhood was far from finished. When the troops of the German *Reich* retreated from the Baltic scene, four competing groups attempted to fill the ensuing power vacuum.[46] First, the liberal national governments headed by Konstantin Päts in Estonia and Kārlis Ulmanis in Latvia organised national patriotic army units.[47] In Estonia, these units were assisted by the British Navy, the regiments of the Baltic Germans, and Finnish volunteers. The forces commanded by the Baltic German nobility in Latvia belonged to a second competing group, acting in conjunction with the retreating troops of the German Reich. Third, after the Bolshevik Revolution in Russia, socialist sentiments also became strong in the Baltic areas, and in both Estonia and Latvia, the local Bolsheviks took over the municipal governments of the capital cities, Tallinn and Riga. Finally, the Socialist government in Russia had

---

42   Garleff, 2001, p. 93; Brüggemann, 2005, p. 129.
43   Probably because of the German occupation of Kurland. Hiden, 1994, p. 30.
44   Garleff, 2001, p. 95; Hiden and Salmon, 1994, p. 32 Raun, 2001, p. 104-105.
45   von Rauch, 1977, p.61; Hiden and Salmon, 1994, p. 32; Plakans, 1995, p. 117-118.
46   von Rauch, 1977, p. 42-75; Hiden and Salmon, 1994, p. 32-38; Plakans, 1995, p. 118-120; Garleff, 2001, p. 100-102; Raun, 2001, p. 107-111.
47   Both of these were important political figures throughout the interwar period, and both installed authoritarian regimes in the 1930s. See also chapter 2.3.3.

not yet given up 'its' Baltic Provinces and sent the Red Army to recapture these areas.

In the Estonian case, the Red Army was strong and enjoyed the support of the local Bolsheviks. Within few months, they occupied most of mainland Estonia, with the exception of Tallinn, but the Bolsheviks could not hold onto the power in the face of the united opposition of Estonians, Baltic Germans, and the Allies. By February 1919, all of Estonia had been liberated once again. On the day before the Red Army fled Tartu, it executed several prisoners, including the Orthodox Archbishop Platon (Kulbusch) and other Orthodox and Lutheran clergymen.[48]

In Latvia, the situation was somewhat more complicated. For one, the local Bolshevik Party, under the leadership of Pēteris Stučka, was strong and dominated Riga along with most of Latvia from November 1918 to April 1919. Second, an agreement was reached between the Allied powers and the remaining German troops in Latvia to recognise the national government of Kārlis Ulmanis, evacuated to Liepāja, as the legitimate government in Latvia. This agreement failed when some Baltic Germans revolted, replaced Ulmanis with the German-friendly Andrievs Niedra, and started an offensive push in the direction of Riga. By April 1919, they had taken most of Kurland. In May they entered Riga and drove the Bolsheviks east. At the same time, Estonian-commanded troops, consisting partly of Latvians, launched an offensive campaign from the north. They defeated the German-controlled troops in early June 1919, at the decisive battle of Cēsis.[49] The victory of Estonian-Latvian soldiers over their German and Baltic German adversaries took on a symbolic significance, signalling the end of 700 years of German domination over Latvians and Estonians.[50]

Although the remaining German forces united with soldiers from the Russian Western Army to launch a last attempt to regain Riga and Latvia in October 1919, this attempt was thwarted by the Latvians. By February 1920, even the Bolsheviks had been driven from Latvia. In the peace treaties signed with the Soviet Union over the course of 1920, the Baltic States were accorded more territories than they would have dreamt of some years earlier. The Estonians gained the county of Petserimaa in the southeast and a strip of land beyond the Narva River in the north. Latvia gained the entirety of Latgale.[51] The young nation states of Estonia and Latvia quickly installed a liberal legal framework of

---

48 See Bühmann, 2008 for the discourse on the so-called Baltic Martyrs in the Lutheran Church until the Second World War. See also chapters 2.2.1., 2.2.2. and 2.2.5. for more on Archbishop Platon.

49 Cēsis is the Latvian name – the town is called Wenden in German and Võnnu in Estonian.

50 See Pajur, 2009; Zellis, 2009.

51 See chapter 6.1.2. for a map of the new states.

a sort which had never existed in the Russian Empire. Before turning to any more direct measures, both states promulgated sweeping land reforms, which distributed the land of the Baltic German elites among the Estonian and Latvian peasants working on it, thereby equalising society to some extent.[52]

The Estonian constitution of May 1920 clearly stated that all inhabitants of Estonia were equal before the law.[53] Moreover, in a very exemplary manner, the constitution gave minority communities the right to receive education in their mother tongue, which they could also use in communications with central state authorities. This right was extended to the Russians, the Germans, the Swedes, and the Jews. In the years between 1920-1925, heated discussions concerning the legal provisions for the minorities occurred, which resulted in a law of cultural autonomy for national minorities, unparalleled at the time.[54] Under this law, the minority communities of Estonia received the right to form public organisations, organise education in their languages, and even to collect special taxes from their communities. The German and Jewish communities quickly made use of these provisions, while the Russian minority was too heterogeneous to agree on any cultural autonomy.[55]

In Latvia, the constitution of 1922 also stated that all inhabitants were equal before the law. However, minority populations were granted somewhat fewer protections than in Estonia. In particular, the official use of non-Latvian languages was more restricted.[56] The Latvian parliament – the *Saeima* – never agreed on a general law to govern the national minorities and their specific situations were regulated by a host of individual laws. One of these laws created a system of education that was similar to the one in Estonia. Nonetheless, unlike in Estonia, there were demands for the Latvianisation of all of society in the 1930s, testified by restrictive language policies and vocal Latvian nationalism.[57]

Legislation concerning religious organisations in Estonia had to be developed from scratch, as the new Estonian State was to be a secular and tolerant state. A law on religious organisations and their associations was promulgated in 1925, which confirmed a ruling from 1919 that the churches were no longer corporations under public law, but had to register as associations of congregations.[58] The individual congregations were completely free to enter or leave the church association at will and all religious organisations, regardless of their membership, were treated equally.

---

52   von Rauch, 1977, p. 90-93; Plakans, 1995, p. 124-126; Garleff, 2001, p. 111-113.
53   Plasseraud, 2003, p. 120; Ringvee, 2008, p. 181.
54   Garleff, 2001, p. 127-145; Plasseraud, 2003, p. 122-124; Smith, David J., 2005.
55   Plasseraud, 2003, p. 123; Smith, David J., 2005, p. 211-212. See also chapter 2.2.3.
56   Garleff, 2001, p. 126-127; Plasseraud, 2003, p. 127-128; Smith, David J., 2005, p. 220.
57   Plasseraud, 2003, p. 139. See also chapter 2.3.3.
58   Bensch, 2004, p. 32; Ringvee, 2008, p. 181-182. See also chapter 2.2.4.

In the Latvian case, after the anti-religious campaigns carried out with special vigour during the Bolshevik control over Latvia in 1918 and 1919, a series of laws from 1919 stipulated that, unless conflicting with new laws, the legislation of the Russian Empire should remain in force.[59] For the Lutheran Church, this meant that it largely continued to function under the statutes of 1832, while the Orthodox Church had no legal recognition at all, since the state church regulations of the Russian Empire were incompatible with the secular Latvian State.[60] Although a 1923 law on socal and political organisations was extended to include religious organisations, the state continued to issue separate laws governing each of the large religious communities in Latvia.[61] Not only the relations were thus governed, but even the internal affairs of the churches were from time to time regulated by the state.[62]

In the 1930s, after years of rapidly changing governments in an unbounded multi-party system (25 parties in the *Saeima* of 1928, 21 Estonian governments 1919-1933), radical political movements appeared in both Estonia and Latvia.[63] When these movements threatened to stage a coup, authoritarian counter-coups were carried out. This occurred in Estonia after the para-fascist *Vabadus-sõjalaste Liit* (Union of Independence War Veterans) managed to change the constitution and threatened to take over the state apparatus in 1934. Konstantin Päts, the first Prime Minister of independent Estonia, introduced martial law and banned all political parties except the *Isamaaliit* (Fatherland Union). A presidential constitution was accepted by a referendum in 1937, and Päts was elected the first president of Estonia. Fascistic organisations also appeared in Latvia, and Kārlis Ulmanis proclaimed martial law in 1934 to counter these developments. Although he continuously claimed that a new constitution would be devised, Ulmanis instead concentrated all power in his hands and remained the leader of Latvia until 1940.[64]

2.1.4. Demographics of the Baltic States

As already mentioned, there were significant minority populations in both Estonia and Latvia. Table 1 illustrates the actual ethnic make-up of the two states. In both states the largest minority were the Russians, making up respectively 8.2 and 10.6% of the total population. The Russian minority in Estonia was primarily composed of tradesmen and factory workers who had settled in Tallinn and

---

59   Zariņš, 1939, p. 31-32; Bensch, 2004, p. 28; Runce, 2008, p. 117-122.
60   See chapter 2.2.5. for this discussion.
61   Zariņš, 1939, p. 36-37. See also chapter 2.2.7.
62   Bensch, 2003, p. 29-31; Runce, 2008, p. 123-155.
63   Garleff, 2001, p. 118-123; Plasseraud, 2003, p. 107-108, 126.
64   See also chapter 2.3.3.

Narva during the industrialisation of the late Tsarist era,[65] along with groups of Old Believers, who lived mostly on the Western shores of the Lake Peipsi.[66] The case of Latvia is similar, although Riga had become a multicultural city in the course of the nineteenth century with an almost self-sufficient Russian community.[67] In addition to this long-established Russian minority, a significant number of the Russians in Estonia and Latvia in the early 1920s were refugees from the Soviet Union, who had fled the Bolsheviks and mostly continued west after a time in the Baltic States.

Table 1. National Minorities in Estonia and Latvia.

Nationality	Estonia (1934)[68]		Latvia (1930)[69]	
	Numbers	%	Numbers	%
Estonians / Latvians	992 520	88.1%	1 394 957	73.4%
Russians	92 656	8.2%	201 778	10.6%
German	16 346	1.5%	69 855	3.7%
Swedish	7 641	0.7%	-	-
Polish/Belarusian/ Lithuanian	-	-	121 288	6.4%
Jewish	4 434	0.4%	94 338	5.0%
Other	12 816	1.2%	17 829	0.9%
Total	1 126 413	100.0%	1 900 045	100.0%

The German minority were the remnants of the Baltic German city dwellers and land-owning class, who had controlled the administration of the Baltic provinces and dominated the city population until urbanisation brought Latvians and Estonians to the cities without turning them into cultural Germans in the mid-nineteenth century.[70] Throughout the interwar period, the Baltic Germans refused to call themselves a minority; instead, they used the term 'Volksgruppe' – national group.[71] The Polish, Ukrainian, and Belarusian minorities in Latvia were mainly

---

65 Isakov, 2001, p. 21-22.
66 Berg and Kulu, 1996; Ponomareva, 2006. See also the venturous travel report to this community in Ammann, 1936.
67 Plasseraud, 2003, p. 135-136; von Hirschhausen, 2006, p. 135-151.
68 Numbers from the 1934 Estonian census. Taken from Andrei Sooster, "Pudemeid usuelust meil ja mujal" [Notices on religious life here and elsewhere] in *UjE₂*, 3, 6, 1935, p. 111-112.
69 Numbers from the 1930 Latvian census. Taken from Al.-sch., "Ticība un tautība Latvijā" [Religion and People in Latvia] in *TuD*, 11, 11, 1935, p. 175-176.
70 See Raun, 2001, p. 56.
71 Plasseraud, 2003, p. 130.

concentrated in the southeast – in the Latgale region, which will be discussed in greater detail below. The Swedes in Estonia were a long-established minority, who had settled mainly in a specific area of Western Estonia. They need not interest us any further. The same is true concerning the Jews. Although they constituted a sizeable minority, they were a 'non-existent' minority; that is, they were not readily accounted for in the press and in everyday life.[72] In my sources, there are hardly any mentions of the Jews at all, and therefore, I am also unable to discuss them further.

The large number of minority groups, accounting for such a high percentage of the population in each of the states, alarmed the League of Nations, which had been established in the wake of the First World War. Both Estonia and Latvia were eager to become members of the League, but they had to sign minority protection treaties as a prerequisite for membership.[73] Although these treaties were challenged at times, the promises made were dutifully carried out, especially in the case of Estonia, which went even further than the League required.[74]

In addition to the numbers in Table 1, important regional differences need to be considered. In Estonia, this first and foremost concerns the southeastern region of Petserimaa, which had been part of the Pskov Province until 1917-1920, when it became part of the new Estonian state.[75] Although the majority of the inhabitants in this small region (numbering somewhat above 60,000 in total) were Russians (63.8%) and only 7.2% of them were Estonians, the region was assigned to the new Estonian State. Almost 25% of the population were *Setu*, a Finno-Ugrian tribe, ethnically close to the Estonians but thoroughly Russified after several centuries in the Russian Empire.[76] The political and social integration of this economically backward region into Estonia challenged the government, not least because the Setu often considered themselves Orthodox Russians rather than Estonians.[77]

A similar region in Latvia, Latgale, which formerly belonged to the Vitebsk Province and historically was part of Catholic Poland, was the melting pot of the young Latvian state. While only 29.1% of the total population of Latvia lived in Latgale, 74.6% of the Russians, 51.8% of the Belarusians, and 39.9% of the Poles of Latvia lived in this regions as of 1935.[78] Table 2 depicts the national divisions in Latgale. The concentration of minority groups made the integration

---

72 Wendland, 2008, p. 422.
73 von Rauch, 1977, p. 133; Plasseraud, 2003, p. 120-121. See also Mazower, 1997 or Crols, 2005 for a general overview of this system.
74 See Heikkilä, 2008, for some of these discussions in Estonia.
75 Jääts, 1998, p. 1143-1144; Alenius, 1999, p. 2301-2303; Lõuna, Kalle, 2003, p. 24-29. See also Raun, 1991.
76 Jääts, 1998; Lõuna, Kalle, 2003, p. 13-20.
77 Raun, 1991, p. 531; Jääts, 1998, p. 1524-1529. See also chapter 2.3.1.
78 Benz, 1998, p. 461. On the region of Latgale, see also Apine, 1996; Lukaševičs, 1996.

of Latgale into the Latvian nation state a vital but extremey difficult issue. Ernst Benz, a German church historian, describes the astonishment of census officials when several inhabitants of Latgale answered the question on their nationality with 'Roman Catholic' or '*tutejšij*,' i.e. 'local.'[79]

Table 2. National minorities in Latgale (1935)[80]

Nationality	Numbers	%
Latvians (incl. Latgalians)	347 751	61.3%
Russians	153 976	27.1%
Germans	892	0.2%
Polish/Belarusians/Lithuanian	34 378	6.1%
Jews	27 974	4.9%
Total	567 164	100.0%

Next to these national differences, there were confessional differences, which often ran counter to the ethnic statistics. In Table 3, the confessional distribution in Estonia, Petseri, Latvia, and Latgale is listed. The explanation for the discrepancies between Table 1 and Table 3 will become clear in subsequent chapters.

Table 3. Denominations in Estonia, Petseri, Latvia and Latgale

Denom.	Estonia (1934)[81]		Petseri (1934)[82]		Latvia (1930) [83]		Latgale (1935)[84]	
	Numbers	%	Numb.	%	Numbers	%	Numb.	%
Lutheran	874 026	77.6%	6 018	9.3%	1 057 877	55.7%	42 365	7.5%
Roman Catholic	2 327	0.2%		-	450 210	23.7%	326 162	57.5%
Orthodox	207 488	18.4%	58 306	90.1%	169 625	8.9%	90 702	16.0%
Jewish	4 302	0.4%		-	93 641	4.9%	28 004	4.9%
Old Believer	5 276	0.5%		-	96 802	5.1%	78 582	13.9%
Other	32 994	2.9%	388	0.6%	31 890	1.7%	1 149	0.2%

79   Benz, 1998, p. 443.
80   Numbers from the 1935 Latvian census. Taken from Benz, 1998, p. 461, Table 4.
81   Numbers from the Estonian 1934 census. Taken from Plaat, 2001, p. 148, Table 4.
82   Numbers from the Estonian 1934 census. Taken from Jääts, 1998, p. 1150.
83   Numbers from the Latvian 1930 census. Taken from Al.-sch., "Ticības un tautības Latvijā" [Religion and People in Latvia] in *TuD*, 11, 11, 1935, p. 175-176.
84   Numbers from the Latvian 1935 census. Taken from Benz, 1998, p. 461, Table 4.

2.2. Creating New Orthodox Churches – the 1920s

The Riga Eparchy of the Orthodox Church tried to keep pace with the times in rapidly changing social, political, and cultural circumstances following the First World War. This chapter analyses the structural changes in the Orthodox Church in the decade after the collapse of the Russian Empire. It is divided into eight sections. The first analyses the 'Estonianisation' and 'Latvianisation' of the Orthodox Church in 1917. The following three analyse different facets of the Estonian development. Three sections then follow on the Latvian experience, before the final section compares the two experiences in relation to the first challenge of modernity and considers the question of canon law. The most important developments in the Estonian and Latvian Orthodox Church are visualised in the form of a timeline in chapter 6.2.

2.2.1. Leading up to Fundamental Change – 1917

There had been attempts to 'Estonianise' and 'Latvianise' the hierarchy of Orthodox congregations of the Riga Eparchy since the final quarter of the nineteenth century. The first attempts to install an Estonian vicar bishop in Tallinn[85] occurred in 1887. These attempts were supported by the Governor of Estland, Count Šakhovskoj, who considered the creation of such a Vicariate a way to further the expansion of Orthodoxy among the Estonians.[86] There was even a candidate for the post in sight, the ethnic Estonian Dionissi Tamm. In his letters to Oberprokuror Pobedonoscev, Šakhovskoj wrote, justifying his choice of candidate, that "in Estland, the bishop would have a primarily missionary role, trying, if possible, to fit into the local society. Just as the Apostles to the Slavs, Cyril and Methodius, prepared for their task by learning Slavic customs, so I think that basic knowledge of the Estonian language would be one of the fundamental requirements for an Orthodox bishop with missionary tasks in Estland."[87] However, these plans came to nothing, as the Riga Eparchy Council saw a danger to the Russian-speaking Orthodox of Estland should an Estonian be

---

85   Called Revel' (Ревель) at the time – the Russian version of the German name (Rewal).

86   [Anton Laar], "Lühike ülevaade Eesti ap.-õigeusu elukäigust 75 a. jooksul" [Short overview of 75 years of Estonian Orthodox life] in *UE*, 1/8, 1921, p. 58-59; Pommers, 1931a, p. 75; M. Mäessa, "Kas venestuse kantsiks või Eesti piiskopi esinduskirikuks?" [Fort of Russification or representative church of the Estonian bishop?] in *ET*, 3/3, 1938, p. 28; Brandt, 1956, p. 185-186; Aleksij, 1999, p. 319-322.

87   Quoted in Aleksij, 1999, p. 321.

named Vicar Bishop of Tallinn.[88] Parallel attempts were undertaken by the Orthodox Latvians, but their candidate, Aleksandrs Zaķis, also never administered the Riga Eparchy. Instead, he was consecrated Bishop of Ostrog in 1883 and eventually transferred to the Eparchy of Polotsk in 1893, where he paid special attention to the Latvians living in the area that was later to become Latgale.[89]

The voices calling for more appropriate structures in Estonian Orthodoxy, first and foremost a bishop that understood their language, resurfaced with force in February 1916, at the 200th anniversary of the Transfiguration church in Tallinn. The most prominent guest was Archbishop Ioann (Smirnov) of Riga.[90] This is how Anton Laar, the leading publicist[91] of the Estonian Orthodox nationalists, describes the celebrations, five years later:

> At this festive occasion, which we celebrated with an immense number of visitors, a very unnatural situation struck the eye: the head shepherd does not understand the language of his flock! This was noticed by quite a few commentators. Since there was no use in trying to make him understand the seriousness of the issue, Fr. Kokla, Fr. Paavel, and I decided to make every possible effort at the following Estonian liturgy to improve the congregation's mood.[92]

After waiting for Easter to pass, Laar anonymously published a one-page memorandum which lamented the current situation as indefensible and sketched out possible solutions, including a revival of plans for a Tallinn Vicariate. This memorandum was sent not only to the Riga Eparchy Council, but also to the Orthodox Baltic Brotherhood and the Most Holy Synod in St. Petersburg. As Laar later noted, the memorandum sent to St. Petersburg "was probably put to rest in one of the roomy 'storage facilities' of the Synod, where we Balts have a

---

88 [Anton Laar], "Lühike ülevaade Eesti ap.-õigeusu elukäigust 75 a. jooksul" [Short overview of 75 years of Estonian Orthodox life] in *UE*, 1/8, 1921, p. 58-59; Brandt, 1956, p. 186; Aleksij, 1999, p. 321-322.

89 Testis, "Arķibiskaps Jānis (I.) Smirnovs un viņa darbiba Rīgas jeparhijā" [Archbishop Jānis (I.) Smirnovs and his activities in the Riga Eparchy] in *TuD*, 14/24, p. 378; S. S. [Сергей Петрович Сахаров], "Polockas un Vitebskas biskaps Aleksandrs (Zaķis)" [Bishop Aleksandr of Polotsk and Vitebsk] in *TuD*, 15/16, 1939, p. 246. See also Šejkin, 1997, p. 58-60; Gavrilin, 1999, p. 316-317. See chapter 2.3.3. for more on Latgale.

90 The church itself was originally a Lutheran church, given to the Orthodox in 1716 after the Russian victory in the Great Nordic War. See Konstantin Kokla, "Tallinna Eesti Õigeusu Kiriku 200 aasta juubeli-pidu" [The 200th anniversary of the Estonian Orthodox church of Tallinn] in *UjE₁*, 13/22, 1916, p. 258-259; 13/23, 1916, p. 270-272; 13/25, 1916, p. 294-296.

91 I will use the term publicist to refer to those actors who created and maintained an image of the Orthodox Church in the Baltic States, largely through the publication of journals.

92 [Anton Laar], "Lühike ülevaade Eesti ap.-õigeusu elukäigust 75 a. jooksul" [Short overview of 75 years of Estonian Orthodox life] in *UE*, 1/9, 1921, p. 66.

corner to ourselves."[93] Archbishop Ioann was upset – apparently not because of the content of the memorandum but because it had been sent to St. Petersburg. He jotted a few question marks in the margins of the memorandum and asked Laar and Konstantin Kokla to soften out the accusations made in these sections. Once he had received their reply, he gathered all the Orthodox clergy present in Tartu, where he had been evacuated due to the war:

> First, deacon Dorin read the memorandum itself. A general murmur and unrest spread. Unanimous decision: The letter is not true! – We, the authors of the reply, felt warm all over. What will they say *then*, once they hear our reply! […] It was really embarrassing to hear how Fr. Dorin read even the most spicy sections of the reply with the same soft voice. – But the reaction was unexpected. After he finished reading, we expected the worst from our Russian colleagues but only an awkward silence followed. Finally, Archbishop Ioann turned to Rev. Fr. Leismann and asked him of his opinion. Fr. Leismann was at first a bit taken aback, but he replied without hesitation: it is completely true! Everything happened just as it is described. […]
> This assertion from such an authority as Fr. Leismann struck as lightning from a clear sky. – An even longer silence followed, at the end of which Fr. Ioann said something like: well, we have heard many nice and interesting things. Let's thank the authors and go home. These horrible 'court proceedings,' as they in actual fact had been, thus finished in such a 'nice' manner.[94]

There is an ironic undertone to this description, which is typical for the writing of the Estonian Orthodox publicists. However, it is only because this account was written five years after the event that it was possible to insert such an undertone. At the time, to do so would not have been possible because of wartime censorship. In the Latvian case, no such undertone of malcontent can be detected. The Latvians did not openly voice dissatisfaction with the current structures either. There are several reasons for this difference. First, the Orthodox Church in the territory that would later be Latvia was strongly focussed on Riga, the centre of the Russian-dominated Eparchy Council and the Bishop of Riga. Riga was a multi-national metropolis, and the Latvian population was not significantly more important than the Russian, German, and Jewish parts.[95] The Orthodox portion of Riga's Latvian population was not powerful enough to be heard. The centre of ethnic Latvian Orthodoxy, the region around Madona in south-eastern Livland, was an agrarian region without many urban intellectuals who could argue for Latvian ruled structures within the Orthodox Church.

---

93   [Anton Laar], "Lühike ülevaade Eesti ap.-õigeusu elukäigust 75 a. jooksul" [Short overview of 75 years of Estonian Orthodox life] in *UE*, 1/9, 1921, p. 66.

94   [Anton Laar], "Lühike ülevaade Eesti ap.-õigeusu elukäigust 75 a. jooksul" [Short overview of 75 years of Estonian Orthodox life] in *UE*, 1/9, 1921, p. 67 (Emphasis in original). This episode is also mentioned in N. A. "Eesti õigeusuliste koosoleku" [The gathering of Estonian Orthodox] in *PM*, 61/83, 15.04.1917, p. 4.

95   von Hirschhausen, 2006. See also chapter 2.2.5.

A second important factor for this difference was the First World War. The war devastated Riga, Latvia's later capital.[96] In 1915, with the German Army threatening the city, the military administration decided to evacuate all church valuables in Riga – including the bells – to inner Russia until the war was over. Moreover, the bishop was evacuated to Tartu with most of the clergy, who partly moved on or were further evacuated to inner Russia as well.[97] After the evacuation, Riga was suddenly bereft of the Russian Orthodox presence which had characterised the city. Another two years went by before the German forces took the city in 1917, and the virtual absence of Orthodox clergy in Riga signalled that the Orthodox Church was no longer a living part of the city and of the nascent Latvian state.[98]

The Estonian actors of the Riga Eparchy thus played a much more open and vivid role in the development of the local Orthodox Church from 1915, because they witnessed the political changes around them in their native surroundings. The Latvians were either evacuated to Tartu, where the surroundings were very different from Riga, or marginalised in a wartime atmosphere. In the beginning of April 1917, not long after the February revolution in Russia, an unofficial 'General Advisory Gathering of Orthodox Estonians' was held in Tallinn.[99] At this assembly, twenty-seven priests, four deacons and thirty lay representatives from the Estonian counties discussed the meaning of the new democratic political order for the organisation of the local Orthodox Church. The assembly agreed that "we, Orthodox Estonians, are part of the Estonian people and, as citizens of free Russia, demand the same rights as the entire Estonian people. Therefore, there is a need to reform the organisation of the local Orthodox Church."[100] The final document produced by the meeting consisted of numerous short- and long-term demands, as well as suggestions of an internal nature. These demands ranged from administrative measures, such as equal rights and positions for Estonians, Latvians, and Russians within the church hierarchy to rights and duties of the clergy, and liturgical issues.[101] Another important decision, which had an immediate effect, was a declaration that the official Estonian Orthodox journal (*Usk ja Elu, UjE₁*), edited by Aleksander Värat, would no

---

96   Hatlie, 2009a, p. 16-159; Hatlie, 2009b.
97   Pommers, 1931a, p. 75, 77-78; Testis, "Mūsu pareizticīgā baznīca vācu okupacijas laikā
      – I" [Our Orthodox Church during German occupation] in *TuD*, 15/1, 1939, p. 7-8;
      Bušueva, 1993, p. 49-50.
98   Hatlie, 2009a, p. 314-315. See also chapter 2.2.5.
99   This gathering had been preceded by a smaller preparatory meeting in Tartu some days
      earlier. The decisions of the Tallinn gathering with a commentary were published in
      Laar, 1917. Most of the text was also published in the secular press. A partial English
      translation is available in Papathomas and Palli, 2002, p. 77-81.
100   Laar, 1917, p. 3.
101   Laar, 1917, p. 6. See also chapter 3.1.

longer be considered the official voice of Estonian Orthodoxy.[102] This decision illustrates the division of Estonian Orthodoxy into nationalist (autonomist) and Russian-friendly wings. Värat belonged to the latter group and was decried a Russifier, misleading the Estonian Orthodox flock.[103]

Having discredited the official journal, the autonomists turned to the secular press, where an exchange of articles, regarding the reorganisation of the Orthodox Church in Estonia, followed. The first of these appeared only a few days after Anton Laar published the decisions of the Tallinn gathering in the secular press.[104] The author, 'N.A.,' starts by affirming that "several decisions were made that cause the Orthodox clergy to appear in an altogether different light than what we are used to from these official representatives of the faith."[105] Regarding the future of the Orthodox Church in Estonia, 'N.A.' sees only one option: legal equality between Orthodox, Lutherans, Baptists, and other faiths. "In short, the Estonian people should approach all issues of faith on free, democratic foundations. Priests and pastors, as free citizens, should be able to work everywhere."[106] According to 'N.A.,' the clergy of the Orthodox Church should not involve themselves in politics, for that would not be compatible with their pastoral role. One day later, an article written by a Lutheran Estonian calling himself 'J.' welcomed the Tallinn gathering as a "decisive turn in the life of the Estonian Orthodox."[107] The article is full of praise for the revelation of the deceitful Russification agenda of Aleksander Värat and the heretofore official Estonian voice of the Orthodox Church. The article ends on the positive note that "there is no longer anything dividing us [Lutherans and Orthodox] nor do we owe each other anything. Let us stand together as one and start building the Estonian home."[108]

The tone soon changed, when the Lutheran pastor Jaan Lattik, who later became a prominent Estonian politician, published his opinion on the Orthodox

---

102 Laar, 1917, p. 8.

103 J., "Pööre õigeusuliste eestlaste elus" [A decisive turn in the life of Orthodox Estonians] in *PM*, 61/84, 16.04.1917, p. 1-2.

104 Anton Laar, "Eesti õigeusu-tegelaste kongress Tallinnas" [The congress of Estonian Orthodox actors in Tallinn] in *Tallinna Teataja*, 8/77, 10.04.1917, p. 2; Anton Laar, "Eesti õigeusuliste tegelaste üleüldine nõupidamine Tallinnas" [The general advisory gathering of Orthodox Estonians] in *PM*, 61/81, 13.04.1917, p. 2-3.

105 N.A., "Eesti õigeusuliste koosoleku" [The gathering of Estonian Orthodox] in *PM*, 61/83, 15.04.1917, p. 4.

106 N.A., "Eesti õigeusuliste koosoleku" [The gathering of Estonian Orthodox] in *PM*, 61/83, 15.04.1917, p. 4.

107 J., "Pööre õigeusuliste eestlaste elus" [A decisive turn in the life of Orthodox Estonians] in *PM*, 61/84, 16.04.1917, p. 1-2.

108 J., "Pööre õigeusuliste eestlaste elus" [A decisive turn in the life of Orthodox Estonians] in *PM*, 61/84, 16.04.1917, p. 1-2. Värat had been a proponent of Russification already in the 1880s. See Plaat, 2001, p. 135, fn. 133.

Church under the title 'Prisoner.'[109] Telling the story of his recently deceased mother, who was put in prison for having baptised her children in the 'wrong faith' (her father had converted in the 1840s), Lattik warns the Orthodox Estonians that "becoming free Estonian men overnight takes more than big words about freedom of conscience."[110] Instead of demanding equality with the Lutheran Church for better or for worse, as 'N.A.' had done, Lattik reminds his readers that "the first point in the ABC of the freedom of conscience is to leave others alone. More is needed in order to understand the true greatness of freedom of conscience and to grow into it than wearing a red ribbon and crying hurray."[111]

Alongside this discourse in the secular press, Aleksander Värat published a series of articles in *Usk ja Elu* starting in mid-April 1917 and continuing until the last number of the journal end of November the same year, called 'The Renewal of the Congregations.' This article series seems to be a hybrid of the official opinion of the Russian Orthodox Church and the personal opinions of the publisher.[112] Here, Värat describes to his readers the "way the congregation ought to be, in other words, how the Lord created it, and the apostles set it up."[113] Only the occasional link to the debates going on in Estonia can be detected. For example, when talking about all the good things the Orthodox priests have done for the Estonian people, Värat laments that

> recently, a small party has been forming among these *vehicles of civilisation*,[114] who start destroying everything that has been built up through hard work in the fashion of the revolutionaries with eagerness and impatience even towards those who have been like fathers to us, such as Archbishop Ioann. The intolerance of these men is grounded solely in national feelings, which do not go together well with politeness. [...] The worst thing about it is, however, that this little party is getting really influential.[115]

---

109 Jaan Lattik, "Vang" [Prisoner] in *PM*, 61/92, 26.04.1917, p. 1.
110 Jaan Lattik, "Vang" [Prisoner] in *PM*, 61/92, 26.04.1917, p. 1. See chapter 2.1.2. for the re-conversion problematic.
111 Jaan Lattik, "Vang" [Prisoner] in *PM*, 61/92, 26.04.1917, p. 1. See chapter 4.2.2. for more on the polemic ensuing from this article.
112 Värat had been evacuated to St. Petersburg along with many of the church valuables of the Riga Eparchy and was not really able to participate in the daily life of Estonian Orthodoxy.
113 Aleksander Värat, "Koguduste uuendamine II. Kogudus ja tema uued korraldused" [The renewal of the congregations II. The congregation and its new structures] in *UjE₁*, 14/18, 02.05.1917, p. 185.
114 A direct translation of the German 'Kulturträger'.
115 Aleksander Värat, "Koguduste uuendamine III. Meie preestrid" [The renewal of the congregations III. Our priests] in *UjE₁*, 14/21, 23.05.1917, p. 208.

At the end of May 1917, an Eparchy congress was held in Tartu, where 124 delegates from the entire Riga Eparchy gathered.[116] Six years later, Anton Laar described planning the congress as follows:

> In order to confirm the envisaged reforms [of the Tallinn gathering], we planned to call an official congress of the Estonian Orthodox in May. However, this aroused the Russians, on whose advice the Archbishop called an Eparchy congress for the 25 and 26 May. They apparently thought that a general assembly, where communication would be in Russian, would impede any national ambitions. The Estonians, therefore, made special arrangements, so that the Estonian delegates, appearing in pretty large numbers, had already met on the 24 May to discuss the agenda, taking into consideration the decisions of the earlier gathering (6-7 April). Obviously, the main question was the consolidation of all Estonian Orthodox into a single church unit. Although a couple of voices in the beginning – some of the older ones, unfortunately belonging to ethnic Estonians – declared that separation from the Russians was no good – the common thought finally fought its way through with such a force that the Estonians were able to appear unanimously in defence of their viewpoints.[117]

This unanimity had not been completely clear from the outset, as a note by the sacristan J. Kalmus shows. This note, published first in a Tallinn newspaper and then in Tartu, called all sacristans and Orthodox school teachers to a meeting in connection with the Eparchy congress. This meeting was to be held as "the sacristans and schoolteachers are not to be allowed easy access."[118] Two days later, Anton Laar tried to calm the waves of discontent, explaining that the congregations can delegate as many clergy and lay members as they wish. Moreover, "the goal of the congress is not to defend the interests of the clergy nor that of the sacristans, but to structure Estonia's Orthodox life to fit the times and the situation, where obviously also issues pertaining to church servants belong."[119]

At the congress itself, according to Konstantin Kokla, a moderate nationalist, it was "as if all national, estate, and class differences disappeared to some-

---

116 Anton Laar, "Eesti õigeusuliste ülemaaline congress Tartus" [The general congress of Estonian Orthodox] in *PM*, 61/118, 30.05.1917, p. 3; Konstantin Kokla, "Baltimaa õigeusuliste üleüldine koosolek" [The General Gathering of Baltic Orthodox], in *UjE₁*, 14/29-30, 25.07.1917, p. 277-279; Anton Laar, "Ülevaade Eesti ap.-õigeusu kiriku elukäigust" [Overview of the life of the Estonian Orthodox Church] in *UE*, 3/7-8, 1923, p. 6.

117 Anton Laar, "Ülevaade Eesti ap.-õigeusu kiriku elukäigust" [Overview of the life of the Estonian Orthodox Church] in *UE*, 3/7-8, 1923, p. 6. See also the call to participate in this congress in "Teadaanne Eesti õigeusu kogudustele" [Notice to the Estonian Orthodox congregations] in *PM*, 61/100, 05.05.1917, p. 3.

118 J. Kalmus, "Üleskutse" [Call] in *PM*, 61/102, 08.05.1917, p. 3. See also J. Kalmus, "Üleskutse Baltimaa õigeusu köstritele" [Call to the Baltic Orthodox Sacristans] in *Tallinna Teataja*, 8/89, 25.04.1917, p. 3.

119 Anton Laar, "Selgituseks" [Clarification] in *PM*, 61/104, 10.05.1917, p. 3.

where far away."[120] However, in the course of the gathering, it became clear that this romantic unity would not last, and on the third day, the discussion broke into three different groups, according to the language (Estonian, Latvian, and Russian). The decisions of the groups would later be accepted or rejected in plenum. The final decisions of the gathering were therefore very general, stressing the wish to have an apolitical clergy, subordinated to an All-Russian Synod or Church Council.[121] The parish structure would remain the same; however, it was decided that an independent bishop for each of the three national groups was desirable. In consideration of the ongoing war, this demand would be tabled for the time being, but a provisional council with representatives from each of the three nations should assist the bishop. Moreover, two delegates from each nation were selected to participate at the upcoming All-Russian Congress of Orthodoxy in Moscow.[122]

According to Anton Laar, the mood at the congress was not that harmonious:

> I cannot conceal the discontent of the Russians, even a certain 'tearfulness' when they anxiously shouted: the Estonians are destroying our congress, the Estonians are dividing the Riga Eparchy! There was, however, no time to listen to the Russian complaints – the Estonian section returned to its toils [...]
> Elected as Estonian speaker, I had to explain the Estonian viewpoints a dozen times over. The Latvians retracted some of their demands, under the influence of the Russian speeches, but the Estonians retained their unanimity as solidly as a rock.[123]

Laar's version of the congress developments posits the Estonians as the main protagonists, struggling to free themselves from the Russian 'oppressors,' who were unwilling to introduce the administrative and structural reforms necessary to achieve equality between the three nationalities of the Riga Eparchy. He concludes: "we had won the first battle for the Estonian Church."[124] In the Latvian

---

120 Konstantin Kokla, "Baltimaa õigeusuliste üleüldine koosolek" [The General Gathering of Baltic Orthodox], in *UjE₁*, 14/29-30, 1917, p. 278.

121 See Konstantin Kokla, "Koguduste uuendamine IX. Baltimaa õigeusuliste üleüldise kongressi otsused" [Renewal of the congregations IX. The decisions of the General Congress of Baltic Orthodox] in *UjE₁*, 14/31-32, 08.08.1917, p. 285-289.

122 Konstantin Kokla, "Koguduste uuendamine IX. Baltimaa õigeusuliste üleüldise kongressi otsused" [Renewal of the congregations IX. The decisions of the General Congress of Baltic Orthodox] in *UjE₁*, 14/31-32, 08.08.1917, p. 289. One of the Estonian delegates to this congress in Moscow, Aleksander Kaelas, reported from it to the secular press: "Ülevenemaaline Gr.-õigeusu vaimulikkude ja ilmalikkude liigete kongress 1.-12. juunil 1917. a." [The All-Russian congress of Gr.-Orthodox clergy and lay people 1-12 June 1917] in *PM* 61/139, 23.06.1917, p. 2.

123 Anton Laar, "Ülevaade Eesti ap.-õigeusu kiriku elukäigust" [Overview of the life of the Estonian Orthodox Church] in *UE*, 3/7-8, 1923, p. 6.

124 Anton Laar, "Ülevaade Eesti ap.-õigeusu kiriku elukäigust" [Overview of the life of the Estonian Orthodox Church] in *UE*, 3/7-8, 1923, p. 6. Nigul Hindov, writing his theologi-

case, press sources are scarce for this first period, due to the devastation of the First World War. The analysis of the events in Tartu in later descriptions is usually accompanied by the comment that the Latvians were also eager to have a bishop who was able to speak their language.[125] However, the sources do not further elaborate on this wish.

Although no concrete reforms had been worked out, the Orthodox Estonians decided to plead for a Tallinn Vicariate in a meeting to be held at the end of June. They named a widowed ethnic Estonian provost, Paul Kulbusch, who had headed the Estonian parish of St. Petersburg from its establishment in 1893, as their desired candidate for bishop.[126] The plea was signed by Archbishop Ioann and sent to St. Petersburg, where the Most Holy Synod, in its very last session in the city, accepted it on 26 July.[127] The official election of the vicar bishop was then carried out at the Riga Eparchy assembly, gathering in Tartu from 8 through 10 August. This assembly was originally convened to elect delegates to the Moscow *sobor*, which would start later that month, and to discuss necessary reforms.[128] The Estonian section of the assembly duly elected Paul Kulbusch as Vicar Bishop of Tallinn. However, the Russian Synod, influenced by the former Bishop of Riga, Archbishop Agafangel (Preobraženskij), retracted from its previously promised concession and refused to confirm Kulbusch as bishop.[129] On 31 December 1917, Paul Kulbusch was finally consecrated as Bishop Platon of Tallinn.[130] The Latvian efforts to get Bishop of Penza Jānis (Pommers), an

---

cal diploma dissertation on Bishop Platon some years later, adopts this rhetoric of an Estonian battle that was won at last. Hindov, 1929.

125 Pommers, 1931a, p. 75; Testis, "Arķibiskaps Jānis (I.) Smirnovs un viņa darbiba Rīgas jeparhijā" [Archbishop Jānis (I.) Smirnovs and his activities in the Riga Eparchy] in *TuD*, 14/24, 1938, p. 378; Balevics, 1987, p. 43-45.

126 Anton Laar, "Ülevaade Eesti ap.-õigeusu kiriku elukäigust" [Overview of the life of the Estonian Orthodox Church] in *UE*, 3/7-8, 1923, p. 6. Hindov, 1929, p. 156-157. See Škarovski, 2005 for the history of the Estonian parish of St. Petersburg.

127 Anton Laar, "Teadaanne Eesti õigeusu kogudustele" [Notice to the Estonian Orthodox congregations] in *PM*, 61/167, 27.07.1917, p. 3. For the entire administrative procedure, see Hindov, 1929, p. 155-158.

128 Keegi, "Piiskopkonna koosolekult" [From the Eparchy Gathering] in *UjE₁*, 14/37-38-39, 26.09.1917, p. 343.

129 Anton Laar, "Ülevaade Eesti ap.-õigeusu kiriku elukäigust" [Overview of the life of the Estonian Orthodox Church] in *UE*, 3/7-8, 1923, p. 7-8; Hindov, 1929, p. 163; Saard, 2008, p. 1544.

130 For the consecration see Konstantin Kokla, "Esimene Eesti piiskopi pühitsemine Tallinnas 31. detsembril 1917 a." [The consecration of the first Estonian bishop in Tallinn on 31 December 1917] in *UE*, 0/1, Dec. 1918, p. 10-11; Anton Laar, "Ülevaade Eesti ap.-õigeusu kiriku elukäigust" [Overview of the life of the Estonian Orthodox Church] in *UE*, 3/7-8, 1923, p. 8; Hindov, 1929, p. 167-168.

ethnic Latvian, as Latvian vicar bishop failed, in part because of the restrictive German occupation of Riga.[131]

In the meantime, Aleksander Värat continued to fill *Usk ja Elu* with his ideas of reform. 'The Renewal of the Congregations' in the numbers 33-39 were devoted to a booklet the 'Provisional Council' had sent him. This Provisional Council is most probably the one set up in the May congress. However, Värat seems oblivious to this fact, despite having mentioned it in the previous number, stating that "there is no mention of where this 'Provisional Council' operates from, nor of whom it consists, or who maintains it. But let that be. However, when, as it seems, the 'Provisional Council' wants to play first fiddle, then it is worthwhile to dwell on its toils."[132] Värat then reproduced the entire content of the booklet, which consisted of an Estonian translation of the congregation statutes worked out by the Synod in St. Petersburg and the statutes of the 'Union of Estonian Orthodox Congregations,' which was to be created. He included commentary on the booklet, with remarks concerning the incorrect translation of certain words or the lack of points important to his mind.[133] His main criticism was the *raison d'être* of the union itself:

> The cohesion of the local congregations is given through the priory and its council, as well as through the bishop and the Eparchy council, and most perfectly in the *täiskogu*[134] of the Eparchy. In other words, there is no need for a further union.
> I would go even further – creating a union in or between congregations is harmful, because it draws a secular line through spiritual matters and shatters the unity which we need most at this time.[135]

While Värat and the central administration of the Russian Church were eager to uphold the principle of territorial structures in the church at all costs, the Estonian nationalists were eager to create structures where they were free from what

---

131 Pommers, 1931a, p. 76.
132 Aleksander Värat, "Koguduste uuendamine X. Kogudus ja tema korraldus" [The renewal of the congregations X. The congregation and its structure] in *UjE₁*, 14/33-34, 22.08.1917, p. 301.
133 See Aleksander Värat, "Koguduste uuendamine XI. Eesti õigeusu koguduste Ühisuse põhjuskirja project" [The renewal of the congregations XI. The designated statutes of the Union of Estonian Orthodox Congregations] in *UjE₁*, 14/35-36, 05.09.1917, p. 318-319; Aleksander Värat, "Koguduste uuendamine XII. Eesti õigeusu koguduste Ühisuse põhjuskirja project (eelnõu)" [The renewal of the congregations XII. The designated statutes of the Union of Estonian Orthodox Congregations (comment)] in *UjE₁*, 14/37-38-39, 26.09.1917, p. 333-337.
134 The *täiskogu* denotes a regular meeting, where clergy and lay delegates from all parishes of Estonia met to discuss important issues, such as the election of bishops.
135 Aleksander Värat, "Koguduste uuendamine XII. Eesti õigeusu koguduste Ühisuse põhjuskirja project (eelnõu)" [The renewal of the congregations XI. The designated statutes of the Union of Estonian Orthodox Congregations (comment)] in *UjE₁*, 14/37-38-39, 26.09.1917, p. 337.

they perceived as Russian meddling. However, the Bolshevik Revolution made further publication of *Usk ja Elu* impossible, and Värat disappeared from the Estonian scene. The attempts to have him hand over the publishing rights of *Usk ja Elu* to Anton Laar or Konstantin Kokla were unsuccessful, as he "clung to the journal with hands and feet."[136] Värat claimed that this was not the case; he was simply not willing to hand the journal to anyone but the institution from which he had received it several years earlier, the Peter and Paul Brotherhood of Riga. Since the Brotherhood had been dispersed all over Russia as a result of the war, this could not be conveniently accomplished.[137]

All in all, the eventful year 1917 revealed a continuum of opinions regarding the future democratic organisation of the Orthodox Church on Estonian soil. On one end of the scale was Aleksander Värat, the publisher of the previously official journal of Estonian Orthodoxy, conservative, and loyal to the Russian-dominated hierarchy.[138] On the other was Anton Laar, a staunch liberal nationalist, who pressed for as much independence as possible. In between was Konstantin Kokla, who tried to hold to both of the afore-mentioned actors.[139] Alongside of these three publicly active men were a host of others who did not write much, or wrote under pseudonyms. Some of them, like Aleksander Kaelas, who was a delegate to the Moscow *sobor*, and the bank director Aleksei Nõu, can be clearly placed in the nationalist camp. Others, such as Nikolai Leismann and Jüri Truusman, both experienced clergy, are more difficult to assess. Both of these men had acted as censors for Estonian-language publications during the Tsarist era, and it is clear that Anton Laar and his other relatively young companions were unsure how to judge these 'seasoned men.'[140] When Laar remembered the 'horrible court proceedings' of 1916, he ended with a note on Leismann and Truusman:

> I cannot leave unsaid a comparison of two former school friends: we, the fighters for a free Estonian church, were warm all over at the just and direct judgement Fr. Leismann gave about the church's politics until then. However, we received a splash

---

136 Aleksander Värat, "Surma otsus!" [Death sentence] in *UjE₁*, 14/18, 02.05.1917, p. 189.

137 Aleksander Värat, "Surma otsus!" [Death sentence] in *UjE₁*, 14/18, 02.05.1917, p. 189-190.

138 Värat was later involved in the 'Living Church' movement. See "Vene patriarhi – Sinodi ja Soome kirikuvalitsuse kirjavahetus" [The correspondence between the Russian Patriarch and Synod and the Finnish church leadership] in *UE*, 4/3, 1924, p. 5.

139 See the note to his "Baltimaa õigeusuliste üleüldine koosolek" [The General Gathering of Baltic Orthodox], in *UjE₁*, 14/29-30, 25.07.1917, p. 277-279, where he mentions that "as a participant of the Tallinn gathering, although I myself was against the decision, I ought not write for *Usk ja Elu*. However, having been asked from several parties, I do it anyhow, for I do not want to let my sense of justice be violated."

140 Laar was born in 1885, whereas Truusman and Leismann were born in 1856 and 1862 respectively.

of cold water from the just as respectable Mag.[141] Truusman, who thundered that this all, especially the demand for an Estonian bishop, was completely unacceptable! We later understood that Fr. Truusman argued as an academician; at the Tartu congress the following year, to the joy of the Russian delegation, he declared that celebrating the liturgy in one's mother tongue cannot be considered appropriate; he himself would receive the most out of reading the Gospels in Greek! [...] Later Mag. Truusman changed his mind, when he decided to sign the letter we had prepared as our last sally before the occupation demanding an Estonian bishop. The academician understood that this was a question of life and death and looked up from behind his books.[142]

Interestingly, the Moscow *sobor* of the Russian Orthodox Church, which is elsewhere praised as the highest echelon of the hierarchy within the Russian Church, was of very little interest to the Estonians. Apart from the election of delegates, there is no mention of it at all in 1917. Even the election of Patriarch Tikhon received only mention in small notices.[143] There was too much happening in Estonia end of 1917 to be much concerned with the Orthodox Church in Moscow.

2.2.2. Estonia: the Road towards Autocephaly

Once the Orthodox Estonians were given their own national bishop, everything would be set for them to construct the structures of an independent church. However, the German occupation interrupted the consolidation of Estonian Orthodoxy in the beginning of 1918. Even though the war did not facilitate his work, Bishop Platon managed to fulfil his episcopal duties, travelling widely in spite of the restrictions in place.[144] He managed to visit over seventy congregations throughout the entire Riga Eparchy, of which he had been named the temporary administrator.[145] These visits were primarily to help implement the

---

141 Magister – Truusmann had a degree from the St. Petersburg Theological Academy.
142 [Anton Laar], "Lühike ülevaade Eesti ap.-õigeusu elukäigust 75 a. jooksul" [Short overview of 75 years of Estonian Orthodox life] in *UE*, 1/9, 1921, p. 67.
143 Such as "Patriarhi valimine" [The election of the Patriarch] in *PM*, 61/258, 11.11.1917, p. 2.
144 Since Platon was later canonised as a Martyr Saint, there is an abundance of material on him. Most of this material repeats the information found in Anton Laar, "Eesti piiskop Platon" [The Estonian Bishop Platon] in *PM*, 63/5, 20.01.1919, p. 1; Anton Laar, "Esimese Eesti piiskopi mälestuseks" [In memory of first Estonian bishop] in *UE*, 0/2, 1919, p. 21-26. See also Kumyš, 1999.
145 Eesti Piiskop Platon, "Mõni lehekene minu päevaraamatust" [Some pages from my diary] in *UE*, 4/8, 1924, p. 1-2. See also chapter 2.2.5. for more on his visit to Riga.

church statutes that had been decided upon in the Moscow *sobor*.[146] The first Estonian Orthodox *täiskogu*, which had been planned for 8-10 February 1918, had to be cancelled due to the occupation.[147] It was, therefore, impossible to carry out any restructuring of the Orthodox Church in Estonia as a whole. Every time Bishop Platon asked for permission to assemble or rebuild the Orthodox Church adminstration that had been evacuated to Russia in 1915, the occupation authorities declined. This prompted the bishop to write a letter of complaint to the exiled Estonian government in London – the only such letter to be sent by any representative of an Estonian religious organisation.[148]

The reception of independence after the end of the First World War in November 1918 was all the more euphoric. One day after the German capitulation, on 12 November 1918, Bishop Platon composed an appeal to Orthodox Estonians, which was printed in the major newspapers.[149] This appeal, written in a romantic and optimistic tone, called on the Orthodox Estonians to help build a free, democratic, and prospering Estonian homeland, which included the local Orthodox Church. The national myth of the Estonian awakening to independence after 700 years of slumber was repeated also among the Orthodox.[150] In addition to the great task standing before the Estonians as such, Orthodox Estonians also had work to do. The first number of the new Orthodox journal *Uus Elu* was devoted entirely to the manifold tasks at hand. These included the restructuring of the Orthodox community from a state institution to a free Christian Church with an Estonian national basis, the question of the fate of the former parish schools, and the relationship with the Russian Orthodox Church.

---

146 This aspect is not stressed in the Estonian accounts of Bishop Platon. However, the Latvian accounts focus on this implementation. For the discussion on the statutes at the *sobor*, see Schulz, 1995, p. 133-167.

147 Konstantin Kokla, "Esimene Eesti piiskopi pühitsemine Tallinnas 31. detsembril 1917 a." [The consecration of the first Estonian bishop in Tallinn on 31 December 1917] in *UE*, 0/1, Dec. 1918, p. 11; Eesti Piiskopkonna ajutine Nõukogu [The Provisional Council of the Estonian Eparchy], "Teadaanne Eestimaa õigeusu kogudustele" [Notice to all Orthodox congregations of Estonia] in *UE*, 0/2, Feb. 1919, p. 27; Hindov, 1929, p. 176-177.

148 The letter was reprinted as "Eesti piiskopi protest väljamaale Saksa okkupatsioni võimude tegevuse vastu" [The international protest of the Estonian bishop against the activities of the German occupation authorities] in *UE*, 0/1, Dec. 1918, p. 7-9. See also "Piiskop Platon surnud" [Bishop Platon is dead] in *UE*, 0/2, Feb. 1919, p. 17-21; Platon, "Mõni lehekene minu päevaraamatust" [Some pages of my diary] in *UE*, 4/9, 1924, p. 1-2; Saard, 2007b, p. 123.

149 The appeal was also reprinted with a commentary as "Eesti rahvale" [To the Estonian people] in *UE*, 0/1, Dec. 1918, p. 5. An English translation is available in Papathomas and Palli, 2002, p. 92-93.

150 Kirjastuse ühisuse 'Uus Elu' asutav toimekond [The founding editorial committee of the printing union 'Uus Elu'], "Üleskutse Eesti apostliku kogudusele" [Invitation to the Estonian Apostolic community] in *UE*, 0/1, Dec. 1918, p. 1-4. See also chapter 4.1.1.

However, the euphoria was short-lived, for the War of Estonian Independence began. Bishop Platon, constantly travelling to organise church life, fell ill and was trapped in Tartu as the Bolsheviks took the town 21 December 1918. A week later, they outlawed all religious services and on 2 January 1919, Bishop Platon was arrested and jailed in a cellar, along with fourteen others. Among the fellow prisoners were two other Orthodox clergy and several Lutheran pastors. Late on 13 January, the captives were called down into the cellar one by one, tortured, and shot. The Estonian liberation army arrived in Tartu before all fifteen had been executed and freed the remaining captives. However, none of the clergy remained alive.[151]

The Estonian Orthodox Church had received a blow. It was, however, not willing to let this stop its attempts to reorganise, and a *täiskogu* was organised for March 1919.[152] This clarification of the need for a *täiskogu*, written by an anonymous author, leaves no room for doubt:

> The Estonian people no longer agree to their former position: living as 'foreigners' in the Russian 'Lifländskaja' and 'Estländskaja' gubernijas, even under the name of 'Estonia.' An independent, free country and people – that is the highest call and ultimate goal of every Estonian. [...]
> Our Estonian apostolic community has also received a kind of independence through our own bishop, albeit under the circumstances of war and almost impossible communication with Russia. Formally, we are still only the Estonian part of the Russian Orthodox Church, or even less; we are but a vicariate of the 'Rizhskaja Eparhia' operating in the former 'Lifländskaja gubernija.' The Russians keep to this former power position of theirs, where they were the A and O – just like the Germans, who tried to keep their power base in the Baltic States. [...]
> Our position is thus clear as the day: *Complete independence (autocephaly) for the Estonian Apostolic Church, cost what it may.*[153]

The attempts to receive autocephaly had begun with a meeting of the 'Provisional Eparchy Council' in Tallinn at the beginning of February 1919, where Aleksander Kaelas was suggested as the new candidate for bishop and a *täiskogu* was scheduled for March.[154] Several avenues to have him consecrated while avoiding the Russian Orthodox Church were discussed, such as turning to the Patriarch of Serbia or the Russian Church in exile administered in Sremski

---

151 See Anton Laar, "Eesti piiskop Platon" [The Estonian Bishop Platon] in *PM*, 63/5, 20.01. 1919, p. 1. A German version of this story was published as Schabert, 1932. All later accounts repeat the same chronology of events.

152 See "Teadaanne Eestimaa õigeusu kogudustele" [Notice to all Orthodox congregations of Estonia] in *UE*, 0/2, Feb. 1919, p. 27-28. An English translation is available in Papathomas and Palli, 2002, p. 95-99.

153 "Lähem piiskopkonna täiskogu" [Details on the *täiskogu*] in *UE*, 0/2, Feb. 1919, p. 30 (Emphasis in original).

154 Saard, 2008, p. 1544-1545.

Karlovci. Kaelas had been Professor at the University of Moscow and a delegate to the Moscow *sobor*, but there was no reliable information on his location since he had been evacuated to Siberia.

The *täiskogu* arrived at decisions in five categories: the relationship with the Russian Orthodox Church, the election of a candidate for bishop, the revision of the statutes of the Estonian Orthodox Church, the constitution of the Eparchy Council, and the relationship with the Estonian secular authorities.[155] Regarding the first point, the *täiskogu* characterised the current situation as extremely difficult and the continuation of the existing organisation as impossible. Moreover, it declared the Estonian Orthodox Church to be autocephalous, maintaining that this would depend on canonical recognition by the other autocephalous Orthodox Churches. At the same time, however, the assembly claimed that the difficulty of maintaining communication with Russia allowed them to look for avenues to gain this recognition outside of the Mother Church. Concerning a new bishop, Aleksander Kaelas was unanimously elected, with Archpriest Aleksander Paulus as his vicar bishop. The Russian delegates abstained from the vote during the latter's election. The assembly then decided to send a delegation to the Anglican Church to ask for help consecrating the two elected bishops.[156]

On the third point, the *täiskogu* decided to ratify the church statutes worked out by the Moscow *sobor*, with some minor modifications. Until the independence of the Estonian Orthodox Church was recognised by the other autocephalous churches, the church would regard itself as *de facto* independent. With regard to the Eparchy Council, it was decided that there should be four members in addition to the bishops. A fifth member should be elected as the representative of the Russian parishes. If the latter was accepted by the *täiskogu*, he would become a full member of the council. Otherwise, he would only be consulted on questions concerning the Russian parishes. The church declared itself in favour of a completely independent Estonia but would not involve iself in party politics. In relation to the secular state, it demanded the right of a juridical person and the right to retain its current property. Moreover, it asked the new authorities to thoroughly reform religious education in state schools – making it Christian, but non-confessional. Confessional education would be the responsibility of the churches.

These discussions set the scene for some of the key areas of conflict during the rest of the interwar period. First, the emphasis on the independence of the Estonian Orthodox Church, second, the 'concessions' granted the Russian minority, enabling it to participate in the organisation of the church, and finally, the demand to be left alone by the state with the same rights as other religious

---

155 The decisions are reprinted in *UE*, 0/3, 1919, p. 44-46. An English translation is available in Papathomas and Palli, 2002, p. 105-109.
156 Sõtšov, 2009, p. 64-65.

organisations. These three fields of conflict are analysed in this and the following sections.

After the *täiskogu*, the newly elected Eparchy Council took steps to carry out the decisions which had been made. Its tasks included notifying the bishop-elect Aleksander Kaelas and contacting the Anglican Church, as well as other Orthodox churches, to ask for help in consecrating the bishop. The council failed in the first task. Kaelas died in April 1920, apparently without receiving the message of his election.[157] The other task, finding help to consecrate him, was taken in several directions. The delegation to the Anglican Church never left Estonia, and attempts to receive help through the Estonian Ambassador to London, Ants Piip, an Orthodox believer, also did not achieve any positive results, nor did talks with the Serbian delegation at the Paris peace conference.[158] These failures prompted Anton Laar and the other Estonian nationalists to look to co-operate with their Finnish sister church, where similar nationalist aspirations were fuelling a search for ways to achieve ecclesiastic independence.[159]

The Eparchy Council did send a letter to Patriarch Tikhon of Moscow asking him to recognise the Estonian Orthodox Church as an independent church.[160] Seeming to ignore this plea, in August 1919 Patriarch Tikhon appointed Bishop Gennadij (Tuberozov) over the Eparchy of Riga, which still included the Estonian territory. The press commented on the appointment with resignation, as yet another attempt to retain Russian influence in the Baltic region.[161] This trope also occurs in the mentions of the Moscow *sobor* by the Estonian nationalists:

> This is only one example of how far the Russian representatives at their *sobor* were willing to go in relation to foreigners, as I have been told by the Latvian delegate A. Maršan [Pēteris Maršans], later confirmed by Prof. A. Kaelas. We wanted to form a committee to discuss the division of the Riga Eparchy into an Estonian and a Latvian Eparchy, and at that time, we asked for nothing more. However, the mood was still so oppositional that the Russians refused to hear this plea, claiming that the Riga Eparchy must remain indivisible, obviously with Russians at the helm (just like Germans in the Baltic Provinces) and *bol'še nikakikh!*[162] But how to arrive at a decision while circumventing the annoying Estonians and Latvians, which one cannot ignore without referring to Imperial politics? Then they found a 'loophole' and did it the simple, Russian way: The meeting was announced at one place and

---

157 Saard, 2008, p. 1547.
158 Saard, 2008, p. 1548-1552.
159 Setälä, U.V.J., 1962, p. 55-60; Setälä, U.V.J., 1972, p. 7-9; Saard, 2008, p. 1550-1552.
160 Saard, 2008, p. 48.
161 X, "Vene piiskopp Baltimaal" [A Russian bishop in the Baltic Lands] in *PM*, 63/157, 29.07.1919, p. 3. Bishop Gennadij (Tuberozov) was apparently not granted entry to Latvia, and another appointee, Serafim (Čičagov), was likewise refused entry. See Purviņš, 1929, p. 58-59; Kalniņš, Jānis, 2001, p. 84-85.
162 This is the Russian phrase for 'no discussion!'

then held at another, enabling an unobstructed Russian-friendly decision. The Russians later even reproached the Latvians and Estonians: just when we needed you, you did not come![163]

Bishop Gennadij never actually arrived in Riga, but the Tartu peace treaty, which was signed between Estonia and the Soviet Union at the beginning of February 1920, once again brought the issue of a bishop to the fore. Since it had not been possible to establish contact with Aleksander Kaelas in Siberia, the Eparchy Council decided to push for a quick consecration of Aleksander Paulus, the other candidate. The festivities were set for early February, with Archbishop Serafim of Finland presiding, but the consecration did not happen, as Serafim refused at the last minute and Paulus refused to take a post to which he had not been elected.[164]

After this plan failed, the Eparchy Council sent a delegation to Moscow, demanding a canonical reorganisation of the Estonian Orthodox Church.[165] This strategy worked, and in May 1920 Patriarch Tikhon of Moscow recognised the former Vicariate of Tallinn, as well as the parts of the Pskov Eparchy which were now situated in the Estonian State, as the autonomous Eparchy of Tallinn.[166] This was not the autocephaly – complete independence – the Estonians were hoping for, but it was a step in the right direction. Patriarch Tikhon applied to the Soviet authorities for a travel visa in order to come to Estonia at the end of June to personally consecrate the new bishop.[167] The visa was refused and another couple of months passed without resolution. In the beginning of September 1920, the newly recognised Tallinn Eparchy organised a *täiskogu*, where a number of organisational questions were discussed.[168] These included the calendar issue, the organisation of the Russian parishes, and the church statutes.

Most important, however, was the unanimous election of Aleksander Paulus as the new Bishop of Tallinn, a result that was communicated directly to Patriarch Tikhon, who acknowledged it at the end of October. Since he was still denied a visa, he delegated the task of consecration to Metropolitan Veniamin of

---

163 Seletuseandja [Clarificator], "Õigeusuliseks eestlaseks" [As Orthodox Estonian] in *PM*, 64/40, 14.02.1920, p. 3.

164 Paljud, keda asi huvitab [Many, who are interested], "Rohkem selgust" [More clarification] in *PM (hommikuväljaanne)*, 64/11, 14.01.1920; Setälä, U.V.J., 1962, p. 56-57; Kaljukosk, 1994, p. 30.

165 Õigeusuline [Orthodox], "Eesti ap.-õigeusu koguduse" [The Estonian Orthodox congregation] in *PM*, 64/69, 09.03.1920, p. 3; Anton Laar, "Ülevaade Eesti ap.-õigeusu kiriku elukäigust" [Overview of the life of the Estonian Orthodox Church] in *UE*, 3/7-8, 1923, p. 8; Saard, 2008, p. 1552-1553.

166 Aleksij, 1999, p. 376-377, 530-531. See also chapter 2.3.1. for more on these territories.

167 Aleksij, 1999, p. 377; Saard, 2008, p. 1553-1554.

168 "Eesti Apostliku-usu kiriku congress" [The congress of the Estonian Orthodox Church] in *UE*, 0/4, 1920, p. 3-7.

Petrograd,[169] Archbishop Serafim of Finland, and Evsevij of Pskov, who resided in Estonia as a Soviet refugee at the time.[170] Veniamin was also denied a visa, and Serafim needed some convincing that travel to Estonia was safe, but Paulus was finally consecrated in December 1920 in Tallinn.[171] Two months later, Patriarch Tikhon once again confirmed the autonomy granted the Estonians, elevated Bishop Aleksander to Archbishop, and promised that the question of autocephaly would be discussed at the next Russian *sobor*.[172]

With an ethnic Estonian now leading the Estonian Orthodox Church, plans to create an autocephalous Pan-Nordic Church reemerged. These plans included uniting the Finnish, Estonian and Latvian Eparchies into one independent Orthodox Church, consisting of three autonomous Eparchies.[173] Discussions continued throughout 1921, not openly, but in correspondence among members of the Estonian Synod,[174] the Finnish ecclesiastic authorities, and diplomats from all three countries. The plans were openly debuted in November 1921, when the Estonian Archbishop Aleksander (Paulus) officially invited the Archbishops Serafim of Finland and Jānis (Pommers) of Latvia to organise a joint Orthodox conference. Although both Serafim and Jānis were apprehensive about the merits of such a conference,[175] it was decided that the conference would be held in Helsinki in May 1922. The delegates from Estonia and Latvia had already been elected, when Jānis declined to participate, which caused Serafim to bow out and to forbid the other Finnish delegates from participating in the meeting.[176] The failure of this conference ended any concrete plans to unite the Baltic Orthodox churches.[177]

In June 1922, the Estonian Orthodox Church organised another *täiskogu*, where new statutes were to be adopted. However, the assembly was dominated

---

169 The name of St. Petersburg at the time (1914-1924).

170 The Patriarch's reply is reproduced in Prekup, 1998, p. 61-63.

171 "Eesti apostliku usu ülempiiskopi ametisse pühitsemine" [The consecration of the Estonian Orthodox Archbishop] in *PL*, 15/278, 06.12.1920, p. 4; Osavõtja [Participant], "Isa Aleksandri Pauluse pühitsemine esimeseks Eesti iseseisva kiriku peapiiskopiks" [The consecration of Fr. Aleksander Paulus as the first bishop of the independent Estonian Church] in *UE*, 0/4, 1920, p. 7-10.

172 Gubonin, 1994, p. 173; Sõtšov, 2004, p. 30. A *sobor* had been planned for 1921, which obviously could not be held because of the antagonistic Soviet regime.

173 Setälä, U.V.J., 1962, p. 58-62; Setälä, U.V.J., 1972; Saard, 2008, 1558-1559.

174 The *täiskogu* of September 1920 had agreed to rename the 'Eparchy Council,' 'Synod,' regardless of protests that the word *synod* could only be used for the highest organ of an independent church unit, consisting of mainly its bishops. "Täiskogu protokollid", *Eesti Ajaloo Arhiiv* [Estonian Historical Archives], f. 1655, n. 3, s. 6.

175 A sceptical letter from Archbishop Serafim to Archbishop Jānis concerning the invitation is reproduced in Sidjakov I, 2008, p. 134-135.

176 Setälä, U.V.J., 1962, p. 63.

177 Setälä, U.V.J., 1972, p. 11.

by the Russian parishes' demand for independence from the Estonian Orthodox Church and insecurity about relations vis-à-vis the state authorities.[178] The most important decision, which almost got lost amongst the other discussions, was a mandate for Archbishop Aleksander and the Estonian Synod to do everything in their power to achieve canonical recognition of autocephaly from the other Orthodox Churches.[179] It was planned to send Archbishop Aleksander together with a representative from the Estonian government to Constantinople in September 1922, but this plan was not carried through.[180] Nonetheless, the perceived need for a canonical solution for Estonian autocephaly without Russian approval was continuously strengthened by the chaotic situation of the church in the Soviet Union. Not only had Patriarch Tikhon been imprisoned by the secret services, but a parallel church hierarchy, calling itself the 'Living Church,' was on the rise with apparent support from the Soviet government.[181] The Estonian Synod composed a long letter to Patriarch Meletios IV of Constantinople in April 1923, recounting the history of the Estonian Orthodox Church with a plea to grant this church canonical security and make it autocephalous.[182] A reply is unattested.

In June 1923, a Finnish delegation consisting of Emil Nestor Setälä, representing the Finnish government; Sergei Solntsev, representing the Finnish Orthodox Church; and Hermann Aav, an ethnic Estonian and candidate for the post of Finnish vicar bishop, left for Constantinople to settle the status of the Orthodox Church of Finland.[183] Archbishop Aleksander of Tallinn joined them in Berlin, and the delegation arrived in Constantinople early on 2 July 1923. The situation at the Patriarchate was chaotic. The Turkish government had pushed through a clause in the Treaty of Lausanne requiring Patriarch Meletios IV to leave the Patriarchate, originally scheduled for 4 July 1923.[184] However, the Swedish embassy successfully arranged a delay of another week, in order for the Finnish-Estonian delegation to have their case heard by the Patriarch.[185]

---

178 "Eesti ap.-õigeusu kiriku Täiskogu" [The *täiskogu* of the Estonian Orthodox Church] in *UE*, 2/6, 1922, p. 1-3. See chapters 2.2.3. and 2.2.4. for more on these discussions.

179 "Eesti ap.-õigeusu kiriku Täiskogu" [The *täiskogu* of the Estonian Orthodox Church] in *UE*, 2/6, 1922, p. 2.

180 Setälä, U.V.J., 1962, p. 65.

181 Emhardt, 1929; Pospielovsky, 1984, p. 43-92. These developments were well known in Estonia, see C. v. Kügelgen, "Die lebendige Kirche" in *Revaler Bote, Russland-Beilage*, 4/135, 21.06.1922; C. v. Kügelgen, "Der Versuch einer bolschewistischen Kirchenrevolution" in *Revaler Bote, Russland-Beilage*, 4/140, 28.06.1922.

182 The letter (in Estonian) is reprinted in Prekup, 1998, p. 64-67.

183 Setälä, E. N., 1923.

184 Plank, 2007, p. 263-266.

185 Setälä, E. N., 1923, p. 6; Anton Laar, "Ülevaade Eesti ap.-õigeusu kiriku elukäigust" [Overview of the life of the Estonian Orthodox Church] in *UE*, 3/7-8, 1923, p. 8; Setälä,

A detailed description of the actual progression of these talks is contained in the travel report of E. N. Setälä.[186] After initial talks with the Patriarch himself, the delegation was informally briefed by protonotary and patriarchal managing director Papaioannou on how to present their case. He warned against insisting on full autocephaly, as there was an unwritten agreement among the Metropolitans in the Holy Synod of Constantinople that no new autocephalous churches should be declared before the planned Pan-Orthodox council, which was scheduled for the occasion of the 1600th anniversary of the First Ecumenical Council of Nicaea in 1925.[187] Wide autonomy within the jurisdiction of the Patriarchate of Constantinople could more easily be granted. The delegation finally accepted this alternative after having looked through the statutes of the recently autonomous Czechoslovakian Orthodox Church.

On 5 July 1923, the delegation was received by the Holy Synod of Constantinople, where each of the members again stated their case. Then they were required to leave, while the Holy Synod made a decision, which turned out to be in favour of the delegation on all points. The documents were prepared for the delegation on 10 July, when Patriarch Meletios IV had to leave for Mount Athos. Regarding the talks, Prof. Setälä concluded that "the solution concerning the status of the Finnish Church is as good as it can be, considering that there is apparently an agreement that no Orthodox Church shall be granted autocephaly at this point. Moreover, the Patriarch would only consider autocephaly for churches that constitute a majority of the local population, and currently there are no such churches without autocephaly."[188] Although, strictly speaking, this comment concerns only the Finnish side, the Estonian view would not have been very different.

In September, the Estonian Apostolic Orthodox Church, as it would now be called, celebrated an 'independence festival,' in which representatives from most Estonian parishes, the Estonian political authorities, and the other confessions took part.[189] However, delegates from three communities were missing. Archbishop Jānis of Latvia declined the invitation with a reference to 'difficult times.'[190] Archbishop Serafim of Finland also refused to send an official Finnish delegation. Nevertheless, Bishop Hermann (Aav), who had been consecrated as

---

U.V.J., 1966, p. 145. The Finnish diplomatic services used Swedish embassies as contact points where no Finnish diplomatic presence was available, such as Constantinople.

186 Setälä, E. N., 1923, p. 5-55. See also Sergei Solntsev, "Suomen kreikkalais-katolisen kirkon asialla Konstantinopolissa" [On business for the Finnish Orthodox Church in Constantinople] in *Aamun Koitto*, 6/14-15, p. 110-112.

187 Setälä, E. N., 1923, p. 29-31.

188 Setälä, E. N., 1923, p. 71-72.

189 Piduline K., "Eesti ap.-õigeusu kiriku iseseisvuse püha Tallinnas" [The independence festival of the Estonian Orthodox Church in Tallinn] in *UE*, 3/9, 1923, p. 1-3.

190 See also chapter 2.2.6.

Finnish vicar bishop in Constantinople against Serafim's will, had not yet taken up residence in Finland and, therefore, participated in the festivities.[191] Third, the Russian parishes of Estonia did not send a delegation.

In December of the same year, Metropolitan Aleksander (he had been named Metropolitan by Patriarch Meletios IV) and the Estonian Synod wrote a letter to Patriarch Tikhon of Moscow, explaining the events of the summer.[192] The Patriarch had been released from prison while the Estonian-Finnish delegation was in Constantinople. No reply to this letter has survived. In an interview given to the Russian-language newspaper *Segodnja* (Today) of Riga in April 1924, Aleksander expressed regret at having not heard from Patriarch Tikhon for more than two years:

> After the return from Constantinople and the release of Patriarch Tikhon from prison, Metropolitan Aleksander sent a detailed presentation to the Patriarch of all that had happened in the Estonian Church during the last few years and the declaration of autocephaly from the Ecumenical Patriarch for the Estonian Orthodox Church. [...]
>
> As has recently become clear, these papers lay a long time in Moscow and could not be handed on to the Patriarch, for reasons unconnected with the Estonian Orthodox Church. Finally, at the end of February, the papers were given to Patriarch Tikhon; moreover, as our partial report says, the Patriarch thought of the Estonian Orthodox Church with the good nature and Christian love so characteristic of him and promised to study the documents given to him very carefully.
>
> Metr. Aleksander has not received any official reply from Patriarch Tikhon so far.[193]

Almost twenty years later, in November 1940, he once again maintained that he never received any reply.[194] Although no reply came from Moscow, Antonij Khrapovitskij from the Russian Orthodox Church Outside Russia based in Sremski Karlovci did write a letter of protest end of July 1923, in which he declared that the independence of the Estonian, Latvian, Finnish, Polish, etc. Churches was neither desirable nor acceptable.[195] However, the Russian Hierarchy in Exile did not pursue this matter beyond empty threats. Their argument

---

191 "Viron kreikkalaiskatolisen kirkon itsenäistymisjuhla" [The independence festivities of the Estonian Orthodox Church] in *Aamun Koitto*, 6/20, 1923, p. 159-160.

192 This letter is reproduced in Prekup, 1998, p. 72-74. An English translation is available in Papathomas and Palli, 2002, p. 118-120.

193 А. Ш., "Патриарх Тихон и эстонская церковь" [Patriarch Tikhon and the Estonian Church] in *Seg*, 6/77, 02.04.1924, p. 4.

194 Letter from Metropolitan Aleksander to the deputy locum tenens of the Patriarch of Moscow, Metropolitan Sergij, 16.11.1940, reproduced in Prekup, 1998, p. 76-78. See also chapter 2.2.8.

195 "Kirik poliitika sõjariistaks" [The church as a political weapon] in *VM*, 6/184, 15.08.1923, p. 1; "Eesti ap. õigeusu kiriku iseseisvus" [The independence of the Estonian Orthodox Church] in *UE*, 3/6, 1923, p. 2.

was, however, taken seriously by many local Russians, whose reactions will be the content of the following section.

In the quote above, the author calls the document from Constantinople 'a declaration of autocephaly.' However, strictly speaking, it only declared the Estonian Orthodox Church autonomous. This is not necessarily a misunderstanding, as the Estonian Church considered itself *de facto* independent once autonomy under Constantinople had been achieved:

> 7 July 1923 will remain an important day in the history of the Estonian Orthodox Church. On that day, Patriarch Meletios IV of Constantinople made a decision with his Synod, declaring the Estonian Church an independent and self-sufficient church under the name of the Estonian Metropolia, equal in rights with all the other Eastern Orthodox Churches. [...]
> Our head of the church, together with representatives of the Finnish Orthodox Church, travelled to Constantinople on 16 June, arriving on 2 July. The situation was presented on the basis of written documents, and five days later, i.e. 7 July, a decision was arrived at, saying that the Estonian Church, retaining canonical relation with the entire Eastern Church, can organise its life with complete independence. The canonical relations consist, next to the common faith, in the duty of each new head of the church to inform the Patriarch of Constantinople of his elevation to office. Moreover, bishops who are convicted by an Estonian ecclesiastical court have the right to appeal to the Patriarch. [...]
> With this declaration, we have achieved our final goal of external organisation.[196]

This was the official interpretation of the Constantinople documents in the Estonian Orthodox Church. The Finnish Orthodox journal reported on the independence festivities of the Estonian Church, which were celebrated "because this church had received effective autocephaly from the Ecumenical Patriarch."[197] The Finnish interpretation of the result differed markedly, as the Estonian Orthodox journal *Uus Elu* reported:

> The Estonian Church received the Constantinople act as an act of complete independence, regarding the Patriarch of Constantinople simply as an honorary head. This interpretation is sustained by the documents, but the Finns went a different way and explained that they switched from being an autonomous Eparchy under the Patriarch of Moscow to an autonomous Eparchy under the Patriarch of Constantinople. That was also the reason why the Finnish Church did not send official representatives to our independence festival. Naturally, both the Estonian and the Finnish churches sent letters of explanation to the Patriarch of Moscow.
> The Finns received a reply from Moscow as expected: Moscow demands a return of the Finnish 'Eparchy' (no more talk about autonomy), justifying the demand with reference to the return of Patriarch Tikhon to daily business, which invalidates the

---

196 "Eesti ap. õigeusu kiriku iseseisvus" [The independence of the Estonian Orthodox Church] in *UE*, 3/6, 1923, p. 1.
197 "Viron kreikkalaiskatolisen kirkon itsenäistymisjuhla" [The independence festivities of the Estonian Orthodox Church] in *Aamun Koitto*, 6/20, 1923, p. 159.

stated reason to turn to Constantinople in the first place. It is not yet known what reply Estonia can expect.

Obviously, Finland has reacted dismissively. The weak point in their argument remains the central one: Constantinople. Although Meletios decided in favour of Finnish autonomy, could his successor Gregorios not, in the same manner, withdraw his predecessor's decision, giving Finland back to Moscow? That this is more than likely, considering Moscow's protest, is beyond doubt. And if that happens, Finnish diplomacy is at a dead end, from which only two exits possible: either back to Moscow's bosom or follow the example of Estonia, implementing the Constantinople decisions correctly, forming an independent Finnish Orthodox Church and arguing accordingly. The Finns considered this Estonian orientation somewhat – well – revolutionary, which they did not hide. But time will show who is right.

In any case, the Estonian Church remains on a firm foundation of independence, and, if the Finnish Church does not follow us, now that they have received their first lesson, it will happen automatically. No other road to peace for our churches exists.[198]

In order to settle the issue of independence, a fourth *täiskogu* was organised for September 1924.[199] The need to restore order in the Estonian Orthodox Church is clearly described by Anton Laar:

Now, even though we have an independent church, we are still nothing but an Eparchy. Our Metropolitan is still the only bishop in Estonia. Our highest assembly – the Synod – is still only an Eparchy council. There lies the chief problem; that this internally and externally weak institution must carry out the duties of ecclesiastic authorities. First, overworked with running tasks, [...] we often lose track of the most important issues, which should constitute the tasks of the Synod. Although they are placed on the agenda, they seldom pass the stage of discussion, for example on the issue of the episcopal church, where we talked, then talked, and talked some more without effect.[200] Moreover, making important decisions with weak authority, little strength, and short of time has resulted in some unsuitable decisions. [...] Nobody wonders any longer when a parish – even entire priories – uses foul language towards the Synod, even in official papers. – Recently, a priory even declared the Synod non-existent. – How the workings of the church suffer under these conditions is clear and understandable to every child. [...] The collapse of church regulations has gone so far that there are parishes and priories that have not handed in a single review in three years, not even about the newborns and member fluctuation. [...] This is an emergency, we must improve our organisation; we cannot let things go on like this.[201]

---

198 "Vene patriarhi – Sinodi ja Soome kirikuvalitsuse kirjavahetus" [The correspondence between the Russian Synod and the Finnish church leadership] in *UE*, 4/3, 1924, p. 5-6.
199 It was originally planned for 1923, but had to be postponed for various reasons.
200 See chapter 2.2.3. and 3.2.3. for more on this issue.
201 "Tänavune kiriku Täiskogu ja selle ülesanded" [This year's *täiskogu* and its tasks] in *UE*, 4/9, 1924, p. 3.

The article continued with an explanation of the canonical requirements for autocephaly, written in a pedagogic language:

> The fundament of Orthodox Christianity is that each independent church has several bishops, for Orthodoxy is based on community and strictly opposed to the power of an individual, such as the Pope in Rome. [...] Only two bishops together can consecrate a new bishop. Therefore, we need at least three bishops, so that, if one of them dies, the remaining two can consecrate a successor.[202]

In the Estonian Church, this meant opening up two new Eparchies, one in Narva and one in Petseri.[203] After the *täiskogu*, where the new statutes were passed, Laar concluded contentedly, "thus, the work on the exterior of our church is brought to an end."[204]

Six years later, in 1930, Laar wondered whether the Estonian Church had received an invitation to a preparatory commission at Mount Athos, where representatives from all autocephalous churches had gathered to discuss the possibility of a future Pan-Orthodox council: "If not, then how should our church leadership react to that? Not having received an invitation would mean not being recognised as autocephalous."[205] Anton Laar and his companions truly believed in having reached the state of autocephaly. However, after Laar's death in 1933, I have not been able to find any mention of such status anywhere.[206] Laar's opinion it seems, was not necessarily widely shared in Estonian Orthodoxy.

2.2.3. Estonia: the Russian Question

Alongside the Estonian aspirations for independence, there was a strong counter current among the Russians living on Estonian territory. This opposition feared

---

202 "Tänavune kiriku Täiskogu ja selle ülesanded" [This year's *täiskogu* and its tasks] in *UE*, 4/9, 1924, p. 3.

203 The *tomos* of Patriarch Meletios IV specified that the Estonian Orthodox Church should open up Eparchies in Petseri and Saaremaa, which Laar rejects as being impossible due to financial constraints. "Tänavune kiriku Täiskogu ja selle ülesanded" [This year's *täiskogu* and its tasks] in *UE*, 4/9, 1924, p. 4. See also the following sections for the new Eparchies.

204 "Eesti kiriku IV Täiskogu 9-11 septembril s. a." [The fourth *täiskogu* of the Estonian Church 9-11 September] in *UE*, 4/10, 1924, p. 2.

205 "Teised lehed" [Other papers] in *UE*, 10/7, 1930, p. 8. See Jensen, 1986, p. 27 for the preparatory commission.

206 In a collection dedicated to the centenary of the Estonian Orthodox Church, written in exile in 1951, an author claims that "the Patriarch of Constantinople gave the Estonian Church autocephaly (independence) as a metropolitanate." The idea thus, still existed, but not in the published interwar discourse. Tõnissoo, 1951, p. 20.

that 'the Estonians' were slowly eroding the Orthodox Church, not only with attempts at structural reform, but also with what they considered innovations in the liturgy, the calendar, and other questions of Orthodox life.[207] Most of the Estonians perceived this counter current as typical Russian political agitation, which could be ignored with a clean conscience, especially as long as the Estonians remained a majority. The first signs of Russian opposition to the Estonian reformation of the local Orthodox Church appeared in May 1917, at the Eparchy congress in Tartu.[208] Resistance continued, and even Bishop Platon was eyed with suspicion by some Russian voices, which saw him as an Estonian patriot, not an Orthodox bishop.[209]

Until Patriarch Tikhon officially recognized the Tallinn Eparchy as autonomous in May 1920, the main actors in Estonian Orthodoxy considered only the parishes of the former Riga Eparchy as their constituency. In the Eparchy assembly of August 1917, the sixth decision of the Estonian section was "that the Estonian Eparchy should have an ethnic boundary, i.e. all Estonians in the entire Russian Empire should together form the Estonian Eparchy."[210] The complete incompatibility of this idea with the canonical norms of the Orthodox Church[211] did not interest the Estonians. They wanted an avenue to customise Orthodox Christianity in a way that made it more acceptable to the mostly Lutheran Estonians around them, removing the stigma of Russification and backwardness.[212] While this is analysed more thoroughly in the later chapters, it is important as a reference point for the efforts to re-organise the Estonian Orthodox Church under the new circumstances. At the *täiskogu* following the death of Bishop Platon in March 1919, Konstantin Kokla thoroughly criticised the decision to aspire to complete autocephaly.[213] For Kokla, it was unnatural for the tiny Estonian Orthodox congregation to break all links with the Russian 'sister congregation' by declaring autocephaly. It should rather aspire to autonomy within the folds of the Russian Church.

---

207 See chapter 3.1. for more on these issues.
208 See chapter 2.2.1.
209 A letter of complaint, sent to Patriarch Tikhon by Estonian Russians, is mentioned both by Poska, 1968, p. 23 and Kumyš, 1999, p. 27 without any further references. I have not been able to find any information on this complaint in the contemporary sources. Saard, 2007b, p. 123 mentions that Patriarch Tikhon may have secretly consented to the murder of Bishop Platon for this reason, referring to an article by Anton Laar from 1933. However, there is no mention of such a link in this article.
210 Keegi [Somebody], "Piiskopkonna koosolekult" [From the Eparchy Gathering] in *UjE₁*, 14/37-38-39, 26.09.1917, p. 344.
211 See chapter 1.2.1. on phyletism.
212 See chapter 3.1. for this customisation process and chapters 3.2.3. and 4.1.2. for the external perspective on Estonian Orthodoxy.
213 Saard, 2008, p. 1546.

Once Patriarch Tikhon raised the Estonian Vicariate to a full Eparchy in May 1920, the tables were turned. Now it was the Russian parishes' turn to demand autonomy for their co-nationals within the Estonian Orthodox Church. Their first official demand for autonomy came at the *täiskogu* of September 1920. The discussion was heated, and in the end a resolution, put forward by Anton Laar, was agreed upon: "The organisation of purely Russian parishes into a separate ecclesiastic unit should be welcomed in principle. The exact configuration of this separation will be worked out by a separate committee."[214] Moreover, the Russian delegates were successful in electing a vicar bishop for the Russian parishes and put forward hieromonk Joann Bulin of the Monastery of Petseri. This was one of the reasons why Aleksander Paulus, whom the Russian delegates did not support in 1919, was elected unanimously this time around. Bulin was elected unanimously. Only Konstantin Kokla was sceptical, expressing doubt that the Russian members of mixed Estonian-Russian parishes, especially in Petserimaa, would not want to follow the decisions of the *täiskogu*, but subordinate themselves to the Russian vicar bishop.[215]

Of the two elected bishops, only Aleksander Paulus was accepted by Patriarch Tikhon, who refused to accept Joann Bulin because of his young age. Bulin was only twenty-seven years old in 1920 and the minimum age for consecration of clergy according to canon law is thirty years.[216] As such, the Russian demands could only partially be met; they had to subordinate themselves to Bishop Aleksander.[217] However, the 'Clerical Council of the Russian Parishes of the Estonian Apostolic Orthodox Church' (CCRP) was created, and started functioning next to the Synod as an autonomous unit.[218] This worked out fine through 1921, but a row over the role of the CCRP erupted during the *täiskogu* of June 1922. This is how the journal *Uus Elu* introduces a description of the 1922 *täiskogu*:

> One of these questions was the relationship with the Russian parishes. As our neighbours – Finland and Latvia – have no problems with separatist Russian parishes, we experience here the opposite. The Russians arrived to the *täiskogu* in 1920 with an extremely agitated attitude. They almost could not find enough words to blackmail the church leadership and demanded no less than a completely independent church. Since this was a completely impossible demand, we had to give some

214 "Täiskogu protokollid", *Eesti Ajaloo Arhiiv* [Estonian Historical Archives], f. 1655, n. 3, s. 6. See also "Eesti Apostliku-usu kiriku congress" [The congress of the Estonian Orthodox Church] in *UE*, 0/4, 1920, p. 4, 6.

215 "Täiskogu protokollid", *Eesti Ajaloo Arhiiv* [Estonian Historical Archives], f. 1655, n. 3, s. 6. See also chapter 2.3.1. for the Petserimaa problematic.

216 See the reply by Patriarch Tikhon reprinted in Prekup, 1998, p. 61-63.

217 See the editor's note under "Eesti Apostliku-usu kiriku congress" [The congress of the Estonian Orthodox Church] in *UE*, 0/4, 1920, p. 7.

218 Saard, 2008, p. 1568.

concessions in order to achieve an unanimous bishop's election. Instead of independence, the Russians were thus given limited autonomy. [...] The process of working out this autonomy was a long-drawn one. Lacking a precise agenda, the Russians did not hesitate to discuss every tiny point very heatedly. Moreover, it became clear towards the end that the Russians were not willing to accept any limits to their autonomy next to a common bishop. – As this last point showed how the Russians understand 'autonomy' the Synod did not have any option but to halt this dubious autonomy and convert it into a normal priory, although it was obvious that the Russians would not let this decision pass easily. The Estonian-Russian issue thus proved to be the most thrilling question of the *täiskogu*.[219]

The author continues, describing the *taiskogu* itself. The Russians contributed "long, boring speeches *à la russe*, designed to impede the workings of the meeting" before "leaving the meeting, for 'technical' reasons, as they affirmed later."[220] According to Laar, the Russians did not want independence in order to improve their religious life, but to support the Russian national cause, which was not an acceptable motive to the Estonians.

That the Russians and Estonians were drifting apart was mentioned in *Uus Elu* as early as February 1922, in an outline of the possible repercussions of the First Russian All-Diaspora Council meeting in Sremski Karlovci at the end of 1921, which had established the Russian Orthodox Church Outside Russia.[221] Chief among these was the concern some of the Russians of Estonia, especially among the émigrés from the Soviet Union, might consider it necessary to subordinate themselves to this church. Moreover, the CCRP decided to delay the planned handover of the Aleksander Nevskij Cathedral in Tallinn to the Estonian Synod, in order to let it be the episcopal seat, claiming that they could not be sure whether the Estonians were really Orthodox anymore. The Estonians countered that "this indecency is all the more inexcusable since the Estonian ecclesiastic authorities have always been accommodating to the Russian minority's demands, sometimes even beyond measure. When the Russians mix up their ideas of church with Imperial and Tsarist politics, then they should not be surprised when the ecclesiastic authorities in Estonia act less friendly."[222]

The conflict broke out in full after the 1922 *täiskogu*, when a stormy verbal exchange appeared in a number of Estonian newspapers. The CCRP refused to accept the decision of the *täiskogu* that its days were numbered and continued meeting, asserting various further demands. These included, first and foremost, autonomy for the Russian parishes, independent of the Estonian Synod, subordi-

---

219 "Eesti ap.-õigeusu kiriku Täiskogu" [The *täiskogu* of the Estonian Orthodox Church] in *UE*, 2/6, 1922, p. 1.
220 "Eesti ap.-õigeusu kiriku Täiskogu" [The *täiskogu* of the Estonian Orthodox Church] in *UE*, 2/6, 1922, p. 1.
221 "Tallinnast" [From Tallinn] in *UE*, 2/2, 1922, p. 5. See also Pospielovsky, 1984, p. 113-117.
222 "Tallinnast" [From Tallinn] in *UE*, 2/2, 1922, p. 5.

nated only to the common Archbishop.[223] The Estonian Synod, through publicist Anton Laar, replied that these demands could not be accepted, because first, the Archbishop alone was not the head of the Estonian Orthodox Church, according to its statutes, but only together with the Synod. Second, the new priory rules adopted at the *täiskogu* would, according to the Synod, provide a framework in which broad autonomy would be possible, if the Russians wished to establish a purely Russian priory.[224]

However, when the parishes were to elect a council for the ethnically defined Russian priory in August, only two delegates appeared, and the election had to be postponed.[225] Prior to this meeting, the CCRP had called upon all Russian parishes to refrain from sending delegates, as this would imply that they agreed to the degradation from autonomy to the status of priory.[226] According to Laar, the CCRP had misunderstood Archbishop Aleksander's statement that no one would be forced to join the Russian priory as an invitation to reject the creation of a priory entirely and insist on continuing autonomy for the CCRP.[227] The Synod, meeting a week later, declared all the Russian demands inadmissible and called upon the Russians to maintain the unity of the Estonian Orthodox Church. Moreover, it decided that the CCRP woul no longer be recognised by the church and requested that any further communication with the Synod and the Archbishop be passed through the territorial priory councils.[228]

This did not impress the CCRP, which continued to function well into September, when it was forcefully disbanded with the help of the Estonian police.[229] The last CCRP chairman, Boris Agapov, claimed an injustice had been committed against the CCRP and that the Synod itself had been illegally elected and

---

223 "Kirjad toimetusele" [Letters to the editor] in *VM*, 5/169, 24.07.1922, p. 7; --f--, "Lahkuminek Eesti ap.-õigeusu kirikus" [Divergences in the Estonian Orthodox Church] in *VM*, 5/191, 18.08.1922, p. 3.

224 Anton Laar, "Vene koguduste nõukogu seletuse puhul vahekorra kohta Eesti kiriku-ga" [Regarding the CCRP letter on the relationship with the Estonian Church] in *VM*, 5/175, 31.07.1922, p. 5.

225 f., "Lahkhelid apostlik-õigeusu kirikus" [Divergences in the Orthodox Church] in *VM*, 5/185, 11.08.1922, p. 3-4.

226 "Воззвание русского духовного совета" [An appeal of the CCRP] in *Последния Известия*, 3/178, 06.08.1922, p. 2; "Русские приходы против выборов 10 августа" [Russian parishes against the elections on 10 August] in *Последния Известия*, 3/178, 06.08.1922, p. 2.

227 Anton Laar, "Eesti-Vene kirikutülid" [The Estonian-Russian church wars] in *Kaja*, 4/197, 29.08.1922, p. 2.

228 "Обращение" [Decision] in *Жизнь*, 1/90, 23.08.1922, p. 2.

229 "Vene vaimulik nõukogu ajutiselt kinni pandud" [The CCRP temporarily closed down] in *PM*, 66/215, 20.09.1922, p. 1; "Vene koguduste nõukogu tegevus siseministri poolt lõpetatud" [The activity of the CCRP stopped by the Minister of the Interior] in *PM*, 66/227, 04.10.1922, p. 2; Saard, 2008, p. 1568.

ratified.[230] According to the Estonian Synod, Agapov represented only a minority of the Russian parishes in Estonia, a view shared by an editorial in the Russian-language newspaper *Žizn'* (Life). Here, the divergences were depicted as a 'misunderstanding' that had been turned into a conflict by the personal enmity among a handful of Orthodox clergy: on the Russian side, Boris Agapov and Vladimir Čumikov, another leading CCRP-member, had pressed for their (personal) understanding of the situation while on the Estonian side, Anton Laar had seemed "not to consider it a sin to propagate schism in the church."[231]

This editorial was the exception to the polemical rhetoric of the other articles in this exchange. Articles in favour of the Russians claimed that the Estonians did not keep their promises; thus, the Russians must have autonomy, in order to avoid the innovations and paternalism of the Estonians.[232] The articles from the Estonian side used the opposite rhetoric. The Russians are annoying; they cannot come to terms with no longer being the masters within the Orthodox Church or with living in a democratic society.[233] After the CCRP was forcefully disbanded, and Laar and Agapov had published their respective understandings of recent events, the polemical articles stopped.

Priests who were not Estonian citizens were barred from serving in November.[234] However, the Aleksander Nevskij Cathedral of Tallinn was still not the episcopal seat but a purely Russian parish church. In February 1923, the parish council decided in a plenary meeting that the Cathedral would not be handed over to the bishop.[235] The report on this meeting in the Estonian secular press did not conceal its disapproval of the methods used:

> The refugee Ivanov [...] delivered a drawn-out, venomous speech. He called on those present to protest against the legal infringement and, in no circumstances whatsoever, to hand over church property to the Synod. If the Aleksander Nevskij parish council showed a tendency to agree to the Synod's demand, it must be

---

230 Борис Агапов, "Синод и русские православные приходы в Эстонии" [The Synod and the Russian Orthodox parishes in Estonia] in *Последния Известия*, 3/230, 05.10.1922, p. 2; 3/231, 06.10.1922, p. 2; 3/234, 10.10.1922, p. 2.

231 Editorial in *Жизнь*, 1/81, 07.08.1922.

232 See the almost daily articles in *Последния Известия* from end of July until mid-August 1922 and especially, Борис Агапов, "Синод и русские православные приходы в Эстонии" [The Synod and the Russian Orthodox parishes in Estonia] in *Последния Известия*, 3/230, 05.10.1922, p. 2; 3/231, 06.10.1922, p. 2; 3/234, 10.10.1922, p. 2. See also chapter 3.1. for more one the issue of innovation.

233 See especially M. K., "Kas niiviisi edasi lasta?" [Should we let this go on?] in *Kaja*, 4/191, 22.08.1922, p. 2; Anton Laar, "Eesti-Vene kirikutülid" [The Estonian-Russian church wars] in *Kaja*, 4/197, 29.08.1922, p. 2.

234 Saard, 2008, p. 1571.

235 "Poliitika kirikus" [Politics in church] in *VM*, 6/36, 13.02.1923, p. 4. See also the public letter to Archbishop Aleksander in Владимир Чумиков, "Вопрос о соборе" [The question of the cathedral], in *Последния Известия*, 4/43, 14.02.1923, p. 2.

immediately dissolved. [...] Some officer from the Northwestern Army demanded, just as Mr. Ivanov, that under no circumstances must the property be given away. The chairman of the meeting, Agapov, could even tell those present that no voluntary handover of the property would happen and that this decision was final.

Then actual members of the parish were invited to speak, but their statements were ignored. [...] Two ladies explained insistently that they had been members of the Aleksander Nevskij Parish for several decades and would stay members. They could not see what was so bad about becoming episcopal church, and would it really be so destructive having an Estonian-language liturgy there once in a while? However, these requests from parishioners far removed from politics did not make an impression on the meeting chairmen.[236]

As can be seen in this article and the following ones, a distinction between 'local Russians' and refugees from the Soviet Union was becoming important for the Estonians discussing the 'Russian issue.'[237] The Estonian neologism '*maruvene-lane*' (extreme Russian) was coined to denote Soviet refugees who refused to acknowledge the Estonians as the masters of Estonia. This story ended when Archbishop Aleksander barred the Russian Archpriest Aleksej Aristov of the Aleksander Nevskij Cathedral from serving and dissolved the parish council.[238] The cathedral was still not handed over and did not become the episcopal seat until 1936. However, this delay was not primarily due to Russian resistance but to the high costs involved in maintaining such a large church.[239]

The 'Russian issue' returned to the newspapers when Metropolitan Aleksander returned from Constantinople at the end of July 1923. In the meantime, the Russians had organised a delegation to the administration of the Russian Exile Church in Sremski Karlovci. Under the leadership of Archpriest Aristov, who had been barred from serving earlier that year, a parallel church structure was created for the Russians in Estonia.[240] Archimandrite Joann Bulin, the candidate for the Russian Vicariate of the Tallinn Eparchy in 1920, was put forward as candidate for bishop of this parallel Eparchy. However, the Estonians remained confident that they would achieve a victory: "It is very questionable

---

236 "Poliitika kirikus" [Politics in church] in *VM*, 6/36, 13.02.1923, p. 4.

237 Such as "Võitlus Aleksander-Nevski kiriku umber" [The battle of the Aleksander Nevskij church] in *VM*, 6/37, 14.02.1923, p. 3; "Tüli kirikumeest vahel" [Conflict between church men] in *PM*, 67/56, 28.02.1923, p. 5; K., "Vene mustasajaliste tegutsemine piiririikide õigeusu kirikutes" [The dirty activities of the Russians in the Orthodox Churches of the border states] in *Kaja*, 5/56, 01.03.1923, p. 2.

238 "Ap. u. k. ülempiiskop skandaali tegijaid karistanud" [The Orthodox Archbishop punished the scandal actors] in *VM*, 6/43, 22.02.1923, p. 3.

239 "Katedraali saatus otsustatud" [The fate of the cathedral is sealed] in *ET*, 1/41, 1936, p. 5; "Переходъ русскаго таллинскаго Александро-Невскаго прихода въ Симеоновскую церковь" [The transfer of the Russian Aleksander Nevskij parish to the Simeonov church] in *PS*, 6/11, 1936, p. 156-160. See also chapter 3.2.3. for more on the Aleksander Nevskij Cathedral.

240 See the almost daily notices in *VM*, 6/169, 28.07.1923 to 6/185, 16.08.1923.

whether there is really a chance of a major schism, for all this Russian rambling is not so much religious as political, and the state cannot ignore it."[241] The issue was put to rest by a thorough audit of the inventory and activities of the Petseri Monastery. This audit revealed a number of inconsistencies and a number of monks were expelled from Estonian territory.[242] This row accounted for the previously mentioned absence of official Russian representatives at the independence festival in September.

An author, writing under the pseudonym 'Quidam,' explained the situation after the parish council of the Aleksander Nevskij Cathedral in June 1924 once again refused to make the Cathedral episcopal seat, as follows:

> First, it is impossible to influence the refugee actors in our church with normal moral means. [...] There is no use in trying anything except for brute force, as we saw during the CCRP-struggle in 1922. Second – and most importantly – we still lack a legal foundation for the activities of the church, settling once and for all the relationship between church and state and the rights of parish members. [...] Although our constitution contains some guidelines in this regard, our parliaments have so far not been able to settle this issue; and they do not yet seem to be in a hurry.[243]

When this turmoil calmed down, the Russian agitation did not create uproar for several years. During the *täiskogu* of September 1924, Archbishop Evsevij of Pskov, who had spent more than five years in Estonia as a Soviet refugee, was unanimously elected bishop of the new, ethnically defined Eparchy of Narva.[244] The election was dependent on a number of conditions, such as Estonian citizenship and the permission of Patriarch Tikhon. Moreover, only Estonian citizens could vote and be elected to the council of the Russian Eparchy. The Russians further agreed to remove the question of parallel church structures and a return to the jurisdiction of the Patriarchate of Moscow from their agenda.[245] By the end of November 1925, all the administrative hurdles had been met, except the permission from Patriarch Tikhon, but Evsevij nevertheless officially accepted the post of Bishop of Narva on 1 December 1925.[246]

---

241 "Eesti Apostliku-usu kirik ei ole iseseisev?" [The Estonian Apostolic Church is not independent?] in *VM*, 6/180, 10.08.1923, p. 3.

242 "Petseri klooster puhastustules" [Cleaning the Petseri Monastery] in *VM*, 6/191, 23.08. 1923, p. 5; "Mitropoliit Aleksander Petserimaal" [Metropolitan Aleksander in Petserimaa] in *VM*, 6/194, 26.08.1923, p. 4. See also chapter 2.3.1.

243 Quidam, "Mitte kirikuvalitsuse süü, vaid seaduse puudus" [Not the fault of the ecclesiastic authorities, but rather the lack of law] in *PL*, 19/157, 14.06.1924, p. 4. For the church-state relationship, see chapter 2.2.4.

244 "Eesti kiriku IV Täiskogu 9-11 septembril s. a." [The fourth *täiskogu* of the Estonian Church 9-11 September] in *UE*, 4/10, 1924, p. 2-5; Saard, 2008, p. 1572.

245 "Vene piiskopkonna nõukogu tahab edasi töötada" [The council of the Russian Eparchy wants to work on] in *PL*, 19/275, 11.10.1924, p. 3.

246 Saard, 2008, p. 1572-1576.

Although Bishop Evsevij remained largely loyal to the Estonian Church, and there were no further serious arguments with the Russians, Anton Laar continued to insist on the incompatibility of the two nations:

> We are not interested in blaming the Russians. Their viewpoint is understandable. The shock of having lost power prevents their hearts from being appeased. Their contempt for the 'potato republic' is well known, as is their condemnation of any 'Estonian Russian' Church. May God stay with them, may they live and act. The only problem is that they do this under the flag and responsibility of our Estonian Church. [...] We have always been of the opinion that the only viable basis of the Estonian Orthodox Church is a purely national one. This is not really in accordance with the internationality of Christianity, but it is necessary, in this case, precisely because of the extreme nationalist politics of the Russians. [...]
> Our only way to salvation now, when church and state have been separated, is to finalise our relationship with the Russians. And this would be: *the Estonian Church must rid itself of its Russian part!* [247]

Laar repeated his demand in 1932 commenting on an article on the Finnish Orthodox Church, where the relationship with the 'Russian element' had apparently found a harmonious end: "Reading all this and thinking about it, I cannot help but asking the hurtful question: *Why do we not yet have a relationship like that?*"[248] However, Laar was the most ardent supporter of a nationally divided Orthodox Church.[249] Most other Orthodox clergy were more moderate and hoped that time would calm the Estonian-Russian tensions.

2.2.4. Estonia: Church and State

The relationship between the Estonian Orthodox Church and the secular authorities of the young Estonian State fell into three large areas of contact. The first concerned the legal status and position of the Estonian Orthodox Church within the state, which remained unclear until 1926. Second, the Estonian Orthodox Church was heavily affected by the implementation of land reform. Third, a heated debate about the desirability and content of religious instruction led to a referendum on the question in spring 1923. In each of these areas, the Estonian Orthodox Church fully participated in the questions of the state,

---

247 Anton Laar, "Vene kirikuasjad" [Russian church issues] in *UE*, 7/10, 1927, p. 1-2 (Emphasis in original).
248 „Eestlane", "Rahvuslikkusest meie ap.-usu kirikus" [Nationalism in our Orthodox Church] in *UE*, 12/9, 1932, p. 3-4 (Emphasis in original). See also Anton Laar, "Sõnad ja teod" [Words and Acts] in *UE*, 12/7-8, 1932, p. 7-9. See also chapter 2.3.1. for more on the 'Russian question' in the early 1930s.
249 Konstantin Kokla, "Astudes uude aastasse" [Entering the new year] in *UjE₂*, 2/1, 1934, p. 3-4.

although it was often not accepted as a full participant by the majority of Estonians.[250]

The first issue, a good relationship with the state and a stable legal foundation, was very important to Orthodox Estonians from the beginning. The provisional government of Estonia passed a bill in April 1919 that temporarily regulated religious organisations in Estonia until a final law could be passed.[251] The provisional law, passed before the Tallinn Eparchy was first recognised as a full Eparchy by Patriarch Tikhon, only stated that the Orthodox Church of Estonia act according to the statutes of the Moscow *sobor*, so long as they did not contradict Estonian laws. Regulations pertaining to existence under the Russian Church, such as the higher ecclesiastic authorities, were examples of contradictions between Estonian law and church statutes. Because the law was so short, interpretations of it varied. For the 'Russian faction' of the Estonian Orthodox Church, any change to the statutes of the *sobor* entailed a violation of the law,[252] while the Estonians claimed that it gave them the freedom to adapt these statutes to the local situation.[253]

After his consecration as Archbishop of Tallinn in December 1920, Aleksander Paulus gave an interview to the Estonian newspaper *Vaba Maa*. He clearly favoured full separation of church and state as this was the only canonically acceptable solution.[254] The *Riigikogu*[255] appointed a committee in the following year, which was to be responsible for working out a draft law on religious organisations. This committee consisted of representatives from the large churches and various ministries. The Orthodox journal *Uus Elu* accompanied a presentation of the committee's work with a short summary of the 1905 French 'Law on the Separation of Church and State.'[256] By the end of 1921, the committee had agreed on a draft law, which was accepted by the responsible

---

250 See chapter 3.2.3. for more on this external perception.

251 "Greeka-katoliku (Vene õigeusu) kiriku valitsuse ja koguduste omavalitsuse ajutine korraldus" [Provisional regulations of the ecclesiastic authorities and self-government of the Greek Catholic (Russian Orthodox) Church] in *Riigi Teataja*, 2/28-29, 1919, p. 227; Saard, 2008, p. 1548.

252 Борис Агапов, "Синод и русские православные приходы в Эстонии" [The Synod and the Russian Orthodox parishes in Estonia] in *Последния Известия*, 3/230, 05.10.1922, p. 2; 3/234, 10.10.1922, p. 2.

253 "Meie kirikuseadus" [Our church statutes] in *UE*, 2/4, 1922, p. 1-2; "Eesti ap.-õigeusu kiriku Täiskogu" [The *täiskogu* of the Estonian Orthodox Church] in *UE*, 2/6, 1922, p. 2-3.

254 K., "Jutuajamine ülempiiskop Aleksandriga" [Conversation with Archbishop Aleksander] in *VM*, 3/297, 28.12.1920, p. 4.

255 The Estonian Parliament.

256 "Kiriku ja riigi vahekordade lahendamiseks" [Finding a solution to the church-state relationship] in *UE*, 1/5-6, 1921, p. 37-39.

Riigikogu-commission on the first reading.[257] However, debates dragged on, and when the new law finally came up for discussion in the *Riigikogu* itself in the autumn of 1922, it was opposed to such an extent that it had to be rewritten.[258]

A new draft law was worked out two years later, this time without consulting representatives of the various churches. This draft was heavily criticised by the Orthodox journal *Uus Elu*:

> Now, we hear how the administration of the Ministry of the Interior has written a new draft law and shown it to the government. – Separation is still separation, but now with a completely different agenda: the church as such, i.e., the union of parishes, can only be registered as a union. In other words, only as the collective of the parishes of which it consists. Being only a union, the church is nothing more than a node, which the parishes can recognise or not at will. – Consequently, in a first step, only individual parishes are registered, for a union is only a union if it unites something. [...]
>
> It is too early to tell how this draft will fare in the *Riigikogu*. However, more attention to real life would be welcome. In our opinion, destroying the unity of the church in order to revive it as a 'union' is a disadvantaging step for Estonia. However, such steps are usually only regretted when it is already too late.[259]

The drawn-out discussions concerning this new draft were the main reason behind the Synod's postponement of the planned *täiskogu* of 1923 to September 1924.[260] However, even that did not help, as the discussion in the *Riigikogu* only ended in October 1925, when the 'law on religious societies and their unions' passed after controversial debates.[261] This law was a hybrid of the first and second drafts, allowing both individual parishes and unions of at least three local religious congregations to register with the Ministry of the Interior.[262] The law was sceptically welcomed by Anton Laar, who could not imagine it making a great difference to the everyday life of the Estonian Orthodox Church, which

---

257 "Riigi ja kiriku vahekorra" [The relationship between state and church] in *UE*, 1/10, 1921, p. 73-75.

258 "Seadus kirikute ja usuühingute kohta" [Law on the churches and religious societies] in *PL*, 17/236, 27.09.1922, p. 2; "Riigikogu" [Parliament] in *PL*, 17/248, 11.10.1922, p. 5; "Riigikogu" [Parliament] in *PL*, 17/260, 25.10.1922, p. 6.

259 "Kiriku ja riigi vahekord Eestis" [The church-state relationship in Estonia] in *UE*, 4/2, 1924, p. 6-7.

260 "Sinodi korraldus" [Synod decision] in *UE*, 4/6-7. 1924, p. 12; "Eesti kiriku IV Täiskogu 9-11 septembril s. a." [The fourth *täiskogu* of the Estonian Church 9-11 September] in *UE*, 4/10, 1924, p. 2-3.

261 "Usuühingute küsimus põhimõttelikult otsustatud" [The question of religious unions principally decided] in *PL*, 20/293, 29.10.1925, p. 6; "Üldkirik ja üksikkogudused" [Church and individual parishes] in *PL*, 20/294, 30.10.1925, p. 7.

262 "Usuühingute ja nende liitude seadus" [Law on religious associations and their unions] in *Riigi Teataja*, 8/183-184, 1925, p. 1050-1054.

officially registered as a union of parishes on 3 July 1926.[263] In an interview Metropolitan Aleksander gave to the newspaper *Päevaleht* end of 1926, he expressed satisfaction with the current situation, in which only a single parish had not yet managed to register itself properly.[264]

In relation to the land reform, *Uus Elu* explained the problem as follows in 1921:

> The church lands are, as we know, all expropriated on the basis of §1 of the Constitutional Assembly's land reform law. §39 of the by-law on the implementation of the land reform, however, says that church lands should remain in the hands of the parish except in case the local government needs the land for its purposes. This situation soon became very unnatural: if the Ministry of Agriculture wants the church lands, they are easily expropriated, for the by-law does not invalidate the law. [...] This led to a juridical question: what use is there in a by-law if it is not followed, although its content is clear? [...] If §39 is eliminated, the story has come to an end, but the lands are still gone.[265]

Regarding the school houses, there was disagreement on whether the law required an expropriation of all properties where school education had happened or only those which had been used exclusively for school education. According to the former interpretation, the Estonian Orthodox Church would suffer huge losses, since most of its schools had been organised within the parish halls, which had also housed the priest.[266] In the following years, the Orthodox journal occasionally published 'unbelievable' examples of state arbitrariness regarding expropriation.[267] However, the issue was more or less settled by 1926, when it was decided that the state should return a certain amount of expropriated land to the parishes. Payment for the expropriated land began only in 1935 and was to last 20 years.[268]

---

263 Anton Laar, "Uuel alusel" [On new foundations] in *UE*, 5/11-12, 1925, p. 8-9; Sõtšov, 2004, p. 32.
264 "Mitropoliit Aleksander õigeusu kirikutest Eestis" [Metropolitan Aleksander on the Orthodox churches in Estonia] in *PL*, 21/341, 15.12.1926, p. 2. See, however, chapter 2.3.1. for the problems this law caused in Petserimaa.
265 "Meie kirikumaade ja koolimajade küsimus" [The question of our church lands and school houses] in *UE*, 1/8, 1921, p. 68.
266 "Aasta algul" [The year's beginning] in *UE*, 2/1, 1922, p. 2-3.
267 "Aasta algul" [The year's beginning] in *UE*, 2/1, 1922, p. 2-3; "Veel pildikene meie varanduste likvideerimisest" [More on the liquidation of our property] in *UE*, 2/6, 1922, p. 3-5; "Ap.-õigeusu koguduste esitus Riigikogus" [The representation of the Orthodox parishes in the *Riigikogu*] in *UE*, 2/7, 1922, p. 2-4; "Kiriku ja riigi vahekord Eestis" [The church-state relationship in Estonia] in *UE*, 4/2, 1924, p. 6-7; Konstantin Kokla, "Meie kirikukoolide saatus" [The fate of our church schools] in *UjE₂*, 2/11, 1934, p. 179-180.
268 "Riigivanem usaldusküsimuse üles tõstnud" [The Prime Minister asked for a vote of confidence] in *PM*, 70/323, 27.11.1926, p. 7; "Kirikutele 30.000 krooni" [30 000 kroons to the churches] in *PM*, 79/313, 16.11.1935, p. 6.

On the issue of religious instruction, the discussions were more heated. Whereas education before 1917 had been confessional, with separate schools for the Orthodox and the Lutherans, this arrangement changed in the new secular state. In July 1917, Aleksander Värat emphasised the importance of religious education in very theological terms.[269] Religious instruction was necessary to understand the God-given human nature, not because it would provide the students with more exact knowledge, but rather because it would make them appreciate knowledge and the world in which they lived. Moreover, Värat refuted the argument that religion is a private matter and explained that freedom, solidarity, and fraternity are Christian categories. Without understanding the Christian message, one cannot really aspire to any of these ideals. Konstantin Kokla also published on the question of religious instruction in 1917, presenting an overview of recent developments in Russia and Estonia.[270] Kokla distinguished three tendencies at a congress on education in Tartu:

> First, the modern slogan, 'religion is bankrupt!'; second the Protestant and Orthodox attempts to prove the opposite; and finally a middle way, which, let it be said, won a narrow majority: let the religious instruction in the schools be inter-denominational, i.e. without confessional colour. But what is religious instruction without confession? It is something our current teachers cannot teach! [...]
>
> But since this decision has not yet been implemented, we continue to demand free religious instruction in a free school. The implementation should be left to the local administrators. That would be the only just basis and actually feasible option concerning religious instruction in our schools.[271]

Anton Laar favoured a system in which religious instruction was the responsibility of the religious organisations, not the state schools.[272] However, there are indications that Laar put forward the idea of inter-denominational religious instruction at the education congress of 1917. For him, this was the only acceptable possibility if religious instruction were to be given in the schools at all, as the Lutheran Church demanded. Since Laar was the public voice of Estonian Orthodoxy throughout the 1920s, his ideas were the ones that were most influential.

The integration of the Orthodox parish schools into the state school system, or rather the abolition of the Orthodox parish schools, was completed by 1920, when the new law on primary education was passed.[273] The Estonian political

---

269 Aleksander Värat, "Koguduste uuendamine VIII. Usk ja kool" [The renewal of the congregations VIII. Religion and Education] in *UjE₁*, 14/29-30, 1917, p. 269-274.

270 Konstantin Kokla, "Kas on usuõpetus koolis tarvilik?" [Is religious education useful?] in *UjE₁*, 14/31-32, 1917, p. 291-292.

271 Konstantin Kokla, "Kas on usuõpetus koolis tarvilik?" [Is religious education useful?] in *UjE₁*, 14/31-32, 1917, p. 291-292. See also Valk, 1997, p. 18-19.

272 "Usuõpetuse küsimus" [The question of religious instruction] in *UE*, 2/7, 1922, p. 1-2.

273 Andresen, 1995, p. 168; Valk, 1997, p. 20-24.

elites of the time, who tended to view the issue of religious instruction critically, decided to exclude the subject of religion from the primary school curriculum.[274] This exclusion was met with strong protests from the Lutheran Church, but in an interview, Archbishop Aleksander claimed that "the turmoil concerning the question of religious instruction is somewhat exaggerated. As a matter of the heart, confession cannot be forced on or denied to anybody."[275] Opposition from the Lutherans continued, and when the *Riigikogu* attempted to exclude religious instruction from the secondary schools in 1922, the Christian People's Party started to collect the 25,000 signatures necessary to put the issue to a referendum.[276] The first Orthodox reaction to this appeal was sceptical:

> Religious instruction, as the teaching of higher morality of mankind, cannot be replaced by anything else and its absence in education is a painful blow to the cultural progress of humankind. Therefore, each Christian community must provide its members, especially the adolescent ones, with religious instruction by all possible means and not only see to it that they remember certain rules, events, and sermons, but that their hearts are influenced. The congregations have numerous possibilities to achieve this aim, even within the Estonian laws, although this obviously means harder work for the clergy. Previously, as part of the state, the religious communities were left rather worry-free: the school did all the work, and the clergyman simply had to control it once in a while. As to the contents of this work, that is another question. It is a controversial topic, whether the religious instruction in the schools did provide the churches with deeply religious and church-friendly members. Only one thing is definite: the current anti-religious and anti-church attitude is very often a fruit of compulsory religious instruction, which was frequently regarded as a pain rather than a step towards salvation.[277]

The Orthodox Church could not, therefore, support a referendum which wished to re-introduce compulsory religious instruction: "that this is sometimes less about the Kingdom of God than it is about the power position of the majority church is very clear to the competent part of the people."[278] The 25,000 signatures were, however, collected, and there was a heated discussion in the *Riigikogu* about whether the referendum should be organised or not.[279] In the end, a referendum was organised for February 1923, asking whether to remove the words 'without religious instruction' from the law on primary education.[280]

---

274 Valk, 1997, p. 23-24.
275 K., "Jutuajamine ülempiiskop Aleksandriga" [Conversation with Archbishop Aleksander] in *VM*, 3/297, 28.12.1920, p. 4.
276 "Usuõpetuse küsimus" [The question of religious instruction] in *UE*, 2/7, 1922, p. 1; Valk, 1997, p. 28-29.
277 "Usuõpetuse küsimus" [The question of religious instruction] in *UE*, 2/7, 1922, p. 1-2.
278 "Usuõpetuse küsimus" [The question of religious instruction] in *UE*, 2/7, 1922, p. 2.
279 "Riigikogu" [Parliament] in *PL*, 17/285, 19.11.1922, p. 5.
280 "Riigikogu" [Parliament] in *PL*, 17/296, 30.11.1922, p. 5; Valk, 1997, p. 30.

In the lead-up to this referendum, a fierce exchange of articles between the supporters and the opponents of religious instruction erupted in the major Estonian newspapers. Anton Laar participated in this debate with an open letter to the Estonian people, expressing doubts as to the use of the referendum.[281] His major criticism was the complete lack of any idea about the content of this instruction. Laar now favoured inter-denominational religious instruction, which,

> according to a recent article in *Postimees* can only be carried out in high culture countries. Consequently, the reader must conclude that our shallow cultural level only allows denominational instruction. [...] Moreover, it is no secret in our leading circles – ecclesiastical and political – that a united Estonia should be mono-confessional, and this is most easily achieved through schooling, where obviously only the majority confession should be taught."[282]

Another Orthodox author with the pseudonym '–nd' published an article abolut the referendum, where he maintained that the best approach to religious instruction was to leave its organisation completely up to the churches.[283] Nevertheless, the referendum ended as could be expected, with a 70% majority for the re-introduction of religious instruction in primary schools.[284] The curricula for these courses was developed in the following months and implemented for the academic year beginning in 1923, despite criticism by Metropolitan Aleksander and the Synod of the Orthodox Church for being overly Lutheran.[285] Looking back in 1934, Konstantin Kokla characterised the developments following the referendum as follows:

> It was agreed that when there are at least ten children of one faith, then it is possible to organise religious instruction for them. However, it remained unclear who was responsible for this organisation, and it was sometimes difficult or even impossible to carry out because of the opposition of some religiously fanatic or intolerant school director. This situation mobilised the Orthodox faithful, so that slowly but steadily, the Orthodox confession had entered the schools: finally a minimum of two weekly teaching hours was secured. The curricula allowed for ten weekly teaching hours, which the Lutherans quickly claimed for themselves. The two Orthodox hours had to be paid for separately.

---

281 Anton Laar, "Usuõpetuse rahvahääletus ja vähemuskirikud" [The referendum on religious instruction and minority churches] in *VM*, 6/24, 1923, 30.01, p. 5, reprinted in *UE*, 3/2, 1923, p. 3.

282 Anton Laar, "Usuõpetuse rahvahääletus ja vähemuskirikud" [The referendum on religious instruction and minority churches] in *VM*, 6/24, 1923, 30.01, p. 5. See also chapter 3.2.2.

283 -nd, "Usuõpetuse rahvahääletamise puhul" [On the referendum on religious instruction] in *UE*, 3/2, 1923, p. 3-5.

284 Valk, 1997, p. 30-33.

285 "Usuõpetuse kava" [The religious instruction curriculum] in *UE*, 3/9, 1923, p. 5-6; "Usuõpetuse kavad" [The religious instruction curriculum] in *UE*, 3/10, 1923, p. 1-3.

The Minister of Education, Mr. Hünerson, however, [in 1930] declared this situation costly to the state funds and decided that all necessary confessional teaching hours must fit within the ten hours allowed. The Minister promoted inter-confessional teaching and left the choice of the content up to the teachers. This spelled a sudden death to most Orthodox religious instruction. It is both easier and cheaper for teachers to turn to inter-confessional instruction, regardless of the impossibility of inter-confessional instruction. That way, the actual religious instruction became Lutheran and the Orthodox faithful were left lamenting: the state uses the money from the multi-confessional nation for the good of one single confession![286]

The official regulations about religious instruction were not the only subjects of discussion. Methodology was also a sore point. Among the Lutheran teachers, methodology improved markedly over the years, even though the Orthodox Church occasionally criticised it.[287] A very self-critical article on the way Orthodox schoolchildren were taught by the teaching priests appeared in 1932 by the nationalist schoolmaster Peeter Laredei:

> Every believer understands that school cannot remain too distant from church if the children are to become good congregation members. It is all the more estranging, therefore, to note that in most places, the church leadership has shown no interest in the school and its pupils throughout the entire independence period.
> There are many occasions when the pupils could get to know and appreciate church life. […] As is known, such occasions must be well prepared. Otherwise, they will not make an impression and could even be counterproductive. When the pupils tell their teacher after the Eucharist: that was pretty boring and my feet hurt – I did not understand a word of the sermon – were there no shrifts? We were not asked, are we then still sinners? […] When the children express such thoughts, then the clergyman lacks basic comprehension of children's spiritual life.[288]

The article continues to complain about the lack of schoolbooks for Orthodox pupils. Although an Orthodox book for the first and second grades had been published by J. Rõbakov (Randvere) in 1928, Laredei did not think this book would meet the needs of teachers. In the higher classes, he advised teachers to use parts of the major Lutheran schoolbook along with parts of the extremely conservative and anachronistic Orthodox schoolbook of J. Mõttus from 1915.[289]

---

286 Konstantin Kokla, "Usuõpetus koolis" [Religious instruction in school] in *UjE₂*, 2/8, 1934, p. 131-132.

287 Such as "Riik ja kirik teelahkmel" [State and church at the crossroads] in *PL*, 21/19, 20.01.1926, p. 3; Md., "Usuõpetus ja ap.-õigeusu kiriku ülemus" [Religious instruction and the head of the Orthodox Church] in *PM*, 70/212, 08.08.1926, p. 4. For the Lutheran side, see Valk, 1997, p.108-112.

288 Peeter Laredei, "Kirik ja kool" [Church and school] in *UE*, 12/9, 1932, p. 1.

289 Peeter Laredei, "Kirik ja kool" [Church and school] in *UE*, 12/9, 1932, p. 1. For an overview of the content of these books, see Valk, 1997, p. 99-100. On the talks between Lutheran and Orthodox representatives on the problem of textbooks, see Sõtšov, 2009, p. 72-73.

This article shows that there was still much to be done in the field of religious instruction in the 1930s.[290]

Another issue of growing importance was the education of new clergy. After the Riga Orthodox Seminary was evacuated to Nižnij Novgorod in 1915, where it closed three years later, there were no possibilities for Estonians to become Orthodox priests following ordinary procedures.[291] Recognising the problem, the Estonian Orthodox Church in September 1919 successfully established a Chair of Orthodox Theology at the national University of Tartu.[292] Although young Orthodox Estonians were encouraged to study in Tartu and a scholarship programme was instated in 1928, not a single student had graduated in Orthodox theology by 1932.[293] To remedy the situation a theological seminary based on the Finnish example was opened at the Petseri Monastery in 1933.[294] In the following seven years, more than forty Orthodox Estonians completed the two-year course at the Petseri Seminary, but only about a third of them were consecrated as priests.[295]

Finally, before turning to the developments in the Latvian Orthodox Church, a few words should be said about the involvement of Orthodox Estonians in state politics. Anton Laar was a member of the Constitutional Assembly, although he left after the Christian People's Party, on whose ticket he had been elected, demanded that he change his mind on the question of religious instruction.[296] The idea of an Orthodox list for elections to the *Riigikogu* did surface during the *täiskogu* of 1922 and was widely commented on in the secular press, but it was not realised.[297] In 1929, Metropolitan Aleksander, Bishop Joann (Bulin), and a third Orthodox priest were elected to the *Riigikogu* on different lists. For the next elections in 1932, only Bishop Joann was re-elected, and he did not serve to the end of the legislative period.[298] Apart from a couple of appearances in defence of the Orthodox Church and, in the case of Bishop

---

290 See also chapter 2.3.3. for more on the second half of the 1930s.

291 Raudsepp, 1998a, p. 36. See also the letters concerning the Riga Seminary to Archbishop Jānis of Riga from 1921, reprinted in Sidjakov I, 2008, p. 43-45, 50.

292 Sõtšov, 2009, p. 73.

293 Anton Laar, "Paar tõsist sõna kõigile ap.-õigeusulistele eestlastele" [A couple of serious words to all Estonian Orthodox] in *UE*, 8/12, 1928, p. 1-2; Konstantin Kokla, "Kõik õigeusulised, käed külge"[All Orthodox, join hands!] in *UE*, 12/3, 1932, p. 6.

294 "Vaimulik akad. kloostrisse" [Clergy academy in the monastery] in *Petseri Uudised*, 2/28, 15.07.1933, p. 2; Konstantin Kokla, "Astudes uude aastasse" [Entering the new year] in *UjE₂*, 2/1, 1934, p. 3-4. See also chapter 2.3.1. for more on the Petseri Monastery.

295 Karjahärm and Sirk, 2001, p. 115.

296 "Usuõpetuse küsimus" [The question of religious education] in *UE*, 2/7, 1922, p. 1-2.

297 "Ap.-õigeusu koguduste esitus Riigikogus" [The representation of the Orthodox parishes in the *Riigikogu*] in *UE*, 2/7, 1922, p. 2-4.

298 See chapter 2.3.1. for more on Bishop Joann (Bulin).

Joann, on issues pertaining to the Russian minority, they did not cause a stir in the *Riigikogu*.

Among the main reasons for this diffidence towards politics is the fact that there were already a number of Orthodox Estonians in high political positions. The first commissioner of the united Estonian province after the February revolution in 1917, Jaan Poska, was Orthodox.[299] Also Konstantin Päts, who served repeatedly as Prime Minister and then ruled as the authoritarian president from 1934, came from an Orthodox family. Although his brother, Nikolai Päts, was the chairman of the Estonian Synod throughout the interwar period, there are no suggestions of any tendency of the former to be especially Orthodox-friendly, however. Moreover, Ants Piip, ambassador in London and multi-term Prime Minister along with a number of other ministers and mayors came from Orthodox families and had received their education from the Riga Orthodox School and/or Seminary.[300] They were not necessarily deeply religious Orthodox Christians, but an Orthodox background was not unusual in Estonian high politics, which diminished the antagonistic attitudes towards the Orthodox Church to some extent.

2.2.5. Latvia: Rebuilding the Church – 1917-1921

Turning to the Latvian case, several important differences to Estonia need to be mentioned from the beginning. First, there is a different body of primary source material. In the sense that it was less dominated by individual opinions the Latvian press was more modern than the Estonian one. More importantly, the national newspapers, which were all published in Riga, did not extensively cover developments within the Orthodox Church of Latvia. Second, there is an abundance of secondary sources available; although, these texts were often written with ulterior motives as well as partly under ideological and methodological constraints. The emphasis on the state-church relations in interwar Latvia is very strong in this secondary source material. This relationship has been virtually ignored in research on both large confessions in Estonia. Other secondary sources include a large amount of published material by and about the very industrious Archbishop Jānis.[301] A third point of difference is that almost all of Latvian political and intellectual life occurred in the capital, Riga, and therefore, made developments less heterogeneous. At least, developments outside Riga

---

299 Laaman, 1998 [1935].
300 Raudsepp, 1998a, p. 94-150.
301 This includes biographies (Kalniņš, Jānis, 2001; Požidaev, 2004; Žitie, 2008) along with published papers and documents from his personal archives (Kalniņš I-II, 1993; Sidjakov I-III, 2008-2011 and others).

received much less coverage. The Latvian case can thus be analysed more chronologically.

The First World War had a much greater impact on Latvia – especially the city of Riga – than on Estonia further north, where the German occupation did not last as long and was not followed by as fierce a struggle for independence.[302] In 1915, with the German Army threatening the city, the military administration decided to evacuate all church valuables in Riga, including the bells, to inner Russia until the war was over. Moreover, Bishop Ioann (Smirnov) of Riga was evacuated to Tartu with most of the clergy, who moved on or were evacuated further to inner Russia as well.[303] The activities of the Bishop and the evacuated clergy in Tartu have been mentioned in a previous section. The Latvian dele-gates to the Moscow *sobor* were Jānis Namnieks and Pēteris Maršans, who established contact with Archbishop Jānis (Pommers) of Penza, a native Latvian and tried to convince him to become the Latvian Vicar Bishop of Riga.

This was the situation when the Germans arrived in late 1917. As can be seen in Table 4, the population of Riga had plummeted due to famine, evacua-tion, and wartime diseases; only about half the population of 1913 was left in the city. Whereas 17% of the Riga population had been Orthodox in 1913, this dropped to 7% by 1920, which means that only one sixth of the pre-war Ortho-dox population remained in Riga. This number more than doubled by 1925 as the war refugees returned, although the percentage stayed below 10%.

Table 4. Orthodox Population of Riga[304]

Year	Total Pop.	Orthodox Pop.	Orthodox %
1913	472 068	80 252	17%
1918	210 590	-	-
1920	ca. 185 000	12 974	7%
1925	ca. 370 000	30 323	8%

The German occupation was not a good period for the Orthodox Church, which had lost most of its leadership and power base. Early in 1918, the German Army confiscated the Riga Orthodox Cathedral and turned it into a Lutheran garrison church. The Alekseev Monastery (previously the Orthodox bishop's residence)

---

302 Hatlie, 2009a, p. 16-159; Hatlie, 2009b.
303 Pommers, 1931a, p. 75, 77-78; Testis, "Mūsu pareizticīgā baznīca vācu okupacijas laikā – I" [Our Orthodox Church during German occupation – I] in *TuD*, 15/1, 1939, p. 7-8; Bušueva, 1993, p. 49-50. See also chapter 2.2.1.
304 Numbers compiled from Ozoliņš, 1997, p. 25; Hatlie, 2009a, p. 54-55, tables 2, 4 and 6.

was confiscated and used as Catholic garrison church.[305] Decimated and without leadership, the Latvian Orthodox Church did not even protest the confiscation. Bishop Platon of Tallinn, who had been named administrator of the entire Riga Eparchy, wished to introduce the parish statutes that had been passed at the Moscow *sobor* in Latvia as well. The authorities of the German occupation did not want him to travel around, but he somehow managed to obtain a travel permit and appeared unexpectedly in Riga on 6 June 1918. This is how an eyewitness recalls the arrival twenty years later:

> I also did not know anything about Platon's arrival in Riga. Provost N. Tikhomirov came to see the editorial office of the 'Rīgas Ziņas' and asked the editor [...] to insert a three-line notice that Bishop Platon had arrived in Riga and that he would celebrate the Liturgy at 5 p.m. on the following day in the Pokrova church. [The editor] was very tolerant towards believers, so he complied to the request...
>
> Thus, I heard about the bishop's arrival to Riga; although, I did not know anything about his person or deeds. That I had not is obvious, for the Rigans had not had any news from outside for a long time, the German occupation authorities and severe censorship saw to that...[306]

Bishop Platon actively reorganised the internal life of the Riga parishes, explaining the role of the parish council and how to organise its election. The last two days of his visit were spent just receiving faithful, before he left on the morning of 15 June. According to the author 'Testis,'

> Metropolitan Agafangel, who was Bishop of Riga before the war, had a lot of time in order to bring the Orthodox Church in Latvia to full bloom, for he worked here *more than ten years* and in very favourable times at that.
>
> Bishop Platon, in contrast, had to renew our completely disintegrating church life in *only some ten days*.
>
> And even so, the work he did here was a great miracle, which showed us what an eminent personality can do in spite of difficult times, guided only by his conscience and duty as head priest – not even fearing banishment by the almighty authorities of the German occupation.[307]

The last church in which Platon celebrated the Liturgy before returning to Tartu was the Ascension church, the only Latvian-language parish of Riga. The Ascension parish was conscious of its role as the most wealthy and powerful of the Latvian Orthodox parishes, as it repeatedly showed over the following years.

---

305 Pommers, 1931a, p. 77; Testis, "Mūsu pareizticīgā baznīca vācu okupacijas laikā – I" [Our Orthodox Church during German occupation – I] in *TuD*, 15/1, 1939, p. 7-8; Bušueva, 1993, p. 50; Ozoliņš, 1997, p. 25; Hatlie, 2009a, p. 318-319.

306 Testis, "Mūsu pareizticīgā baznīca vācu okupacijas laikā – III" [Our Orthodox Church during German occupation – III] in *TuD*, 15/2, 1939, p. 26. The unidentifiable author says he was a journalist in Riga at the time.

307 Testis, "Mūsu pareizticīgā baznīca vācu okupacijas laikā – VI" [Our Orthodox Church during German occupation – VI] in *TuD*, 15/8, 1939, p. 122 (Emphasis in original).

According to 'Testis,' the bishop told the local priest that "he hoped that the Orthodox Latvian Ascension parish becomes the nucleus for the future of the entire Latvian Orthodox Church, for this parish is the leading one, in which there are many intelligent members, who even preach brotherly relations with the Orthodox faithful of Russian nationality."[308]

When the First World War ended in November 1918, the Latvians declared their independence. In the quickly appointed interim government, led by Kārlis Ulmanis,[309] there was one Latvian Orthodox member, Jānis Zālītis. His appointment has been sentimentally described as follows:

> For all the other state departments, a suitable minister could be found, only the Ministry of War remained vacant and nobody wanted to take this post. And really, taking this post in wartime, with the noise of machine guns and cannons shooting everywhere, was more than risky... Minister of War?!... Minister of War without an army, without even soldiers, Minister of War without munitions, guns, not even thinking about cannons; [...] can anybody knowingly risk these kinds of circumstances?! – But time was precious, hesitation was impermissible, and Jānis Zālītis, wiping away his tears, said: 'I'll take that post!'[310]

However, he was one of the few Latvian Orthodox believers with any political fame for the next ten years, and he died in December 1919, having been Minister of War only for the first, crucial months of Latvian independence.

The struggle over Riga was far from finished. The Germans were intent on staying in power; the Latvians had proclaimed their independence; and the Red Army along with local Bolsheviks was eager to take control of the city.[311] By January 1919, the Red Army had taken Riga, and the Latvian interim government had gone into exile to Liepāja,[312] where a coup by German military representatives replaced Ulmanis' government with a German-friendly puppet government in April 1919. The revival of the Orthodox Church of Latvia could not be centred either in Soviet controlled Riga or in German controlled Western Latvia, but was housed in the region of Madona, were the largest number of Latvian Orthodox believers lived.[313] In Lazdona in late 1918 and in Bērzone in January 1919, the most active parishes of the region organised meetings with representatives from surrounding parishes:

---

308 Testis, "Mūsu pareizticīgā baznīca vācu okupacijas laikā – V" [Our Orthodox Church during German occupation – V] in *TuD*, 15/4, 1939, p. 57.
309 See also chapter 2.3.3. for more on Ulmanis.
310 Purviņš, 1929, p. 56.
311 Hatlie, 2009a, p. 95-102.
312 See maps in chapter 6.1.
313 In 1935, the percentage of Orthodox in the region of Madona was 17.5%. In several of the municipalities around Madona, the majority of the inhabitants were Orthodox. See Ozoliņš, 1997, p. 16; Strods, 2005, p. 30.

Remember, when the representatives of the Baltic Orthodox parishes met in Jurjev [Tartu] for the first time after the revolution in the summer of 1917, they decided that the bishop ought to understand the local language, which then displeased many. Now, in Bērzone, they already wanted to establish that the Orthodox Church would be free; but then came the Bolsheviks and the matter failed.[314]

In Riga, the Red Terror "lasted less than five months, but left a miserable imprint on the Latvian land and people. Those months were horrible – much worse than the German occupation. With regard to our Orthodox Church, one must say, however, that the Bolsheviks displayed a more tolerant attitude than the Germans, not persecuting priests [...] and not impeding religious services."[315] The former congregation of the Orthodox Cathedral re-occupied it after the Germans left, but the Alekseev Monastery and its church remained in the hands of the Catholics.[316] In spite of initial problems due to the lack of liturgical items after the evacuation and Lutheran use, in 1919 Orthodox Easter was celebrated in the cathedral. The continuing struggle over the city of Riga in the summer of 1919 included air raids and artillery shootings, which damaged the cathedral so that it had to be closed, opening again only in January 1920.[317]

In the meantime, the parish council of the Ascension church had petitioned the interim Latvian government to give all the property of the former Riga Eparchy to the Latvian Orthodox Church, which should be established under the leadership of the Ascension parish.[318] Preparations for the establishment of a Latvian Church continued in the Madona region, where a meeting of representatives from most of the Latvian Orthodox parishes was organised for January 1920 in Mārciena. At this gathering, Pēteris Maršans reported from the Moscow *sobor*, and those assembled decided to call all parishes to an ecclesiastic *saeima* in order to reorganise the Latvian Orthodox Church.[319] This first *saeima* of the Latvian Orthodox Church occurred at the end of February in the assembly room of the Latvian parliament, the *Saeima*, and discussed many organisational issues.[320] Its main decisions were that the canonical link to Moscow should be retained, and Archbishop Jānis (Pommers) of Penza should be invited to become Bishop of Riga. Moreover, an interim synod was elected and charged "with

314 "Latvijas pareizticīgās baznīcas pirmie, brīvie soļi" [The first free steps of the Latvian Orthodox Church] in *Krusta Ēna*, 1/1, 1920, p. 5.

315 Testis, "Pareizticīgā baznīca Latvijā lielinieku valdibas laikā" [The Orthodox Church in Latvia during Bolshevik rule] in *TuD*, 15/9, 1939, p. 137. See also Balevics, 1987, p. 46-47; Kalniņš, Jānis, 2001, p. 82; Hatlie, 2009a, p. 117-123.

316 Bušueva, 1993, p. 53-56; Ozoliņš, 1997, p. 25.

317 Bušueva, 1993, p. 55-56.

318 Purviņš, 1929, p. 57-58.

319 "Latvijas pareizticīgās baznīcas pirmie, brīvie soļi" [The first free steps of the Latvian Orthodox Church] in *Krusta Ēna*, 1/1, 1920, p. 5. A *saeima* is a council of delegates, the highest administrative organ in the Latvian Orthodox Church.

320 The protocol was published in *Krusta Ēna*, 1/1, 1920, p. 9-24.

three main tasks: 1) to organise the parishes, 2) to see to it that the church gets a new bishop and 3), to lead the Orthodox Church until the next *saeima*, at which the life of the church will be definitely organised on new foundations."[321]

The discussions regarding canonical independence had been heated.[322] Jānis Dāvis, the chairman of the parish council of the Ascension church, presented the findings of the commission that had discussed this issue. The majority favoured retaining canonical subordination to Moscow, whereas Dāvis had been in the minority, arguing for complete independence for the Orthodox Church of Latvia in all respects. Many delegates, such as Provost N. Tikhomirov, responded that it was impossible to break the canonical link with Moscow:

> It is true that each nation has its own tendencies and characteristics, such as Monte-negro, Serbia, and others. But in Latvia there are also people of Russian nationality, not only temporarily, but as worthy Latvian citizens. We want to live in friendly harmony with the Latvians. An Orthodox Latvian means more to us than a non-Orthodox Russian, who would be more foreign to us. If we look to Moscow, then we do not have nationalistic opinions and feelings, no, but rather, brotherly Christian solidarity. The Russian Orthodox Church is important to us, as our spiritual mother and not otherwise. Living in Latvia, we cannot suddenly become Latvians, since we are Russians. Where would we get books, crosses, myrrh, antiminse, etc.? Can we get along without the Orthodox Church in Russia? [...] We have nothing to fear from the Patriarch, for what could he wish or force upon us, free citizens of free Latvia? Nothing at all.[323]

When the final vote remained in favour of retaining the canonical link with Moscow, Jānis Dāvis declared that he was not prepared to work for a church that was not independent and left the meeting. In a history of the Ascension parish, published in 1929, the chapter on the first *saeima*, possibly written by Dāvis himself, describes the meeting as thus:

> The meeting was very well attended. However, it did not provide the expected results. If the Latvian delegates were unanimous in almost all questions, then this cannot be said about the Russian delegates. Their opinions, especially on ecclesiastic autocephaly (independence) were strongly opposed. Since the majority followed the Russian line and many decisions displayed the Russian spirit instead of the due respect for the Latvian state, the Latvian delegates left the meeting and asked the government to annul its decision, as they did not reflect the thoughts of the majority of the Orthodox Latvians.[324]

The government did not recognise the Synod, and two days after the *saeima* concluded, the Latvian Minister of the Interior, Arveds Bergs, decided to seal

---

321 "Latvijas pareizticīgās baznīcas pirmie, brīvie soļi" [The first free steps of the Latvian Orthodox Church] in *Krusta Ēna*, 1/1, 1920, p. 5.
322 *Krusta Ēna*, 1/1, 1920, p. 12-17.
323 *Krusta Ēna*, 1/1, 1920, p. 13-14.
324 Purviņš, 1929, p. 60. Only Dāvis had actually left the meeting, though.

the Riga Orthodox Cathedral until its status was cleared.[325] The ensuing protests from the Russian congregation of the Cathedral were to no avail. Instead, Jānis Dāvis and the congregation of the Ascension parish were occasionally permitted to use it for Latvian-language celebrations. During these celebrations, the Orthodox priest Jānis Bormanis and the Lutheran pastor Voldemārs Maldonis would engage in unusual ecumenical activities, such as issuing calls for unity in the one 'Latvian national faith.'[326] In the summer of 1920, the Latvian government took the organisation of the Orthodox Church in Latvia into its hands. The reasons for this were clear, at least to Dāvis:

> During the Tsarist regime in Latvia, the Orthodox Church was a special pet: not only did she receive extraordinary privileges, but even *great wealth, which at the current exchange rates exceeds hundreds of millions.*[327] Obviously, from the point of view of the state, we cannot passively regard this wealth, in whose hands it is held, and with which intentions it is used. Looking at the Latvian Orthodox Church, the Russians obviously seek to Russify its Latvian members, thereby strengthening the power of the Russian state. Our native history has taken a very different course to the Russian one. Therefore, the Orthodox Church of Latvia, if she wants to become a national church, must join hands with the Latvian people and *must work in the spirit of the Latvian state, completely renouncing any Russian orientation.*
>
> By contrast, the gathering of Latvian Orthodox parish representatives from 25-27 February, thanks to the large number of Russian 'contributors' with voting rights, the mobilisation efforts and agitations of the Russian faction, the weakness of the Latvian countryside parishes, and the lack of organisation on their part, [...] decided, with 52 votes for and 32 against, that the Orthodox Church of Latvia should remain *hierarchically dependent on the Russian Patriarch* and even elected *people of the Russian orientation* to the Synod! If the government had recognised this meeting as the legitimate 'ecclesiastic *saeima,*' then the Russian Patriarch would be able to decide on our bishop, who would have to follow all the decisions of the Russian Patriarch, regardless whether they would please or displease the Latvian government.[328]

Dāvis published articles in different newspapers calling on the Latvian parishes not to let the church down by failing to send delegates to the expected government-backed *saeima*. He counseled that "to this meeting you should send

---

325 "Latvijas pareizticīgās baznīcas tiesiskais stāvoklis Pagaidu Valdības laikā" [The legal status of the Latvian Orthodox Church under the provisional government] in *Krusta Ēna*, 1/2, 1920, p. 11-14; P. Maršans, "Vairāk taisnības" [More clarity] in *Krusta Ēna*, 1/2, 1920, p. 21-23; Pommers, 1931a, p. 79; Balevics, 1964, p. 61; Bušueva, 1993, p. 57-58; Kalniņš, Jānis, 2001, p. 85.

326 "Iz L.U. Teoloģijas fakultātes pareizticīgo nodaļas vēstures" [From the history of the Latvian University, Faculty of Theology, Orthodox section] in *TuD*, 16/7, 1940, p. 108-109; Bušueva, 1993, p. 59-60. See also chapters 3.2.2. and 4.1.2.

327 There is no mention what kind of millions.

328 J. Dāvis, "Latvijas pareizticīgā baznīca" [The Latvian Orthodox Church] in *Latvijas Sargs*, 2/123, 04.06.1920, p. 1 (Emphasis in original).

only brave and unwavering delegates who understand that in an independent state there can only be an independent church. In other words, people who are not liable to listen to the opinions of the enemies of the independence of either Latvia or its Orthodox Church."[329] The provisional Synod of the Latvian Orthodox Church, which had been unanimously elected by the February *saeima* (although after Dāvis had left), tried, at the same time, to convince the provisional government that it was legitimate and ought to be treated similarly to the administration of the Catholic and Lutheran Churches. Synod member Jānis Svemps published an open letter "to Jānis Dāvis and his brothers, who see the splinter in others' eyes but fail to see the plank in their own."[330] In this letter, he explained that there was no use in trying to circumvent the canons, but rather, Dāvis should work together with the current leadership of the Latvian Orthodox Church in order to achieve greater ecclesiastic independence.

The state-sponsored *saeima* was organised for end of August, but it did not exactly proceed as the government had planned. The *saeima* was opened by Arveds Bergs, Minister of the Interior. Fridrihs Mīlenbahs (Friedrich Mülenbach), head of the department of ecclesiastic affairs and a Lutheran pastor, presided over its sessions. When Mīlenbahs refused to allow alleged Russian monarchists to participate in the discussions, many delegates protested such illegitimate government interference by emphatically confirming the Synod elected at the February *saeima*.[331] The attempt of the government to divide the church in two according to nationality failed. Instead, it was decided "that the Latvian Orthodox Church should become a people's church, which operates on the basis of self-government."[332] On the question of the canonical link to Moscow, it was decided that the Latvian Orthodox Church would be completely independent but would organise its life according to the canonical regulations of the Orthodox Church. This last addition ensured that links with Moscow remained, since only the Patriarch of Moscow could grant the Latvian Church autocephaly, according to the canons.[333]

The Latvian Orthodox Church thus achieved a first *modus vivendi* with the government, which by November had recognised the Synod that had been elected in February.[334] However, the situation was far from perfect. First, the government had still not reopened the cathedral and second, the question of a

---

329 J. Dāvis, "Latvijas pareizticīgās baznīcas autokefālija" [The autocephaly of the Latvian Orthodox Church] in *Baltijas Vēstnesis*, 51/118, 29.05.1920, p. 1.

330 J. Svemps, "Atklāta vēstule J. Dāvam un brāļiem, kuri redz skabargu tuvāka acī, bet baļķi savā acī neredz" [Open letter to J. Dāvis and his brothers, who see the speck in others' eyes but fail to see the plank in their own] in *Krusta Ēna*, 1/2, 1920, p. 23-25.

331 This is the reading of Balevics, 1964, p. 61.

332 Balevics, 1964, p. 61. See also Kalniņš, Jānis, 2001, p. 85-86.

333 Balevics, 1964, p. 62.

334 Zariņš, 1939, p. 31; Balevics, 1964, p. 62.

new Bishop of Riga was still unresolved. More importantly, however, the Synod was caught in a dilemma, nicely summed up by Synod member Upesleja end of 1920: "The government wants us to become its property, together with our possessions and real estate. If we, as Synod members, accept the offer of becoming state functionaries, then we may no longer protest the arbitrariness of the state. If we do not become state functionaries, we can do so. However, then we have to renounce all state support."[335] In the end, the Synod diplomatically declared the church internally independent, but canonically reporting to the Patriarchate of Moscow, without really giving the government the clarity for which it hoped. Nevertheless, in March 1921 the government agreed to reopen the Riga Cathedral, on the condition that it remained in the hands of the Synod and would not be given to any organisation or congregation.[336]

2.2.6. Latvia: under the Leadership of Archbishop Jānis – 1921-1925

Archbishop Jānis (Pommers) of Penza had now been invited three times to take up the post of Bishop of Riga: once at the Moscow *sobor* and twice at the *saeimas* of February and August 1920. Jānis sent a positive reply in early April 1921, and by the end of April, Patriarch Tikhon of Moscow also accepted the request, transferring Jānis to Riga.[337] Jānis passed through Moscow and received an act of autonomy from Patriarch Tikhon, before entering Latvian territory in July 1921.[338] The arrival was commented on in the Riga press, which mentioned the large procession and Jānis' liturgy at the cathedral. The commentary in the newspaper *Latvijas Kareivis* (The Latvian Soldier) ended with a note that "the Archbishop settled down in the rooms of the cathedral cellar, for the bishop cannot stay in private homes or in hotels according to Orthodox traditions."[339] In the leading Russian newspaper of Riga, *Segodnja* (Today), a longer article titled 'The Archbishop in the Cellar' provides the reader with several additional reasons for this unusual housing arrangement:

> Unfortunately, the representatives of the government did not understand the momentousness of this occasion for the Latvian national self-esteem. Except for the mayor of Riga, Mr. Andersons, nobody from the government welcomed the new Orthodox Archbishop, while the ministers had travelled all the way to Latgale to

---

335 Balevics, 1964, p. 62-63; Runce, 2008, p. 157.
336 Bušueva, 1993, p. 60-61.
337 The relevant correspondence is reproduced (in Russian translation) in Sidjakov I, 2008, p. 42-46. See also Balevics, 1964, p. 63; Kalniņš, Jānis, 2001, p. 85-87.
338 Pommers, 1931a, p. 79, Kalniņš, Jānis, 2001, p. 97-98; Runce, 2008, p. 157.
339 L., "Latvijas pareizticīgo arķibiskapa ierāšanās" [The arrival of the Latvian Orthodox Archbishop] in *Latvijas Kareivis*, 2/164, 26.07.1921, p. 3.

meet with the Catholic Archbishop as if it was the most natural thing to do! This obviously does not diminish the value of our new Orthodox head shepherd, but rather reflects the contemptuous attitude towards the 250,000 Orthodox in this country, whose patriotic value for Latvia should be obvious. [...]

After the prayer, the masses poured out on the streets in order to see the Archbishop to the domicile the Synod had prepared for him in a house on Zamkovaja Street [M. Pils iela] 13, situated directly opposite the Orthodox Archbishop's residence, which had been taken away on the instructions of the government on the evening before the arrival of the Lord Bishop in order to be handed over to the Catholic Arcibiskup.[340]

The surprise was all over when the Archbishop declined the offer of the Synod and instead descended to the damp cellar of the cathedral, entering the rooms next to the watchman's apartment, humbly announcing that 'the dwelling foreseen for me is located in a private home. I do not want to cause any inconvenience and prefer my own cellar, until the government finds it fitting to provide me with the residence to which I am entitled and the Alekseev Monastery.'

The decision of the Lord Bishop aroused mixed feelings among the faithful. Some were delighted by his self-sacrificing mind, others experienced shame over such discriminative government practices concerning the Orthodox and Catholic Latvians.

This inadvertently underlined the former relations between the two churches: the feudal Catholic Arcibiskup shall live in the mansion that is selected and furnished for him while the democratic Archbishop must accept the damp, musty, and gloomy cathedral cellar.[341]

Making his home in the cathedral cellar is mentioned in almost all biographies on Archbishop Jānis. In the following years, he repeatedly used this home as an instrument to pressure the Latvian government. He signed all his letters with 'Archbishop Jānis – Riga Cathedral Cellar.' Some accounts even maintain that he moved into the cellar to avoid having the cathedral confiscated.[342]

The reorganisation of the Orthodox Church was perceived very differently by the Latvian Roman Catholics, who commented on the August 1920 *saeima* as follows:

In Riga, a conference of *prawoslawu* parish delegates has taken place (In Latvia, the *prawoslawus* are called '*pareizticigim.*'[343] From a Catholic point of view this word is not at all appropriate, for this terminology implies that *prawoslawija* is the 'right' faith, which is not correct. All foreign faiths should be called by their own name. Therefore, we call the Greek-Eastern faith of Russia *prawoslawim*. The word

---

340 The author uses a Polonised version of *Archbishop*, indicating that Roman Catholicism is a Polish faith.

341 Д.В., "Архиепископ – в подвале" [The Archbishop in the cellar] in *Seg*, 3/166, 26.07. 1921, p. 1. The article is reproduced in Sidjakov I, 2008, p. 52. See also "Läti ap.-kiriku elust" [From the life of the Latvian Orthodox Church] in *UE*, 1/8, 1921, p. 60-61.

342 Kalniņš, Jānis, 2001, p. 99.

343 This article is written in the Latgalian dialect and the differentiation between the Russian word '*prawoslawiha*' and the Latvian '*pareizticiba*' for Orthodox is important, as it calls attention to how the Catholic Church saw the Orthodox faith. In the original language, both mean 'the right worship.'

'*pareizticiba*' is a remainder from the bad times of Latvian history, which we cannot put in our Latgalian dictionaries). [...]

The *prawoslawajs* congress asked the government to return their former cathedral church in Riga and the former possessions of the Archbishop (probably also the Church of Mary-Magdalene with its grounds). However, we also know that the Catholic Church asserts its claim on the church and the grounds [...]

Therefore, maybe, the government, standing between two claimants will have difficulty finding a position and deciding between the two sides. We can only guess who our Lutheran government will support: the Catholics or the *prawoslawi*.[344]

The article in the Latgalian newspaper relating the arrival of Archbishop Jānis to Riga ended by exclaiming that "it looks like the Orthodox cannot yet leave the ancient regime behind."[345] For the next few years, Jānis and the Orthodox Synod struggled bitterly for the Alekseev Monastery. However, the Lutheran Church made such a loud protest concerning the Peter-and-Paul church, which had been handed over to the Catholic Church as episcopal seat that the Orthodox complaints all but drowned.[346] The *Saeima* settled both questions in favour of the Catholic Church in April 1923, but the Latvians demanded a referendum on the issue. In spite of loud agitation on both sides, in the end not enough voters participated in the referendum and the earlier decisions remained in force.[347]

The Alekseev Monastery was not the only pressing concern for the Archbishop. According to the city council and the government, an Orthodox chapel on the square in front of the Riga railway station was insupportable. The decision to demolish the chapel was made in September 1920, but its execution was delayed until July 1925. In the meantime, Orthodox Latvians sent numerous pleas to the government and wrote articles unsuccessfully protesting the demolition.[348]

A third sore point was the legal status of the Latvian Orthodox Church. The government had not yet legally recognised the Orthodox Church, since it had retained its subordination to the Patriarch of Moscow. Moreover, the authorities could not be comfortable with Archbishop Jānis' unrelenting and uncompromising views, which were repeatedly criticised as un-Latvian.[349]

---

344 Letigallus, "Prawoslawiha Latwijâ" [Orthodoxy in Latvia] in *Latgolas Wōrds*, 2/51, 07.09.1920, p. 4.

345 "Kriwu archirejs" [The Russian Hierarch] in *Latgolas Wōrds*, 3/29, 27.07.1921, p. 2.

346 "Ap. usu koguduste elust väljamaalt. Lätis" [Orthodox life abroad. Latvia] in *UE*, 3/4, 1923, p. 5; Ozoliņš, 1997, p. 25-28; Runce, 2008, p. 140. The parliament discussions concerning the Alekseev Monastery were reproduced in "К истории Православия в Латвии" [On the history of Orthodoxy in Latvia] in *ViŽ*, 1/3-4, 1923, p. 18-50, 1/5-6, 1923, p. 15-28. See also the protest letters from all over Latvia reproduced in Kalniņš I, 1993, p. 28-34.

347 Runce, 2008, p. 140-142.

348 Ozoliņš, 1997, p. 22-25. See also the special issue of *TuD*, 3/8, 1925.

349 Runce, 2008, p. 158.

According to the official historian of the Latvian Orthodox Church, Antonijs Pommers, Jānis' younger brother, the Ministry of the Interior is supposed to have answered the queries with "there is nothing in the Latvian laws about any Orthodox Church and its organs, nor is there anything about protection of this church. On the head shepherd's question of legal recognition for the church, the answer was that national interest and the current political situation did not necessitate such a move."[350]

While struggling for government recognition, Jānis began to organise the internal structure of the Orthodox Church in Latvia. This included visiting Latgale, which had previously not been part of the Riga Eparchy. The Latgalian (Roman Catholic) newspapers mentioned his visit in the parish of Kokorova with contempt:

> On 25 September of this year, the Orthodox Archbishop Iwans[351] Pommers visited the Kokorova Orthodox, which are really few. The people meeting the Archbishop were relatively manageable, about 200 persons. They all hoped to hear some affirmative words, about strong love, peace, mutual co-operation, and so on. But out came horrible, cursing, and rough words about the errors of the Catholics and others.[352]

The parish council of Kokorova found it necessary to correct the article at a meeting in November. Their argument was that Jānis had not insulted the Catholics but had only questioned the intentions of the Jesuits in Latvia and called on the Latgalian Orthodox to join the Lutheran battle against Latgalian separatism.[353] The conflict between the two Latvian minority churches was all-consuming, each threw accusations at the other to discredit the enemy in the eyes of the government.

This mud-slinging continued into 1922, when Archbishop Jānis wrote a long memorandum to the government, accusing it of treating the Orthodox faithful as stepchildren of Latvia and thereby disregarding the freedom of conscience guaranteed by the constitution.[354] Listing the buildings expropriated from the Orthodox, including the Riga Orthodox School and Seminary, he despondently referred to the situation as worse than in Soviet Russia, where at least all confessions were in the same situation. However, no notice was taken of the memorandum, and the Latvian state signed a concordat with the Vatican end of May 1922, making the Catholic Church the first church with complete legal recogni-

---

350 Pommers, 1931a, p. 80. This quote is uncritically repeated in almost all later accounts on the Latvian Orthodox Church, but there is no archival evidence of the saying.

351 Using the Russian form of the name 'Jānis.'

352 Radzatojs, "Kokorowa" in *Latgolas Wōrds*, 3/42, 26.10.1921, p. 4.

353 The protocol of this meeting is reproduced in Kalniņš I, 1993, p. 43-44. See also Pommers, 1931a, p. 85; Benz, 1998, p. 468; Kalniņš, Jānis, 2001, p. 111; Runce, 2008, p. 135-136.

354 The memorandum was reprinted in Pommers, 1931a, p. 80-84.

tion in Latvia.[355] Once the situation of the Catholic Church in Latvia was normalised, debate turned to the Orthodox Church, as the following article by 'Civis' in the secular press shows:

> If we use all possible means and do not hesitate in spending large sums of money in order for the Latvian Catholic Church to not have to take its orders from Rome via Warsaw and Vilnius, but directly from our capital Riga, how much more should we then not invest in making the Orthodox Church break its links to Moscow. We have already received a lot of misfortune from that corner and threat looms still... But we ignorantly accept that the highest shepherd of the Latvian Orthodox Church remains dependent on Moscow's rule. [...] Did Jānis come to us only at the invitation of our Synod? And who inaugurated him into the office of the highest Orthodox hierarch in Latvia? Was it not the Patriarch of Moscow, since the Most Holy Synod does not exist anymore? On these important questions, the majority of our society cannot give an informed answer. A secure and satisfactory clarification is only possible if the Orthodox Church of Latvia becomes autocephalous. [...] However, the 138,000-strong Latvian Orthodox Church cannot become a completely independent, autocephalous church. And the government cannot afford to have several bishops on its payroll. The only possibility is to reach an agreement with the other Baltic States on a *Baltic autocephalous Orthodox Church*.[356]

The establishment of a Baltic Orthodox Church, uniting Latvia with Estonia and Finland, was discussed not only in the press but also in diplomatic circles. As the plans became less realistic, the Latvian government sought help and advice from neighbouring countries. The Estonian president Konstantin Päts recommended the Latvians accommodate some of Archbishop Jānis' material demands in order to encourage him to cut ties with Moscow.[357] In another article, 'Civis' repeated his opinion that a joint Baltic Orthodox Church would be the best solution, but he brought the Patriarchate of Constantinople into play as an alternative to Moscow's oversight. However, he mentioned that the chances of reform from within were dim, since "our Jānis more or less demonstratively continues his life as an imprisoned guard and maybe even as a martyr in the cathedral cellar, where he obviously can never find clear and enlightened thoughts about the future of the Latvian Orthodox Church..."[358] The mood in the Latvian Orthodox Church in 1923 was well described by 'An Orthodox Latvian':

> The current 'church wars' in Latvia concern not only Catholic and Lutheran, but also Orthodox Latvians. Among the latter, there is a growing division, and although the conflict is still in its beginning and cannot be seen from outside, one must admit

---

355 Zariņš, 1939, p. 32, 35-36; Runce, 2008, p. 132-137.
356 Civis, "Pareizticīgo baznīca Latvijā" [The Orthodox Church in Latvia] in *JZ*, 12/141, 30.06.1922, p. 1 (Emphasis in original). See also chapter 2.2.2.
357 Runce, 2008, p. 160.
358 Civis, "Pareizticīgā baznīca Baltijas valstīs" [The Orthodox Church in the Baltic States] in *JZ*, 13/38, 16.02.1923, p. 1.

that the Orthodox Church in Latvia stands on the brink of reform. It is about the Latvianisation of Orthodoxy and the renunciation of everything Russian. On the traditionalist side we find our compatriot from Prauliena, Archbishop Jānis Pommers, with his priestly entourage, while the reforming side is rallied around Archpriest Bormanis of the Ascension parish, including much of the clergy in the countryside and most of the intelligentsia. As we have noticed, it is difficult for Archbishop Jānis to understand the workings of a democratic system, and he contaminates the Latvian spirit with a foreign element.[359]

Another article by Pāvils Gruzna, a well-known Latvian author, linked the 'Living Church' movement in Russia with the developments in Latvia. He urged the Latvian Orthodox Church to follow suit and

cut the fictional imagined bonds, with which it is linked with Moscow, [since the Patriarch] has become a historical anachronism. [...] Instead of being led by a hierarch installed by the Patriarch, the church needs to elect an independent *Church Synod*. Not bureaucratically, as was the case in Russia, [...] but democratically. The first task of this Synod would be to reform and renew the church. Also our government expects such a Synod, as it has no choice in the current situation but to ignore the unreformed Orthodox Church.[360]

Earlier the same year, Gruzna had attracted attention by talking negatively about the Orthodox Church in spite of having received his education from the Riga Orthodox Seminary.[361] The Orthodox Church thus had many enemies in the Latvian public of the time.

Archbishop Jānis summoned an All-Latvian gathering of clergy in mid-June, where he clearly argued that the times of dependence on Patriarch Tikhon were past, because the document, which he had received from the Patriarch on the way to Latvia, stated "that in religious, economical, educational, organisational, and political questions, the Latvian Church shall serve God and the Fatherland as best it can."[362] The remainder of the meeting consisted in agreeing on new statutes for the church, discussions on religious instruction in schools, and avenues to theological education in Latvia. On the question of reforming the liturgy in light of the demands of the 'Living Church' movement in Russia, the gather-

---

359 Pareizticīgais Latvietis, "Pareizticīgo baznīca Latvijā" [The Orthodox Church in Latvia] in *JZ*, 13/88, 25.04.1923, p. 2.

360 Pāvils Gruzna, "Pareizticīga baznīca" [The Orthodox Church] in *JZ*, 13/119, 05.06.1923, p. 4 (Emphasis in original).

361 Jānis Lapiķens, "Pareizticīga baznīca (Atbilde Pāvilam Gruznam)" [The Orthodox Church (An answer to Pāvils Gruznam)] in *TuD*, 1/5, 1923, p. 5-11. I was not able to find the article which this reply referenced. See also Vāvere, 1992, p. 25-26.

362 "Neatkarīgā pareizticīgā baznīca" [An independent Orthodox Church] in *JZ*, 13/133, 21.06.1923, p. 6. The protocols of this meeting were published in *TuD*, 1/8-9, 1923, p. 1-14. It is impossible to say what triggered this change of mind, although the complicated situation in Soviet Russia including Tikhon's imprisonment might be a reason. See also chapter 2.2.8. for the relationship between Jānis and Tikhon's successor.

ing decided that "the Orthodox Church follows Christ and reforms are to be achieved by way of evolution, not revolution."[363] Finally, it was decided that an ecclesiastic *saeima* was to be held later in 1923, where the decisions of the gathering would be confirmed and the Latvian Orthodox Church would be constituted. By then, the church had regained enough strength to open a publishing house and started to print two journals, one in Latvian and one in Russian.[364] Moreover, the recovery of church property and Orthodox clergy, which had been evacuated to Soviet Russia, progressed and the material situation of the church seemed to improve.[365]

The Archbishop opened the first *saeima* under his auspices, where 170 delegates from 107 parishes had gathered, with a long speech, in which he accounted for the two years since his arrival in Latvia.[366] This speech used highly sophisticated rhetoric and provides a key to understand the interwar Latvian Orthodox Church. In the short introduction, the Archbishop prepared the audience that what was to follow would be "that which will not be said in the coming reports" (11-12).[367] Repeatedly dealing side blows at the communists, who he described as degenerated evil-doers (12-14, 55-67, 107-109), Jānis continued with a recounting his long way to the post of Archbishop of Riga. His superiors, including Patriarch Tikhon of Moscow, tried everything to discourage him from accepting this post (20-35), but he was standfast in his love of the Fatherland (35-43), even teasing out full ecclesiastic independence for the Latvian Orthodox Church from the Patriarch (43-55). Moreover, citing negative examples from Poland (68-85) and Estonia (85-97), he claimed that the independence he achieved was canonically worth more than the two neighbours' attempts, and at the same time, was much cheaper to the Latvian State (99-105).

A long section followed, where the Archbishop listed all his activities in the past two years and the difficulties he encountered (111-185), ending with the observation that "if all the above is converted into working hours, then it becomes obvious that the entire day of a bishop consists of working hours and that his work cannot be limited to eight hours a day" (186-188). In the next sec-

---

363 "Neatkarīgā pareizticīgā baznīca" [An independent Orthodox Church] in *JZ*, 13/133, 21.06.1923, p. 6. See also chapter 3.1. for more on liturgical reform in Latvia.

364 Teodors Būcens, "Ticība un Dzīve" [Faith and life] in *TuD*, 1/1-2, 1923, p. 1-4; Kalniņš, Jānis, 2001, p. 111. See also chapter 1.3.

365 Ozoliņš, 1997, p. 19-21. For the material situation of the Orthodox parishes in Vidzeme (the Latvian part of Livland), see Pazāne, 2008, p. 40-42. See also the re-evacuation story of Augustīns Pētersons in Strods, 2005, p. 70-71.

366 The entire speech is reproduced as chapter 6.3. Contemporary reports on the speech can be found in „iks", "Latvijas pareizticīgā baznīca" [The Latvian Orthodox Church] in *JZ*, 13/244, 01.11.1923, p. 2; R.S., "Latvijas Pareizticīgas Baznīcas Saeima" [The *saeima* of the Latvian Orthodox Church] in *TuD*, 1/12, p. 9-16. In almost all works on the Latvian Orthodox Church, this speech is cited at least once.

367 This and all further citations are given with line numbers from chapter 6.3.

tion, Jānis reminded his audience about the circumstances in which he had to work, about his unsuitable apartment and the enemies all around. He dismissed the communists as envious political adventure-seekers (189-201). Such people would call him an "enemy of Latvian freedom and independence" and "the leader of some political movement" (201-207). They would do this because they were unable to understand why anyone in such a potentially powerful position would practice self-humiliation and restraint for the prosperity of the society as a whole (208-225).

From this point on, Jānis directed the attention of his audience to the presumed 'Russianness' of the Orthodox Church, where the religious buildings were Tsarist remnants to be demolished (226-229). He ridiculed this presumption, maintaining that all Christian churches in Greece and Palestine then would be Russian and that the only real Tsarist remnant in contemporary Latvia was the liquor monopoly, which was not objected to as such (229-237). For Jānis, it is obvious that the enemies of Orthodoxy in Latvia were short-sighted, not considering to what their enmity might lead. The Orthodox Latvian citizens were important parts of Latvian society, and their loyalty should be sought, not declined (238-256). The Archbishop had always been loyal and kept his Christian virtues in everything he did, resisting the temptation to use his position as a weapon (257-266). In the last section of his speech, Jānis called on the faithful to continue to counter all evil attacks with Christian love and patience. He compared the situation in Latvia with the early Christian Church and nourished the hope that God's love would someday encompass the enemies of Orthodoxy and all would be well (267-323).

Without going too deeply into rhetorical analysis, there are a few points in this speech that immediately meet the eye, such as the astute arrangement of topics. In the introduction, the speaker captivates the audience by suggesting the extraordy nature of the speech, claiming it is something they will not hear elsewhere. He then polishes his own image by detailing his numerous activities and the opposition he met in accomplishing them. Once that is done, the enemies, loosely sketched as 'red barons' and degenerate evil-doers, are depreciated in a typically Christian manner as unable to grasp the consequences of their actions. The final section then is designed to encourage the audience, recalling God's love, peacefulness, and eventual, inevitable victory. Throughout, the continuous references to the 'common enemy,' the degenerate evil of the communists, binds the audience together and identifies the speaker with them, as do repeated references to the Archbishop's solidarity with the poor and needy.

The effect of this speech is difficult to ascertain. Commentators stress that in 1923 the *saeima* passed without the national antagonism that had characterised the Orthodox Church in independent Latvia so far.[368] It is possible that Archbishop Jānis convinced both the Latvian and the Russian nationalists in the Orthodox Church that they would be stronger standing together. Excepting some individual dissenting voices from within, the church was no longer on the brink of disintegration.[369] The majority of Latvian society did not follow Jānis' argumentation as readily. His assertions that the autonomy granted by Patriarch Tikhon of Moscow entailed full independence were simply not accepted as the truth. Diplomatic attempts to herd Jānis to the Ecumenical Patriarchate, on the one hand, and public suspicion of Jānis' personality and the independence of the Latvian Orthodox Church, on the other, continued unabated.[370]

Nevertheless, in March 1924, the Ministry of the Interior accepted the ecclesiastic statutes that had been passed during the 1923 *saeima*.[371] The claim that "the church was still not officially legalised and persecution continued," mentioned in most histories of the Latvian Orthodox Church is an exaggeration.[372] Jānis Zariņš, an Orthodox legal specialist, showed in 1939 that although this was a *de jure* truth, almost all the activities of the Orthodox Church were covered by other laws, and it was *de facto* equal with the Lutheran and Roman Catholic Church.[373] The most important problem was not the legal standing of the church,

---

368 „iks", "Latvijas pareizticīgā baznīca" [The Latvian Orthodox Church] in *JZ*, 13/245, 02.11.1923, p. 3; Hermann (Aav), "Latvian Ortodoksisesta kirkkokunnasta" [The Latvian Orthodox Church] in *Aamun Koitto*, 7/15, 1924, p. 117; Pommers, 1931a, p. 85.

369 N., "Kāds vārds par pareizticības nostiprināšanu pastāvošās draudzēs Latvijā" [Some words on the consolidation of Orthodoxy in the existing congregations in Latvia] in *TuD*, 4/5, 1926, p. 7-11; Jānis Jansons, "Vai Pareizticība pie Latviešiem var palikt par nacionalu ticību?" [Can Orthodoxy among the Latvians remain a national faith?] in *TuD*, 4/5, 1926, p. 12-13; Pareizticīgais Latvis, "Vai pareizticīgo baznīca Latvijā ir apdraudēta?" [Is the Orthodox Church in Latvia threatened?] in *Latvijas Sargs*, 8/195, 02.09.1926, p. 1. See also the eight contributions by Archbishop Jānis in *TuD*, 4/9, 4/10, 1926 and *ViŽ*, 4/10, 1926 (Kalniņš I, 1993, p. 44-56, 67-70); Runce, 2008, p. 165.

370 B. "Vai Latvijas pareizticīgo baznīca ir neatkariga?" [Is the Latvian Orthodox Church independent?] in *Brīvā Zeme*, 6/182, 14.08.1924, p. 1; Balevics, 1964, p. 59, 67-68; Runce, 2008, p. 160-161. Balevics presents documents claiming that Jānis was a monarchist, closely cooperating with the white Russians in exile. This assessment is definitely tainted by the Soviet ideology underlying Balevics' text, although there can be no doubt that the Archbishop was more white than red. See Balevics, 1964, p. 69-70. See also the assessment of the canonical question in chapter 2.2.8.

371 "Paziņojums" [Announcement] in *Valdības Vēstnesis*, 7/78, 03.04.1924, p. 1.

372 Pommers, 1931a, p. 86. This source seems to be at the basis of most later accounts. See also chapter 1.4.2.

373 Zariņš, 1939, 36-39. The presentation of attorney Bērziņš at the 1923 *saeima* had already come to this conclusion. „iks", "Latvijas pareizticīgā baznīca" [The Latvian Orthodox Church] in *JZ*, 13/245, 02.11.1923, p. 3. Bērziņš' speech is not mentioned in the official account of the ecclesiastic *saeima*. N. S., "Latvijas Pareizticības Baznīcas Saeima" [The *saeima* of the Latvian Orthodox Church] in *TuD*, 2/2, 1923, p. 1-8.

but the discrepancy between the self-perception of some Orthodox as belonging to the 'ruling church' and the national pride that led some Latvians to deride Orthodoxy as the 'Russian faith.'[374]

In specific questions, such as religious education in schools or expropriation of parish land, the Latvian Orthodox Church had firm legal standing. The debates seem to have been conducted more soberly and directly than in Estonia, and the results were less heatedly contested. Regarding the schools, the Latvian government never considered removing religious instruction from the curriculum, leaving the content and form of this instruction up to the various confessions.[375] The gathering of the clergy in June 1923 agreed that "the old methods are no longer suitable; hammering contents into the heads of pupils kills religious intellectual life. To make the instruction serious, it was decided to create a post of Inspector of Religious Instruction."[376] One of the most important questions at the *saeima* was the re-opening of the Riga Seminary to alleviate the shortage of priests. The inventory of the seminary had been evacuated to Nižnij Novgorod in 1915, and the buildings had been taken over by the Latvian government and turned into Riga University's Faculty of Medicine.[377] Appeals to the government were not successful, however, and the seminary remained closed.

Altogether, the 1923 *saeima* created some order within the Latvian Orthodox Church and, by and large, rallied the various factions of the church behind their Archbishop. In relation to the non-Orthodox Latvians, however, the *saeima* did not have the intended effect. The privileging of the Roman Catholic Church continued and the Orthodox Church still lacked legal recognition. Much more damaging, however, was the negative image of the Orthodox Church that was propagated by the press. At the same time, the Archbishop repeatedly communicated his housing situation in the cathedral cellar to visitors and descriptions of it appeared in several foreign publications.[378] One could get the impression that Jānis brazenly instrumentalised his living conditions in order to dishonour the

---

374 See chapter 3.2.3.
375 Hermann (Aav), "Latvian Ortodoksisesta kirkkokunnasta" [The Latvian Orthodox Church] in *Aamun Koitto*, 7/14, 1924, p. 112; Zariņš, 1939, 35.
376 "Neatkarīgā pareizticīgā baznīca" [An Independent Orthodox Church] in *JZ*, 13/133, 21.06.1923, p. 6.
377 „iks", "Latvijas pareizticīgā baznīca" in *JZ*, 13/244, 01.11.1923, p. 2; N. S., "Latvijas Pareizticības Baznīcas Saeima" [The *saeima* of the Latvian Orthodox Church] in *TuD*, 2/1, 1923, p. 2; Kalniņš I, 1993, p. 56-57. See also the letters between Nižnij Novgorod and Latvia, reproduced in Sidjakov I, 2008, p. 43-45, 50.
378 See Hermann (Aav), "Latvian Ortodoksisesta kirkkokunnasta" [The Latvian Orthodox Church] in *Aamun Koitto*, 7/14, 1924, p. 111-112; 7/15, 1924, p. 117-119. See also the article exchange on the Latvian Orthodox Church in *The Church Times*, London, 19.09. 1924-05.12.1924. See chapter 4.2.1.

Latvian government. This is how the Finnish Archbishop Hermann (Aav) describes them in 1924:

> Archbishop Jānis is an active, tall and warmblooded man. He speaks eloquently and demonstrates willingness, strength and life experience. He lives in the cellar of the cathedral, in a room that is only about 8.5 m long, 3 m wide, and 3 m high. The room is illuminated through three small cellar windows with iron crosses like a prison. They are so small that there is not enough light in order to read or write. The windows are so high that they do not help ventilate the room. The wooden floor is partly rotten and, in springtime, completely wet. The walls are damp and mouldy. There is no running water, sewage, or other comforts.
>
> [... However, the Archbishop was] proud and satisfied, saying that 'in difficult times, people often become dishonest – there has been an embezzlement scandal in Latvia; many high state officials had to go to jail – however, among these embezzlers, there was not a single Orthodox, even though also Orthodox people were in higher offices. Even the current Minister of Justice is Orthodox, having received seminary and law school education. This shows the growing influence of Orthodoxy.'[379]

At the same time, Archbishop Jānis actively continued to work towards the full recognition of the Latvian Orthodox Church, against the privileges of the Catholic Church and, especially, against the politics of the Social Democrats.[380] As he was so active in the political scene, a gathering of Orthodox Latvians decided to put the Archbishop himself on the ballot for the next parliamentary election, scheduled for October 1925. Jānis was elected and entered the highest body of Latvian politics, the *Saeima*, where he would remain until his death nine years later.[381]

2.2.7. Latvia: an Archbishop in Parliament – 1926-1934

In a sermon on New Year's Eve 1925, Archpriest Jānis Jansons mentioned the election of the Archbishop to the *Saeima* as an important event of the past year:

> Our esteemed head shepherd Archbishop Jānis has been elected to the highest body of the state, the *Saeima*, as a delegate. The Orthodox Congregations now have their own representative with the government. Until now, we were like orphans, abandoned, and pushed aside. Let us then support His Eminence and pray to God that He

---

379 Hermann (Aav), "Latvian Ortodoksisesta kirkkokunnasta" [The Latvian Orthodox Church] in *Aamun Koitto*, 7/14, 1924, p. 111; 7/15, 1924, p. 119. He is talking about Jūlijs Arājs, who was Minister of Justice from 10.04-18.12, 1924.

380 Most of his political letters and articles between 1925 and 1927 are reproduced in Kalniņš I, 1993, p. 44-71.

381 "Pareizticīgi un visi citi ticīgie vēletāji!" [Orthodox and all other religious voters!] in *TuD*, 3/9, p. 15. The time in the *Saeima* has been analysed by Kalniņš, Jānis, 2001, p. 116-134; Runce, 2008, p. 162-164.

give him strength and wisdom to unrelentingly and successfuly fulfil the work He has granted him.[382]

Another commentator reminded the Orthodox Latvians of a time four years earlier, when

> the Orthodox Church was an orphan in the fullest sense of the word. It did not have any representatives and when somebody spoke on its behalf, their voice was not heard. [...] Now, after four years, even though we cannot say that the needs of the Orthodox Church have been satisfied and even though it has suffered much injustice during this time, the scene is a different one, much more pleasant than four years ago. A portion of the Latvian people has showed their reason and civility by electing Archbishop Jānis to the *Saeima*. He was elected in two different electoral districts. This shows that the people did not turn all their attention to the scandal makers, the political careerists, and the instigators but, rather, to the apartment in the cathedral cellar, where dwells an authentic man, a rightful son of his nation, a friend of humanity, and a benefactor. The people have showed that they have had enough of the scandal making that characterises many of their chosen delegates, that their minds want simplicity, cordiality, and truthfulness.[383]

In an obvious reference to the Social Democrats, the Latvian left-wing parliamentarians, who, as the largest faction, commanded almost one third of the seats in the *Saeima*, the commentator continues:

> It seems to me that it does not carry weight to have a seat in the *Saeima*, it does not carry weight to hide oneself behind widely attuned slogans, but it does carry weight to take a determined stance on the important questions of the state and society. Archbishop Jānis has correctly grasped the importance of this and has chosen a determined stance on the issue of his heart – the integration of the minorities in Latvian society. In spite of being a Latvian, he sits among the Russians [in the *Saeima*], in order to actively show Latvian goodwill in relation to the Russians in our independent Fatherland.[384]

Archbishop Jānis was a very active member of the Latvian *Saeima*. He did not give many speeches in his three terms, but when he spoke, this was a celebrated event in the Orthodox Church. His speeches were edited and republished by the Latvian Orthodox journals. The actual speeches must have been events as well, for the Social Democrats did not refrain from showing their disapproval of the Archbishop by interrupting his speeches with numerous objections and com-

---

382 Jānis Jansons, "Tā Kunga žēlastibas gads" [The year of the Lord's mercy] in *TuD*, 4/1, 1926, p. 2-4.

383 A. Akmentiņš, "Arhibīskaps Jānis Saeimā" [Archbishop Jānis in the *Saeima*] in *TuD*, 3/11-12, 1925, p. 1-3 (Kalniņš I, 1993, p. 79-80).

384 A. Akmentiņš, "Arhibīskaps Jānis Saeimā" [Archbishop Jānis in the *Saeima*] in *TuD*, 3/11-12, 1925, p. 1-3 (Kalniņš I, 1993, p. 79-80).

ments.[385] In his *Saeima* speeches, the Archbishop continued the line of his 1923 speech, focusing on three main topics: the yet unrecognised legal status of the Latvian Orthodox Church, the incompetence of the Social Democrats (in Latvia and in the Soviet Union), and the value, in spite of the past, of the Russian nation.

The first topic claimed the centre of his first two speeches, given as part of the debate concerning the state budget for 1927.[386] Both of these speeches pertained less to the budget and more to the position of the Latvian Orthodox Church:

> I will speak in the name of the confessional minority who gave me my mandate. We still are peace-loving, tolerant, and enduring, but circumstances press me to register several objections to the situation, in which this government and a range of earlier governments have left us.[387]

During this first speech on 19 May 1926, which was repeatedly interrupted by interjections from different Social Democrats, Jānis offered a reading of history which understood the Orthodox Church positively as a defender of Latvian nationality.[388] Moreover, he questioned why both the other churches of Latvia, as well as the Orthodox Church in neighbouring countries, had a better legal standing than the Latvian Orthodox Church. The speech continued by claiming that not only the Ministry of the Interior but also the Ministries of Agriculture and Education discriminated against the Orthodox Church, and then it ended with an eloquent rejoinder:

> I have presented all these facts to you, dear Parliament, so that you may see for yourself what obvious injustice is practiced in relation to the Orthodox Church. We get the impression that we are to be suppressed with juridical and economical means and left in the darkness. But as I already mentioned, we are tolerant, we are enduring, and we are peaceful people. And therefore, regardless of all that which has been, we vote for this government and for this budget in the hope that the government will turn its attention to us once the budget has been made public and will no longer allow that which it has allowed until now.[389]

A couple of days later, the Social Democrat delegate K. Dēķens spoke negatively about the three large churches in Latvia, arguing against giving them

---

385 Finartijs, 1976, p. 71-72. See also Neo-Sil'vestr, 1971, p. 77-78; Kalniņš, Jānis, 2001, p. 120-121.

386 See *Saeimas Stenogrammas*, II/iii, 14.04.1926-04.06.1926, c. 690-704, 773-781. Edited versions of the two speeches were published in *TuD*, 4/7, 1926, p. 1-15 (Kalniņš I, 1993, p. 80-87).

387 *Saeimas Stenogrammas*, II/iii, 14.04.1926-04.06.1926, c. 690.

388 See also chapter 4.2.2.

389 *Saeimas Stenogrammas*, II/iii, 14.04.1926-04.06.1926, c. 694.

state support.[390] Archbishop Jānis would not allow the insults against the Orthodox Church stand and replied in the beginning of June, after the Lutheran and Catholic representatives in the *Saeima* had defended their churches:

> A great amount was said here about my alleged ambitions and those of my church, but only once was concrete evidence about these allegations mentioned. Unfortunately, I must state that even this once, the factual material produced was not factual. As you yourself heard, your speaker said: 'he would very much like the government to give him all those former Russian magnates' castles, in which there has ever been an Orthodox Church; he even wants to claim the President's palace, for there was once an Orthodox Church within its walls.' There is a Russian saying which goes 'do lie, but know when to stop!' The Social Democrats have forgotten those wise words. They lie without measure. Neither I nor anyone in my church have ever claimed any castle and would never do so, for we, my dears, are led by the Biblical commandment that 'you shall not covet your neighbour's house.' The commandment which circulates among some Social Democrats: 'rob the robbed' is no commandment to us. We would leave all castles to those Social Democrats who strive for castles.[391]

In this same speech, Jānis repeated much of what he said during the 1923 ecclesiastic *saeima*, refuting the Social Democrats' allegations that he had arrived in Latvia as a refugee. "I had no need to flee from anything and no need to flee anywhere, for in Moscow I already knew the political situation in Latvia very well. I knew: persecution there, persecution here. I knew that under the influence of the Social Democrats the persecution in Latvia was often worse than in Soviet Russia."[392] In mixing political and theological language, the Archbishop discredited his political opponents while preaching tolerance to his flock.

Such harsh verbal exchanges were characteristic of Jānis' appearances in the *Saeima* and were most directly experienced in this concrete debate. It is difficult to ascertain the influence of the Archbishop's rhetorical strategy and powers of persuasion, but during the following *Saeima* recess, the Latvian government issued a decree on the status of the Latvian Orthodox Church, finally making it a regularly legalised body in the Latvian State.[393] Less than a month later, the church convened a new regular *saeima*, elected a new Synod, and thanked the government for legal recognition.[394] At the same time, the meeting complained

---

390 The section against the Orthodox Church can be found in *Saeimas Stenogrammas*, II/iii, 14.04.1926-04.06.1926, c. 707-709.

391 *Saeimas Stenogrammas*, II/iii, 14.04.1926-04.06.1926, c. 779.

392 *Saeimas Stenogrammas*, II/iii, 14.04.1926-04.06.1926, c. 778.

393 *Valdības Vēstnesis*, 9/228, 11.10.1926, p. 1; Zariņš, 1939, p. 40. According to Kalniņš, Jānis, 2001, p. 118, this was a direct result of Jānis' political efforts. Runce, 2008, p. 161-162 does not mention such a direct link, but rather the weakness of the Moscow Patriarchate. This is also the opinion of Balevics, 1987, p. 60-62.

394 Sinode, "Latvijas pareizticīgās baznīcas koncila (Saeimas) 28. un 29. oktobrī 1926 g." [The council (*saeima*) of the Latvian Orthodox Church 28 and 29 October 1926] in *TuD*,

that "of the 137 Orthodox congregations in Latvia, thirty-two do not currently have any priest" and mentioned the poor material status of the clergy and the lack of new priests.[395] However, on this last point, the decree of legal recognition was the first step towards resolution. On 1 December 1926, the Riga Orthodox Seminary was re-opened. This news was welcomed by Archbishop Jānis in the Orthodox journal with the following words:

> The Great War forced the evacuation of the Riga Orthodox School to inner Russia. Unfortunately, this enlightener of the Latvian and Estonian national spirits, rich in achievements, has not only remained in evacuation, but it is not even certain that those to whom it was evacuated are keen on returning the school. And that is not all. When we repeatedly applied for the possibility to open a theological seminary with our own means and powers, the answer was always a simple no. We were only given the formal permission to restart the work of our theological school this autumn. However, practically from the outset, everything was done to hinder the work of renewal. The building of the theological school, built with the church's own means, was taken away from us without permission. The rich library and schoolbook collection was destroyed. The inventory lists are not available. In those circumstances, formal permission to start working sounds like irony, even if it was, maybe, not intended. Accepting such a retarded permission, we feel as one does after a fire or after an earthquake, or like the sacrifice of some unknown goddess, who, destroying our achievements, can now rub her hands, saying: 'Well then, let us see how they manage this one'...[396]

The Archbishop continued the report on the reopening of the Seminary with another article, fending off the critics who saw the Riga Orthodox Seminary as an institution of Russification. The Seminary alumni "are not Russified and no Russifiers, but they always were opponents of Germanisation and the Germanisers. This they will be also in the future."[397] Although this reversal of the official attitude towards the Latvian Orthodox Church was not reflected widely in Latvian society, the Archbishop could consider the 'new era of persecution,'[398] which he had raged against until then, past. He could therefore, turn to his two

---

4/8, 1926, p. 14-16; T., "Pareizticīgās baznīcas koncils" [The council of the Orthodox Church] in *Latvijas Kareivis*, 7/244, 29.10.1926, p. 3.

395 "Pareizticīgās baznīcas koncilā" [At the council of the Orthodox Church] in *JZ*, 16/244, p. 29.10.1926, p. 4. See also Pazāne, 2008, p. 34-37, 40-42.

396 Jānis (Pommers), "Rīgas Garīgā semināra darbības atjaunošana" [The renewal of the work of the Riga Orthodox Seminary] in *TuD*, 4/11-12, 1926, p. 3-7 (Kalniņš I, 1993, p. 56-57).

397 Jānis (Pommers), "Pasaka par rusifikāciju" [A story about Russification] in *TuD*, 4/11-12, 1926, p. 7-11 (Kalniņš I, 1993, p. 57-59). See also chapter 4.2.2.

398 Jānis (Pommers), "Jauns graušanas laiks" [A new era of persecution] in *TuD*, 4/10, 1926, p. 1-3 (Kalniņš I, 1993, p. 54-56). This is the introduction to a special issue of *TuD*, full of articles on this subject written by Archbishop Jānis.

other main subjects, arguing against the Social Democrats and improving the image of the Russians, especially those living in Latvia.

These two topics were closely intertwined, as is shown by his 'crusade' against the Social Democrats in the *Saeima* and in the local Russian-language press. Following his first speech in the *Saeima*, he published an article on the Social Democrats in the newspaper *Slovo* (Word):

> We have always sensed that the Social Democrats are unappeasable enemies of all that is Orthodox and all that is Russian. The faction has officially dismissed all such statements as individual prejudices, but in the beginning of this *Saeima* session, we could feel a change among the delegates from the Social Democratic Party. We noticed that they started organising a veritable campaign against the Orthodox Church and all that is Russian. Even at times when nationally-minded Latvians implement unacceptable policies, it is the Social Democrats who appear as the main enemy to us. As we can observe, they have radically changed their politics. [...]
> From the Social Democrats, we have heard that they both orally and in written form call the Russian nation's most holy sanctuary the 'boot of a Russian monarchist.' We have heard that the entire Russian culture, which is studied and admired all over the world, was contemptibly called Asian. We have heard calls not only to raze all that is Russian to the ground, but also anything that somehow might remind someone of something Russian. We have seen that in this international hatred of all things Russian, the Social Democrats have overcome even the most qualified of the internationalists, Lenin and Trotsky. When our Social Democrats speak about their love and loyalty towards the Russians, they obviously have in mind some particular Russians, who have been cleansed of everything specifically Russian. Where these un-Russian Russians live, we all know very well and do not doubt the least that these are very dear to our Social Democrats, for they hail denationalisation as one of the fundamental principles not only in relation to the Russians, but equally with the Latvians and all other nations. Their ideals, just as their hymn, are called 'the Internationale.'[399]

In order to fully appreciate Jānis' criticism, it is important to explain the political system of interwar Latvia. After the terror of large parts of Latvia under the communist Pēteris Stučka in 1919, the Communist party was outlawed in Latvia. Its moderate wing formed the Latvian Social Democratic Party, which was the largest faction in the *Saeima* throughout the 1920s. The party never formed a government coalition, because of "its reluctance to take on political responsibility. Blinded by Marxist dogma, it maintained that Latvia was not yet ready for 'democratic socialism,' and the party, therefore, ought to remain as the opposition. It criticised the bourgeoisie and simply waited for the conditions of

---

399 Reproduced as "Архиепископ Иоанн о социал-демократах" [Archbishop Jānis on the Social Democrats] in *ViŽ*, 4/7,1926, p. 10-12 (Kalniņš II, 1993, p. 62-63). The 'Internationale' had been the Marxist battle song and became the first Soviet Anthem until the Second World War.

social democracy to ripen."[400] The beginning of the second *Saeima* in 1926 was a swing to the left for the Social Democratic Party.

Jānis continued to publish very critical articles on the Social Democrats in various newspapers.[401] His speeches in the *Saeima* followed the same rhetoric. According to an eye-witness,

> all the speeches of his Excellency in the *Saeima* took on a passionate character as soon as they touched upon the Marxists (as he always used to call the Bolsheviks) and their willing or unwilling accomplices. In the speeches, Jānis opened his soul, bubbling with violent anger, at times seemingly far from displaying monastic humility, but always truthful and uncompromising in the face of the godless, regardless of who they were.[402]

He gave the most paradigmatic speech of this style during a debate regarding the violent police reaction to a labour demonstration in Riga in January 1929. Here, in obvious reference to the Social Democrat reaction to all his actions in the *Saeima*, Jānis told the story of how a coachman in southern Russia reassured him not to be afraid of the barking and howling dogs: "Do not worry, Father, the dogs simply greet you with dogs' manners, it is their instinct."[403] The newspapers noted that "during the entire speech, there was a virulent storm of interjections from the left and laughter from the right."[404] The chairman of the *Saeima* had to intervene five times in order to calm the agitation. Another newspaper commented on the *Saeima* session that

> the debate about the Ministry's reply to the interpellation, which has already lasted for two days, took on a purely personal hue yesterday. Particularly spicy criticism of the Social Democrats came from J. Pommers. Many delegates from outside Riga unhappily began wandering around the Chairman's seat. Then some delegates, both from the coalition and from the opposition disappeared one by one. [...] This was the first occasion on which a government response had caused such a heated debate in the *Saeima*.[405]

---

400 Bleiere et al., 2008, p. 157.

401 Most of Jānis' texts on this topic are collected in Kalniņš II, 1993, p. 62-76.

402 Neo-Sil'vestr, 1971, p. 78.

403 *Saeimas Stenogrammas*, III/ii, 22.01.1929-22.03.1929, c. 180-181 [Original in Russian]. In the version published in the Orthodox journal, the reference to the Social Democrats is made explicit. Moreover, the legend says that the ensuing 'barking' and 'howling' made any communication in the meeting hall impossible for a while. See *ViŽ*, 7/2, 1929, p. 17-22 (Kalniņš II, 1993, p. 78-81). See also Neo-Sil'vestr, 1971, p. 82-83; Kalniņš, Jānis, 2001, 128-129; Požidaev, 2004, p. 85-86.

404 "Pieprasījuma lietā – jautra Saeimas sēde" [Debating the interpellation – a cheerful *Saeima* session] in *JZ*, 19/27, 02.02.1929, p. 6.

405 "Vakar vēl neizbeidzās debates par iekšlietu ministra atbilde" [The debate on the reply of the Minister of the Interior did not end yet yesterday] in *Latvijas Kareivis*, 10/27, 02.02. 1929, p. 1.

In the further debate, the chairman of the Social Democrats Bruno Kalniņš accused the Archbishop of being an opportunistic monarchist:

> Here in Latvia, delegate Pommers has a page in [the Russian-language newspaper] 'Slovo' (*J. Pommers*, from seat: 'there is no such page!'); this is his *Leiborgan*, printing everything that comes from this mister. This time, his speech from the last session was printed *in extenso* only in 'Slovo.' (*J. Pommers*, from seat: 'and what about [the Russian-language newspaper] 'Segodnja'?'[406]) Even 'Segodnja' was partly critical of your speech. Delegate Pommers has published more in 'Slovo' than he would admit here! [...] Sirs, is this not opportunism?
>
> This same delegate Pommers, who criticises and denounces us for opportunism is himself a firm anti-Semite, as he has showed in the *Saeima* and the *Saeima* committees. At the same time, this delegate sits in the minorities' bloc together with the Jews. Why!? Because you have several common interests, you need money, etc.; therefore, you have to sit together with them. Thus, on the one hand you are an anti-Semite, but on the other, you vote together with them.
>
> Moreover, delegate Pommers, your situation here, in this High House, is a bit funny. You are here as a representative of the *Russian* monarchists, but on several occasions, you try to appear as a Latvian. [...] When you need money for your church or other activities, you find it fitting to go together with the Latvians, but in your political activities, you have never wanted, and never tried to leave your Russian, I would even say Tsarist, orientation.[407]

Replying to these accusations, Archbishop Jānis cited various newspaper articles written by or about several of the Social Democrats from the civil war period, in which they had repeatedly argued against independence and worked hand in hand with the Communist party.[408] Both the Social Democrats and Archbishop Jānis refuted the accusations thrown against them by the other. The vote of confidence, in the end, overruled the leftist agitation and confirmed the government. The newspapers noted that "after three days of debate, the *Saeima* can now finally return to its legislative activities."[409] The editors of the Orthodox journal noted that Jānis' recent speech had reached far beyond Latvia's borders, to the Polish newspaper *Russkij Golos* (Russian Voice) based in Lwów:[410]

---

406 The main Russian-language newspaper of Riga.

407 *Saeimas Stenogrammas*, III/ii, 22.01.1929-22.03.1929, c. 204.

408 *Saeimas Stenogrammas*, III/ii, 22.01.1929-22.03.1929, c. 212-219. The edited version reads more like a sermon than a political speech. See "Ответ опортунистскам-марксистам" [Answering the opportunist Marxists] in *ViŽ*, 7/3, 1929, p. 33-39 (Kalniņš II, 1993, p. 81-84).

409 "Vakar pēc triju dienu debatēm valdībai izteica uzticību ar 51 pret 40 balsim" [Yesterday, after three days of debates, the confidence in the government was confirmed with 51 votes against 40] in *Latvijas Kareivis*, 10/30, 06.02.1929, p. 1.

410 This city in western Ukraine, called Lemberg in German, Львов in Russian, and Львів in Ukrainian, was Polish at the time, thus the name Lwów.

Jānis is a member of the *Saeima* from among the Russians in Latvia, a fearless fighter for the rights of the oppressed Russian minority, an ascetic, and a talented orator. Our careerist Polish Orthodox clergy try to hide their 'Russianness' as much as they can, ready to call themselves 'Ukrainians,' 'Belarusians,' or anything else, just to savour the most of the 'this-worldly good.' Archbishop Jānis is nothing like these servants of the Polish Orthodox Church. Originally a Latvian, he still directly defends the rights of the Russian ethnic inhabitants as firmly as a rock, for they need this support the most.[411]

While these appearances in the *Saeima* might have positively impacted the image of the Archbishop among the Orthodox faithful of Latvia and elsewhere, it is doubtful whether they really affected the image of the Orthodox Church in Latvia.[412] It is beyond doubt that Jānis' political activities and his stubbornly uncompromising attitude provoked many negative reactions from his enemies. When the Social Democratic Party in July 1931 proposed to drop state pensions for clergy, Jānis once again thundered against the delegates from the left.[413] He mentioned the most active ones by name and read out newspaper articles discrediting them. The Social Democrats' faction became more and more unruly until

> F. Cielēns and other delegates stormed the speaker's desk, crying something to the speaker and throwing paper at him. A ruler also flew onto the speaker's desk. When the session chairman saw that the racket continued, he left the hall, signifying a break. After the departure of the chairman, the Social Democratic delegates stopped in front of J. Pommers and cried 'go away!' When Pommers did not move but peacefully smiled, several delegates pushed him from the hall. Pommers' faction comrade S. Kirilovs happened to be in the way, claiming also to have been pushed.[414]

---

411 Cited in *ViŽ*, 7/3, 1929, p. 39 (Kalniņš II, 1993, p. 84).

412 The journalist Neo-Sil'vestr remembers how the Archbishop was revered and idolised among the Orthodox inhabitants of Latvia. Neo-Sil'vestr, 1971, p. 79.

413 *Saeimas Stenogrammas*, III/ix, 22.04.1931-22.10.1931, c. 1294-1301. The edited version is very close to the original speech, including the interjections and agitation in the *Saeima* hall. *ViŽ*, 9/8, 1931, p. 121-132 (Kalniņš I, 1993, p. 93-97).

414 K.,"Valdības atbildes un jautājumi" [Answers of and questions to the government] in *Latvijas Kareivis*, 12/144, 04.07.1931, p. 1. See also "Vēl nepiedzīvots skandals saeimā" [A completely new kind of scandal in the *Saeima*] in *JZ*, 21/144, 04.07.1931, p. 10. According to an eyewitness, who used to visit the *Saeima* sessions during breaks from classes, "Archbishop Jānis with his large frame had no difficulty shoving them aside." Finartijs, 1976, p. 71. In the recollection of Neo-Sil'vestr, Jānis' speeches of February 1929 and the one from July 1931 were intermingled, so that the 1931 speech, "revealing secret documents," led to an uproar in the *Saeima*, which Jānis countered with his story of the dogs in southern Russia. Moreover, Neo-Sil'vestr claims that this scene happened only a few weeks before the *Saeima* was disbanded, as if it was an omen. In reality, the *Saeima* met until May 1934. Neo-Sil'vestr, 1971, p. 81-83. Later accounts repeat this version of the 'legend': Kalniņš, Jānis, 2001, p. 127-129; Požidaev, 2004, p. 85-86.

The official excuse of the *Saeima* chairman, P. Kalniņš, following this incident was that he could not have done otherwise, for "as I allowed delegate N. Kalniņš to personally attack delegate J. Pommers, I could not stop delegate J. Pommers from returning the attacks. The delegates should know the boundaries of their passion, in order to avoid undesirable incidents. The chairman alone is completely powerless in such cases."[415] The Archbishop called the incident a wake-up call for the Latvian democracy. "I think that those who struggle for the freedom of the word should not fight this freedom with such methods as we saw yesterday. [...] Personally, I am quite sure that I have nothing to fear following this incident."[416] The Baltic German politician Paul Schiemann, however, called the incident a black day for Latvian democracy and criticised Jānis, claiming that the latter was "not a friend of parliamentarianism and democracy."[417] In the following *Saeima* session, when the Archbishop wanted to continue his speech, the chairman did not allow him and reprimanded every subsequent speaker who mentioned the last session.[418]

It is certain that the Latvian Orthodox Church of the interwar period could thank Jānis for its stability and status in the Latvian state. However, his double role as representative of a national minority and of an incongruent religious minority casts some doubt on his political integrity.[419] One might argue that his two *Saeima* re-elections in 1928 and 1931 were not necessary for the status of the Orthodox Church of Latvia. His first election in 1925 on the list of the 'United Russian Minority' had been the result of a decision in the Synod of the Latvian Orthodox Church to give the church a stronger voice in national politics than had previously been the case. Within one year, the Latvian Orthodox Church had been legally recognised and could operate normally within the Latvian state. On the occasion of his first re-election on the list of the 'Orthodox and Old Belief Voters and United Russian Organisations,' Jānis justified his involvement in politics with historical examples and with the argument that the Bolshevik anti-church campaign had not yet reached its apogee and must not be

415 "Balsis par vakardienas skandalu saeimā" [Voices on yesterday's scandal in the *Saeima*] in *JZ*, 21/144, 04.07.1931, p. 17; "Aizvakardienas notikumu *Saeimā*" [The incident in the *Saeima* the day before yesterday] in *Latvijas Kareivis*, 12/145, 05.07.1931, p. 3.
416 "Balsis par vakardienas skandalu saeimā" [Voices on yesterday's scandal in the *Saeima*] in *JZ*, 21/144, 04.07.1931, p. 17.
417 "Kādus likumus vēl pieņems saeimā?" [Which laws are yet to be accepted in the *Saeima*?] in *JZ*, 21/145, 05.07.1931, p. 12.
418 "Saeimas lielā trača atskaņas vakardienas sēdē" [The great *Saeima* row reverberated in yesterday's session] in *JZ*, 21/147, 08.07.1931, p. 5; K., "Saeima pieņēmusi pensiju likuma pirmos pantus" [The *Saeima* accepted the first paragraphs of the pension law] in *Latvijas Kareivis*, 12/147, 08.07.1931, p.1. Jānis had prepared a short speech for this session. See Kalniņš I, 1993, p. 97-98.
419 See "Ko stāsta Arhibīskaps Jānis par savu personu" [What Archbishop Jānis said about himself] in *TuD*, 15/13, 1939, p. 195-197 (Kalniņš I, 1993, p. 16-18).

facilitated.[420] The campaigns for both of his re-elections faced heavy anti-Jānis propaganda.[421] However, his popularity among the Orthodox flock did not dwindle. At least, no critical voices from within the church could be heard.

2.2.8. The 1920s Compared

The first challenge of modernity concerns the design and role of political institutions, the relationship between religious and secular authorities, and the advent of the modern ideologies of nationalism and socialism. In the Baltic States of the 1920s, all three aspects contributed to a fundamental reshaping of social and political life as compared to that under the Tsarist Russian Empire. The role of the Orthodox Church in this changing context differed markedly between Estonia and Latvia, at least on the surface. In Estonia, strengthening nationalist ideology within the Orthodox Church was detectable. The Russians were decried an unsuitable element, which must be kept under control. Externally, this pro-Estonian orientation was fixed by a jurisdictional switch from hostile Moscow to far-away Constantinople. Internally, the Russian priory (later Eparchy) was established, with limited external rights. Otherwise, the Russians were left alone and undisturbed. In Latvia, Archbishop Jānis managed to drown the nationalistic tendencies which existed among the Orthodox Latvians before they could become influential. The immense productivity of the Archbishop and his successful anti-socialist rhetoric managed to consolidate Russian and Latvian Orthodox faithful in Latvia, or at least stifled any attempts at division. His political career, moreover, made him a target for external criticism, which helped to consolidate those supporting him.

Another very important difference was the relationship to the Patriarchate of Moscow. In Estonia, although Metropolitan Aleksander had sent two letters to Moscow during 1923 regarding the question of jurisdiction, he never received a reply and had no contact with Moscow until 1940. The Finnish Orthodox Church did receive a condemning reply from Moscow to its announcement that it had switched jurisdictions. Moreover, the Moscow Patriarchate continued to exchange letters with the Finnish Bishop Hermann (Aav) and the head monk of the Orthodox Valamo Monastery (Finland) throughout the interwar period.[422] Nevertheless, the Finnish and Estonian ecclesiastic authorities seemed to lose

420 Arhibīskaps Jānis, "Baznīcas tiesības un pienākumi" [The rights and duties of the church] in Kalniņš II, 1993, p. 61-62.
421 See Neo-Sil'vestr, 1971, p. 120-121; Kalniņš II, 1993, p. 72-76; Kalniņš, Jānis, 2001, p. 127, 133.
422 Riikonen, 2007, p. 22-24.

interest in the ecclesiastic developments in Soviet Russia after their switch to Constantinople.

Archbishop Jānis of Riga and Latvia, on the other hand, continued to take a vivid interest in the fate of the Patriarchate of Moscow. Especially after the death of Patriarch Tikhon in April 1925, the Archbishop repeatedly and publicly questioned the canonicity of the current developments within the Russian Orthodox Church. The 1927 declaration of the clergy's loyalty to the Soviet regime was, for example, harshly criticised as a Soviet plot designed to appear as a unilateral capitulation by the church.[423] Jānis increasingly turned away from the Moscow Patriarchate and considered the Latvian Orthodox Church independent so long as there was no canonically elected Patriarch in Moscow. When the deputy locum tenens of the Patriarch, Metropolitan Sergij (Stragorodskij) of Moscow sent a letter to Archbishop Jānis in September 1927, asking him to sign the declaration of loyalty, the latter refused and clearly distanced himself from the Russian Orthodox Church in Soviet Russia as an institution while asserting his loyalty to the faithful Soviet citizens as individuals.[424] Jānis continued his extensive correspondence with various hierarchs of the Orthodox Church outside the Soviet Union, in which he staunchly defended his specific view of canonical relations.

The reasons for these different attitudes towards contact with Moscow can be found in the differing approaches to the national question. While in Estonia (and Finland), the Russian minority within the church was neutralised in order to nationalise the church, the Latvian case saw the consolidation of the two ethnic groups. Since an orientation towards Russia prefaced any interest in the situation of the Patriarchate of Moscow, the Estonians did not need to occupy themselves with the Moscow Patriarch. Only in the Russian-language journal of Estonian Orthodoxy, founded 1931, were developments in Russia reported prominently and discussed in vivid detail. In Latvia, where Jānis retained a pronounced orientation to Russia, the developments in Russia were also prominently featured by the Orthodox press. It is difficult to ascertain what the Latvian nationalists in the church thought about this state of affairs, because Jānis' personality dominates the Orthodox press to such an extent that all other voices are silenced.

The relationship each of the two churches entertained with their respective state also seems different. Whereas in the Estonian case, the church met the state at an equal footing, the Latvian Orthodox Church had to fight for recognition

---

423 "Архиепископ Иоанн об обращении временного патриаршего совета" [Archbishop Jānis on the installation of the provisional patriarchal council] in *ViŽ*, 5/9, 1927, p. 1-3 (Kalniņš II, 1993, p. 116). Jānis' articles on this topic are collected in Kalniņš II, 1993, p. 98-116. For the developments as such, see Pospielovsky, 1984, p. 108-191; Sidjakov III, 2011, p. 71.

424 The letter is reprinted in Sidjakov III, 20122, p. 73-74 (Kalniņš II, 1993, p. 117-118).

and was treated like a criminal organisation, at least in the self-understanding of
Orthodox Latvians. Again, the rhetoric of persecution so dominates the history
of the Latvian Orthodox Church that it is difficult to arrive at an objective
assessment of the situation. According to contemporary legal specialists, there
was no persecution, at least in a juridical sense.[425] Once the Archbishop had a
seat in parliament, however, the situation quickly changed, with the Latvian
Orthodox Church gaining legal recognition in a specific legal act. This series of
events shows a very different approach from that of Estonia, where all faiths
were grouped under a general law on religious organisations, without legally
distinguishing between them. While the Latvian state, therefore, did not fully
embrace secularism but continued to occasionally interfere in the internal affairs
of the religious organisations, the Estonian state formed an entirely secular
system. Consequently, unlike the Estonian Orthodox Church, the Latvian
Orthodox Church was partly financed by the state, especially in the case of
repairs to the churches that had suffered during the war.

In both cases, however, there was a debate regarding religious education.
Although the Latvian state left confessional education entirely up to the
churches while the Estonian state introduced inter-confessional classes, discussions on how to improve religious instruction were conducted in both Orthodox
churches. Unfortunately, my sources do not give an extensive insight into these
discussions, other than stating that they took place. Another similarity was that
both Orthodox churches recognised the need to have representatives in national
politics. In the Estonian case, this was relatively easy, because a number of
Estonian graduates from the Riga Orthodox Seminary had gone on to higher
education and were now influential politicians. In Latvia, this was not the case.
Although the Latvian Orthodox Church was proud of its 'heros,' the need arose
to have a representative in the Latvian parliament, a role Archbishop Jānis
successfully played. Metropolitan Aleksander of Tallinn and Bishop Joann
(Bulin) of Petseri also became members of the Estonian parliament, but they did
not exercise political influence to the same extent as Jānis.

Finally, there are also important differences in relation to the modern ideologies of socialism and nationalism. On the one hand, both churches, especially
the Latvian one, strongly rejected socialism. The extreme anti-socialist attitudes
of Archbishop Jānis makes such opposition to socialist ideology as existed
within the Estonian Orthodox Church seem inconsequential. However, the
Estonian Orthodox Church did not need to be anti-socialist, as the socialists in
Estonia did not have the same position as in Latvia.[426] Moreover, the Estonian

---

425 „iks", "Latvijas pareizticīgā baznīca" [The Latvian Orthodox Church] in *JZ*, 13/245,
02.11.1923, p. 3; N. S., "Latvijas Pareizticības Baznīcas Saeima" [The *saeima* of the
Latvian Orthodox Church] in *TuD*, 2/1, 1924, p. 1-8; 2/2, 1924, p. 1-8; 2/3, 1924, p. 1-8;
Zariņš, 1939, 36-39.
426 Parming, 1981.

Church was not involved in politics to the same extent as the Latvian Church. In the early 1920s, there were discussions on whether the Estonian Orthodox Church should have an official representative in parliament. These discussions did not have an ideological background but simply intended that the representative should stand against injustice suffered by the Orthodox Church. While this might also have been the thought behind Archbishop Jānis' election, his rhetoric and passion made him a representative of the Russian community and traditional ideology and a target for criticism from both the right and the left, accusing him of lacking any ideological foundation to his positions.

On the other hand, nationalist ideology enjoyed great popularity among the Latvians and Estonians in general. This popularity passed on to the dominant forces within Estonian and Latvian Orthodoxy. However, ethnic Russians and those Estonians and Latvians with more of an orientation towards Russia did not embrace nationalism, setting the scene for a conflict. In Estonia, nationalism won and led to an Estonian-dominated church with an autonomous Eparchy for the ethnic Russians. In Latvia, the conflict was stifled by the arrival of Archbishop Jānis, who diverted internal opposition to nationalism onto the common enemy of socialism. In parliament, the Archbishop was repeatedly criticised for not clearly associating himself with a national grouping. And, in the words of Paul Schiemann, a very distinguished Baltic German publicist and politician, Jānis was "not a friend of parliamentarianism and democracy."[427]

2.3. From Crisis to Crisis: the Structures of the Orthodox Church in the 1930s

Towards the turn of the decade, following the international economic crisis of 1929, there was a general lack of confidence in the democratic political order. The anti-democratic mood was most discernible in Latvia, but the global depression also touched Estonia and destabilised the political system. In both states, a quasi-authoritarian regime was installed in 1934, and the entire political environment became more restrictive of discourse.[428] The changing political context was not lost on the Orthodox churches, which can be discerned in the arguments and rhetorical style of their journals. This chapter analyses developments in the two churches during the 1930s against the background of this general political mood. The chapter title refers to the fact that there were considerable internal

---

427 "Kādus likumus vēl pieņems saeimā?" [Which laws are yet to be accepted in the *Saeima*?] in *JZ*, 21/145, 05.07.1931, p. 12.

428 Plakans, 1995, p. 132-133; Raun, 2001, p. 115-116; Bleiere et al., 2008, p. 160-163. Calling the regimes 'quasi-authoritarian' takes their relative leniency, as compared to fascist Italy, Nazi Germany, or the Stalinist Soviet Union, into account. See also chapter 2.3.3.

crises within both churches during the first half of the 1930s, and the Second World War brought forth a renewed internal crisis, this time externally induced. Between these two crises, the churches were rebuilt under more restrictive quasi-authoritarian governments.

The chapter is composed of four sections. First, a section considers the relationship between the Estonian Orthodox Church and the Petserimaa region in south-east Estonia, leading to the 'Monastery War' of 1932. This conflict was closely intertwined with the continuing Russian opposition to the Estonian church leadership, which is analysed here as well. The second section covers the crisis of the Latvian Church, which had a long developmental period and a more dramatic apogee, namely the assassination of Archbishop Jānis. This section also briefly analyses the debate about his succession in the power triangle between ecclesiastic leadership, secular politics, and Orthodox faithful. The third section considers the second half of the 1930s, when the churches had to redefine their role in the authoritarian context. The last section characterises the 1930s as a whole and hints at the developments from 1940 onwards.

2.3.1. Crisis in Estonia: the *Setu* in Petserimaa and the 'Monastery War'

The integration of Petserimaa was an area of complex interaction between the Estonian state, the Orthodox Church, and the ethnic Russians of Estonia. The lands around the city of Petseri, in the southeast of Estonia, never belonged to the German dominated Baltic Provinces of the Russian Empire, but rather to the Pskov *Gubernija*.[429] Alongside the many ethnic Russians living in the region, there was also a number of so-called *Setu*, a Finno-Ugric tribe closely related to the Estonians. The *Setu* had already aroused the interest of the Estonian nationalists in the early years of the twentieth century. When Estonia unexpectedly won the entire Petserimaa from the Russians in the Tartu Peace Treaty of February 1920, the state authorities made plans for the integration of the *Setu* into majority society, regarding them as Estonians who had been led astray.[430]

Since the *Setu* were almost without exception Orthodox believers, the church was destined to play an important role in their integration. Within the church there were attempts to 'win over' the *Setu* from Russian agitation. Among the most important actors in this context was Karl Ustav, an Estonian Orthodox priest who had been actively involved in furthering Estonian intellectual life in Petseri since at least 1909.[431] At the beginning of 1917, he became disillusioned as a result of the war and left for western Estonia. A resolution

---

429 Печёры in Russian and Petschur in German. Raun, 1991.
430 Alenius, 1999, p. 2303-2306; Lõuna, Kalle, 2003, p. 61-70.
431 Ustav, 1914; Lõuna, Kalle, 2003, p. 19-20.

adopted at the gathering of the Orthodox Estonians in April 1917 in Tallinn, included the demand that "the situation of the Pskov Estonians [the *Setu*] be considered intolerable – since their only Estonian priest was forced to leave – and that the necessary steps for the salvation of their souls be taken."[432]

The decision of the 1919 *täiskogu* of the Estonian Orthodox Church to strive for autocephaly was especially welcomed by Karl Ustav, who saw an autocephalous Estonian Church as the only way to avoid separatism in Petserimaa.[433] Patriarch Tikhon, in his May 1920 act of autonomy, officially made Petserimaa part of the newly created Tallinn Eparchy.[434] In the ensuing discussions on Petserimaa, the Estonian state, although officially denying any direct involvement in religious issues, did exert some pressure on the Orthodox Church. This included the wish to integrate *Setu* parishioners in Estonian-language parishes and separate them from Russian-language parishes, as well as prescribing the use of the Gregorian calendar.[435]

In the following years, it became clear that the image of Petserimaa as the 'wild east' was not going to disappear quickly.[436] In *Uus Elu*, several articles appeared, depicting the situation in Petserimaa in a positive light; however, the stigma attached to the region remained.[437] Among the most difficult issues was local Russian agitation, for Petserimaa was the main channel for Soviet refugees. According to the Estonian press, the Russians had even taken control of some parts of Petserimaa. Conversely, according to the Soviet press, the Russians were thoroughly oppressed everywhere.[438] The Orthodox Church tried to minimalise Russian influence by sending four Estonian Orthodox priests to Petserimaa in 1920 to provide the *Setu* with Estonian-language liturgy. Due to difficult conditions, however, only one of them remained by 1923.[439] With financial backing from the government-sponsored *Piirimaade Selts* (Border Region Society), the Synod employed a wandering Estonian priest, who visited the *Setu* parishes and held Estonian-language liturgies.[440]

---

432 Laar, 1917, p. 6.
433 Saard, 2008, p. 1546.
434 Aleksij, 1999, p. 530-531.
435 Grichin, 2003, p. 168-169; Lõuna, Kalle, 2003, p. 152-153. See also chapter 3.1.3.
436 Alenius, 1999, p. 2317-2321.
437 Such as Izborska Ivan, "Petseri maakond minevikus ja olevikus" [Petseri County past and present] in *UE*, 1/4, 1921, p. 26-27 and 1/5-6, 1921, p. 34-38; 'setulell', "Petserimaast ja setudest" [Petserimaa and the Setu] in *UE*, 1/8, 1921, p. 58-62.
438 Lõuna, Kalle, 2003, p. 90-91.
439 "Petseri Eesti koguduse korraldus" [The organisation of the Estonian congregation in Petseri] in *UE*, 1/8, 1921, p. 67; "Vene monarhistid Eestisse omale piiskopkonda asutamas" [The Russian monarchists are setting up their own Eparchy in Estonia] in *VM*, 6/170, 29.07.1923, p. 4; Samuel Sommer, "Setude venekeelset jumalateenistused" [The Russian-language liturgies of the *Setu*] in *PM*, 69/131, 16.05.1925, p. 5.
440 Lõuna, Kalle, 1999, p. 60; Grichin, 2003, p. 173.

Another difficult issue was the Petseri Monastery, which was the oldest monastery on Estonian territory. Most of the monks were ethnic Russians, holding pro-monarchist views, "seeing the monastery as a piece of the Russian Empire, existing within the borders of the Estonian Republic."[441] In 1921, the Estonian Orthodox Church complained to the government about the latter's decision to use some of the monastery buildings for offices of state departments. The decision to place the county court and military barracks within the monastery walls was perceived as a sacrilege by the Petseri inhabitants:

> How far the Latvian government goes to satisfy the demands of the Catholic Church in order to integrate Latgale will be well known by the newspaper reader.[442] However, when we ask our government in the name of the entire Orthodox population of Petseri to leave the monastery in peace, it is like a voice crying in the wilderness. And when the people become unruly and agitated because of this, then everything is at fault, just not the breach of the monastery peace. Anyway, we would recommend the government to listen to the Petseri people.[443]

The head monk from 1920 was Joann Bulin, a *Setu* by birth, with ambivalent views on sovereign Estonia. In 1919 he was described as very Estonian-friendly; three years later, he was regarded as very dangerous for Estonia; whereas by 1926, he was again assessed positively.[444] Bulin had been elected as candidate for the post of Vicar Bishop of Narva at the *täiskogu* of 1920, but he was not accepted by Patriarch Tikhon due to his young age.[445] When the *täiskogu* of 1924 again had to choose a candidate for the post of Bishop of Narva, Bulin was not even nominated.[446] Probably the reason was that the plans to create a Petseri Eparchy were also discussed at this meeting, and Bulin preferred to become Bishop of Petseri.[447] His wish was granted two years later, when Joann Bulin was consecrated Bishop of Petseri by Metropolitan Aleksander of Tallinn and Archbishop Evsevij of Narva, "thereby completing the canonical requirements for full autocephaly of the Orthodox Church of Estonia."[448] The Eparchy of Narva and Izborsk gathered all purely Russian congregations on Estonian terri-

---

441 Lõuna, Kalle, 2003, p. 43.
442 See chapter 2.2.6.
443 "Petseri Eesti koguduse korraldus" [The organisation of the Estonian congregation in Petseri county] in *UE*, 1/8, 1921, p. 68.
444 Lõuna, Kalle, 2003, p. 43, 45.
445 See chapter 2.2.3. Bulin was 27 years old at the time.
446 "Eesti kiriku IV Täiskogu 9-11 septembril s. a." [The fourth *täiskogu* of the Estonian Church 9-11 September] in *UE*, 4/10, 1924, p. 3.
447 Saard, 2008, p. 1573.
448 Koguduseliige, "Uus piiskop Eesti ap.-õigeusu kirikus" [A new bishop for the Estonian Orthodox Church] in *UE*, 6/7-8, 1926, p. 14. See also Risch, 1937, p. 126; Isakov, 2001, p. 49. See also chapter 2.2.2. for the autocephaly issue.

tory, including those in Petserimaa, while the Bishop of Petseri was responsible for the other parishes of Petserimaa, be they mixed, *Setu*, or Estonian.[449]

A complex interplay of three more factors led to the so called 'Monastery War' of 1930-1932. First, the 1926 law on religious organisations required all congregations to register with the Ministry of the Interior. However, nothing was said regarding the registration of monasteries, and disagreement followed over the subordination of the Petseri Monastery. While the Estonian Synod considered it a legal part of the Estonian Orthodox Church, Bishop Joann regarded the monastery as an independent unit, which he "ruled as a king in his kingdom."[450] According to the Synod, the monastery should play a more important role in the Estonian Orthodox Church, since the 1929 *täiskogu* had decided that a theological education institution, preparing Orthodox Estonians for the priesthood, should be opened there. The stubborn Bishop Joann hindered these plans.

The second important issue developed in Narva. Bishop Evsevij of Narva and Izborsk died one and a half months after the 1929 *täiskogu*.[451] Another three years remained until the next regular *täiskogu*, when an election could take place, and the ecclesiastic authorities did not consider it necessary to call an extraordinary *täiskogu*. The Narva Eparchy Council named Metropolitan Aleksander of Tallinn and All Estonia the temporary administrator of the Eparchy, a post he accepted. However, a meeting of the full Eparchy revoked this decision and named Bishop Joann of Petseri instead. The Estonian Synod did not accept the Eparchy's appointment and overruled it.[452] Considering the general political mood at the time, the Russian parishes understandably feared the loss of their autonomy.

Third, due to the specific history of Petserimaa, no registry of land existed until the appointment of a registration commission in 1927.[453] One of its members was Peeter Päts, the younger brother of Nikolai Päts, chairman of the Estonian Orthodox Synod, and Konstantin Päts, an influential politician. In an article on the occasion of Peeter Päts' sixtieth birthday in 1940, the author describes how Päts "applied all his energy and the work experience he had gathered in order to fulfil the task at hand, as if he had always been longing to do this kind of work. With his simple and friendly attitude, he quickly managed to gain popularity and trust among the Petserimaa peasants, who turned to him not only concerning the land registry, but with all kinds of questions and con-

---

449 Risch, 1937, p. 125-126; Lõuna, Kalle, 1999, p. 58.
450 Suur, 1940, p. 83. See also Lõuna, Kalle, 1999, p. 61-62.
451 "Vene kõrgem vaimulik Eestis surnud" [The highest Russian cleric in Estonia died] in
    PL, 24/217, 14.08.1929, p. 6; Risch, 1937, p. 126; Lõuna, Kalle, 1999, p. 62.
452 X., "Нарвская Епархия" [The Eparchy of Narva] in *PS*, 2/6, 1932, p. 89-90; Risch,
    1937, p. 126-127; Lõuna, Kalle, 1999, p. 62.
453 Suur, 1940, p. 82.

cerns."[454] The land registry commission obviously came into contact with the Petseri Monastery and its inventory. The commission found that the monastery bookkeeping showed numerous irregularities. Since Päts was Orthodox and had direct links to the Estonian Synod, he reported these irregularities to the ecclesiastic authorities. At the same time, in Petseri, rumours of changes began to circulate.[455]

An investigation commission headed by Synod chairman Nikolai Päts arrived at the monastery in June 1930 inaugurating changes in its operation and oversight. The commission concluded that not everything was as it should be in the monastery and appointed a standing committee under the leadership of Peeter Päts to bring order and transparency to the monastery finances and subordinate the monastery to the Synod.[456] His charge brought Päts into direct conflict with Bishop Joann, who claimed that the financial situation of the monastery was in the best order. According to the Päts-laudator, "how much 'in order' the finances were was easily established as the monastery, in spite of its extensive external property, was not self-sufficient but needed to take out loan after loan."[457] The continuous reluctance of Bishop Joann to allow Päts to carry out his charge, as well as the inability of the Estonian nationalist Päts to create friendly inter-ethnic relations in the multi-ethnic Petseri region led to conflict, which became known as the 'Monastery War.'[458] Metropolitan Aleksander explained to the Estonian press the reason for opposition to the Synod's attempts to bring order into the monastery finances:

It is obvious that some *Russians seem to think that the monastery is their private property* and do not want to accept any oversight from the Synod. This kind of reasoning is also found in Bishop Joann's explanation in the Tallinn Russian newspaper. In fact, however, they have nothing to worry about, for the monastery administration remains the same and all its income continues to go through the treasurer of the monastery funds. The only difference is that outgoing cheques need to carry the signature of the Synod representative next to that of the head monk. This is normal practice. No other institutions allow cheques with only a single signature. [...]
[The rumours about the pending sale of the entire monastery] have also reached the Metropolitan, namely through Bishop Joann himself. When Bishop Joann visited an exposition of church art in Riga, the rumour that an icon from the monastery had been sold for a large sum quickly spread. There should be an end to this kind of rumours, when the inventory lists have been correctly compiled. [...]

454 Suur, 1940, p. 82.
455 Lõuna, Kalle, 1999, p. 63.
456 Suur, 1940, p. 83; Lõuna, Kalle, 1999, p. 63.
457 Suur, 1940, p. 83.
458 "Kloostrisõda Petseris" [The Monastery War in Petseri] in *VM*, 14/278, 27.11.1930, p. 3; "Tüli Petseri kloostri inventeerimisega" [The conflict around the inventory of the Petseri Monastery] in *VM*, 14/280, 29.11.1930, p. 5. Suur, 1940, p. 84; Risch, 1937, p. 127; Lõuna, Kalle, 1999, p. 63-64.

[An ethnic Russian member of the Synod, who was sent to Petseri to investigate the conflict] got the impression that *the entire 'monastery fight' has been greatly puffed up* and the rumour about a rebellion in the monastery and outside is an exaggeration. Mr. Päts equally denies having threatened to flatten the monastery with cannons.[459]

To ameliorate the conflict, an influential monk named Benjamin was expelled from Estonia in early December 1930. Benjamin had been responsible for the finances of the monastery and, reportedly, the leader of the Russian monarchist faction among the monks.[460] With his 'assistant' gone, Bishop Joann became active in the conflict. He instituted legal proceedings against the Estonian Synod, arguing that it was illegally interfering in the internal affairs of the monastery. However, the secular courts dismissed the charges, in part because the statutes of the church stipulated that Bishop Joann should have appealed to the Patriarchate of Constantinople in this case and not the secular courts.[461]

It was hoped that the *täiskogu* planned for June 1932 would elect a new Bishop of Narva settle the issue of the Petseri Monastery. Konstantin Kokla described why these two issues came about and how they were interwoven:

We were under one bishop. But one bishop alone cannot overturn old traditions and replace them with new ones. We needed two bishops. We got that. Meeting the spiritual needs of our Russian brothers, we allowed them an ethnically defined Eparchy. This is not defined in the holy canons but necessary in actual life. And our Rus-

---

459 "Mis sünnib Petseri kloostris?" [What happens in the Petseri Monastery?] in *VM*, 14/279, 28.11.1930, p. 1 (Emphasis in original). A full page feature on the monastery in *Vaba Maa*, the most 'yellow' of the interwar Estonian newspapers, notes that "since the Great Russian orientation has taken over power in the monastery, access to dissenters is closed off. Those of the monks who are not ethnic Russians, but belong to the *Setu* are second order men in the monastery; the *Setu*fellows [Setulelled] among the monks are sent to work on the monastery farmland tens of miles away in summer and they *are not allowed to enter the monastery for days*. Formerly, there were also Estonian monks, but they have been driven out in the course of time." "Kloostri müüride taga" [Behind the monastery walls] in *Esmaspäev*, 9/48, 01.12.1932, p. 3 (Emphasis in original).

460 "Võitlus Petseri kloostri pärast" [The fight for the monastery of Petseri] in *VM*, 14/283, 03.12.1930, p. 5; Risch, 1937, p. 128; Lõuna, Kalle, 1999, p. 64-65. An interesting article in an important Latvian newspaper shows how Benjamin was perceived: "Bishop Joann worked hand in hand with the irreconcilable Russian nationalists and his right-hand-man was a former officer and friend of [the Anti-Bolshevik] general Judenič [of 1919], the adventurer B[enjamin], who was the actual leader of the Petseri Monastery and the head agitator among the Russians. This same B[enjamin] also maintained links with Russian emigré circles. As later became clear, the means to undertake his travels abroad came from the sale of valuables from the monastery treasury. B[enjamin]'s activities were unmasked in 1930, and he was expelled from Estonia. Now, he has taken up an important position in Jerusalem." H. Velners, "Pareizticīgā bīskapa dumpis Igaunijā" [The rebellion of an Orthodox bishop in Estonia] in *JZ*, 22/208, 15.09.1932, p. 11.

461 "Vene marurahvuslaste kihutustöö kannab vilja" [The agitation attempts by Russian chauvinists bears fruits] in *PL*, 27/99, 12.04.1932, p. 4; Risch, 1937, p. 128.

sian brothers happily accepted the offer. Fortunately, there was a bishop in Estonia, who, although stuck in old Russian era traditions, was open minded and without blood on his hands. That was the beginning of the Narva Eparchy.

We thus lived peacefully, brotherly. Our young church, formed by the natural and social context in which it operated, began to set goals for itself. To achieve the complete canonical requirements, we elected a third bishop, a young monk, Joann of Petseri.

But now, severe obstacles appeared on this peaceful road. The Russian faction, having found complete security and freedom in Estonia, came out of hibernation. The Russians found that several religious practices are different from what they were used to; it was impossible for them to accept the interests of the Estonian Church as their own. [...] As if to put the young church to the test, God called the liberal Archbishop Evsevij away from this world. The young Bishop of Petseri was left completely at the mercy of the Russian nationalists.

And we ask: what are the consequences of this internal victory? In the Russian parishes, the religious die-hards have great success; the parishes do not find any clergy [...]; the Petseri Monastery, regardless of belonging to the ecclesiastic authorities by order of the state, works as an independent entity, making a fuss and raising objections when the Synod sends its auditor there...

If you ask me, I think that all this disorder could be cleared up and the life of the Estonian Church could be brought onto the right tracks, if only the *täiskogu* will ensure that the following maxim is followed: there should be no difference of opinion between the Estonian bishops. If one of them finds that he cannot follow the general direction of the church, he should make it his moral duty to officially step down from his office into his chamber, asking God to help the truth He has prepared to victory without his help.[462]

Regarding the Petseri Monastery issue, the *täiskogu* voted in favour of the Synod and against Bishop Joann's proposal to make the monastery an autonomous legal entity.[463] Concerning the Bishop of Narva, a majority of the *täiskogu* delegates voted against the candidate put forward by the Narva Eparchy Council, the ailing Anatolij Ostroumov, mainly on the grounds that he did not understand the national language and that his election 'would not conform to the Estonian national interest.' The *täiskogu* then proceeded to elect Bishop Joann of Petseri, although he had categorically refused to accept the candidacy. He was elected with an overwhelming majority, because all the Russian delegates had left the meeting in protest.[464] In the months following the *täiskogu*, the Synod

---

462 Konstantin Kokla, "Kõik õigeusulised, käed külge!" [All Orthodox, get ready!] in *UE*, 12/3, 1932, p. 5-6.

463 "Apostliku-õigeusu kiriku täiskogu istungjärk" [The session of the Orthodox Church *täiskogu*] in *PL*, 27/162, 17.06.1932, p. 4.

464 "Piiskop Johannes Narva piiskopiks" [Bishop Joann to become Bishop of Narva] in *PL*, 27/163, 18.06.1932, p. 5; *Memorandum*, 1932; *K voprosu*, 1933, p. 60-64; Risch, 1937, p. 128; Lõuna, Kalle, 1999, p. 67; Isakov, 2001, p. 50. For this and the following, see also А. Ш., "Волнения в эстонских православных кругах" [Unrest in Estonian Orthodox corners] in *Seg*, 14/240, 30.08.1932, p. 8.

and the Metropolitan unsuccessfully attempted to convince Joann to accept the post in Narva.[465] On 1 August, then, the Synod dismissed him from the post of head monk. He refused to comply with the decision, locked himself in the monastery, and denied Peeter Päts and others access.[466] The first week of August 1932 was "the Petseri 'Monastery revolt,' second act" which ended only when "the Petseri Monastery was finally captured [and] Joann was considered a secularised person to be removed by order of court at some point."[467] Sensationalism in the Estonian press directed special focus on Petseri and its monastery, resulting in an influx of tourists.[468]

Once Joann was forcefully deposed as head monk on 11 August, the waves of conflict continued because the ex-bishop was intent on remaining in the monastery. His position as a member of the Estonian *Riigikogu*, elected to represent Russian interests, made the whole situation look like an anti-Russian campaign. He filed a complaint with the secular courts, arguing that his deposition was not in the jurisdiction of the Estonian Orthodox Synod. He also organised a petition, which was signed by thousands of Petserimaa Russians who had been told that the monastery would be desecrated if Bishop Joann was forced to leave.[469] The court proceedings were followed with great interest by the population. Ultimately, however, his suit did not succeed.[470] Bishop Joann visited Narva at the end of November 1932, but finding no suitable lodgings there, he returned to the Petseri Monastery again. The Estonian Synod made a final decision end of December to defrock Bishop Joann, since he had let more than half a year pass without accepting any negotiations or compromise solutions regarding his move to the Narva Eparchy.[471] The ex-bishop continued to periodically turn up in the

---

465 "Piiskopp Joann ei liigu Petserist" [Bishop Joann will not move from Petseri] in *PL*, 27/190, 15.07.1932, p. 1.

466 Lõuna, Kalle, 1999, p. 66-67.

467 "Petseri 'kloostri-mässu' järgmine vaatus" [The Petseri 'monastery revolt', second act] in *PL*, 27/212, 06.08.1932, p. 1, 4; "Petseri klooster võeti lõpuks siiski üle" [The Petseri Monastery was finally captured] in *VM*, 16/183, 06.08.1932, p. 3.

468 K. Eh., "Kloostriga ja kloostrita Petseri" [Petseri with and without a monastery] in *PM*, 76/181, 05.08.1932, p. 3; "Petseri kloostri majapidamine revideerimisel" [The accountancy of the Petseri Monastery is under revision] in *VM*, 16/185, 09.08.1932, p. 7.

469 "Mitropoliidi märgukiri ja Petseri asjad" [The official note of the metropolitan and the Petseri matters] in *PL*, 27/255, 18.09.1932, p. 4.

470 "Piiskopp Joanni väljatõstmise protsess" [The lawsuit on the removal of Bishop Joann] in *PL*, 27/260, 23.09.1932, p. 4; "Joanni protsessid mitropoliidiga luhtusid" [Joann's lawsuits against the metropolitan failed] in *PL*, 27/273, 06.10.1932, p. 4.

471 "Narvas ei leiduvat piiskopile kohaseid ruume" [In Narva, there are 'no suitable rooms' for the bishop] in *PL*, 27/329, 01.12.1932, p. 1; "Kas Joann asub Narva piiskopi kohale?" [Will Joann take the position as Narva bishop?] in *PL*, 27/339, 11.12.1932, p. 5; "Piiskop Joanni intriigide selgitamine vana-aasta lõpul" [Explanation for bishop Joann's intrigues before year's end] in *PL*, 27/344, 16.12.1932, p. 1; "Petseri sai piiskopi" [Petseri has a

Estonian press, repeatedly associated with Russian-minded agitation. In January 1934, Joann took leave of absence from the *Riigikogu* for 'health reasons' and travelled to the Patriarch of Constantinople to complain about his treatment. The latter also dismissed the complaint, but informed him that the Estonian Church agreed to allow him to return as Bishop of Narva if he repented. Joann refused, stayed in Yugoslavia, and later turned up as a bishop of the Russian exile hierarchy in Sremski Karlovci.[472]

The conflict around the Petseri Monastery and Bishop Joann was reported exclusively in the secular press. The Estonian Orthodox journals did not mention the occurrences and only tangentially referred to them, for example in the run-up to the 1932 *täiskogu* or as editor's comments to articles reproduced from the secular press. The conflict was not considered an important issue for the everyday life of the Estonian Orthodox Church, but rather as a marginal within the Russian minority. The Synod obviously closely monitored the secular press, however, and when an article did not reflect the official narrative, it sent a correction to the responsible editors.[473] The 'Russian faction' of the church published flyers, memoranda, and booklets about the perceived canonical transgressions of the Estonian church leadership. Instead of their earlier argument, that the Estonian Orthodox Church had no right to switch from the jurisdiction of Moscow to that of Constantinople, these texts argued that the *tomos* of auton-

---

bishop] in *VM*, 16/297, 17.12.1932, p. 1; "Joann Bulin ametita piiskopiks" [Joann Bulin is a bishop without a see] in *PL*, 27/355, 30.12.1932, p. 1; Risch, 1937, p. 128. See also *K voprosu*, 1933, p. 66-71.

472 "Piiskop Joann ei loe end tagandatuks" [Bishop Joann does not consider himself suspended] in *PL*, 28/87, 29.03.1933, p. 1; "Joann ei loobu ässitustööst" [Joann does not refrain from agitation] in *PL*, 28/95, 06.04.1933, p. 1; "Piiskop Joann tegutseb Petseris väljakutsuvalt" [Bishop Joann operates loudly in Petseri] in *PL*, 28/100, 11.04.1933, p. 3; "Piiskop Joann õiendab" [Bishop Joann makes a correction] in *PL*, 28/102, 13.04. 1933, p. 4; "Ajakirjanduse keskel"[Among the newspapers] in *UjE₃*, 1/1, 1933, p. 12-13; "Piiskop Joann õiendas oma asju Petseri kloostriga" [Bishop Joann clarifies matters with the Petseri Monastery] in *PL*, 28/306, 09.11.1933, p. 3; "Piiskop Joann sõitis kaebama Istanbuli patriarhile" [Bishop Joann travelled to the Patriarch in Istanbul to complain] in *PL*, 29/15, 16.01.1934, p. 1; "Piiskop Joann jatkab Eesti mustamist välismaal" [Bishop Joann continues to blackmail Estonia abroad] in *PL*, 29/46, 16.02.1934, p. 3; "Joann ei saa Narva piiskopiks" [Joann wo not become Narva bishop] in *PL*, 29/99, 12.04.1934, p. 3; "Konstantinoopoli patriarhi kiri mitropoliit Aleksandrile" [The letter from the Constantinople Patriarch to Metropolitan Aleksander] in *PL*, 29/146, 31.05.1934, p. 3; "Piiskop Joanni käik patriarhi juure nurjus" [Bishop Joann's trip to the Patriarch failed] in *PL*, 29/216, 08.08.1934, p. 3. See also Hirvoja and Pau, 2002, p. 43-44; Šor, 2008.

473 D. Samon, "Piiskop Joanni sõidust Konstantinoopoli ja tema seletustest" [About Bishop Joann's trip to Constantinople and his explanation] in *PL*, 29/19, 20.01.1934, p. 2 (also published in Russian in *Seg*, 16/20, 20.01.1934, p. 8); "Märkmeid Petseri kloostrist" [Notes about the Petseri Monastery] in *PL*, 29/50, 20.02.1934, p. 2.

omy, which the Estonian Orthodox Church had received from the Patriarch of Constantinople in 1923 was not correctly applied.

The most comprehensive of these texts spanned seventy-one pages and described the transgressions of the Estonian Church in detail.[474] It claimed that the rules set forth in the Constantinople *tomos* had been violated without exception, beginning with the application of the adjective 'independent,' or even 'autocephalous,' to the Estonian Orthodox Church and continuing through the non-canonical structure of the church and its decision-making processes. The last quarter of the text concretely analysed the events surrounding Bishop Joann of Petseri, concluding that "in this case, the secular courts have committed a blatant abuse of their formal possibilities, dealing canonical justice a blow in the face, that is, showing contempt of the highest canonical court of the Ecumenical Patriarchate, to which Bishop Joann has now turned to be rehabilitated and protected."[475]

In the meantime, the new Bishop of Petseri, Nikolai (Leismann), had a very different approach to the monastery administration. He made his appointment conditional on the removal of commissioner P. Päts from the monastery, and followed a much less nationalist policy. On his enthronement in April 1933, the press reported that "the Estonian hymn was heard in the Petseri Monastery for the first time."[476] After this time, Bishop Nikolai and the Petseri Monastery only appeared in the press in positive terms. The new bishop allowed the municipality to install a gas storage facility in the monastery cellar, opened a home for retired priests on a farm belonging to the monastery, and gave one of its chapels to the newly established Estonian-language parish of Petseri.[477] However, the ethnically defined Eparchy of Narva and Izborsk remained without a bishop.

---

474 *K voprosu*, 1933.

475 *K voprosu*, 1933, p. 71.

476 "Esmakordselt kõlas Petseri kloostris vabariigi hümn" [The Estonian hymn heard in the Petseri Monastery for the first time] in *VM*, 07.04.1933, p. 6; "Petseri tervitas uut piiskoppi" [Petseri welcomed the new bishop] in *PL*, 28/96, 07.04.1933, p. 1. See also Risch, 1937, p. 129; Lõuna, Kalle, 1999, p. 68.

477 "Klooster asutas Juuriku tallu vanadekodu" [The monastery opened a retired people's home at the Juuriku farm] in *Petseri Uudised*, 2/38, 23.09.1933, p. 1; P. O. Ü. Juhatus, "Petseri kloostrivalitsus nõus gaasivarjendite ehitamisega" [The administration of the Petseri Monastery agrees to build a gas storage facility] in *VM*, 17/232, 04.10.1933, p. 4; "Setu on kangekaelne" [The *Setu* is hard in the taking] in *Esmaspäev*, 15/21, 22.05.1934, p. 5; Nikolai Raag, "Enne ja nüüd – Ülempiiskop Nikolai juhtimisel kultuuristub Petseri klooster" [Before and now – under the leadership of Archbishop Nikolai, the Petseri Monastery is brought to cultural bloom] in *ET*, 2/19, 1937, p. 231; Risch, 1937, p. 129; Raag, 1938, p. 32; Lõuna, Kalle, 1999, p. 68.

2.3.2. Crisis in Latvia: an Assassination and its Consequences

As already noted, Archbishop Jānis was described by Paul Schiemann in 1931 as "not a friend of democracy and parliamentarianism."[478] The official view of the Latvian Orthodox Church on the democratic ideals were aptly described by an article published in the run-up to the 1929 ecclesiastic *saeima*. Proposing a change in the statutes, to revoke the right of a congregation to elect its clergy, the author[479] noted:

> This regulation was originally introduced in an era when all of Latvia was crazy about democratic order, i.e. the rule of the crowd: everywhere the majority of the votes, everywhere elections! That was the slogan of that time. The Social Democrats especially venerated this slogan. In the beginning of socialism, the convinced socialists may actually have considered the majority principle good, that it would bring new winds into politics, make the people happy. By now, this principle has shown its complete defectiveness. Nevertheless, the Social Democrats keep holding on to it, maybe because of old habit, maybe because it allows them to hold up the banner of democracy, take high political office, keep profit-making habits, and earn a lot of money. The citizens hold on to the principle, only a few raise their voice against it, because they are afraid of being called reactionaries or supporters of the Black Hundreds.[480] The citizens are afraid of a 'ghost,' like children. Also, in the life and statutes of the Latvian Orthodox Church, this principle remains, thanks to fear of changes... But in Moscow, as we know, this principle has long since been replaced and governance happens now only with the help of despotism. It is time for the Latvian Orthodox Church too, to remove this inappropriate method. From church history, we know that the principle was introduced ages ago and since then discarded as inept. Also in the Latvian Orthodox Church, it has been tested for long enough (10 years), found bad and evil, and it must therefore be removed.[481]

In addition to the public visibility of Archbishop Jānis and the move towards authoritarianism within the structures of the Orthodox Church, a number of factors led to a crisis in Latvian Orthodoxy in the early 1930s. One factor was the increasingly popular Russian Christian Students' Movement [Russkogo Studenčeskogo Khristianskogo Dviženija, RSKhD], based in Paris. It mainly considered itself a supporter of the rights of the Russian minority and acted

---

478 "Kādus likumus vēl pieņems saeimā?" [Which laws are yet to be accepted in the *Saeima*?] in *JZ*, 21/145, 05.07.1931, p. 12. See also Hiden, 2004, for more on Schiemann.

479 Signing with 'A. P.', this is possibly either the younger brother of Archbishop Jānis, the historian Antonijs Pommers or the later Metropolitan of Riga, Archpriest Augustīns Pētersons.

480 A Russian ultra-nationalist movement.

481 A. P., "Nākošai Latvijas Par. Draudzes Saeimai" [To the coming *saeima* of the Latvian Orthodox Church] in *TuD*, 7/10, 1929, p. 116-117.

relatively independently of the ecclesiastic authorities in Latvia and Estonia.[482] In Estonia, it had few dealings with the ecclesiastic authorities, since it catered primarily to ethnic Russians, but in Latvia, Archbishop Jānis maintained friendly relations with its leadership throughout the 1920s. However, in the early 1930s, the increasingly suspicious political climate began to make life difficult for the RSKhD.[483] For some reason, Archbishop Jānis fell out with a high official of the RSKhD, A. I. Nikitin, during the latter's visit to Riga in 1931, and his relationship with the RSKhD cooled drastically.[484]

The two main supporters of the RSKhD among the Latvian Orthodox clergy were Jānis Jansons, the rector of the re-established Riga Orthodox Seminary, and Kirils Zaics, the head priest of the Riga Cathedral parish. Jansons was among the most visible and powerful Latvian Orthodox priests at the time but remained loyal to the Archbishop until his death.[485] Zaics, on the other hand, was more difficult to judge. Having actively supported reform in the church after 1905 and being a participant in the Moscow *sobor* of 1917, he had risen to the position of editor of both the Latvian- and Russian-language Orthodox journals of Latvia and head priest of the Cathedral in Riga.[486] There are several indications that Zaics might have presented a danger to the Archbishop, and the latter, therefore, sought a way to diminish his influence. End of 1931, the organisation 'Brotherhood,' which had financed the two Latvian Orthodox journals until then, ran into financial difficulties. Zaics proceeded to give the Latvian-language journal away and declared his willingness to manage the Russian-language one on his own initiative. There was no successor for the Latvian-language journal, which did not appear for two years. Moreover, Zaics turned the focus of the Russian-language journal to international Orthodox missions, scarcely reporting anything at all about developments in Latvia during 1932 and 1933.[487] The general anti-Jānis mood on the political left and right as

---

482 This movement was closely associated with the American YMCA and YWCA. See Pljuchanov, 1993; Aleksij, 1999, p. 380-383; Sidjakov III, 2011, p. 174-175. See also Balevics, 1962, p. 7-21 for a Marxist reading of the Latvian crises.

483 Pljuchanov, 1993, p. 165-166.

484 Balevics, 1987, p. 67-70; Sidjakov, III, 2011, p. 174-175. The relevant letter are reproduced in Sidjakov, II, 2009, 31-34 and in Latvian translation in Kalniņš II, 1993, p. 123-127. Interestingly, Pljuchanov, writing primarily a review of his own role in the RSKhD, only mentions that Nikitin was no longer invited because of problems with the Baltic governments. Pljuchanov, 1993, p. 147.

485 Balevics claims that there were voices within the RSKhD claiming that Jansons would be better suited to represent Russian interests than the current Archbishop. Balevics, 1987, p. 68.

486 Balašov, 2001, p. 50; Golikov and Škarovskij, 2002.

487 See "Указ Синода" [Synod decision] in *ViŽ*, 10/1, 1932, p. 14-15; Кирилл Зайц, "Просьба" [Plea] in *ViŽ*, 10/1, 1932, p. 15-16; Кирилл Зайц, "'Вера и Жизнь' в 1933

well as the absence of an official journal makes any attempt at objective assessment of the events that followed even more difficult. Finally, since Jānis was later praised as a martyr and Kirils Zaics achieved great popularity as the head of the Pskov Mission, objective treatments are also rare in later years.[488] The best source is probably a newspaper account of the 'Zaics affair' from the opening of the court proceedings in March 1936:

> In 1932, the then Archbishop, now deceased, Jānis Pommers, filed a complaint about the activities of the accountant of the cathedral, Archpriest Kirils Zaics. Z[aics] took this post in 1922 and always enjoyed the full confidence of the congregation and Archbishop. Although Zaics' activities had to be audited twice a year, he always managed to find a reason to delay the audits, which remained undone. The most important commercial activity of the church was the sale of candles, which Zaics managed. That the revenue was large can be seen by the enormous amount of candles sold; from 1924 to 1931, 800 boxes of candles were sold for 160,000 Ls.[489] The money was taken by Zaics and he kept the books himself. Apart from the candle sales, offerings, and fees for weddings and funerals, Zaics organised the collection of donations for the restoration of the bells. Since Provost N. Tikhomirov's audit did not yield any results, in April 1933 Archbishop Jānis made a special decision to examine the financial transactions of Zaics, in order to finally get real clarity. The audit was carried out by Archpriest Balodis and lasted several months. Here again, Balodis came across Zaics' reluctance to show the account books. Nowhere could the books monitoring the candle sales be found, and the actual number of candles sold remained unclear. The cash till books were found in disorder, and the books documenting the income of the cathedral never turned up anywhere. Notwithstanding the disordered book-keeping, the audit could still detect a loss of 8,448 Ls, which Z[aics] could not account for in any documents. The case of K. Zaics was handed over to the Riga prosecution department, and the lawsuit began yesterday.[490]

Zaics had published an open letter to the Latvian clergy following the Synod decision to defrock him in November 1933, in which he voiced his disappointment with the secrecy of the proceedings:

> I do not understand that *in the course of the entire process, nobody ever wished to listen to my version of the story.* On 26 April, when the full Synod discussed my case, I was locked out of the meeting once there was talk about defrocking me, and I had no possibility to say anything to my defence. On 17 August, I was not invited to the full Synod meeting with the esteemed fathers, when the extraordinarily important question of referring my case to the ecclesiastical courts for breach of the 25th Apostolic Canon, providing for the deprivation of clerical ranks, was discussed, and

---

году" ['Vera i Žizn' in 1933] in *ViŽ*, 10/12, 1932, p. 234-235. See also the editor's note in Kalniņš II, 1993, p. 138.

488 See Golikov and Škarovskij, 2002. For the Pskov mission, see Oboznyj, 2008.

489 Ls = *Lats*, the Latvian currency.

490 S., "Vakar sāka iztiesāt virspriestera Zaica prāvu" [Yesterday began the process against Archpriest Zaics] in *Latvijas Kareivis*, 17/69, 24.03.1936, p. 5. A position paper, prepared by Archbishop Jānis can be found in Kalniņš II, 1993, p. 138-140.

I could not give any explanation. And finally, on 1 November, when the clergy was to have its say, I again was not invited to give an account. Tell me, dear servants of God, *how am I to sacrificially and humiliatingly endure this most severe decision of yours, throwing your oldest colleague out of your midst?*[491]

In the course of the process, which was followed by the Latvian newspapers with great interest, it became clear that the charges against Zaics were much more severe than simple financial fraud. A small notice in the left-wing Russian-language newspaper *Trudovaja mysl'* (Worker's Thought) from January 1933 had triggered the whole case. This note describes how Archbishop Jānis accused Zaics of publicising a threatening letter directed at the Archbishop:

K. Zaics replied that Archbishop J. Pommers himself was the author of this letter. He named a woman, whom the Archbishop had engaged to present the letter to the Synod. J. Pommers went quiet. In our opinion, this proves that the fuss about the purported danger, in which Archbishop J. Pommers claims his life to be, in reality is nothing more and nothing less than a naïve trick in order to get attention.[492]

Without justifying either side of the conflict, the internal communication in the Latvian Orthodox Church suffered because of the case against Zaics. From the beginning of 1932 until end of 1934, no Orthodox journals had reported on Latvian issues, and when Zaics was removed, he apologetically wrote in his journal:

Issue number 12 of this year was already with the typographer and parts of the material were already set when I received the decision of the Synod that after eleven years of hard work, I was relieved of my duties as publisher-editor. Therefore, the current issue is only half the normal size. [...]
Thus, my work as editor and, for the last two years, also as publisher (without subsidies) has ended. I thank God that I was given the possibility to complete this year's issues. The reason of my dismissal is unknown.[493]

The Synod decided to restart both the Latvian-language and the Russian-language Latvian Orthodox journals in 1934 with two separate editors. Apart from an article reporting on the Synod meeting of 1 November 1933, when Kirils Zaics was suspended, the journals did not mention the internal problems

---

491 Кирилл Зайц, "Письмо прот. К. Зайц православному духовенству Латвии" [An open letter from Archpriest K. Zaics to the Latvian Orthodox clergy] in *Seg*, 15/208, 07.11. 1933, p. 2 (Emphasis in original).

492 И. Б. "В царстве Поммера" [In the Pommers' kingdom] in *Трудовая Мысль*, 6/3, 22.01.1933, p. 3 (Kalniņš II, 1993, p. 136-137). See also S., "Zaica sveču prāvā atklājās jaunas lietas" [New issues appeared in the candle process against Zaics] in *Latvijas Kareivis*, 17/71, 26.03.1936, p. 3; "День сенсационных заявлений на процессе прот. К. Зайц" [The day of sensational requests in the court case against K. Zaics] in *Seg*, 18/87, 27.03.1936, p. 6.

493 This last claim is very unlikely, as he knew by then very well what the Synod thought about him. Кирилл Зайц, "'Вера и Жизнь' в 1934 году" ['Vera i Žizn' in 1934] in *ViŽ*, 11/12, 1933, p. 217-218. See also the editor's note in Kalniņš II, 1993, p. 138.

of the Orthodox Church of Latvia, but rather focused on external enemies, who "attempt to take away our laurels and good press in the eyes of the population, the Latvian government, and foreign countries."[494] The discourse on these external enemies, especially the Social Democrats on the political left, but also, the extreme right, became increasingly aggressive and authoritarian, following the general political climate in Latvia.[495]

The high point of this discourse was reached about five months after the disbandment of the *Saeima*, when the Archbishop was murdered on the night between 11 and 12 October 1934.[496] The murderer was never identified. Three main theories on the motive began to circulate: The first one related the murder to the previously mentioned conflict between Jānis and the RSKhD leadership. The second version involved the conflict between Jānis and Zaics, and the third held Soviet agents to be responsible.[497]

The assassination threw the Orthodox Church of Latvia into turmoil, since it had not made any preparations for the potential of losing its bishop, as the Estonians had done by electing more bishops. After turning to the Estonian Orthodox Church for help in the matter of consecration, the Synod began a discussion regarding the future path of the Orthodox Church of Latvia.[498] The hopelessness of its situation was commented on by Pēteris Gredzens, the new editor of the Latvian-language Orthodox journal in his editorial for the year 1935. After analysing the political changes in Latvia of 1934, he exclaimed:

---

494 "Из церковной хроники" [From the church chronicles] in *ViŽ*, 12/26 1934, p. 38-40 (Kalniņš II, 1993, p. 130).

495 See "Esiet modri!" [Be moderate!] in *TuD*, 10/2, 1934, p. 17-18 (Kalniņš II, 1993, p. 131-132). See also the other articles collected in Kalniņš II, 1993, p. 127-129, 131-136. For the political changes in Latvia in 1934, see chapter 2.3.3. Jānis had continued his political agitation against the left throughout the years. In one of his last speeches, in June 1933, he accused the Marxists of not realising the scope of the case against Zaics and of inconsistent arguments. See *Saeimas Stenogrammas*, IV/vi, 01.05.1933-06.07. 1933, c. 837-843. See also Runce, 2008, p. 164.

496 The literature on the assassination, the funeral, and the commemoration of Jānis abounds, but is often tainted by him being considered a martyr saint. See the contemporary documents collected in Kalniņš II, 1993, p. 144-159. See also Cherney, 1985, p. 41-43; Kalniņš, Jānis, 2001, p. 189-240; Požidaev, 2004, p. 124-150.

497 This short and concise listing of the theories is taken from Sidjakov III, 2011, p. 175.

498 "Kaks mõrva" [Two murders] in *UjE₂*, 3/1, 1935, p. 10-13; Balevics, 1987, p. 74-75. The Moscow Patriarchate reacted by charging Metropolitan Elevferij of Vilnius to provisionally administer the Riga Eparchy and see to the election of a successor. However, the Latvian authorities refused to allow Elevferij's agents to conduct any business in sovereign Latvia. No reports about this reaction reached the press, but it can be reconstructed through archival material. See Balevics, 1964, p. 231-244; Kulis, 1993, 69-70.

Oh, how I would like to stop here and not have to write anything more! Then we would keep the year 1934 as a most happy memory and could enter the new year thanking God for His great benevolence that He grants us...
But...
After the morning of 15 May,[499] there came also the morning of 12 October... and brought us the terrible news of the death of our leader and head shepherd... [...]
1935 provides us, Orthodox Latvians, with hard and important work. We must first of all heal the wound that 1934 gave us. We need to find a new head of the church; although, it is already clear that the election will be very difficult. Archbishop Jānis was an exceptional individual, who is not easily replaced. And yet we must get a new bishop, for a church without a bishop is untenable. While the Latvian Orthodox Church is autonomous and independent from foreign influence from a legal point of view, without a bishop, we are entirely dependent on foreign help, for without the help of foreign bishops, we cannot consecrate a single clergyman.[500]

Since the common Latvian citizen could not detect any progress on the issue of a new Latvian bishop, the editors of the Orthodox journals were assailed with letters asking about it. The latter also had to explain to the faithful that the question was much more difficult than it seemed. An anonymous author, signing with 'Cand. jur. J.,' expressed the problems and fears in detail:

The fundamental question is: where to find the means to resolve this situation? [...] Apparently, the Synod turns to specific persons in such a manner that if one declines, they turn to the next one etc., but also on this issue we know nothing, since the Synod does not inform us about anything. [...] The result of this procedure might be that the chosen candidate, far from being the one best suited for the position, would be the one who agrees to take the post, which could even turn out to be only one single person. [...] Obviously, this kind of procedure is not adequate and summoning a *saeima* to elect a new head of the church under these auspices is risky.
Let us try to clarify the problems. The first fundamental question is: whose duty is it to organise this matter and execute it? The answer is straightforward: [the Synod] But on the one hand, the three-year mandate of the Synod has passed,[501] and in order to elect a new Synod, we need a *saeima*. On the other hand, the Synod currently has no legitimate chairman to lead its activity.[502] Thus, for both of these matters, a *saeima* must be summoned. However, it is questionable whether such a *saeima* would yield desirable results in the current situation on the question of candidates for the head of the church. From our own experience, we know that an election always is a very problematic issue, but even then, in order for the election process to

---

499 The day of the political *coup d'état*. See also chapter 2.3.3.
500 Pēteris Gredzens, "Jaunā Gadā" [New Year] in *TuD*, 11/1, 1935, p. 1-3.
501 Archbishop Jānis had requested preparations for a *saeima* in a letter written four days before his death, although a regular *saeima* should have met already two years earlier. Kalniņš II, 1993, p. 143; Strods, 2005, p. 90.
502 The Archbishop should have been the chairman, and the second chairman, Archpriest A. Makedonskis, had also been charged with embezzlement and excluded from the Synod. Kulis, 1993, p. 68.

succeed, it is vital that it is led by a competent and authoritative personality, such as the deceased Archbishop Jānis. [...] Moreover, the current political era is not at all suited for large gatherings, such as an ecclesiastic *saeima*. [...] If we now do not have any authoritative person that could become *saeima* president, this is because we are caught in a vicious circle, from which it is difficult to escape.[503]

The article continues by proposing to introduce a post similar to the *Oberprokuror* of the Russian Orthodox Church. According to the author, this would solve all the problems, for then there would be one authority for correct procedures and good order in the Synod but uninvolved in the content.[504] The editor added in his comments that, although he understood the good intentions behind the author's views, he did not see an *Oberprokuror* as the solution, since the Russian Synod consisted of bishops, whereas the Latvian problem was the lack of any bishop:

> If our synod also consisted of bishops, then I would not have any objections to a Synod that rules the Orthodox Church without any *ruling* head shepherd, but living without any bishops, having to ask for foreign help for every consecration of priests or deacons, is an extremely abnormal situation for an independent Orthodox Church. The sooner it finds a conclusion, the better. But how to end it, if the Synod and society is unable to find a suitable candidate for the bishop's post? You see, that is a vicious circle, from which there is no exit. And if currently there is no suitable candidate to be found, then certainly, we have no option but to somehow renew the Synod constitution and wait for a candidate to appear. That may take a few more years.[505]

In July 1935, the church journal euphorically reported that an ecclesiastical *saeima* would happen soon, where a new bishop would be elected from two candidates.[506] The next issue then had to report that the Latvian Minister of the Interior, V. Gulbis, had prohibited the gathering, because "the technical preparations for a canonical *saeima* have not been completed [and] many parishes have

---

503 Cand. jur. J., "Ka kārtojams virsgana vēlešanas jautājums?" [How to organise the election of the head of the church?] in *TuD*, 11/6, 1935, p. 84. See also Pēteris Gredzens, "Virsganu vēlešanu jantājums" [The question of electing a new archbishop] in *TuD*, 11/3, 1935, p. 43; "По поводу избрания Архиепископа" [On the way to the election of an Archbishop] in *ViŽ*, 13/3, 1935, p. 67-69; Pēteris Gredzens, "Kad dabusim virsganu" [When do we get a head of the church?] in *TuD*, 11/5, 1935, p. 72.

504 Cand. jur. J., "Ka kārtojams virsgana vēlešanas jautājums?" [How to organise the election of the head of the church?] in *TuD*, 11/6, 1935, p. 85-86.

505 Pēteris Gredzens, *editor's comment to* Cand. jur. J., "Ka kārtojams virsgana vēlešanas jautājums?" [How to organise the election of the head of the church?] in *TuD*, 11/6, 1935, p. 86.

506 See all the articles in *TuD*, 11/7, 1935, p. 97-103. The two candidates were Augustīns Pētersons and Jānis Jansons. For the selection of candidates, see also Balevics, 1987, p. 75-82; Kulis, 1993, p. 71-72; Strods, 2005, p. 96-101; Runce, 2008, p. 193-194, 196-197.

not yet provided the government with the names of their delegates."[507] Within the Synod, two camps had been forming, the so-called 'government orientation' and the 'Orthodox opposition.' The delayed *saeima* enabled the Latvian government to replace three members of the latter group, including the acting chairman, allowing the government-loyal group to become dominant. Moreover, the government installed lawyer P. Elksnītis as its representative in the Synod.[508] The ecclesiastic *saeima* was originally delayed until September, but by then, the Synod had turned to Ecumenical Patriarch Fotios II for help organising the Latvian Orthodox Church and the *saeima* was further delayed.[509]

In November 1935, Metropolitan Germanos (Strenopoulos) of Thyateira, the Exarch of Western Europe of the Patriarchate of Constantinople, based in London, came to Riga. He stayed three weeks and began the re-organisation of the Latvian Orthodox Church. The journal *Ticība un Dzīve* noted with noticeable relief:

> This way, we have now, thanks be to God, been given a way to organise the election of our head of the church as quickly as possible. In the near future, we may gather at a *saeima* and elect for ourselves a head shepherd. It is very possible that our church will be organised as a Metropolia, with the Metropolitan of Riga and all Latvia at its head and two vicar bishops at his side.[510]

Patriarch Fotios II died shortly before finalising the declaration of autonomy for the Latvian Orthodox Church, to which he had agreed. Nevertheless, his successor, Patriarch Veniamin signed the documents as one of his first acts in office.[511]

---

507 "Valdošā virsgana vēlešanas atliktas" [The election of a ruling bishop delayed] in *TuD*, 11/8, 1935, p. 123.

508 Balevics, 1964, p. 234-237; Kulis, 1993, p. 68-69; Runce, 2008, p. 193.

509 V. Rušanovs, "Konstantinopoles patriarhija" [The Patriarchate of Constantinople] in *TuD*, 11/11, 1935, p. 163-164; "Pudemeid usuelust mujal maailmas – Lätimaal" [Notices on religious life elsewhere in the world – Latvia] in *UjE₂*, 3/12, 1935, p. 209; N., "Mūsu pareizticīgās baznīcas autonomija" [The Autonomy of our Orthodox Church] in *Pēdējā Brīdī*, 9/1, 01.01.1936, p. 10.

510 "Vispasaules Patriarha sūtnis Rīgā" [The envoy of the Ecumenical Patriarch in Riga] in *TuD*, 11/12, 1935, p. 183-185. See also "Jauna pareizticīgo archibīskapa izraudzīšana" [The enthronisation of the new Orthodox Archbishop] in *Rīts*, 05.11.1935, p. 7; Ludvigs Adamovičs, "Rīgas metropolija – Latvijas pareizticīgo baznīcas patstāvība" [The Metropoly of Riga – Independence for the Latvian Orthodox Church] in *JZ*, 25/291, 21.12.1935, p. 5. See chapter 2.3.3. for the election of vicar bishops.

511 "Sinodes plenarsēde 23. janvarī" [The plenary session of the Synod on 23 January] in *TuD*, 12/2, 1936, p. 23-24; "Латвийская православная церковь принята в юрисдикцию константинопольской патриархии" [The Latvian Orthodox Church is accepted in the jurisdiction of the Constantinople Patriarchate] in *Seg*, 18/43, 12.02.1936, p. 1; Vērotājs, "Latvijas pareizticīgās baznīcas stāvoklis" [The Situation of the Latvian Orthodox Church] in *Svētdienas Rīts* 17/9, 23.02.1936, p. 68; "Mitropolita vēlešanas 10. martā" [The election of the Metropolitan on 10 March] in *TuD*, 12/3, 1936, p. 44-45;

The Latvian Orthodox Church organised an ecclesiastic *saeima* for March 1936, at which Augustīns Pēterson was elected Metropolitan of Riga. He was consecrated and enthroned at the end of March, with extensive coverage by the press.[512] These events were great sensations in both the Latvian and the Russian-language press. In the Orthodox journals, the joy at no longer being orphans also predominated. The trial of Kirils Zaics, which also took place at the end of March 1936, received equally extensive coverage by the press. It ended with an acquittal on the charges of destruction and concealment of documents, but Zaics was convicted to eight months on probation for embezzlement. He appealed and was acquitted, but was not allowed to return to his former post at the Riga Cathedral, because he remained loyal to the Patriarchate of Moscow.[513]

2.3.3. The Orthodox Church and the Authoritarian Regimes

On 12 March 1934, Konstantin Päts staged a *coup d'état* in Estonia, and on 15 May 1934, Kārlis Ulmanis did the same in Latvia. Both forceful leaders re-organised the political system from parliamentary democracy to quasi-authoritarian presidential rule. In both cases, this regime change was preceded by a general lack of confidence in the national parliament and societal unrest due to

---

"Vispasaules patriarha vēstijums Latvijas Pareizticīgās Baznīcas Saeimai" [The message of the Ecumenical Patriarch to the Latvian Orthodox Church *saeima*] in *TuD*, 12/4, 1936, p. 50; "Patriarha tomoss Latvijas Pareizticīgai Baznīcai" [The patriarchal *tomos* to the Latvian Orthodox Church] in *TuD*, 12/4, 1936, p. 50-51.

512 "Mitropolita vēlešanas 10. martā" [The election of the Metropolitan on 10 March] in *TuD*, 12/3, 1936, p. 44-45; "Latvijas Pareizticīgās Baznīcas Saeima – Mitropolits Germanos Rīgā." [The *saeima* of the Latvian Orthodox Church – Metropolitan Germanos in Riga] in *TuD*, 12/4, 1936, p. 51-56; "Pirmā Rīgas un visas Latvijas Mitropolita Augustīna iesvētišana" [The consecration of the first Metropolitan of Riga and all Latvia, Augustīns] in *TuD*, 12/5, 1936, p. 67-70; "Mitropolita Augustīna intronizacija" [The enthronisation of Metropolitan Augustīns] in *TuD*, 12/5, 1936, p. 70-73; "Kirikuelu teateid – Osavõtt Läti Kiriku suursündmusest" [Notes from ecclesiastic life – participation in a major event of the Latvian Churcht] in *UjE₂*, 4/4, 1936, p. 50; "Õigeusk Lätimaal" [Orthodoxy in Latvia] in *ET*, 1/8, 1936, p. 10. See also the articles in all Latvian newspapers from 26. to 30.03.1936.

513 S., "Jāņa Pommera liecība par Zaicu" [Jānis Pommers' accusations about Zaics] in *Latvijas Kareivis*, 17/72, 27.03.1936, p. 5; "Katedrales sveču prāvas noslēgums" [The conclusions of the 'Cathedral Candle Case'] in *JZ*, 26/72, 27.03.1936, p. 6; "Прот. К. Зайц оправдан по обвинению в уничтожения и сокрытий документов" [K. Zaics acquitted of charges of destruction and concealment of documents] in *Seg*, 18/88, 28.03.1936, p. 6; "Virspr. K. Zaics attaisnots" [Archpriest K. Zaics acquitted] in *TuD*, 12/12, 1936, p. 186. See also Golikov and Škarovskij, 2002.

economic depression.[514] Moreover, in both cases, the new leaders had been distinguished politicians since before independence. Assessing the two regimes objectively is difficult, for "characterizing the years of [...] authoritarian rule as positive or negative depends on which aspects of the era is emphasized."[515] For example, there was no violence, although society was more closely monitored than before, including censorship of the public press and a ban on all political parties but one. The ideology of the authoritarian presidents is summarised by the slogan 'the nation must be strong!' In order to achieve this strength, "it must act unitarily, keeping the goals of the state and the nation in sight and avoiding fragmentation into political, social, economic, and cultural groups."[516]

The new ideology impacted on the Orthodox Estonians and Latvians considerably, though it was welcomed, especially in Latvia. Although the relationship between Archbishop Jānis and Kārlis Ulmanis was ambiguous, in June 1934, the Latvian Orthodox journal *Ticība un Dzīve* wrote:

> We have suffered many ideological and material losses over the last years because there was no strong and authoritative state government. The government was weak since it always had to account for specific wishes from a variety of political parties, who did not have Latvia's but only their own interests in mind. [...] Obviously, this situation could not last. And look, the turning point has arrived. [...] 15 May 1934 is the boundary which divides the past, with its cowardly fragility and exaggerated democracy from the future. [...]
>
> We are no politicians, we are no lawyers, therefore we leave the political and juridical component of the new government activities to the politicians and lawyers. We are Christians, friends of the church, interested in the contemporary situation and future perspectives from *our* viewpoint and especially what the new governmental direction can offer the Christian Faith and Church in general and the Orthodox in particular? Will our position in the Latvian State be better or worse than before? [...] These are the questions that interest our readers. And we can answer them directly and clearly, without idle gossip: The first steps of the new power holders show that *this government does not oppose the Christian Faith, but even plans to support it more* than was earlier the case. [...] We, as Christians, may now relax and look into the future with the best hopes.[517]

---

514 Plakans, 1995, p. 132-135; Raun, 2001, p. 115-119; Pajur, 2001, p. 165-172; Feldmanis, 2001, p. 218-222.

515 Plakans, 1995, p. 133. See also Raun, 2001, p. 118-123; Oberländer, 2001, p. 5-8, 13; Pajur, 2001, p. 178-213; Feldmanis, 2001, p. 222-243; Butulis, 2001.

516 Pajur, 2001, p. 183. See also Plakans, 1995, p. 135; Butulis, 2001, p. 250-251.

517 P. Kaltiņš, "Jauns laikmets Latvijas vēsturē" [A new era in the history of Latvia] in *TuD*, 10/6, 1934, p. 81-82. Kaltiņš wrote numerous articles for the journal during 1934, speaking warmly about the new regime. On the relationship between Archbishop Jānis and Ulmanis, see Runce, 2008, p. 191-192. See also the ideologically tainted view in Balevics, 1987, p. 64-65.

Neither Ulmanis nor Päts excluded the Orthodox from the nation. On the contrary, the states de-secularised and introduced something akin to state churches, mainly in order to better control religious life. In the Estonian case, this included a new law, which introduced a distinction between a 'church' and a 'religious organisation.' Since a 'church' had to have more than 100,000 members, only the Lutheran Church and the Orthodox Church could enjoy the privileges this status entailed, such as official representatives in government and some limited state support.[518] In Latvia, no new law regarding religion was passed until 1940, but *Vadoņis* (The Leader), as Ulmanis was called, installed the secular lawyer Edvards Dimiņš as head of the Department of Religious Affairs of the Ministry of the Interior. Dimiņs energetically entangled himself in internal church affairs and wrote propaganda articles for all ecclesiastical journals, aimed at strengthening the new authoritarian ideology.[519]

Within the Orthodox Church, the language of the journals changed and became more nationalistic. The editorials of the new official journal of the Estonian Orthodox Church from 1936, *Elutõde* (Truth of Life), were primarily devoted to topics such as 'church and state,' 'faith and nation,' 'patriotism,' and 'where lies the future of the nation?' Incidentally, the editor in chief of the new journal was Nikolai Päts, the brother of regime head Konstantin Päts. However, apart from passing mentions of their common education at the Riga Orthodox School and Seminary, there is nothing to suggest any close relationship between the two brothers.[520] In the Latvian Church, especially after Archbishop Jānis' assassination and the cleansing of the Synod of 'subversive' actors, strong

---

518 "Kirikute ja usuühingute seadus" [Law on churches and religious organisations] in *Riigi Teataja*, 17/107, 1934, p. 1821-1826; Konstantin Päts, "Kirik pole täitnud temale pandud lootusi" [The church has not fulfilled the hopes put in it] in *ET*, 3/3, 1938, p. 29; Ringvee, 2008, p. 182.

519 P. Kaltiņš, "Izglītibas ministrs L. Adamovičs par baznīcas un valsts attiecibām Latvijā" [L. Adamovičs, Minister of Education, on state-church relations] in *TuD*, 10/7, 1934, p. 98-99; "Visas Latvijas pareizticīgo garidznieku sapulce" [The Meeting of all Latvian Orthodox clergy] in *TuD*, 12/8, 1936, p. 119-120; E. Dimiņš, "Latvijas 20 gadu pastāvēšanas svētkos" [The 20th anniversary of the Latvian existence] in *TuD*, 14/21, 1938, p. 322-324; E. Dimiņš, "Jaunam laikam, - jaunas sirdis" [New era, - new heart] in *TuD*, 14/24, 1938, p. 370-371; E. Dimiņš, "Религиозная жизнь Обновленной Латвии" [Religious life in New Latvia] in *ViŽ*, 17/6, 1939, p. 127-128; Runce, 2008, p. 180-184. For the role of Dimiņš in the reorganisation of the Latvian Orthodox Church 1934-1936, see also Balevics, 1964, p. 237-244.

520 In fact, it is impossible to say whether Konstantin Päts felt any link with his Orthodox past. In his biographies, the years at the Riga Orthodox School and Seminary are always mentioned, but the Orthodox Church does not figure in later years. According to the Lutheran pastor and *Riigikogu* member L. Raudkepp, Päts was among the most energetic Estonian politicans when it came to the concerns of the church. However, Raudkepp always talked only about the Lutheran Church, never mentioning the Orthodox. Raudkepp, 1934, p. 365-368.

'Latvianising' tendencies came to the fore. This was especially notable in relation to the Latgale region, which now took on a role similar to Petserimaa in Estonia in the 1920s. When an Orthodox liturgy in Latgale was held in Latvian for the first time, this was mentioned in the Orthodox journal.[521] P. Kaltiņš had written about the Latvianising of Latgale as early as in October 1934:

> There cannot be disagreement that the Latgalian movement to return to their nation [i.e. to become Latvians] is to be welcomed and supported. It is first and foremost to be welcomed from the point of view of the state, for a unitary nation is the strength of a state. It is also to be welcomed from cultural, social, and economic points of view, for the Latgalians will achieve cultural and economic prosperity much quicker together with the Latvians than in their region alone. But we also regard this movement (if only it is serious) from the point of view of the Orthodox Church. And from this point of view, we can only welcome the movement. In much of Latvia, there are still such politicians, whose wisdom's alpha and omega is that Orthodoxy is a Russian faith and adverse to the Latvian national interests. [...] If the Russified Orthodox Latgalians are re-Latvianised, then that would be a sign forcing our politicians to pay much more attention to the Orthodox Church than what has so far been the case in independent Latvia.[522]

Another important topic for the Orthodox journals in this context during the second half of the 1930s was a renewed debate concerning religious instruction. This was connected with the new regimes' emphasis on creating better citizens.[523] In Estonia, a new law on education was adopted in 1934, slightly raising the amount of religious instruction in the curriculum. The Lutheran Church welcomed the move, but the commentators in the Orthodox journals were sceptical as to its efficiency as long as the question concerning confessional or inter-confessional religious instruction was not solved.[524] Assurance that everything was

---

521 "Dievkalpošanas Latgalē latviešu valodā" [Liturgy in Latgale in Latvian] in *TuD*, 13/23, 1937, p. 365; "Latviski Dievkalpojumi Baltinavā" [Latvian Liturgy in Baltinava] in *TuD*, 14/4, 1938, p. 62; Balevics, 1964, p. 246-247. See also chapter 3.1.1. for the language issue.

522 P. Kaltiņš, "Tautiskā atmoda Latgalē" [The national awakening in Latgale] in *TuD*, 10/10, 1934, p. 147-148. See also Balevics, 1964, p. 244-251. For more on the general perception, see chapter 3.2.3.

523 Pajur, 2001, p. 191, 207-208; Feldmanis, 2001, p. 237-238; Butulis, 2001, p. 263-264, 279-281.

524 Konstantin Kokla, "Usuõpetus koolis" [Religious education in schools] in *UjE₂*, 2/8, 1934, p. 131-132; Konstantin Kokla, "Pisikesed pahed kiriklikus asjaajamises" [Tiny sins in the administration of the church] in *UjE₂*, 3/4b, 1935, p. 75-76; Konstantin Kokla, "Mõnda kirikuelu pisipahedest" [Some words on the mini-sins of ecclesiastic life] in *UjE₂*, 3/5, 1935, p. 94-96; K. "Usuõpetus vähja-käiku tegemas!" [Religious instruction shows cancerous sprouts!] in *ET*, 1/6, 1936, p. 2-3; Peeter Laredei, "Usuõpetus koolis" [Religious instruction in the school] in *ET*, 1/9, 1936, p. 6-7; Nikolai Päts, "Usuline kasvatus ja kool" [Religious upbringing and the school] in *ET*, 3/15-16, 1938, p. 169-

in order by Nikolai Kann, Minister of Education 1933-1936 and an Orthodox Estonian, did not calm the discussions.[525] Next to the discussion on the formal framework of religious instruction, the debate occasionally included a much more universal valuation of religious instruction as a counterweight to the pitfalls of the modern world:

> In our current times, in the post-world-war era, we can observe developments never seen before to the same extent. We can see attempts to bring the youth in line with one's own political, national and governmental organisations. Many organisations lure the youngsters into their bosom, not considering whether growing minds need such links. The youth are often ruined, alien goals and tasks are cultivated in them, destroying their morality and even their creativity, breeding individualism, separatism, pessimism, international enmity, and fraternal hatred instead.
>
> This is where religious instruction comes in and where the church is called to co-operate in education. Church and school should find each other here.[526]

The editorial continues to condemn the modern focus on physical strength, external beauty, and material wealth while praising religious and cultural history and authority.

In the Latvian case, the discussion was similar. A letter to the editor from 1934, signed with 'A. K. from Laubere,' described the unsatisfactory situation of religious instruction in Latvia:

> Before the great World War, each parish had a school, where the children not only learned all the necessary academic subjects, but were equally brought up in a strict Orthodox spirit and taught to love their church and its songs [...] That was once. But now! Now, only the songs and prayers of alien faiths are sung and spoken in the schools and sometimes even anti-Orthodox ones. And then, when the Orthodox children finish school, they are in a state far from their faith. And that is only natural, for they know nothing about the faith. The Orthodox Church is entirely foreign to them; they know nothing about either the function or the order of our holy service. [...] They are more acquainted with the Lutheran Church and Faith than with their own [...]
>
> It is true that the current laws allow Orthodox pupils classes in their own faith. However, it is not so easy to get a teacher of Orthodox religion, because the school needs ten Orthodox children. In those cases where a borough has two schools and each of them only nine Orthodox pupils, there will be no Orthodox teacher. But there exist even schools where fifteen to twenty or even thirty-five Orthodox pupils

170; Anton Angerjas, "Kool ja konfessionaalne usuõpetus" [The school and confessional religious instruction] in *ET*, 3/18, 1938, p. 202-203. See also chapter 2.2.4.

525 Nikolai Kann, "Usuõpetuse tähtsusest ja korraldamisest koolides" [The importance and organisation of religious instruction] in *ET*, 1/1, 1936, p. 2-3.

526 "Kirik ja kool" [Church and school] in *ET*, 2/15, 1937, p. 181.

learn, where there is also no Orthodox teacher. Here, the children's parents, who accept such a situation, are to blame.[527]

Instead of complaining about the lack of official instruction, the journal soon published a long article about how to teach one's own children the basics of the Orthodox faith at home.[528] A new law from July 1934 stipulated that religious instruction should be obligatory, together with participation in certain religious ceremonies, while it had earlier been only optional. Moreover, the new law allowed a much closer control of the teachers by the relevant ecclesiastic authorities, so the latter welcomed it:

> As we see, the new law is very promising for us, and only those Orthodox children, who go to schools with less than ten Orthodox pupils remain in an unfortunate position. In such cases, there is no other way than teaching the children about Orthodoxy at home with the help of the parents and local clergy, as we wrote about earlier.[529]

However, at the first opportunity to test the new law, the opening ceremony of the 1934 academic year, there were only Lutheran services available, and angry parents complained in the Orthodox journal that their children were required to participate in the Lutheran ceremony. More complaints about the implementation of the new law followed, claiming that in reality, nothing had changed.[530] The last treatment of religious instruction in the Latvian Orthodox journal was a notice reporting a Synod resolution that had been sent to the Ministry of Education, bringing these deviations to its attention.[531] The Latvians then turned to the question of theological education. The Riga Orthodox Seminary, which had reopened in 1926 and had educated more than eighty priests for the Latvian Church since then, was closed in 1936.[532] Instead, a theological institute was

---

527 A. K. no Lauberes, "Pareizticības stāvoklis Latvijā" [The situation of Orthodoxy in Latvia] in *TuD*, 10/3, 1934, p. 38-39. This same reader explained the concrete situation in his home parish in the next number: A. K. no Lauberes, "Grūti izvedams likums" [A law, difficult to implement] in *TuD*, 10/4, 1934, p. 58.

528 Pēteris Gredzens, "Laidiet bērniņus pie Manis nākt" [Let the children come to Me] in *TuD* 10/6, 1934, p. 86-87.

529 "Ticības mācība skolās pēc jaunā izglītibas likuma" [Religious instruction in schools according to the new law on education] in *TuD*, 10/9, 1934, p. 136-137; Jānis Jansons, "Латвийская Православная Церковь и 1934-1939 г.г." [The Latvian Orthodox Church from 1934 to 1939] in *ViŽ*, 17/6, 1939, p. 126.

530 Vairāku vecāka vārdā K. [K. in the name of many parents], "Vēstule redakcijai" [Letter to the editor] in *TuD*, 10/10, 1934, p. 158; P. Kārkliņš, "Jaunais likums vecās sliedēs" [The new law on the old tracks] in *TuD*, 11/1, 1935, p. 8-9.

531 "Ticības mācibas jautajumā" [On the question of religious instruction] in *TuD*, 12/9, 1936, p. 138.

532 Bursaks, "Rīgas Garigais Seminars likvidets" [Liquidation of the Riga Orthodox Seminary] in *TuD*, 12/9, 1936, p. 136. *Bursaks* was the nickname of the alumni of this seminary. See also Pazāne, 2008, p. 36-38.

established and, later, a Department of Orthodox Theology within the Faculty of Theology in the predominantly Lutheran University of Latvia.[533] Metropolitan Augustīns later praised this department as a way to diminish confessional hatred:

> We want our church's future servants, who are to serve God and the people in the folds of Orthodoxy, to receive their higher education from that same institution where the other servants of our nation deepen their academic knowledge. All those working among people have one and the same task – serving our nation, form it spiritually and materially and look after its spiritual and material well-being. It is good when the new workers learn to respect and appreciate their co-workers in different life areas and specialisations while preparing for their life's work. This prevents misunderstanding and its accomplices, hatred and secession. Our nation is divided into various faiths. This religious plurality was often the reason for hatred and division. We do not want any of that in the life of our Latvia.[534]

Compared to the University of Tartu, the department was pretty successful, with twelve students in the first year and twenty-one in the following. However, no students were able to finish their course due to the Second World War.[535]

Both the Estonian and the Latvian Orthodox Church developed new statutes after the regime changes. In Estonia new statutes, corresponding with the 1934 law on churches and religious organisations, were written by Metropolitan Aleksander and the Synod and filed with the Ministry of the Interior in 1935.[536] According to the German political scientist Helmut Risch, the changes to previous statutes were fundamental: "Although the statutes keep a parliamentary-conciliar appearance, they are totally authoritarian-episcopalian in essence. The

533 "Garidznieku sagatavošanas jautājums Sinodē" [The question of preparing clergy in the Synod] in *TuD*, 12/9, 1936, p. 138; "Pareizticīgo teoloģiskā Instituta atklāšana" [The opening of the Orthodox Theological Institute] in *TuD*, 12/10, 1936, p. 154-155; "Latvijas Universitātes Teoloģiskās fakultātes pareizticīgo nodaļa uzsākuši darbību" [The Orthodox Department of the Latvian University Theological Faculty started work.] in *TuD*, 13/18, 1937, p. 283-284; "Kā darbosies pareizticīgo nodaļa universitātē" [What happens in the Orthodox Department of the University] in *Brīvā Zeme*, 12.01.1938, p. 10. The former rector of the Riga Orthodox Seminary, Archpriest Jānis Jansons, was transferred to the University. According to some commentators, this transfer was staged in order to diminish Jansons' influence, for he had been seen as the most dangerous enemy to Metropolitan Augustīns. See Balevics, 1964, p. 248-249; Gavrilin, 2009, p. 91.

534 Augustīns Pētersons, "Mitropolīta Augustīna runa pirmā pareizticīgo dievkalpojumā Latvijas Universitātē" [Metropolitan Augustīns' speech at the first Orthodox service at the University of Latvia] in *TuD*, 14/19, 1938, p. 290. See also "Pirmais pareizticīgo dievkalpojums Latvijas Universitātē" [The first Orthodox service at the University of Latvia] in *TuD*, 14/19, 1938, p. 300.

535 "Iz L. U. Teoloģijas pareizticīgo nodaļas vēstures" [From the history of the L. U. department of Orthodox Theology] in *TuD*, 16/8, 1940, p. 121-122.

536 "Eesti Apostliku-õigeusu Kiriku põhimäärus" [The statutes of the Estonian Apostolic Orthodox Church] in *Riigi Teataja*, 18/48, 1935, p. 1354-1376.

authority, with which the almost monarchically ruling [Metropolitan] is vested, is now extended to include the last word on all important questions."[537] The fact that these statutes were prepared and passed without any *täiskogu*, demonstrates that democratic procedures had become discredited in Estonia by 1935. The new statutes changed the frequency of the *täiskogu*, which would now meet only every five years. Moreover, the Metropolitan could now deny an elected delegate the right to participate. *Elutõde*, the official journal of the church, noted in autumn of 1936 that "although the new statutes are still young, their positive consequences are already evident; organising church life has definitely become more predictable and the inner order more secure, which in turn has made religious life much more intensive."[538] The only *täiskogu* meeting under these new auspices occurred in 1937, and there was no criticism voiced from within the church regarding the new statutes.[539]

In Latvia, new statutes were necessary to account for the changed canonical status of the church and its new role in the state. Once Metropolitan Augustīns was consecrated, he called a regular ecclesiastic *saeima* for July 1936, at which new statutes could be confirmed. These statutes were prepared by a commission of which E. Dimiņš had been an active member.[540] The *saeima* was planned to last only one day. In order for all urgent matters to be decided in only one day, "the Synod, in close co-operation with Dimiņš, prepared 'rules of procedure' worthy of the fascist government. According to these rules, the *saeima* delegates were not allowed to criticise the *saeima* and its draconian agenda or even 'the activity of any other instance.'"[541] We need not rely on the above Marxist account, although its essence is certainly correct. The official account noted that:

> The *saeima* showed great trust in the head of the church also on the question of electing a new Synod. Metropolitan Augustīns read a notice to the *saeima*, listing the Synod members and deputies he would prefer. There was not a single vote against the clerical candidates, and although some few isolated votes opposed one or the other lay candidate, also this list was accepted with an overwhelming majority.[542]

According to the official account, the new statutes, which were unanimously confirmed, were "better suited to life's demands" but did not include funda-

---

537 Risch, 1937, p. 136. The original speaks about the 'Patriarch,' which is obviously an error. See also chapter 4.2.1. for more on Risch.

538 "Õigeusu kiriku elust Lätis ja Eestis" [From Orthodox Church Life in Latvia and Estonia] in *ET*, 1/35, 1936, p. 1-2.

539 Üks neist, "Usuelu teateid kohtadelt – Eesti Apostliku Õigeusu Kiriku Täiskogu" [Notes from local church life – The Estonian Church *Täiskogu*] in *UjE₂*, 5/8, 1937, p. 126-127.

540 Balevics, 1987, p. 85; Gavrilin, 2009, p. 86.

541 Balevics, 1964, p. 86. See also Gavrilin, 2009, p. 86-87.

542 "Latvijas Pareizticīgās Baznīcas Saeima" [The *saeima* of the Latvian Orthodox Church] in *TuD*, 12/8, 1936, p. 122. See also Balevics, 1987, p. 88.

mental changes.[543] According to Balevics, all discussion on the statutes was stifled, and they "completely eliminated parish autonomy."[544]

In both the Estonian and the Latvian Orthodox Church, there was new
emphasis on filling all bishops' seats. In the Estonian case, a Bishop of Narva
was finally elected during the *täiskogu* of 1937 after a vacancy of almost ten
years.[545] The new bishop, Pavel Dmitrovskij, was elected without discussion. An
anonymous *täiskogu* participant described the process as thus:

> The most exciting point on the agenda was the election of the Bishop of Narva. At
> almost every break, this issue was discussed and arguments for and against ethnic
> Eparchies were exchanged, especially since such an Eparchy does not benefit the
> church as a whole. Just prior to the election session, the information was orally
> transmitted that the Metropolitan himself would take personal responsibility for the
> future episcopal activities of the candidate of the Russians, attaching importance to
> an election without discussion. And thus it happened. One hundred twenty-five
> votes in favour, forty-six against. Archpriest P. Dmitrovski entered the speaker's
> podium, thanking the assembly for their trust and promising to serve the church and
> Estonia, where he had found a home, as bishop. The gathering sang 'Axios' –
> deeming him worthy. In the name of the Russians, Archpriest J. Bogojavlenskij
> thanked the Estonians for their trust, seeing the election of their preferred candidate
> as an opportunity for better inter-ethnic relations.[546]

The election of the first Latvian vicar bishop at the one-day *saeima* of 1936
mentioned above was even more surreal:

> Metropolitan Augustīns read the notification of the department of religious affairs,
> accepting the two candidates for vicar bishop, Jēkabs Karps of Koknese and Pēteris
> Barbans of Viļķene, and defining Riga as the vicar bishop's seat. The voting began,
> but seeing as the *saeima* delegates could not agree on either of the candidates, a
> motion was submitted to leave the confirmation of either candidate to the personal
> decision of the Metropolitan. The motion was justified with reference to the role of
> the vicar bishop as the Metropolitan's assistant. The Metropolitan himself would
> then decide who was best suited to help him. The motion was welcomed
> euphorically and passed. This way, the election of a vicar bishop remained open –
> the ruling head of the church, Metropolitan Augustīns, would make a final decision.

---

543 "Latvijas Pareizticīgās Baznīcas Saeima" [The *saeima* of the Latvian Orthodox Church]
    in *TuD*, 12/8, 1936, p. 121.
544 Balevics, 1987, p. 87. See also Gavrilin, 2009, p. 86.
545 Üks neist, "Usuelu teateid kohtadelt – Eesti Apostliku Õigeusu Kiriku Täiskogu"
    [Notices from local church life – The Estonian *täiskogu*] in *UjE₂*, 5/8, 1937, p. 126-127.
546 Üks neist, "Usuelu teateid kohtadelt – Eesti Apostliku Õigeusu Kiriku Täiskogu"
    [Notices from local church life – The Estonian Church *Täiskogu*] in *UjE₂*, 5/8, 1937, p.
    126-127. See also "Narva piiskopi õnnistamisele" [The consecration of the Narva
    Bishop] in *Uus Eesti*, 3/156, 11.06.1937, p. 2; Nikolai Päts, "Kiriklikud sündmused seo-
    ses riigieluga" [Church events in connection with state life] in *ET*, 2/20, 1937, p. 241;
    Veritas, "Uus piiskopp – Ülempreester P. Dmitrovski pühitsemine piiskopiks" [New
    bishop – the consecration of Archpriest P. Dmitrovskij] in *ET*, 2/20, 1937, p. 249-250.

The *saeima* thus showed exceptionally strong trust in its bishop, and that is good, for whom to trust, if not one's head shepherd and blessing giver?![547]

Jēkabs Karps was chosen as vicar bishop and was consecrated Bishop of Jelgava.[548] In the summer of 1938, he was joined by Ādams Vītols as Bishop Aleksandrs of Jersika. The latter had not been elected by a *saeima*, but selected by the Metropolitan and the Synod.[549] Before the next regular *saeima* (scheduled for 1939), Metropolitan Augustīns pushed a statutory amendment through the Synod, scheduling the *saeima* to meet only every five years.[550]

In both the Estonian and Latvian cases, it is clear that the official press accounts of the events do not depict the entire reality. Especially in the Latvian case, it is difficult to ascertain the general mood in the Orthodox Church as a whole. A report from the Latvian secret services in January 1937 noted that "the opposition to Metropolitan Augustīns and each of his decisions is growing. The Orthodox express unhappiness that their actual leader and 'metropolitan' is the head of the Department of Religious Affairs of the Ministry of the Interior, E. Dimiņš, not Augustīns, for the latter only carries out the decisions of the former."[551] In the Estonian case, due to the existence of two competing journals, the press coverage is less one-sided and biased. However, Estonian society was still suspicious of the Russian wing of the Orthodox Church. For example, this was the case when the secular press in June 1934 reported about plans for a conference of Orthodox clergy in Narva, where "the separation of the Estonian and Russian parishes will come up for discussion, with the Russians returning under the Soviet Metropolitan Sergij."[552] It soon became clear that such reports were

---

547 "Latvijas Pareizticīgās Baznīcas Saeima" [The *saeima* of the Latvian Orthodox Church] in *TuD*, 12/8, 1936, p. 121. See also Balevics, 1987, p. 87.

548 "Kokneses virspriesteris Jēkabs Karps – Jelgavas Biskaps" [Archpriest Jēkabs Karps of Koknese – Bishop of Jelgava] in *TuD*, 12/8, 1936, p. 122-123; "Jelgavas biskapa Jēkaba iesvētīšana" [The consecration of Bishop Jēkabs of Jelgava] in *TuD*, 12 /10, 1936, p. 153-154. See also Balevics, 1987, p. 87.

549 "Būs trešais biskaps" [There will be a third bishop] in *TuD*, 14/6, 1938, p. 92; "Virspriesteris Adams Vītols – biskapu amata kandidats" [Archpriest Adams Vītols – candidate for bishop] in *TuD*, 14/7, 1938, p. 109; "Jersika biskapa iesvētīšana" [The consecration of the Bishop of Jersika] in *TuD*, 14/13, 1938, p. 205; "Jersika biskapa Aleksandra iesvētīšana und ievešana amatā" [The consecration and enthronisation of Bishop Aleksandrs of Jersika] in *TuD*, 14/14, 1938, p. 214-220. See also Balevics, 1987, p. 93. Jersika was the historical centre of medieval Latvian Orthodoxy, situated in Latgale. In the following year, the designation was changed to Bishop of Madona.

550 "Grozījumi Latvijas Pareizticīgās baznīcas statutos" [Changes in the statutes of the Latvian Orthodox Church] in *TuD*, 15/12, 1939, p. 189; Gavrilin, 2009, p. 89-91.

551 Cited in Balevics, 1987, p. 89. See also Gavrilin, 2009, p. 89.

552 "Ap.-usu koguduste õpetajate konverents Narvas" [Orthodox parish clergy conference in Narva] in *PL*, 29/158, 12.06.1934, p. 5; "Maruvenelased üldkirikust lahti?" [The Russian chauvinists to secede from the main church?] in *VM*, 18/135, 13.06.1934, p. 3.

no more than scaremongering. The conference was organised by the Baltic German *Baltische Rußlandarbeit* and supported by the Estonian Orthodox bishops. Its aims were to improve ecumenical dialogue and to reveal areas where the Baltic German pastors could employ their intellectual and financial resources in the fight against atheism in the Russian parishes.[553]

The move towards more authoritarian language, the stronger emphasis on the national elements in the Estonian and Latvian Orthodox Church, and their alignment of the churches with their respective state apparatuses were accompanied by stronger inter-Baltic Orthodox co-operation. Whereas the Orthodox journals in the 1920s had focussed on developments internal to the respective country, the 1930s saw a rise in foreign news, especially concerning the neighbours. Moreover, joint activities increased markedly.[554] The first joint gathering of clergy happened in 1934, on the occasion of the 40th anniversary of Metropolitan Aleksander's completion of the Riga Orthodox Seminary. All Estonian and Latvian alumni of the Class of 1894 were invited to Tallinn, where they were "received with exceptional hospitality. [...] After the liturgy, there was a litany for the deceased classmates and for the Latvian and Estonian Orthodox Churches. Archpriest Andrejs Jansons of Alūksne spoke about the co-operation between the two churches."[555]

This co-operation was deepened when Archbishop Jānis was murdered and Metropolitan Aleksander temporarily took over the spiritual leadership of the Latvian Orthodox Church. The Latvian journal published a close analysis of the Estonian road to autonomy by the lawyer J. Bērziņš in 1935.[556] A closer co-operation was initiated after the Latvian Church received a *tomos* of autonomy from Constantinople, thirteen years after the Estonian Church received a similar

---

553 "Narvast" [From Narva] in *VM*, 18/136, 14.06.1934, p. 6; "Narvast" [From Narva] in *VM*, 18/138, 16.06.1934, p. 6; "Ap.-usu koguduste mureks usuvastane liikumine" [The worry of the Orthodox parishes is the anti-religious movement] in *PL*, 29/163, 17.06.1934, p. 2. See also Kahle, 1959, p. 236-271, esp. p. 255-258. See chapter 3.2.2. for another discussion concerning the *Baltische Rußlandarbeit*.

554 Such co-operation had already taken place between the Estonian and Finnish Churches for several years, mainly due to the ethnic Estonian Archbishop Hermann (Aav) leading the Finnish Orthodox Church from 1923. See "Soome külalised" [Finnish visitors] in *UE*, 7/7, 1927, p. 2; "Ühte ja teist kiriku ligidalt – Kiriku Täiskogu" [This and that touching church life – the ecclesiastic *täiskogu*] in *UE*, 9/8, 1929, p. 7; "Vastukülaskäigu Soome ap. kirikul" [A return visit to the Finnish Orthodox Church] in *UE*, 10/7, 1930, p. 8.

555 "Latvijas un Igaunijas pareizticīgo garidznieku satikšanās" [The gathering of Orthodox clergy from Latvia and Estonia] in *TuD*, 10/8, 1934, p. 126-127. Alūksne is close to the Latvian-Estonian border and Archpriest A. Jansons was one of the very few Latvian clergy able to read Estonian. He occasionally published translated articles from the Estonian Orthodox journals in *TuD*.

556 J. Bērziņš, "Kā Igaunijas pareizticīgo baznīca dabuja autonomiju" [How the Estonian Orthodox Church became autonomous] in *TuD*, 11/6, 1935, p. 87-88.

tomos. Starting with Metropolitan Augustīns, every new bishop in Finland, Estonia, and Latvia was always consecrated by the bishops of all three churches. Moreover, the head bishops paid each other official visits, which were reported on in detail in the Orthodox journals.[557] Co-operation with the Polish Orthodox Church was occasionally discussed, as well.[558] The *tomos* from Constantinople directed the Estonian, Latvian, and Finnish Churches to hold a yearly joint Synod of Bishops. Such Synods met in 1937 and 1938, before the international situation made further meetings impossible.[559]

Not only among the bishops but also among the ordinary faithful, there was an increase in inter-Baltic co-operation. Travel reports from the monasteries in Estonia and Finland were common-place, as were reports about parish or seminary excursions to or visits from the neighbouring countries. Metropolitan Aleksander welcomed the first excursion from a Latvian parish to Tallinn in Summer 1936 with the words:

> [This excursion] must not be considered as some private group excursion, but it is an excursion that speaks the official language of the growing together of two nations – the Estonians and the Latvians and the strengthening of their spiritual bonds. This is a welcome step, made by the leaders of spiritual life at the Ascension parish in Riga, R. Blodons and P. Bērziņš, together with their congregation. This unifying bond between the Estonian and Latvian nations, whose fate is so close,[...] must be continuously strengthened, for only unity is strength and this unitary strength is especially powerful when it is structured around Christian love and tolerance.[560]

557 "Kirikuelu teateid - Osavõtt Läti Kiriku suursündmusest" [Church life notes - participation in the Latvian Church's major event] in *UjE₂*, 4/4, 1936, p. 50; "Latvijas Pareizticīgās baznīcas Mitropolita Augustīna ceļojums uz Igauniju un Somiju" [Latvian Orthodox Metropolitan Augustīns' travel to Estonia and Finland] in *TuD*, 12/10, 1936, p. 151-153; "Õigeusu kiriku elust Lätis ja Eestis" [From Orthodox Church Life in Latvia and Estonia] in *ET*, 1/35, 1936, p. 1-2; "Mitropolits Augustīns Igaunijas Baznīcas svinībās" [Metropolitan Augustīns at Estonian Church celebrations] in *TuD*, 13/19, 1937, p. 298; "Igaunijas un Somijas augstie Virsgani Rīgā" [The highest bishops of Estonia and Finland in Riga] in *TuD*, 14/14, 1938, p. 220-221.
558 "Poola piiskop Tallinnas" [The Polish bishop in Tallinn] in *ET*, 2/15, 1937, p. 191; -tis, "Veidojas Polijas un pārejo Baltijas pareizticīgo baznīcu kopdarbība" [Forming a co-operation between the Polish and the other Baltic Orthodox Churches] in *TuD*, 13/15, 1937, p. 237.
559 "Baltijas valstu pareizticīgo biskapu sanāksme (koncils) Somijā" [The meeting (council) of the Orthodox bishops of the Baltic countries] in *TuD*, 13/17, 1937, p. 263; J. Välbe, "Mitropoliit sõitis Soome" [The Metropolitan went to Finland] in *ET*, 2/17, 1937, p. 214; "Pareizticīgo biskapu sanāksme Petseros" [The meeting of the Orthodox bishops in Petseri] in *TuD*, 14/19, 1938, p. 304; E. T., "3-me riigi kirikujuhid Petseris" [The heads of the churches of three states in Petseri] in *ET*, 3/19, 1938, p. 216-217. See also Purmonen, 1986, p. 69-72; Larikka, 2004, Rimestad, 2009.
560 "Rīgas Debessbraukšanas draudze Tallinā" [The Ascension parish of Riga in Tallinn] in *TuD*, 12/7, 1936, p. 108-109.

Most of these reports contained other elements alongside the purely descriptive accounts of the visits. Describing a pilgrimage of the Ascension parish of Riga to the Petseri Monastery in Estonia, the author emotionally recounts the bus trip towards the border:

> At four pm, we, the pilgrims, reached the border separating our Fatherland from the neighbouring country. We happily left our Fatherland for a little while, for we knew that this journey was not for shallow pleasure, but in order to accomplish a serious task for the Latvian people and land, the fate of which our people and its leader Dr. K. Ulmanis have placed upon each of us. While organising the border formalities, we sent the following telegram:
>
> > To the Prime Minister Dr. K. Ulmanis – Riga
> >
> > Dear Mr. Prime Minister!
>
> Following your words – that every activity we do should be done for the good of our country and its people – we, the members of the Ascension parish, on our way as pilgrims to our neighbours – the Estonians, believe that this will benefit our country, for we will pray to God that the spirit of renewed Latvia will join us together in a stronger friendship and unity, not only within the Latvian nation, but also in its already friendly relations with the neighbouring Estonian nation. May our mutual friendship become even stronger and inalienable![561]

In the Estonian travel articles, the emphasis was more on the comparative element, as this report on a visit of Finnish seminarians in Tallinn shows:

> The conversation between the head of the Estonian Church and the Finnish visitors happened in Estonian and Finnish, although this produced occasional misunderstandings. It was truly refreshing to see and hear the 'Finnishness' of the visitors, who did not bow down to either West or East. It is unfortunately not like that everywhere. [...] The interest of the Finns was especially directed at the pulpit in the Transfiguration church. They asked their guides numerous questions concerning the pulpit. Hearing that it is usually in use during services, they asked Fr. Lepik about permission to have a closer look while explaining that this innovation might soon take place in the Finnish Church.[562]

The Estonian Orthodox journal repeatedly referred to its southern and northern neighbours as models to look up to, partly because of the state support the Latvian and Finnish Church enjoyed.[563]

---

561 Svētceļnieks [Pilgrim], "Rīgas Debessbraukšanas draudzes svētceļojums uz Pečoriem Igaunijā" [The pilgrimage of Riga Ascension parish to Petseri in Estonia] in *TuD*, 11/8, 1935, p. 124-125.

562 J. K., "Meie armastame Eestit!" [We love Estonia!] in *ET*, 4/12, 1939, p. 141-142. See also chapter 3.1. for the discourse on liturgical renewal in the Estonian Orthodox Church.

563 "Õigeusu kiriku elust Lätis ja Eestis" [From Orthodox Church Life in Latvia and Estonia] in *ET*, 1/35, 1936, p. 1-2; "Soome õigeusu kirik 20 a." [20 years Orthodox Church of Finland] in *ET*, 4/1, 1939, p. 4-5. (The subtitle to this article reads: "The Finnish Ortho-

2.3.4. The 1930s Compared

In general, the 1930s were characterised by a gradual loss of the liberal, democratic and patriotic atmosphere that had characterised the 1920s, especially in Estonia. The crises of the early 1930s, the 'Monastery War' in Estonia and the Zaics case in Latvia, paved the way to more control of suspicious elements within the Orthodox Church both by state authorities and church leadership. In both cases, the crisis preceded the authoritarian *coup d'état* and, therefore, cannot be connected with the authoritarian regimes. More importantly, both crises were communicated not in the ecclesiastic journals but in the secular press. The ecclesiastic journals only attempted to occasionally rectify the picture given in the secular press. Mostly they pretended everything was in perfect order. This signals that an authoritarian mood was spreading through society at large, recognising and putting to use the media as a tool of propaganda and control.

The authoritarian regimes continued this style from 1934, making it official. The apogee of the Latvian crisis, the murder of Archbishop Jānis, happened five months after the Ulmanis coup and provided the new regime with a welcome pretence to increase its intervention in the church's internal affairs. This intervention was secured with the introduction of a government representative in the Synod, which remained more or less influential even after the normalisation of church affairs in 1936. The Päts regime in Estonia did not have such a pretext, but it still indirectly increased its influence on the church through the new law on churches and religious organisations, which required a much closer cooperation between church and state than had hitherto been the case. In the Orthodox press, this could be seen in the proliferation of national-patriotic articles. The journals turned more to subjects like identity, history, and national consciousness, rather than matters of church structure and governance. These matters were, more often than earlier, communicated as *faits accomplis* rather than issues under consideration.

It is difficult to speculate where developments in the two cases would have led if the war had not interrupted them. The approach of war was not lost on the two Baltic Orthodox Churches. However, there was not much coverage of the course of the war in the Orthodox journals. The official policy in both Latvia and Estonia was to pretend that the two countries were safe. This pretense crumbled in June 1940 when the Soviet Union staged peaceful socialist take-overs and occupied the territories later in the summer.[564] Exceptions to the above pol-

---

dox Church is the culturally most developed Christian congregation in the world."); J. K., "Meie armastame Eestit!" [We love Estonia!] in *ET*, 4/12, 1939, p. 141-142.

564 Plakans, 1995, p. 141-144; Raun, 2001, p. 139-146. See also M. Mäessa, "Säilitagem rahu, ärevuseks pole põhjust!" [Let's stay calm, no need to worry!] in *ET*, 4/17, 1939, p. 173.

icy were a mention of the changes the beginning of the war inflicted on the Orthodox Churches of Lithuania, Poland, and Finland[565] and a notice on the occasion of Hitler's call to the Baltic Germans for an *Umsiedlung* (resettlement) to the *Reich*.[566] All Estonian Orthodox journals suddenly ceased publication in June 1940, as did the Russian-language journal of the Latvian Orthodox Church. This was most probably due to the ongoing war and Soviet influence, which involved restructuring of the local Orthodox Church. The developments leading to this restructuring are extremely complex and have been interpreted differently by various scholars.[567] Suffice it to say that by the beginning of the German occupation in the summer of 1941, both Metropolitan Aleksander of Estonia and Metropolitan Agustīns of Latvia had publicly repented in the Moscow Patriarchate of the 'schism' they had instituted and promised to return to the Patriarchate of Moscow. That both retracted these promises under the German occupation and thereby caused a split in the local Orthodox Churches need not interest us here.

As mentioned above, the beginning of the Soviet occupation in June 1940 stifled the printed discourse on Orthodoxy in Estonia. The remainder was either heavily censored or pure propaganda. The Latvian-language Orthodox journal, *Ticība un Dzīve*, however, published three more issues before August 1940, when it suddenly stopped. These three issues allow an interesting glimpse into the mood of at least some Latvian Orthodox circles after the Soviet take-over. In an article titled 'A New Era in Latvian history' from July 1940, the author[568] asked what the new Soviet-friendly government meant to the Orthodox faithful of Latvia:

---

565 "Ārzemes" [Abroad] in *TuD*, 15/24, 1939, p. 383-384; Д. Ишевский, "Возстановление Литовско-Виленской Епархии" [The reopening of the Eparchy of Vilnius and Lithuania] in *PS*, 9/12, 1939, p. 169-173. Vilnius, which had been part of Poland since 1922 was handed over to Lithuania in October 1939. Metropolitan Elevferij of Vilnius and All Lithuania could finally take up residence in the city of his denomination. In Finland, the approaching Soviet army endangered the Orthodox Church, whose members lived primarily in the border regions.

566 "Pareizticīgo vāciešu draudze slēgta" [The German Orthodox congregation closed down] in *TuD*, 15/23, 1939, p. 365; Usumees, "Mõtteid sakslaste lahkumise puhul" [Thoughts on the departure of the Germans] in *UjE₂*, 7/12, 1939, p. 179-180. For the call itself, see von Hehn, 1984, p. 75-135. See also chapter 4.2.2 for the historiography discussion this call caused in the Estonian Orthodox journals.

567 For the Estonian case, see Prekup, 1998, p. 21-22; Aleksij, 1999, p. 401; Sõtsov, 2002, p. 290-297; Sõtsov, 2004, p. 34-35; Kala, 2007, p. 62-68. For the Latvian case, see Balevics, 1987, p. 106-109; Strods, 2005, p. 144-159; Kalniņš, Jānis, 2007, p. 71-80; Gavriļins, 2008; Gavrilin, 2009, p. 107-137.

568 Signing with P. K., this is possibly the same Pēteris Kaltiņš that euphorically welcomed the Ulmanis-regime.

And the answer to those questions has already been given by the new government. Namely, *the new government of Latvia has declared religious freedom and the equality of all faiths.* This declaration satisfies us completely. We Orthodox never strove for the privileges of the other faiths, but freedom of conscience and religion has always been important to us. [...] Although not officially, the Roman Catholic Church has enjoyed priority treatment, not only in relation to the Orthodox faith, but even over the Lutheran Church. Now, these privileges are done with, and we thank our new government for that. [...] If and to what extent the new government will support the churches is not yet decided, but according to the declaration, the treatment will be unitary. That is the main point to us. [...]

Concerning the consequences of the government's declared strengthening of the friendship with the Soviet Union, which has promised to keep Latvia out of the current war – we also have no reason to protest, if only because the Soviet Union has promised not to interfere in Latvia's internal affairs. On the contrary, we should start thinking whether the Orthodox Church of Latvia can do anything to help strengthen this friendship. First of all, has the time not come to think about a return to the jurisdiction of the Patriarchate of Moscow? The switch to the Ecumenical Patriarch's jurisdiction happened [...] because of the political circumstances at the time. And currently, a return to the jurisdiction of the Moscow Patriarchate can only benefit us, obviously if the internal autonomy we have achieved by the Ecumenical *tomos* is not restricted again. [...]

We look into the future with confidence in God and trust in our new government and the principles of its declaration.[569]

Whether this is pure propaganda or real belief in the goodwill of the communist regime is difficult to ascertain. The editor of the journal, Pēteris Gredzens, wrote an answer in the second number from July 1940, emphasising that a return to the Patriarchate of Moscow, as the Mother Church of the Latvian Orthodox, would be the only correct solution. This return could occur in three ways, according to Gredzens:

The best and easiest way would be if the Metropolitan and the Synod take the initiative, or even the Metropolitan only, without the Synod, who would be able to say: 'Here we are, I and these children God has given in my care.' If the Metropolitan and the Synod do not do that, then it is possible for the Orthodox population to become active. Considering the current political situation, they will doubtlessly succeed, but that would not be as smooth and neat, as with the Metropolitan and Synod doing it. Finally, if not the clerical leadership and not even the population, then the proposition might come from Moscow, that is the third possibility.[570]

---

569 P. K., "Jauns laikmets Latvijas vēsturē" [A new era in the history of Latvia] in *TuD*, 16/13, 1940, p. 194-195. The same issue also brought a long article on the occasion of the 350th anniversary of the Moscow Patriarchate: "Maskavas Patriarhijas 350 gadi" [350th anniversary of the Moscow Patriarchate] in *TuD*, 16/13, 1940, p. 202-203.

570 Pēteris Gredzens, "Ņemiet vērā to laiku" [Take heed in these times] in *TuD*, 16/14, 1940, p. 210-211.

This was the first time that the journal indirectly criticised the Latvian ecclesiastic leadership, and the division between those loyal to Moscow and those suspicious of Moscow, which had been suppressed until then, became apparent. More importantly, this division did not conform to but transcended the ethnic boundary. In the very last issue of the journal, Kirils Zaics appeared again, writing about his hope that the Latvian Church would return to Moscow. The same issue presented a Latvian translation of the Act of Re-Admission of the Polish Bishop Aleksej (Gromadskij) to the Moscow Patriarchate, under the heading 'an interesting document.'[571] However, the beginning of this new discourse no longer occured in a liberal context and did not have a chance to develop. It was, therefore, no more than an appendix to the interwar discourse on Latvian Orthodoxy, revealing a certain criticism of the way the Latvian Orthodox Church structures developed after 1934.

A similar appendix to the interwar discourse undoubtedly circulated in the Estonian Orthodox Church, but there are no published records of it. The first free publications follopwing the occupation were the reminiscences of Orthodox Estonians and Latvians in exile, which were heavily biased by personal experiences of war and exile.[572] The 'natural' development of the Orthodox Church in Estonia and Latvia was hindered by the power play of the great European powers and the result was unfinished ecclesiastic structures. The structural debates of the 1920s and 1930s were never carried through to their conclusion and had to be taken up anew when Estonia and Latvia regained independence in 1991. In Estonia, this nearly resulted in a schism of the worldwide Orthodox Church and a situation that is still canonically delicate.[573] In Latvia, although there are voices of discontent and criticism, the church is ruled with a strong hand that keeps it unified.[574]

---

571 "Lasitāju balsis" [The voice of the readers] in *TuD*, 16/15, 1940, p. 239; "Interesants documents" [An interesting document] in *TuD*, 16/15, 1940, p. 239-240. The Polish Orthodox Church had received full autocephaly from the Patriarch of Constantinople in 1924.
572 See Starcs, 1954; Juhkam, 1961; Laatsi, 1966; Cherney, 1985.
573 Rimestad, *forthcoming*, 2013a; Rimestad, *forthcoming*, 2013b.
574 See Kalniņš, Jānis, 2007; *Latvijas Pareizticīgā Baznīca*, 2009.

3. Orthodox Baltic Identity: Language and Tradition

The second challenge of modernity refers to the way modern organisations, including religious organisations, manage the identity of their members. It is no longer enough to refer to tradition and divine will in order to legitimise demands for conformity. Rather, justification has to be rooted in rational arguments and their management monitored and facilitated by the organisation. This challenge arises in two main dimensions: within the organisation and externally to it. The internal dimension includes issues of reform and appropriation; the external dimension is more concerned with identity preservation and uniqueness. In order to understand the discussions regarding the internal and external dimensions in the Baltic periphery of the Orthodox world, it is important to analyse their pre-history in the Russian Empire. The following chapters each provide such an analysis before turning to the specific Baltic case study.

3.1. The Internal Dimension

The discourse concerning the internal dimension of Orthodox identity centres on the question of whether adaptations of the liturgy and church life are possible and what they should look like. The idea of reforming ecclesiastic life had existed in the Russian Empire since Tsar Aleksander II initiated a range of sweeping societal, economic, and agrarian reforms in the 1860s.[1] Once Russian society started to modernise as a result of these reforms, a critical discourse began to form within the Russian Orthodox Church.[2] This discourse complained that the church was disintegrating into three groups: the lay parishioners, the white clergy (married parish priests), and the black clergy (unmarried bishops and monastics). The large majority of lay parishioners were peasants, who had been freed from serfdom only in 1861 and were to a large extent analphabetic.[3] The white (i.e. parish) clergy were a relatively closed social estate. However, they were often just as poor as the parishioners and, therefore, dependent on them.[4] The black clergy, i.e. the monks and the bishops, were often viewed as conservative worldly despots rather than as spiritual leaders. This impression

---

1   I call these reforms sweeping; although they were carried not as acts of geniality but rather as responses to social unrest. Tsar Aleksander II signed the reform proposals of his ministers rather half-heartedly and brought a certain modernisation to Russian society without really fighting for it. See Eklof et al., 1994; Engelstein, 2009.

2   Jockwig, 1971, p. 31-55; Weber, Renate, 1993; Manchester, 2008.

3   The peasants in the Baltic region constitute an exception here, with their relatively high literacy rate.

4   Jockwig, 1971, p. 52; Manchester, 2008.

was especially accentuated during the authoritative term in office of *Oberproku-ror* K. P. Pobedonoscev (1880-1905), an ultra-conservative statesman who turned the church into a state department and did not tolerate any bishop who did not follow his line of policy.[5]

However, discourse within the church was hampered by censorship and the frozen structures of the church, especially under Pobedonoscev. Only when Tsar Nikolai II proclaimed freedom of conscience and press as a result of the failed revolution of 1905 did the discourse really gain force. The freedoms granted were far from extensive, but they enabled the Orthodox Church to discuss and criticise its structures much more freely than had heretofore been the case.[6] One of the first actions of the Most Holy Synod after the Manifesto of Tolerance of 1905 was calling for the bishops to comment on current structures and propose improvements. The numerous responses to this call were published as three volumes in 1906.[7] Although James W. Cunningham, an American Orthodox theologian who analysed these replies, called them 'a vanquished hope,' since the plans for ecclesiastic reform again had stalled by end of 1906, they set a starting point for the discussions, which returned with full force after the February Revolution of 1917.

During the short quasi-parliamentary period of Russian history between the February and October Revolutions of 1917, the Most Holy Synod issued new temporary parish statutes and organised a long-needed full council of the Rus-sian Orthodox Church, a *sobor*, to begin in August 1917.[8] Alongside structural questions, this *sobor* also discussed other aspects of internal church life, such as correction of the liturgical books, liturgical order (*bogoslužebnogo ustav*), and participation of the parishioners in the liturgy. These components of the *sobor*, as well as the discussions preceding them, all contributed to liturgical renewal in the Russian Orthodox Church, although no full scale reform of the church was achieved.[9]

The discussions that continued within the Estonian and Latvian Orthodox Churches during the interwar years happened at three different levels. First, the question of whether adaptations were permissible at all repeatedly caused debates in the Orthodox press. The concrete content of these reforms constituted the second level, whereas the third level consisted of the means of bringing changes about and assessments of criticisms. While discussions on the first level occurred primarily in the period prior to 1917, the second two levels constituted much of the interwar discourse. The three levels were closely intertwined and cannot easily be separated. In general, however, they were emphasised at differ-

---

5   Simon, 1969a; Polunov, 1996.
6   Tuchtenhagen, 1995; Hildermeier, 2000; Firsov, 2002.
7   Jockwig, 1971, p. 99-110; Cunningham, 1981; Firsov, 2002, p. 193-215.
8   Schulz, 1995, p. 122-140; Firsov, 2002, p. 485-534.
9   Balašov, 2001; Mojzeš, 2005, p. 25-154.

ent stages of the development of the discourse. The following sections will analyse this discourse with a focus on three main issues: language of the liturgy, the
style of liturgical music, and the calendar.

3.1.1. The Language of the Liturgy

The issue of language appeared throughout the interwar period at all three levels. The first level, whether an Estonian and Latvian liturgy was at all permitted
in the Orthodox Church, belonged primarily to the years before 1917. The
debate had been ongoing since the wave of conversions during the 1840s. The
Estonian and Latvian peasants converting to Orthodox Christianity knew no
Russian since the Baltic Germans had previously been their direct superiors.
Moreover, they were accustomed to the Lutheran Church in which understanding the service is much more important than in the Orthodox Church.
Finally, the literacy and education rate in the Baltic Provinces was many times
higher than in inner Russia. This created a need to provide a translation of the
Orthodox Liturgy, if only to enable the converts to roughly follow the church
Slavonic celebrations. Estonian and Latvian translations of the most important
liturgical texts had been commissioned at the Seminary of Pskov in 1842.[10] The
two young priests charged with carrying out the translations were sent to the
University of Dorpat (Tartu) to improve their rudimentary knowledge of Estonian and Latvian. Unfortunately, the only existing grammars of those two
languages were in German, which the two did not speak. The inspector of the
Pskov Seminary, A. S. Knjazev, offered to translate the grammars into Russian,
although he did not know either Estonian or Latvian himself. The resulting
translations of the liturgy obviously left much to be desired, although they
helped emancipate the nascent Estonian and Latvian native literatures from the
Baltic Germans.[11]

The question of whether the two languages could be used to celebrate the
liturgy itself was answered differently by each new Bishop of Riga. The answer
also varied from priest to priest. In some congregations, liturgy was always
Estonian or Latvian, in others only Church Slavonic, and in numerous congregations, a mixture was practiced. The wartime evacuation of Bishop Ioann
(Smirnov) of Riga to Tartu, firmly in the territory of the Estonian language,
prompted Orthodox Estonian nationalists to protest the absurdity of a spiritual
leader not understanding the language of his flock. One of the major demands of
the Estonian manifesto of 1916 was official endorsement of celebrating the Lit-

---

10 N.R. [Nikolai Raag], "Eesti ja läti keel Pihkva vaimuliku seminaris" [Estonian and Lat-
     vian at the Pskov Seminary] in *UE*, 8/11, 1928, p. 3-4.
11 Aleksij, 1999, p. 237-244.

urgy in Estonian.[12] In Latvia, there was no such public debate on the question of a Latvian liturgy. The only Latvian Orthodox congregation of Riga, the Ascension parish, insisted that the Liturgy in the Riga Cathedral should be in Latvian as often as possible but agreed to the government decision of March 1921 that the Sunday service should be celebrated alternatively in Russian and Latvian.[13] Since the Latvians and the Russians followed different calendars, the major holidays would not collide often.[14]

The second level of the language question was the most sustained discussion in the interwar Orthodox press of Estonia and Latvia. The liturgical translations, which had been prepared in the 1840s, were not very good due to the reasons discussed above, and their language was repeatedly criticised. No official correction was carried out under the Russian Empire, but as soon as the Empire was crumbling, preparations for a new translation began in Estonia and Latvia. In the early 1920s, the Orthodox press asked priests to provide improved language forms for the new liturgical books.[15] However, the churches did not manage to publish new liturgical books before the Second World War broke out. Only *ad hoc* changes were introduced and the practice of individual adaptations to liturgical languages continued. The following excerpt gives an insight into the discussions:

> Resting upon the rule of the Early Church – 'the presbyter does what he thinks best' – we have a situation in which almost every priest tries to remove improperness from the liturgical texts as best he can. However, this often results in new problems: calling the things thus in one church and otherwise in another not only distracts the thoughts of the faithful from the prayer, but may lead them to control, instruct, and even denounce their priests.
>
> I myself experienced such a case last Sunday. A year ago, I started omitting 'ja' [and] at the end of many prayers, ending up with the following wording: "...au nii nüüd kui ikka ja igavesti." [...glory now, as always and forever] My own congregation quickly became accustomed, but the fellow priests thought that this innovation did not suit the liturgy. And soon my special path was criticised even from faraway places. I retracted, taking the wording "...au nüüd, ikka ja igavesti." [...glory now, always, and forever] But last Sunday, I happened to say "ikka, nüüd ja igavesti" [always, now, and forever], and immediately after the service, I was surrounded by critics and teachers: that is not correct; you are destroying the atmosphere of prayer etc. We finally agreed that we would listen to the radio service the following day, letting the Tallinn Cathedral decide. But there we heard very clearly 'ikka, nüüd ja igavesti' [always, now, and forever]. In other words, the Tallinn Cathedral parish

---

12 [Anton Laar], "Lühike ülevaade Eesti ap.-õigeusu elukäigust 75 a. jooksul" [Short overview of 75 years of Estonian Orthodox life] in *UE*, 1/9, 1921, p. 66-67. See also chapter 2.2.1.

13 Purviņš, 1929, p. 61-62; Bušueva, 1993, p. 60-61.

14 See chapter 3.1.3.

15 "Üleskutse" [Appeal] in *UE*, 2/8, 1922, p. 7; "Jaunas lūgšanas grāmatas izdošana" [The publication of new liturgical books] in *TuD*, 1/1-2, 1923, p. 25-26.

use the words we are offended by, just as they are offended by those we use. Moreover, neither of the two corresponds to the liturgical books. [...]
The church is not a place to teach languages but to school the spirit. This can perfectly well be done with archaic words and does not have to follow all new trends.[16]

The question of whether or not to follow trends was discussed not only from a purely linguistic standpoint but was often combined with political, historical, and religious arguments, as the following reaction to a linguistics based article on the liturgy shows:

If we consider the question only from the linguist's perspective, there is nothing to add to the opinion of the honoured colleague – linguistically speaking, he is 100% correct. However, it seems to me that the correction of the liturgical books also needs to take several other concerns into consideration. The language of the church must be serious, solemn, expressive, and elevated. It has to differentiate itself from the colloquial everyday language. If the traditional 'mīlestība' [love] is replaced by the neologism 'mīla,' this does not mean that the church should speak about God's 'mīla' towards mankind: we must continue to use 'mīlestība,' although this – linguistically speaking – is an outdated word. The same can be said about the articles 'tas, ta.' In general, they are useless in Latvian, but they are needed in special cases, such as the word 'Kungs' [Lord], if we designate God. [...]
We also need to consider the historical angle here. Unfortunately, seven hundred years of slavery has left a deep impression in the psychology of the Latvians, which cannot easily be weeded out of the current generation. The Latvian was a slave and the master was a German manor lord. And lo, even today, when the Latvian hears the term 'kungs' [lord], he instinctively imagines the German manor lord. 'Kungs' and manor lord have one single meaning. The article 'tas' is then what helps the Latvian to differentiate between Kungs (God) and kungs (manor lord). For the differentiation between capitalised and lowercase does not appear in the pronunciation. [...]
From the same point of view, in order to provide the ecclesiastic language with a certain kind of solemnity, it seems to me that some ecclesiastic language innovators have gone too far. During the litany they no longer say 'lai lūdzam to Kungu' [let us praise the Lord God] but 'lūgsim Kungu' [Praise the Lord]. Thus, the ecclesiastic language has been humiliated to become some sort of 'marketplace language.' And why was that necessary? 'Lai lūdzam' definitely sounds much more important and solemn. Or is this form maybe not correct? Yet, it is completely correct, completely usable. For example, it is also used in literature and songs, when the language is to convey a sense of solemnity, of vigour.[17]

Difficulty in conceptualising God was attributed to the long period of serfdom under Baltic German landlords. Although the discourse on language renewal continued throughout the interwar period, there was no definite agreement on

---

16 Konstantin Kokla, "Uute jumalateenistuse raamatute" [On the new liturgical books] in *UjE₂*, 5/13, 1937, p. 208.
17 Pēteris Gredzens, "Mūsu baznīcas valoda" [Our church language] in *TuD*, 15/12, 1939, p. 188-189.

the linguistic forms for liturgical reform. In 1940, a new collection of liturgical texts was published in Estonia, but no such publication appeared in Latvia. The issue was not remediated by the new edition; the practice of *ad hoc* adaptation continued, as the preface to the current hymnal from 2003 shows:

> The need for this kind of material has been pressing for a number of years because, at present, the hymnals, service books, and other sources from earlier periods are linguistically dated and are for many difficult to read and harmonize with others because of their gothic script. Such a situation has necessitated all sorts of compromises and accommodations in particular places which are often linguistically or liturgically faulty and internally inconsistent. It is clear that the current redaction will not satisfy everyone and will not be able to reflect the customary language used in every congregation. At the same time, it is unavoidable to make some choices which will serve to unify the liturgical texts of our small church.[18]

The political component of the language question, or its third level, was most clearly seen when the Estonian government in 1934 introduced a simplified procedure for changing German and Russian sounding names to more genuinely Estonian ones, such as Karl to Kaarel or Ivan to Jaan. This also applied to surnames such as Eisenberg to Raudmäe or Sergejev to Salmar. These kinds of nationalistic politics did not have a counterpart in Latvia, where the public debate concerning names was not as salient. Between 1934 and 1939 more than 200,000 Estonians changed their names, but some refused to respond to the call to do so, as can be seen in the Orthodox press. On the one hand, the generous offer of the government to change the names free of charge did not please the Orthodox clergy, who still had to spend time to make the name changes and money to inform the secular authorities.[19] Moreover, the necessity and value of changing a name was discussed. One commentator argued that the Estonian Synod ought to publish a list of acceptable Estonian forms of first names, which took into account the Hebrew, Greek, or Latin origins of the names,[20] and the Archpriest Ilja Adamov in an open letter refused to change his name to Elias, because

> changing the given name is a sin, for the name was fixed to me during a sacrament. Demagogic coercion always alerts the free citizen and fosters suspicion towards the counterpart, even if he is a brother in the faith. [...] If the individual thinks the Russian-sounding name evokes fright and hopes that a change might alleviate prejudice, then he is wrong.[21]

---

18   *Lauluraamat*, 2003, p. 5 (Translation from Engelhardt, 2005, p. 207-208).
19   Konstantin Kokla, "Pisikesed pahed kiriklises asjaajamises" [Tiny difficulties in church administration] in *UjE₂*, 3/4b, 1935, p. 75-76; Hingekarjane, "Nimede eestistamine protseduur" [The procedure for the Estonicisation of names] in *UjE₂*, 4/6, 1936, p. 95.
20   Alg., "Kas rahvusnimed?" [National names?] in *ET*, 1/7, 1936, p. 5-6; 1/8, 1936, p. 5-6.
21   Ilja Adamov, "Seletuseks" [Explanation] in *ET*, 1/19, 1936, p. 12.

Finally, a debate over the way to write the Saints' names erupted in 1940. The young nationalist Eugen Tamm commented regarding the Orthodox Church calendar of 1940 that the Saints' names should not be transcribed from the Russian as *Vassiili*, *Grigoori*, and *Evseevi* but rather from the Greek as *Basileios*, *Grigorios*, and *Eusebios*.[22] Archpriest Konstantin Gustavson, the editor of the calendar, noted in his reply that it is not the original of the name that is important, but proximity to the pronunciation: "A letter-for-letter transcription is not conceivable for the liturgical texts. If somebody pronounces the car maker Renault letter-for-letter (instead of 'rönoo'), this is funny. We cannot allow that in the liturgical books."[23] Instead, for Gustavson, the names must be written exactly as they are pronounced, and a common Estonian orthography must be found. The Second World War made a continuation of this debate impossible, but two camps had been forming, one eager to modernise everything which recalled Estonia's Russian past and another more pragmatic camp.[24]

3.1.2. Song and Music

Concerning song and music in the Orthodox Churches of Estonia and Latvia, a similar discussion took place on all three levels. As with the question of language, the question of whether the Lutheran practice of congregational singing, to which the Estonians and Latvians were acclimated, was permissible in the Orthodox Church arose at an early stage. The very first converts in 1845, for example, belonged to a pietistic Herrnhut brotherhood, headed by Dāvis Balodis. They petitioned Bishop Filaret to be admitted to the Orthodox Church, but made it conditional on being allowed to continue congregational singing, which was granted.[25] After the mass conversions in the second half of the 1840s, a completely new situation arose. Many of the newly converted Orthodox Christians were dissatisfied, as they could no longer go to the (Lutheran) services they knew. Therefore, some of the newly established Orthodox parishes introduced hybrid liturgies, modifying the music used, in order to make the transition from the Lutheran Church easier for the parishioners.[26] Towards the end of the nineteenth century, as Jeffers Engelhardt argues, the practice of congrega-

---

22 E. Tamm, "Märkmeid 1940. A. kalendri kohta" [Notes on the calendar for 1940] in *ET*, 5/5, 1940, p. 60-61.
23 K. Gustavson, "Vastuseks kalendri arvustusele" [An answer to the calendar-critic] in *ET*, 5/7, 1940, p. 77-79.
24 See also chapter 4.2.2.
25 "Dāvids Balodis un 1845. g. kustība" [Dāvis Balodis and the movement of 1845] in *TuD*, 13/7, 1937, p. 98-100; Engelhardt, 2005, p. 117-118.
26 Kalniņš, Pēteris, 1930.

tional singing emerged "as an essential means of creating Estonian Orthodox sacred and social order where both Estonianness and Orthodoxy assumed ever more ideological significance."[27] The Estonian Orthodox priests Andrei Ramul, Peeter Laredei, and others promoted this practice by publishing Orthodox hymnals at the turn of the twentieth century, which "transform[ed] the Lutheran musical world that Orthodox Estonians were familiar with into something Orthodox."[28]

After the Manifesto of Tolerance of 1905, the discourse about church music became more explicit. The newly established Estonian and Latvian Orthodox journals published numerous propaganda articles on the positive relationship between the Orthodox Church and Estonianness and Latvianness. In some of these articles, congregational singing was of prime importance. In these arguments, "congregational songs [...] were a vital means of religious renewal and the purpose of renewal was not only to stem the tide of reconversion to Lutheranism, but also to distinguish Estonian Orthodoxy from Russian Orthodoxy; to make it 'the people's own.'"[29]

This discourse continued after independence, when it diversified, taking on an "apologetic and, at times, defensive tone [which] betrays resistance to or equivocal acceptance of the new canonicities that sanctioned congregational singing, although these dissenting voices were not given a platform in official church publications."[30] This is especially the case in the editor's introduction to an article by Archpriest Martin Viik published in 1922 by the Estonian journal, *Uus Elu*:

> We often hear the opinion that certain national religious practices, which are established in our life, are not acceptable to some Orthodox. There is especially much doubt about congregational church songs, which are slanderously reputed to be a completely Lutheran practice. Unfortunately, these objections are raised without taking the trouble to penetrate deeper into the spiritual life of the nation, which would reveal what each person's urgent wish is: to participate personally in worship services. Versified song is an instrument for this.
>
> That congregational song is usually held in condemnation is due in great part to the narrow perspective of northern Russian church singing which we cannot get beyond. Let us bear in mind the words of the honourable archpriest from Pärnu [Laredei] that

---

27 Engelhardt, 2005, p. 124. The doctoral dissertation of Jeffers Engelhardt convincingly tells the story of Estonian Orthodox church music. There have been no corresponding study of the Latvian case, but it is likely that a similar development happened here, albeit probably less intensive.
28 Engelhardt, 2005, p. 129.
29 Engelhardt, 2005, p. 141-142.
30 Engelhardt, 2005, p. 161-162.

explain the validity of church song through the proverb: every bird has its own song.[31]

A similar idea informs a letter to the editor from 1928:

An important shortcoming in our current Orthodox Church is a deficient and con-
fusing liturgical service, held by some of the more recently appointed young priests.
You pass a church somewhere in the countryside, where the morning liturgy is being
held and, although the priest is indeed clothed in our Orthodox liturgical vestments,
the service is – well, God knows what it is supposed to be. As much as you try, you
cannot make out if it is a prayer session going on, but it is impossible to consider the
event a morning liturgy. [...]
It is sad when the congregation is served by a bad sacristan, but thousand times
worse when the priest was not even a psalm singer before consecration and does not
know anything about the order of the service, because he has never seen one before.
It is laudable when such priests field the excuse that they would like to make the liturgy acceptable to Lutherans, but that is a groundless excuse. Such a priest, who
does not know the basics of the order of the service, should grasp the importance of
the issue and ask advice from an older priest or his provost. If a priest cannot even
hold the morning liturgy or the Divine Liturgy, what will he do on Christmas Eve,
during Holy Lent, or on Easter Sunday? The congregation is well off if at least it has
a good sacristan, but if not, the case is really bad. [...]
There have been many simplifications and renewals in our order of service, which
were desperately necessary, but every novice-priest is not thereby entitled to introduce whatever he sees fit to such an extent that even the Lutherans praise him, saying: 'it is almost impossible to recognise the Orthodox Christianity in this man!'[32]

The interesting thing about this letter, signed by 'a priest from the Pärnu region,'
is that although it did not bring about an extensive discussion in Estonia, the
Latvian journal printed a translation of it and commented:

Thus, innovations in liturgical services have arrived at a point where arbitrariness
and exaggeration are pushing even the most ardent ideologues of modernism from
their high horse. Even the editor of *Uus Elu*, Archpriest Anton Laar, has raised his
voice against the exaggerations, although he himself, during Easter Night Liturgy in
Tallinn, had introduced a brass orchestra next to the choir and congregation singing.
In Pärnu, with the help of Archpriest Martin Viik, there is apparently a balalaika
orchestra accompanying the All Saints' procession and a harmonium during liturgy.
[...] The introduction of balalaikas and a harmonium in the services in Pärnu was
followed by what only a blind mind could fail or refuse to imagine – the congregation split into two antagonistic parts, of which the larger completely distanced itself
from the innovations of Archpriest Martin Viik as exaggerated modernisms, not
suited to the spirit of Orthodoxy, wishing to establish a separate congregation. Do
these sorrowful facts not show once again that experimentation and light-hearted

---

31 Editor's introduction to Martin Viik, "Elupildid ja mõtted õigeusu kiriku laulust" [Still
    lives and thoughts on the Orthodox church song] in *UE*, 2/8, 1922, p. 1 (Translation from
    Engelhardt, 2005, p. 170-171).
32 Preester Pärnumaalt, "Suured puudused" [Large lacunae] in *UE*, 8/11, 1928, p. 4.

modernisation in the liturgical service cannot avoid a negative and schism-provok-
ing character? [...]
They are very mistaken, the reformers, who think that they can strengthen the
Orthodox faith through their liturgical experimentation. Nothing is strengthened,
rather, the congregation is shattered.[33]

This excerpt demonstrates that the discussions in Estonia were regarded with
suspicion in Latvia and that the Latvian discourse took a more moderate path
after 1917. *Vera i Žizn'*, The Russian-language Orthodox journal in Latvia, in
1923 noted with resignation that anti-Orthodox articles had appeared in the Latvian press, which urged the church to modernise and become more Latvian.[34]
The unidentifiable author of the article explains very soberly, that "Archbishop
Jānis, as a true Orthodox hierarch, cannot endorse the introduction of the
reformers' inadmissible experiments, of which some persons, claiming to be
Orthodox but knowing nothing about Orthodoxy, speak so much."[35] This discourse, emanating from Russian(-speaking) circles tried to gain force in Estonia
too, but the prevalence of the Estonian element dismissed it.[36] In the Latvian
case, it was the nationalist discourse of innovations that was shut out. In fact,
nationalist arguments appeared only once in the Latvian Orthodox journal during the 1920s, in an article written by 'N.', aimed at strengthening Orthodoxy
among the Latvians. The main element the author mentions in this respect, is the
necessity of introducing congregational singing, as "standing and listening when
some tiny group of people sing is not for the Latvian spirit and does not satisfy
it."[37] Archpriest Jānis Jansons, commenting on the letter, agreed, but the topic
was not common in the Latvian Orthodox press.

Alongside the discourse on the first level, criticising the exaggerations in
modernisation efforts, there was a constructive debate on the second level. It
focused on how to make the Orthodox service more attractive, especially in
congregations without satisfactory choirs. In Estonia, this discourse occurred
throughout the interwar period, whereas in the Latvian case, it started mainly in
1936. The Estonian discourse focused on methods of disseminating song sheets
and books as well as musical knowledge, often combined with an argument that

---

33   A. Jansons, "Pareizticīgās draudzes Dievkalpojumu reformēšanas lietā" [On the reform
     of the Orthodox Mass] in *TuD*, 7/4, 1929, p. 56-61.
34   Н. И. Ш., "Обновителям церкви" [To the church reformers] in *ViŽ*, 1/5-6, 1923, p. 29-
     32.
35   Н. И. Ш., "Обновителям церкви" [To the church reformers] in *ViŽ*, 1/5-6, 1923, p. 31.
36   See chapter 2.2.3.
37   N., "Kāds vārds par pareizticības nostiprināšanu pastāvošās draudzēs Latvijā" [Some
     words on the consolidation of Orthodoxy in the existing parishes in Latvia] in *TuD*, 4/5,
     1926, p. 10.

the Estonians were closely connected to a tradition of common singing.[38] An author from 1936 approached the issue of congregational singing systematically, calling for a questionnaire to be sent to all parishes:

> This would answer our many questions, such as (1) Does the parish use congregational singing, and if yes, since when? (2) What does the congregation sing and to what melody (note sheet may even be provided) and (3) with how many voices? (4) What facilitates and what hinders the development of congregational singing and (5) what suggestions are there for removing these obstacles? [...] With such a questionnaire, we would have a holistic picture of the situation and would be better suited to make progress in this area.[39]

The difficulties in organising congregational singing were repeatedly mentioned, leading one author to opine that congregational singing, as it was propagated in the Estonian Orthodox Church, was counterproductive:

> The supporters of congregational singing look to the Lutherans as an example, because *congregational singing apparently binds the faithful closer to their church.* Taking the worst case of Lutheran prayer house congregational singing as an example, the Orthodox supporters did not take pains to notice that congregational singing is not that universally praised by our Lutheran brethren. [...] Thus, there is something more needed to bind the faithful to their church, namely *religious schooling* – from the earliest moment. The weakest link in our church is not the lack of congregational singing but insufficient religious schooling, a downright fatal weakness, which unfortunately has not received the kind of attention that congregational singing has had. [We should rather turn to religious schooling], because a believer comes to church to pray, and prayer, if it is not to be empty chatter, requires great spiritual concentration. And if he is supposed to sing at the same time, something he is not properly prepared to do mechanically, such as eating and walking – then his attention is obviously to a large extent turned to the correct singing. Understandably, there is not much attention left for God. [...] Short, *let primary importance be given to choral singing, while congregational singing can take on significance when lacking a choir or as a secondary issue.*[40]

In Latvia, the published discourse was limited to several articles from 1937, initiated by Metropolitan Augustīns' "passionate support for congregational singing" and by the just cited article from *Elutöde*, which had been published in

---

38   K. Ustav, "Kirikulalu korraldamisest Eestis" [On the organisation of church singing in Estonia] in *UE*, 0/3, 1919, p. 40; "Sõnad ja teod" [Words and deeds] in *UE*, 12/7-8, 1932, p. 8; Anton Angerjas, "Laula, laula suukene" [Sing, sing, little mouth] in *UjE₂*, 1/4, 1933, p. 1-2. See also Engelhardt, 2005, p. 154-156, 162-163.

39   Algataja, "Koguduse laulu korraldus" [Organising congregation song] in *ET*, 1/2, 1936, p. 5-6.

40   -nd, "Kirikulaulust" [On the singing in church] in *ET*, 1/35, 1936, p. 4-5 (Emphasis in original).

translation in the Latvian Orthodox journal *Ticība un Dzīve*.[41] Four months after its appearance, the editor had received four comments which he deemed worthy of publication. They all had the same tenor:

> The Latvian nation wants to sing. The parish clergy, chanters, and conductors must take that into account. A choir is necessary, clearly, but it should primarily act as a nucleus from which the other parishioners can orient their own singing. This obviously does not rob the choir of its artistic value – there will always be songs that the congregation had better leave to the choir, for example at special concerts or complex songs of the Cherubim etc.
>
> It is no denying that congregational singing does not attain the same degree of art and perfection as a well disciplined choir, but how many of our congregations can boast of having such a good choir? […] And finally, we need to emphasise that our order of liturgical service includes numerous passages where the congregation can join in the singing. When the priest or the deacon call out 'Let us praise the Lord God in peace,' 'We pray to the Lord God about peace from above and the salvation of our souls,' etc., then it is clear that these calls are not limited to the singers in the choir, but concern all those present.[42]

The article continued:

> I do not know either the Estonian situation or the national spirit of the Estonians that well. It may well be that congregational singing has a lower position there. I only know that the Russian national spirit was completely satisfied when the faithful had been to church and 'stood through' the liturgy. That is not the Latvian spirit: for the Latvian, standing through alone does not satisfy him nor does listening only. He wants to participate in the divine service himself. And nobody can deny him this right, not the priest, not the choir, not the conductor, not the chanter, not the other singers. Quite the opposite, we should support congregational singing with all our power, for only thus can the Latvian be satisfied and come cheerfully to church, for only then does he feel that the church gives him something. He is like the children, of whom Christ said: 'if these should hold their peace, the stones would immediately cry out.'[43]

From these opinions, one forms the impression that the discussion between proponents and opponents of congregational singing that occurred within the Estonian Orthodox Church had been avoided in the Latvian Church, or at least had a much less public character. In the Latvian case, there seems to have been less emphasis on shaping the public opinion in favour of congregational singing and

---

41 -nd, "Sagazīmies no Dievkalpojumu viekāšošanas ar daudzināta kopdziedāšanu. Svarigāka par kopdziedāšanu ir ticības gaļa audzināšana" [Let us not destroy the liturgy with too much congregational singing. More important is spreading the true faith] in *TuD*, 13/1, 1937, p. 7-8.

42 Pēteris Gredzens (ed.), "Baznīcas dziedāšanas jautājumā" [On the question of church singing] in *TuD*, 13/4, 1937, p. 60.

43 Pēteris Gredzens (ed.), "Baznīcas dziedāšanas jautājumā" [On the question of church singing] in *TuD*, 13/4, 1937, p. 60-61. The bible reference is to Lk, 19:40.

a more organic evolution. However, following the article quoted above, more critical voices appeared in the Latvian journal and the issue was nicely summed up by Archpriest Vilimons Ratnieks at a gathering of Latvian clergy in October 1937.[44] Ratnieks emphasised the difficulty of combining artistic and aesthetic perfection with the religious wish to praise God together. His conclusion, after listing all the pros and cons and influencing factors, follows

> First of all, a choir singing in harmony is necessary to musically discipline the congregational singing. Let us therefore support the development of good choirs in every parish in order for the singing spirit, which is the first and foremost expression of the Orthodox Church, to grow among the parishioners. This spirit has brought more than a few outstanding singers to our national culture.[45]

In fact, a similar conclusion shone through in the Estonian debate during the same year. One article praised a specific parish, where the former priest had put a lot of effort into teaching the congregation to sing fifty years earlier, a tradition which was still vividly alive.[46] A couple of months later, the Estonian Synod petitioned the Ministry of Education to introduce conductor's classes at the Tallinn Conservatory, where candidates from both the Lutheran and Orthodox Estonian Churches would learn to lead a choir.[47] Another article from 1939 criticised the practice of paying professionals to sing in the choir during liturgy:

> Since we repeatedly emphasise that the Estonian is a singer and that there are so many good singers in Estonia, then it is somewhat strange that we cannot fill our choirs without resorting to professional singers. […] Church choirs in the city and in the countryside: revise your old understandings! The power and beauty of song are enough in themselves to gather singers and especially those that sing for the musical experience, not for the money they can earn thereby.[48]

In summary, the discussion concerning song and music in the liturgy was very limited in scope, focussing on the ways Orthodoxy could be suited to the Estonian and Latvian national spirits and how to make Orthodoxy attractive to the Latvians and Estonians. Russian voices were barely present in these debates. It occurred, thus, mostly on the second and third levels, whereas the first level was only present as the invisible counterpart of apologetic articles.

---

44 Published as V. Ratnieks, "Kopdziedāšana vaj koris?" [Congregational singing or choir?] in *TuD*, 13/21, 1937, p. 323-325.

45 V. Ratnieks, "Kopdziedāšana vaj koris?" [Congregational singing or choir?] in *TuD*, 13/21, 1937, p. 325.

46 J. R., "Preestrid, õpetage rahvas laulma!" [Priests, teach the people to sing!] in *ET*, 2/10, 1937, p. 130.

47 M., "Ääremärkused Kirikulaulust" [Side notes on church singing] in *ET*, 2/15, 1937, p. 187.

48 M., "Professionaal kooridest asjaarmastajateks!" [From professional choirs to amateurs!] in *ET*, 4/21, 1939, p. 225-226.

3.1.3. The Calendar Issue

The third issue of the internal dimension, the question of the calendar, created the most vivid discussions on the first and third levels. It was a difficult subject in all of Eastern Europe during the interwar years. Until the revolutionary upheavals of the early twentieth century most of Eastern Europe used the Julian calendar, which at that time trailed thirteen days behind the Gregorian calendar used by the West. Estonia and Latvia officially switched to the Gregorian calendar during the German occupation 1917/1918, and Soviet Russia shifted to the new calendar in February 1918. Only the Orthodox Church retained the Julian calendar. In part, the church's decision was based on ecclesio-political reasoning; many theologians refused to follow a calendar instituted by a Roman Pope. The calendar, moreover, especially the Paschalion, the determination of the date of Easter, was considered so important that only an Pan-Orthodox Council could institute a change. The Pan-Orthodox Conference, summoned by the Ecumenical Patriarch Meletios IV in 1923, did make a decision to switch to a new, improved calendar, but many Orthodox Churches did not ratify the decision.[49]

Even before this conference, however, both the Estonian and the Latvian Orthodox Church had received permission from Patriarch Tikhon, in his decrees of autonomy from 1920 and 1921, to celebrate according to the 'new style' if they so wished. However, after this the approach to the question of the calendar differed considerably in the two Baltic churches. In the Estonian Church, the autonomy *tomos* from Constantinople (1923) also granted the Orthodox Church the right to use the new calendar. Since 1920, the church and state authorities had repeatedly declared that the entire Estonian Church should switch to the new style, including the Western Paschalion.[50] This idea was fiercely protested by the Russian minority of the Estonian Orthodox Church. One of the main arguments of the Russian minority in its row since 1921 with the Estonian ecclesiastic authorities had been that the Estonians were not really Orthodox, and the calendar change was seen as definite proof of that.[51] Thus, the Russian parishes ignored the decision and continued to celebrate according to the Julian calendar. Moreover, the Estonian ecclesiastic authorities were too weak to exercise control concerning this question, so those parishes which wished to remain on the Julian calendar did not need to fear any consequences. An article from 1924 complained about the continuing calendar upheavals:

> As much as we would like to not believe it, the calendar question still causes uproar in these days. The culprits this time are some Russian parishes along the river Narva

---

49   Slesarev, 2009, p. 60-71. See also chapter 1.2.3.
50   Grichin, 2003, p. 169.
51   See chapter 2.2.3. For the calendar question in the Finnish case, see Frilander, 1995; Frilander, 1997.

and the Peipsi-lake as well as in Petserimaa. Determined incitement, without any ecclesiastical aim but instigated also by members of the clergy, has succeeded in preventing the bells to ring on new style feast days and in interrupting the liturgy with interjections, inappropriate singing, and other activities. [...] The Synod has always been, and remains firm in the stance that once the new style liturgy has been held [...], there is no prohibition from repeating the service according to the old calendar, as long as it does not disturb the state and societal life.[52]

In the Latvian Orthodox Church, Archbishop Jānis solved the problem differently: He let every congregation decide for itself which calendar would be used for its celebrations: "This permission of the Archbishop follows normal Orthodox practice, stipulating that feast liturgy may be celebrated on days other than the feast itself. The Ascension Monastery [near Moscow], for example, celebrates Easter Night Liturgy every Saturday."[53] In contrast to the Estonian Church, which made a decision and tried to force it through, the Latvian Orthodox Church discussed the calendar lengthily at the 1923 ecclesiastic *saeima*, deciding to opt for the new style with the possibility of exceptions, while keeping to the Orthodox Paschalion.[54] Moreover, the two Orthodox journals of Latvia monitored and discussed the debates on the calendar that happened outside Latvia. In 1924 Mikhail N. Burnašev, an ethnic Russian schoolteacher and future priest, published an extensive article in *Vera i Žizn'*, justifying the decision to switch to the new style and trying to convince its opponents to change their minds.[55] The inclusion of the Russians in the decision making process minimised the opposition to the new calendar in Latvia. A minor row erupted over the date of Easter in 1926, which according to the Western Paschalion fell on 4 April, whereas Orthodox Easter was almost a month later, on 2 May. The discussion appeared in both the Russian- and Latvian-language Orthodox journals; both emphasised the importance of keeping the Orthodox Paschalion.[56]

The differences between the Estonian and Latvian Church on the calendar issue continued throughout the 1920s. The authorities of the Estonian Church

---

52 "Kalendri küsimus" [The calendar question] in *UE*, 4/2, 1924, p. 7.

53 K. L., "Vecais un jaunais stils" [The old and the new style] in *TuD*, 1/1-2, 1923, p. 24-25.

54 N. S., "Latvijas Pareizticības Baznīcas Saeima" [The *saeima* of the Latvian Orthodox Church] in *TuD*, 2/2, 1924, p. 4-6. Archbishop Jānis' presentation on the calendar question at the ecclesiastic *saeima* is reprinted in Kalniņš II, 1993, p. 95-96.

55 М. Н. Бурнашев, "Календарь и его реформа" [The Calendar and its reform] in *ViŽ*, 2/6, 1924, p. 11-16; 2/7-8, 1924, p. 6-8.

56 "Архиепископ Иоанн о дне празднования Пасхи" [Archbishop Jānis on the day of celebrating Easter] in *ViŽ*, 4/4, 1926, p. 1-2; N., "Kāds vārds par pareizticības nostiprināšanu pastāvošās draudzēs Latvijā" [Some words on the consolidation of Orthodoxy in the existing congregations in Latvia] in *TuD*, 4/5, 1926, p. 7-11; Jānis Jansons, "Vai Pareizticība pie Latviešiem var palikt par nacionālu ticību?" [Can Orthodoxy among the Latvians remain a national faith?] in *TuD*, 4/5, 1926, p. 12-13.

tried to persuade all the parishes of Estonia to use only the new calendar but to no avail, as this letter to the editor from 1929 shows:

> If the Russian holders of power would retain the old calendar for nationalistic reasons, the Estonian parishes would not have any reason to react. But when they field religious arguments for the calendar schism and convince many Estonians, who our weak Estonian Church must so-to-speak sacrifice to Russian national interests, then we cannot remain silent. [...]
> There is another reason to change the calendar: the general canons of the church. We know that the canon of subordination to one's hierarch is more important than the calendar issue. No Orthodox Church has yet condemned the Estonian Metropolitan, they all still call him their Brother in Christ. [...] Thus, there is currently no reason to follow the Russian course of action. Rather, we should warn the Russian brothers. If a warning does not help, we should rally around our spiritual head, secure in the knowledge and hope for the future of the Estonian Church, knowing that the Russians have put even religion to the service of their national interests, aiming at using the faith to gain followers.[57]

The issue of the church calendar turned up in the Estonian Orthodox journal every time it touched the Russian minority. The *täiskogu* of 1932 again declared the new calendar compulsive for the entire church, but once again this did not help.[58] The following postscript from a lead article in 1934 illustrates the resignation of the editor, Konstantin Kokla:

> P.S. Just as I finished writing these lines, the bells of the Uspenski church started ringing. The entire city is full of these bells' ringing in the quiet of night. They are celebrating Christ's resurrection, just as we did a week ago. And we supposedly belong to the same church, with a holy and strong liturgical order! Do our Russian brothers in the faith not make our Orthodox constancy weak and laughable?[59]

By that time, however, the question of the calendar had turned into an important issue for state politics, especially concerning the *Setu* of Petserimaa.[60] Since the mid-1920s, it was repeatedly reported in the Estonian press that many of the *Setu* still followed the old calendar, thereby disrupting the course of everyday life; workers did not appear to work, and pupils skipped school on Julian calendar holidays. Moreover, these old style holidays often turned into drunken fights

---

57   Konstantin Kokla, "Pühad vana ja uue kalendri põhjal" [The saints according to the old and new calendar] in *UE*, 9/5, 1929, p. 15-16. The editor's comment to this article is very interesting, because it shows how the editor Anton Laar wished to be the 'voice of Estonian Orthodoxy': "We are very happy that this viewpoint, which we have advocated for so long and which has occasionally been criticised, finds new followers."
58   Risch, 1937, p. 130-132.
59   Konstantin Kokla, "Usk tegurina rahvuslikul kaitserindel" [The faith as an actor in the nationalistic struggles] in *UjE₂*, 2/4, 1934, p. 69.
60   Konstantin Kokla, "Usk tegurina rahvuslikul kaitserindel" [The faith as an actor in the nationalistic struggles] in *UjE₂*, 2/4, 1934, p. 67-68; Grichin, 2003, p. 169-170. See also chapter 2.3.1.

with numerous casualties.[61] The situation was brought under control only after the 'Monastery War' had finished and the new law on religious organisations was promulgated in 1934.[62] This law stipulated ethnic congregations, and the reform of the mixed parishes ensured a decrease of Russian influence on the *Setu*.[63] The calendar issue could now be settled, at least in the Estonian and *Setu* parishes, which mattered to the ecclesiastic authorities. By 1936 the problems of the preceding years did not occur anymore.[64]

In the Latvian case, the 1930s infused new life into the debate about the calendar. In connection with the new regime and its attempts to Latvianise the entire country, a reader asked in the Orthodox journal what to do:

A painful question in Krāslava and all of Latgale is whether to celebrate the church holidays according to the old or the new calendar. The state institutions and schools function according to the new style, but the congregations keep to the old one. As a consequence, the celebrations happen neither in the old nor in the new style, for on old style holidays, we need to go to work and the children to school and the new style holidays are not accepted by the priests. Taking this discomfort into account, a general meeting of the Krāslava parish members decided to celebrate all holidays according to the new calendar. Also the supporters of the old style admit to this discomfort, but wait for an authoritative decision from the ecclesiastic authorities.[65]

In his answer, the editor pointed to the general difficulty of solving this question not only in Latgale, but throughout the Orthodox Church:

Some of the Orthodox, especially the Russians, are very conservative and would never switch to the new style, even threatening to join the Old Believers if the Synod makes such a decision. [...] We, the Orthodox in Latvia, are a minority, and as long as the majority celebrates the holidays according to the new calendar, then we have no real reason to act differently, for there are no obstacles to the new style from a religious point of view. The best solution, obviously, would be if all Christians could celebrate the holidays at the same time.[66]

---

61 "Mida edendab ristikäigutamine-kirmassitamine Setumaal?" [Whom do the procession-festivals in the Setu county benefit?] in *Petseri Uudised*, 2/41, 14.10.1933, p. 2; "Setu on kangekaelne" [The *Setu* is strong in the taking] in *Esmaspäev*, 13/21, 22.05.1934, p. 5; Grichin, 2003, p. 175-178; Lõuna, Kalle, 2003, p. 87-88.
62 See chapter 2.3.1. and 2.3.3.
63 "Ammuoodatud kirikureform teostati" [Long-awaited church reform put into place] in *Petseri Uudised*, 4/28, 13.07.1935, p. 4; Raag, 1938, p. 32-34; Grichin, 2003, p. 178-179; Lõuna, Kalle, 2003, p. 111-112.
64 "Ülestõusmispühad möödusid vaikselt" [Easter passed quietly] in *Petseri Uudised*, 5/16, 17.04.1936, p. 3; Raag, 1938, p. 35; Grichin, 2003, p. 178.
65 "Vecais vai jaunais kalendars?" [Old or new calendar?] in *TuD*, 11/5, 1935, p. 76. See also chapter 2.3.3. for the Latvianising of Latgale.
66 Pēteris Gredzens, "Vecais vai jaunais kalendars?" [Old or new calendar?] in *TuD*, 11/5, 1935, p. 76-77.

However, the answer only expresses that a unitary solution would be desirable, without giving any concrete suggestions. Once Augustīns Pētersons was consecrated Metropolitan of Riga, the Synod did demand a switch to the new style in all the parishes of Latvia, which was followed by propaganda articles on the new calendar in the journal.[67] By then, however, there was no strong opposition from within the church, probably due to the strict political regime.

In both cases, then, a clear distinction appears between the Estonians and Latvians on the one side and the Russians on the other, when it comes to the question of the calendar. One can say that the Estonians and Latvians felt uneasy following an 'outdated' tradition, while the Russians showed their unwillingness to adapt by clinging to a seemingly minor issue such as the calendar. The German scholar Helmut Risch, writing about the Estonian Orthodox Church in 1937, diligently lists the arguments of both sides in this conflict.[68] This list brings to mind the other great schisms in the Orthodox Church, which also arguably occurred over bagatelles, such as: the Great Schism between Rome and Constantinople in 1054 over a word in the Creed and the use of unleavened bread and the Nikonian Schism in 1666, when the Old Believers left the Russian Patriarchal Church over the number of fingers used in the sign of the cross and the pronunciation of the name of Jesus.[69] According to the Russian theologian Vladimir Soloviev, both of these schisms occurred because the conservatives confused relevant and irrelevant issues and "considered the 'irrelevant' – i.e. the 'temporal' and 'contingent' – sufficient to propagate schism."[70] Giorgij Avvakumov, an Eastern Catholic theologian, differentiates between the materialist and the essentialist interpretation of ritual difference. The materialist view postulates that concrete accusations of violating ritual purity function as pretext for some more important 'real' or 'material' issues. On the other hand, the essentialists posit that every ritual difference is "an expression of the abysmal and essential spiritual differences between two conflicting parties."[71]

In the case of the two Baltic Orthodox Churches, the Estonian and Latvian Orthodox Christians clearly tended more towards a materialist interpretation of the conflict, whereas the Russians had a more essentialist outlook. Since the materialist interpretation is associated with modernity, it is possible to say that the Estonians and Latvians were eager to be conceived as modern and therefore did not heed the essentialist protests of the Russians in the church. That the con-

---

67 "Aicinājums pareizticīgiem svinēt svētkus pēc jaunā stila" [Invitation to the Orthodox to celebrate holidays according to the new style] in *Brīvā Zeme*, 19/139, 26.06.1937, p. 6; F. J., "Kalendara jautājums" [The question of the calendar] in *TuD*, 14/16, 1938, p. 243-245.
68 Risch, 1937, p. 130-132.
69 Avvakumov, 2006, p. 197-205.
70 Avvakumov, 2006, p. 205.
71 Avvakumov, 2006, p. 211.

flict in Estonian occurred much earlier and was more dividing than the Latvian one can be explained by the consolidating personality of Archbishop Jānis. He was able to stifle internal conflicts and redirect them to an outside enemy, the state and the politicians of the left. Once he was no longer in charge of the Latvian Orthodox Church, disintegration of the unity among the ethnic groups began to appear.

Since the issue of the calendar was so straightforward, there was no need to discuss it extensively on the second level. The question of which calendar to use, engendered few, if any, secondary questions. An exception to this may be the question of what to do on holy days that are not official holidays. Such days include, first and foremost, the many celebrations of different patron saints. An article from 1931 pointedly describes the dilemma:

> In former times, the great holidays were state holidays, and then there was a liturgy, with numerous visitors. Nowadays we often see that the priest as well as the parishioners must work [on these days]. There is no way but to arrange a meeting in the evening, while the festive morning liturgy is left out. [...]
> In our opinion there is but one way out of the dilemma: to hold the important divine liturgies in the evenings, if no other option is possible. In the countryside, this might happen in some populous village far from the church. This is just one of the demands of our times: to reach out among the people, if it is otherwise not possible to draw them to religious life. A great holy day is a perfect occasion to wake them up. Also in the city, where the church is easily accessible to all, evening services are very welcome.[72]

Generally, howeveer, in all three areas, language, music and calendar, there were strong tendencies to nationalise and modernise the Orthodox service in both Estonia and Latvia. This modernisation was, on the one hand, necessary to attract the faithful to the churches and, on the other, to make the Orthodox Church appear modern and up-to-date in the face of societal antagonism. At the same time, there were voices calling to keep the changes moderate. This was especially the case in Latvia, where the divergence between the ethnic Russians and ethnic Latvians had not resulted in separate church structures. In Estonia, promoting an image of the 'modern' Orthodox Church was seen as more important than satisfying the various factions in the church. The relatively weak and unexperienced central authorities of the church were unable to guide these factions in one direction. Only the attempts to make Orthodox Church music more Estonian, which had been quite successful already in the nineteenth century, continued without such disturbances, as the Russian and Estonian parishes were separated and had little mutual contact.

---

72   "Kirikuelu küsimusi" [Questions of ecclesiastic life] in *UE*, 11/8, 1931, p. 3-4.

3.2. The External Dimension

Externally, the issues of identity and tradition came to the fore each time the Orthodox Church discussed its 'Others.' These 'Others' primarily belonged to two categories. On the one hand, the Lutheran and Roman Catholic Churches repeatedly provoked Orthodox actors in Estonia and Latvia to position themselves and clarify their identity. Secular society and politics, on the other hand, equally challenged the Orthodox identity, which was discursively constructed in opposition to it. This chapter first considers the relations of the Orthodox to the Anglicans and Catholics, then their attitude towards the Lutheran Church, and finally the Orthodox understanding of the secular world.

3.2.1. Orthodoxy and the Discourse of Ecumenicalism

The Estonian and Latvian Orthodox Christians largely shared the same attitudes towards other confessions. The discourse in both cases demonstrates important similarities, although there are differences in intensity. In both cases, the Anglican Church was perceived as the best friend of the Orthodox, while the Lutheran Church was seen as the main partner or adversary, depending on the context. The attitude towards the Roman Catholic Church was officially hostile and wary. In the Estonian case, commentaries on Catholicism took on an apologetic tone, suggesting that the attitude towards the Roman Catholic Church was ambivalent in some circles. Other confessions, such as the Baptists and neo-pagans appear only in negative terms. Interestingly, the Old Believers, who split from the Russian Orthodox Church in the seventeenth century, are hardly ever mentioned in the journals. In the following sections, I will look at each of these confessions in turn.

The optimistic attitude towards the Anglican Church in Estonia has already been mentioned.[73] The idea of a switch to the jurisdiction of the Anglican Church in order to achieve full ecclesiastical independence had been discarded by 1920, but the positive image of the Anglican Church remained, aided by Vassili Martinson, professor of Orthodox Theology at the University of Tartu. Martinson published several lengthy articles in 1925 describing the process of a hypothetical unification between the Anglican and the Orthodox Churches. He opined that "we do not know when the union might take place. Everything is in the hands of God. We only know that it will happen eventually because of the prayer of our Saviour Jesus Christ that all who truly believe in him may be

---

73   See chapter 2.2.2. See also Sõtšov, 2009, p. 63-68.

one."[74] Six years later, he published a collection of documents on the unification in the same optimistic tone.[75]

The Latvian Orthodox Church did not propagate an outlook on the future of the two churches as intensively. However, Anglican bishops visited Riga three times in the late 1920s. Each time they were warmly received by Archbishop Jānis, and their visits were lengthily described in the Orthodox journal by Archpriest Jānis Jansons. Although written in very theological language, these articles focus on the course of the visits, mentioning only in passing that the Anglican and Orthodox Churches have much in common and that preparations are being made for union.[76] The Russian-language journal published an article by Archbishop Jānis in 1926 about the friendship between the Anglican and Orthodox Churches along with his speech for the occasion of the Anglican bishop's visit.[77] Moreover, when two important conferences of the ecumenical movement took place in Oxford and Edinburgh in the summer of 1937, Archpriest Jānis Jansons attended as a delegate of the Orthodox Church of Latvia.[78] In his travel reports, he continued his theological language and emphasised that he had learnt a lot. There were no Estonian Orthodox delegates at this gathering, only representatives from the Estonian Lutheran Church.[79]

74 Vassili Martinson, "Hommikumaa-õigeusu ja Inglise (anglikaani) kiriku vahekorrast" [On the relationship between the Eastern Orthodox and the English (Anglican) Church] in *UE*, 5/2, 1925, p. 4 (Translation from Sõtsov, 2009, p. 67, fn. 182).

75 Martinson, 1931.

76 Jānis Jansons, "Angļu Bīskaps Beri Rīgā" [The English Bishop Bury in Riga] in *TuD*, 4/8, 1926, p. 3-6; Jānis Jansons, "Anglikaņu draudzība ar Pareizticīgo Baznīcu" [The Anglican friendship with the Orthodox Church] in *TuD*, 5/6, 1927, p. 1-3; Jānis Jansons, "Anglikaņu bīskapa Stauntona Betti viesošanās Rīgas Katedrālē" [The visit of the Anglican Bishop Staunton Batty to Riga] in *TuD*, 7/11, 1929, p. 136-138.

77 Иоанн (Поммер) [Jānis (Pommers)], "Ожидая Англиканский епископ" [Waiting for the Anglican bishop] in *ViŽ*, 4/6, 1926, p. 2-4 (Kalniņš I, 1993, p. 70-71); "Приветственной речь Архиепископа Иоанна" [Archbishop Jānis' welcome speech] in *ViŽ*, 4/6, 1926, p. 4-5 (Kalniņš I, 1993, p. 71). In 1930, Archpriest Jānis Jansons wrote that "in England, the 'reunion literature' is flourishing. It would have been beneficial if something was translated into Latvian. However, we might wait long for anything to happen here, for there is still a strong conservativeness among the Latvians and an important section of the Latvian intelligentsia does not spare a thought about religious aims." Jānis Jansons, "Pareizticība un protestantisms" [Orthodoxy and Protestantism] in *TuD*, 8/9, 1930, p. 123.

78 A travel description was published in *TuD*, 13/14, 1937, p. 218; 13/15, 1937, p. 240; 13/16, 1937, p. 255; 13/17, 1937, p. 271. See also Zernov, 2004, p. 658-660.

79 Rohtmets, 2006, p. 144-146, 151-153. For another ecumenical conference in the Netherlands the same year, Metropolitan Aleksander had asked the Lutheran Bishop Rahamägi to be so kind as to keep the Orthodox Church of Estonia in mind. This had been interpreted by some as a unique case of a Lutheran representing an Orthodox Church. See

When the Lutheran Church of Estonia began to discuss unification with the Anglican Church in 1938,[80] an author in the Orthodox journal asked critically:

> It made me think, what kind of wondrous ways could unite these two so dogmatically different theological currents. I thought it a pretentious step by our Lutheran neighbours, since the English Church has hitherto been more inclined towards Apostolic Orthodoxy. The well known Lutheran churchman H. Põld now explains this secret in his journal *Meie Misjon* [Our Mission]. [...]
>
> From this we can see reason blundering about on the matter of religion and winning over those Christians who have placed religious purification and new religious trends on a par with Christ's principles. They think that the divine wedding suit (the principles of faith) has become timeworn and needs adjustment. Obviously the thus mended original suit can hardly be recognised and the Christian Faith is banished to history.[81]

In Latvian Orthodox circles, there is no reflection on this rapprochement between the Lutheran and the Anglican Churches, although this does not imply that the Latvian journals neglected Anglicanism. An article from 1939 is devoted to the Anglican Church, mentioning how even the largest cathedrals are empty on Sundays and how the church is split between a right wing and a left wing.[82] Nevertheless, the author lauds the way Anglican clergy relate to people in their everyday life, for example by organising Sunday schools at football matches and other sporting events.

On the other hand, relations with the Roman Catholic Church were not very friendly. In the case of Latvia, where more intense relations could be expected due to the Catholic majority in the Latgale region, Catholicism was hardly ever thematised, while in the Estonian case the matter of the Catholic Church created an interesting discourse, especially during the years 1930-1935. This discourse was initiated by rumours that union between the Estonian Orthodox Church and the Roman Catholic Church was imminent, because one Orthodox priest had converted.[83] Anton Laar dismissed the rumours, but he included a complaint with an ironical undertone that

---

"Piiskop Rahamägi meie mitropoliidi asemikuna" [Bishop Rahamägi as representative of our Metropolitan] in *UjE₂*, 6/7, 1938, p. 111.

80 See Rohtmets, 2006, p. 70-75.

81 Tiit Saluste, "Eesti luteri-inglise usulisest ühendusest" [Of the religious union of the Estonian Lutherans and the Anglicans] in *UjE₂*, 6/7, 1938, p. 111. See also Konstantin Kokla, "Uuendusi luteriusu kirikus" [Reforms in the Lutheran Church] in *UjE₂*, 5/1, 1937, p. 12-13.

82 „J. S.", "Anglikaņu baznīca un tauta" [The Anglican church and the people] in *TuD*, 15/2, 1939, p. 31.

83 See Sõtšov, 2009, p. 79-80. In the Jesuit archives in Rome, there is a document claiming that the Estonian Orthodox Synod had even made a decision to join the Roman Catholic Church in 1928. Klinke, 2000a, p. 28.

as long as Orthodox Estonians remain second- or even third-order citizens, as long as admitting to being Orthodox remains a confession of sins, there would be no wonder or incomprehension if the Orthodox Church really did enter into union with the Roman Catholic Church in self-defence, although this would not suit the national unity.

Our religious foundations are almost the same [...] we might even retain our religious habits and local autonomy, as was the case with count Scheptitski.[84] [...] Organising a theological seminary would be an easy task. Celibate priests would suit our difficult circumstances much better than our current ones, who have to worry about their families. [...] Maybe we could even achieve a concordat with the Vatican, as they have in Latvia. If the current atmosphere – hoping only for our death – should continue and our independent life should prove impossible (I certainly do not think it has come that far), then maybe this is it: better to form a union with the most influential church in the world than let ourselves be smashed by the fanatics of German learning or disappear in Moscow's bosom.

Time will show.[85]

Apparently, this article was picked up by the Lutheran journal *Meie Kirik* (Our Church) and other journals across Estonia and Europe. These journals mostly misunderstood the irony and took the article as proof of imminent union.[86] Such rumours reappeared at regular intervals, and there are indications that some influential figures within the Estonian Orthodox Church supported the idea of union.[87] Nevertheless, the Orthodox journals repeatedly criticised the Catholic Church, either through articles critical of its Estonian branch[88] or alienating

---

84 The correct writing of this name varies from the Polish Szeptycki to the German Scheptyzkyj or the Russian Шептицкий. Andrey Sheptytsky was the Eastern Catholic Archbishop of Lviv/Lemberg in current Ukraine. For more on him, see Heiler, 1971, p. 410, 585; Suttner, 1999, p. 233-239; Avvakumov, 2007.

85 Anton Laar, "Eesti apostliku-õigeusu ja Rooma-katoliku kiriku ühinemisest" [On the union between the Estonian Orthodox and Roman Catholic Churches] in *UE*, 10/9-10, 1930, p. 12-13. See also Sõtšov, 2009, p. 77-81.

86 At least, this is how Laar and other Orthodox Estonians saw it. See Anton Laar, "Teised lehed" [Other papers] in *UE*, 10/11, 1930, p. 7-8; "Ringvaade usuelule" [Reviewing religious life] in *UE*, 11/2, 1931, p. 8; A. J. Luusmann, "Märkmeid kiriklikkudes asjades" [Notices on ecclesiastical affairs] in *UE*, 11/12, 1931, p. 14-15.

87 Risch, 1937, p. 141; Klinke, 2000b, p. 864-865; Sõtšov, 2009, p. 77-81.

88 "Huvitavat ajakirjandusest" [Interesting things in the press] in *UjE₂*, 3/5, 1935, p. 96-98; Konstantin Kokla, "Huvitavat ajakirjandusest" [Interesting things in the press] in *UjE₂*, 3/6, 1935, p. 111; Konstantin Kokla, "Huvitavat ajakirjandusest" [Interesting things in the press] in *UjE₂*, 3/9, 1935, p. 158-159; Ajaloolane, "Mõtteid isade ja mitteisade kirjutiste puhul eestikeelses katoliiklaste häälekandjas" [Thoughts on the writings of fathers and non-fathers in the Estonian-language Catholic journal] in *UjE₂*, 4/13, 1936, p. 202-203; "Ühisele Kirikule" [To *Ühine Kirik* (the Estonian Catholic journal)] in *ET*, 2/8, 1937, p. 99; Konstantin Kokla, "Püha Tool ja meie" [The Holy See and us] in *UjE₂*, 5/8, 1937, p. 122-124; "Vatikani dogmast" [The dogma of the Vatican] in *UjE₂*, 6/7, 1938, p.

travel reports.[89] Konstantin Kokla even published a page of his personal diary, where he had noted his critical thoughts after a two-hour talk with a papal envoy:[90]

> A drop of water has the same characteristics as all the water in the oceans: this kind of inner unity is what is meant by the Greek word 'catholic.' Nowadays, the Latins understand catholic as the exclusive right of the papacy to explain the faith, whereas the Lutherans see their 'one holy Christianity' as the boundless individual preaching of God's will. However, Christ and his apostles did not preach either version. Their faith was the bounded 'congregation – church' as the Body of Christ. [...]
>
> When the heart (the Orthodox Church) says: 'keep holy unity while denying yourself,' while the head (the Roman Catholic Church) preaches: 'keep the rational faith holy!' – then this is no longer one united catholic church. Just as minerals and salts give the ocean water an aftertaste, the Roman Catholic confession has such an aftertaste. Then, when the body (the Lutherans, Anglicans, Calvinists, Adventists, Methodists, etc. etc. etc.) claim: 'keep the holy unity as it suits each soul!' – then we are dealing with water that has an aftertaste not only of minerals and salts, but equally of rotten swamps and peat.
>
> Everybody can call himself catholic, but not in the sense of the Greek word 'catholic;'[91] not in the sense of inner purity and unity, but only as an external characteristic, for there will always be salty and muddy and stinking waters all over the globe.[92]

Kokla had another opportunity to discredit Roman Catholicism after publishing a report by a young Orthodox Estonian who had planned to convert but interrupted the process after four months.[93] Two issues later, Kokla published a 'correction' from the Roman Catholic Church, together with a long introduction and a postscript about the Catholic priest that had brought it.[94] In this commentary, Kokla made it clear that he was no friend of the Catholic Church, and that the Catholic 'correction' – which was more like a personal attack on the young truthseeker – would not serve its purpose, but rather deepen the antagonism

---

109-110. K., "Katoliikluse püüded Eestis" [The Roman Catholic attempts in Estonia] in *UjE₂*, 6/15, 1938, p. 238.

89 M. Viik, "Muljeid Pariisi reisilt" [Impressions from my journey to Paris] in *UE*, 11/10, 1931, p. 3-5. However, this trip was interpreted by the secular press as an official visit to prepare the union between the churches. See Sõtšov, 2009, p. 81.

90 This was probably the later bishop and martyr Eduard Profittlich. See Klinke, 2000b, p. 865-873.

91 The Estonian version differentiates between 'katoliiklik' and 'kafoliikne', the latter denoting the Greek term.

92 Konstantin Kokla, "Huvitavat ajakirjandusest – Katoliiklus" [Interesting things from the press - Catholicism] in *UjE₂*, 3/7, 1935, p. 127-129

93 "Õppima katoliku vaimulikuks" [Learning to become a Catholic clergyman] in *PL*, 31/310, 15.11.1936, p. 1; N. S., "Tee Rooma" [The road to Rome] in *UjE₂*, 2/10, 1934, p. 168-170.

94 Berard Huber and Konstantin Kokla "Usuteelt, mis tuleb Roomast" [Of the road of faith, which comes from Rome] in *UjE₂*, 2/12, 1934, p. 200-203.

between the churches. This antagonism repeatedly appeared on both sides, and also Andrei Sõtšov concludes, in his overview of Orthodox Ecumenicalism in Estonia, that "the general attitude of the Orthodox press towards the Catholic Church in the 1930s was negative."[95]

Analyses of the Roman Catholic Church are almost absent from the Latvian Orthodox journals. However, a critical attitude towards it was detectable in the *Saeima* speeches of Archbishop Jānis, where Catholic deputies were repeatedly criticised. Also in connection with the debate surrounding the Alekseev Monastery and church, which was given to the Catholic Church in 1921, numerous anti-Catholic voices were heard.[96] An interesting aspect of Orthodox-Catholic relations came to the fore in 1939, in connection with the centenary of the 'vozsoedinenie,' the dissolution of the Uniate Church in the Russian Empire.[97] On this occasion, Juris Kreics, a retired Latvian schoolteacher from the Latgale region, wrote a critical, but informative article about the Orthodox-Catholic Union and its aftermath, warning Orthodox Latvians not to accept such a union too easily, for "the Uniates were neither this nor that, not Orthodox, not Catholic, not full, healthy individuals, but only a kind of half-persons."[98] A year later, on the occasion of the 350th anniversary of the Union itself, Kreics wrote about the Catholic Church's attempts during the last two years to spread Uniatism in Latvia. This article does not appear critical but simply describes the events.[99] Such attempts were also made in Estonia, but were unsuccessful among the ethnic Estonians. They convinces some ethnic Russian parishioners in the 1930s to convert, however.[100]

The smaller Protestant confessions, such as the Baptists and Methodists, were seldom mentioned by the Orthodox journals. An exception occurred during

---

95 Sõtšov, 2009, p. 81.
96 See chapter 2.2.6.
97 For more on the 'возсоединение', see Suttner, 1999, p. 233-239; Weeks, 2001; Dolbilov and Staliūnas, 2005.
98 Juris Kreics, "Daži vārdi par uniju" [Some words on the union] in *TuD*, 15/7, 1939, p. 104.
99 Juris Kreics, "Unijas 350 gadu jubileja" [350th anniversary of the Union] in *TuD*, 16/8, 1940, p. 119-121. Kreics also mentioned the Lithuanian state's attitude to the minority Orthodox Church in a positive light. Following the beginning of the Second World War and the return of Vilnius to Lithuania, the state returned all Orthodox churches and monasteries that the Polish state had handed over to the Catholic Church since 1920. See also D. V. R-s., "Veltīga katolicisma propaganda" [Unnecessary Roman Catholic propaganda] in *TuD*, 10/3, 1934, p. 47; "Uniati mēģina iespiesties arī Latvijā" [The Uniates try to spread also to Latvia] in *TuD*, 14/6, 1938, p. 93; Klinke, 2000a, p. 40; Sõtšov, 2009, p. 78-80.
100 The Russian-language Orthodox journal of Estonia also published critical articles to distance itself from Catholicism. Apostolicus, "Из эстской печати" [From the Estonian press] in *PS*, 6/9, 1936, p. 122-126; 6/10, 1936, p. 132-140.

1931-1933, when the editor of the Russian-language journal in Latvia, Kirils Zaics, turned it into a journal for internal missions and largely published programmatic articles for Orthodox priests fighting various Protestant groups. In the case of Estonia, these groups were mentioned more often in the Russian-language journal than in the Estonian one and always in a very negative tone. The other religious groups of Estonia and Latvia, such as the Jews and Old Believers, were hardly ever mentioned; thus it is impossible to draw any conclusions about the attitude of the Orthodox community towards them.

3.2.2. The Orthodox Church and Lutheranism

The Lutheran Church was a much more present partner to the Orthodox Church than Anglicanism and Roman Catholicism in both Estonia and Latvia, as it had always been the dominant church. Since the beginning of the twentieth century, the Lutheran Church was increasingly divided between the growing number of nationalist theologians and the formerly dominant Baltic Germans.[101] Especially in the Latvian case, this culminated in a discourse on the incompatibility of the Latvian nation with (Baltic German) Lutheranism at the outbreak of the First World War. The Orthodox journals eagerly picked up this discussion and there were attempts to incite a new mass conversion movement to the Orthodox Church.[102] According to Mark Hatlie, an American historian, the "Lutheran church, which had been the target of some criticism before the war but had been for the most part off limits to frontal attacks, now became the focus of Russian Orthodox vitriol."[103] In the Estonian case, competition between the Lutheran and Orthodox Churches was not established with the same vehemence, and anti-Lutheran propaganda was hardly present in the Estonian-language journal before 1917.

Interestingly, in the twenty years following the war, the tables were turned. While the Estonian Orthodox journals repeatedly criticised their 'Lutheran

---

101 von Schrenck, 1933, p. 179-203; Ketola, 2000a, p. 24-33; Saard, 2007a, p. 1263-1268, Talonen, 2008, p. 35-41.

102 Hatlie, 2009a, p. 306-309. For example, a Russian propaganda booklet on the Orthodox-Lutheran controversy (*Pravoslavie*, 1911) was printed in translation by the Latvian-language Orthodox journal over eleven issues in 1913. See also Nikolajs Kļava, "Protestantisma bankrots" [The bankruptcy of Protestantism] in *PLV*, 13/15, 1914, p. 227-236; 13/19, 1914, p. 293-300; 13/20, 1914, p. 311-316; 13/21, 1914, p. 326-329; -???-, "Luteraņu mācitāji atzīst savu bankrotu" [The Lutheran Pastors admit their bankrotcy] in *PLV*, 13/42, 1914, p. 661-663; Kr. Lappuķe, "Luterisma pārkrievošana un nacionālā religija" [Russification of Lutheranism and the national religion] in *PLV*, 13/51, 1914, p. 802-805; "Par tautisko ticību" [On the national faith] in *PLV*, 16/3-4, 1917, p. 20-24.

103 Hatlie, 2009a, p. 306.

neighbours,' the Latvian publications hardly ever mentioned the Lutheran Church. This might be related to Archbishop Jānis' strategy to focus on the Social Democrats as the main enemies, which diverted attention away from any other (religious) rivals.[104] In the following few pages, I will therefore focus on the Estonian case and mention the Latvian case only in passing. The previously mentioned national struggle within the Lutheran Church was complemented by a dispute between two theological schools: the conservative theology of the 'old Tartu University' and the increasingly popular liberal theology.[105] These internal struggles of the dominant Lutheran Church overshadowed most conflicts of inter-confessional relations. For the Orthodox minority, especially in Estonia, this meant that the Lutheran Church was an inflexible giant that could be criticised without fear of consequences. More importantly, it was the 'standard' to which the Orthodox minority compared itself.[106]

In concrete terms, ecumenical relations between the Orthodox and Lutheran Churches in Estonia were friendly and peaceful. Alongside the formal relations in state committees, ecumenicity was lived out in three main areas.[107] First, there was the joint commemoration of the 'Tartu martyrs,' killed by the Bolsheviks in January 1919.[108] Second, at public celebrations for army units, schools, societies, etc., representatives from both confessions were usually actively involved, and third, joint support of the temperance movement. While the relations were mostly peaceful from the outside, the journals were often rather critical. In the Orthodox press, one can identify five themes in this criticism. Every time an article touched upon the Lutheran Church, it mentioned at least one of these themes, even when the article was positively inclined towards the 'neighbour church.'

The first theme was the claim that Orthodoxy was the true Christianity and, consequently, that the Lutheran Faith was less valid. This theme appeared in a variety of contexts and with a number of connotations. A concrete example was the consecration of Jakob Kukk as the first Estonian Lutheran bishop in June 1921.[109] Commenting on the consecration, carried out by two visiting bishops

---

104 The few articles on inter-confessional relations in Latvia are written much more theologically and less polemically than in the Estonian case. See Jānis Bormanis, "Pareizticīgo baznīca attiecībā uz citām ticībam Latvijā" [The relationship between the Orthodox Church and other faiths in Latvia] in *TuD* 8/5, p. 65-69; Jānis Jansons, "Pareizticība un protestantisms" [Orthodoxy and Protestantism] in *TuD* 8/9, p. 121-123. See chapter 3.2.3. for more on criticism of the secular world.

105 von Schrenck, 1933, p. 142-152; Wittram, Heinrich, 1956, p. 234-243; Talonen, 2008, p. 28-35.

106 See also Saard, 2007a, p. 1260-1262.

107 Sõtsov, 2009, p. 68-75.

108 See chapter 2.2.1.

109 Ketola, 2000a, p. 80-83.

from Sweden and Finland, the Orthodox journal emphasised that their Lutheran 'neighbours' could have invited the Orthodox Archbishop Aleksander (Paulus) to co-celebrate the consecration, in order to ensure true apostolic succession.[110] This specific issue arose in Latvia as well, when Teodors Grīnbergs was consecrated as the Lutheran Archbishop of Riga in November 1933. His consecration was performed by a simple provost in the presence of many pastors. Commenting on an apologetic article by the most prominent Latvian Lutheran theologian, Ludvigs Adamovičs, the Orthodox journal *Ticība un Dzīve* noted with relief that

> apostolic priesthood is preserved in the holy Orthodox Church, for all the priests and bishops of this church are legitimately consecrated to their office by some older bishop, who in turn was consecrated by an older one, who again received it from someone older, and thus all the way back to the Apostles and Jesus Christ. The Lutheran pastors lack this exponentiation, this uninterrupted apostolic imposition of hands, just as the Latvian Lutheran Archbishop T. Grīnbergs does not have it.
> Since the Lutherans now cannot ever expect to regain this apostolic blessing, the above mentioned article [by Adamovičs] tries to assure the readers that it is not even necessary, that it does not conform to the Lutheran faith. That may be, that it does not conform to the Lutheran faith, but it does conform to the Holy Scripture and the history of Christianity. And it also conforms to the rational mind, for only he can give his blessing, who has legitimately received it himself.[111]

In most cases where this theme was used, the authors of the articles referred to conversations they had or publications they read. An example of this is the commentary on the publication, in 1928, of extracts from the Protestant theologian Ernst Wilhelm Hengstenberg under the heading 'A Lutheran Opinion on the Orthodox Liturgy.'[112] What the commentator did not mention was that Hengstenberg lived almost a century earlier. When the journal *Uus Elu* published an Estonian translation of the conversion story of Pavel Tiedeboehl in

---

110 "Üks põhiõpetus Ev.-Lutheri kirikus" [A fundamental principle in the Lutheran Church] in *UE*, 1/5-6, 1921, p. 45-46. Although the Swedish and Finnish Lutheran Churches claim true apostolic succession, this is disputed. The opinion was also referred to in Konstantin Kokla, "Kirikliku elu vaatlemisel" [Looking at church life] in *UE*, 10/9-10, 1930, p. 7; Konstantin Kokla, "Mis ajas eestlasi usuvahetusele?" [What drove the Estonians to conversion?] in *UE*, 11/7, 1931, p. 3; Eestlane, "Viimne aeg likvideerida mineviku pärandused" [Now is the last chance to dissolve the past's inheritance!] in *ET*, 4/20, 1939, p. 213.

111 Pēteris Gredzens, "Latvijas luteraņu arķibīskapa iesvētīšana" [The consecration of the Archbishop of the Latvian Lutheran Church] in *TuD*, 10/1, 1934, p. 12. These discussions were even noted in the Estonian Orthodox journal: Konstantin Kokla, "Kirikute vahepiirilt Eestis" [On the boundary between the churches in Estonia] in *UjE₂*, 2/7, 1934, p. 117.

112 K. M., "Protestantlase arvamine ap.-õigeusu jumalateenistusest" [A Lutheran opinion on the Orthodox liturgy] in *UE*, 8/8-9, 1928, p. 8-10.

1937-38, the editor contextualised the text in a postscript, mentioning that
Tiedeboehl was of Baltic German origin and wrote his conversion story in
1902.[113] The articles on the basis of conversations looked like this:

> 'Our Lutheranism,' as one of them told me, 'compared with your Orthodoxy, is pale
> and dim. Look at the splendour of your houses of worship, at their glitter – what can
> surpass that? [...] One can only say in awe: a better faith than Orthodoxy does not
> exist. [...]' A Lutheran woman told me this. And it is not only a solitary opinion, but
> many Lutherans, men and women, feel this way. That is the current tendency among
> the Lutherans, especially among the educated ones, getting acquainted with Ortho-
> doxy and even wishing to convert, as we have noticed in the most recent times. [...]
> Therefore, we can only consider those who leave the Orthodox Church simpletons
> and victims of blindness of the soul.[114]

A final occasion where the theme of true Christianity was used was discussion
of liturgical reform. In these cases, the authors emphasised the steadfastness of
Orthodox Christianity, which had retained the spirit of the Early Church. The
Orthodox Church would remain steadfast in faith and practice while the Lutherans seek forms more suitable to modern life.[115] This trope alos appears when the
ecumenical movement is discussed. The movement is welcomed as a platform
for talks, but "the only way to heal a chronic disease is to remove its causes, and
it is just the same with a mass religious disease. It is caused by divergence from

---

113 The first instalment: Pavel S. Tiedeboehl, "Kuidas leidsin õige Kiriku" [How I found the
correct church] in *UjE₂*, 5/1, 1937, p. 8-9. The postscript: Konstantin Kokla, "Preester
Pavel Tiedeboehl" [Priest Pavel Tiedeboehl] in *UjE₂*, 6/12, 1938, p. 183. See also B. An-
ko, "Protestantline pastor protestantlusest" [A Protestant Pastor on Protestantism] in *UE*,
5/6, 1925, p. 3-4; T. Lepik, "Õigeusu kirikulaulu hinnang võõralt" [Foreigners appreci-
ating Orthodox church song] in *UjE₂*, 6/1, 1938, p. 11-13; J., "Vakareiropas zinātnieka
domas par pareizticību" [A West European's thoughts on Orthodoxy] in *TuD*, 15/3, 1939,
p. 35-37.
114 Kirils Zaics, "Luterticīgās sievietes atsauksme par pareizticību." [A Lutheran woman's
opinion of Orthodoxy] in *TuD*, 6/10, p. 158. See also Joann Paavel, "Ap.-õigeusu õpetus
ja kogudusekorraldus - kõneluses välismaa turistidega" [The teaching and services of the
Orthodox Church – in conversation with foreign tourists] in *ET*, 1/17, 1936, p. 3-5; 1/18,
1936, p. 3-4; Koguduse preester, "Vestlusi usuvahetajatega" [Discussions with converts]
in *UjE₂*, 5/12, 1937, p. 180-181; J., "Vakareiropas zinātnieka domas par pareizticību" [A
West European's thoughts on Orthodoxy] in *TuD*, 15/3, 1939, p. 35.
115 See "Teised lehed" [Other newspapers] in *UE*, 4/4-5, 1924, p. 12-13; Kirils Zaics,
"Pareizticības gaisma" [The light of Orthodoxy] in *TuD*, 7/5, 1929, p. 65-66; "Huvitavat
usuelust kirjanduses" [Interesting facts about religious life in the press] in *UjE₂*, 3/2,
1935, p. 25-26; Konstantin Kokla, "Uuendusi luteriusu kirikus" [Reforms in the Lutheran
Church] in *UjE₂*, 5/1, 1937, p. 12-13; "Kas uus reform?" [A new reform?] in *ET*, 2/6,
1937, p. 69.

the catholic Christian Church. The religious doctors must start healing where the Pope left."[116]

The second theme suggested that Orthodox Christianity was more suitable to the Estonians and Latvians than Lutheranism and the third theme held that Lutheranism was a German faith. Both ideas primarily accompanied the claim that the mainstream view of history was one falsified by the Baltic Germans. This is more elaborately analysed in the next chapter. The theme of Lutheranism as a German faith also appears in other contexts; especially in Orthodox responses to the Lutherans calling them 'the Russian faith':

> Recently, a young Lutheran priest exclaimed in true amazement: 'impossible, an Estonian who converted to the Russian faith in our days!' An older Orthodox priest reacted: 'Is it natural for a free Estonian to be retained by the German faith?'[117]

> After all, no Orthodox Christian would ever call the Lutheran Church 'the Martin faith' or 'the German faith,' although he would have reasons to do so, but he relates to this confession with sincerity and respects its religious traditions. [...]
> And finally: It is nowadays clear to every intelligent person that there is neither a German nor a Russian faith in free Estonia but rather the Estonian Evangelical Lutheran Church and the Estonian Apostolic Orthodox Church.[118]

The fourth theme posited that the Lutherans are arrogant and presumptuous. It was of prime importance in governing the Orthodox analysis of ecumenical relations in Estonia. Concretely, the description of joint celebrations was often coloured by a sad tone about how the relationship was not as it should be. Coverage of the blessing of a new schoolhouse in Tallinn in 1924 provides a concrete example:

> In order to remain impartial, we will let the official correspondence between the municipality and the Orthodox Synod speak for itself. Maybe some historian might use this documentation at a later stage, for it is worth it:

---

116 Konstantin Kokla, "'Oikumeeniline' ja 'katoliiklik'" ['Ecumenical' and 'catholic'] in *UjE₂*, 6/7, 1938, p. 99-100. See also Konstantin Kokla, "Ajakirjanduse keskel" [Among the newspapers] in *UjE₂*, 1/3, 1933, p. 6; Konstantin Kokla, "Huvitavat ajakirjandusest – Katoliiklus" [Interesting things from the press – Catholicism] in *UjE₂*, 3/7, 1935, p. 127-129.

117 Andrei Sooster, "Pudemeid usuelust meil ja mujal – Rahvused Eestis" [Notices on religious life here and elsewhere – Nationalities in Estonia] in *UjE₂*, 3/6, 1935, p. 112.

118 M., "Kas võhiklikkus või sihiklikkus?" [Is that ignorance or deliberate?] in *ET*, 2/13, 1937, p. 157-158. When some Lutheran pastors in 1939 started to advocate Estonianising the German faith (Lutheranism), the Orthodox journal greedily picked up this discourse. "Eesti usk – Saksa usk" [Estonian faith – German faith] in *UjE₂*, 7/3, 1939, p. 47. See also Ketola, 2000b.

From the Estonian Orthodox Synod
12 February 1924, Nr. 353/3314   To the Tallinn city government

Having heard that the municipality plans to invite only a Lutheran pastor to the blessing of
the new schoolhouse in *Raua* Street and considering 1) that there is no privileged faith in
Estonia and 2) that a large portion of the Tallinn inhabitants and taxpayers are Orthodox,
which means that a significant section of the future pupils at this school also belong to this
faith, we consider it biased of the municipality not to invite an Orthodox representative,
who would carry out the blessing jointly with the Lutheran pastor, as it is usually done
elsewhere in Estonia.

Synod member (Signature)
Secretary (Signature)

From the Tallinn city government
14 February 1924, Nr. 1849   To the Estonian Orthodox Synod

In reply to your letter no. 353/3314 from 12 Feb. 1924 concerning the blessing of the *Raua*
schoolhouse, the Tallinn city government announces that there will be no religious act at
this schoolhouse *blessing*,[119] only a speech by Pastor Mohrfeldt.

Mayor (Signature)
Secretary (Signature)

From the Estonian Orthodox Synod
18 March 1924, Nr. 453/3510   To the Tallinn city government

In your letter from 14 February 1924 no. 1849, the city government announced that 'there
will be no religious act at this blessing.' The Synod did not understand how you would go
about 'blessing' something without a religious act, for these two phrases signify the same
thing. After the event, the Tallinn press unanimously announced: the religious act was carried out by Pastor Mohrfeldt. Although we could concede that the secular press might not
have enough expertise to distinguish this act from a real religious act, we should nevertheless believe the authority of the [Lutheran] newspaper *Meie Kirik* [Our Church], which
stated that 'the *religious act* was nicely carried out by Pastor Mohrfeldt: in his *blessing
speech*, he emphasised ... etc. Opening the *blessing service*, the schoolchoir sang 'Let us
praise the Lord, the almighty' (a Lutheran church song) and repeating the *words of the
blessing*: 'Praise the Lord, oh my soul.' Since this issue not only interests us for the sake of
religious discrimination, but also the Tallinn city government for the sake of accuracy, the
Synod would like to know: How can we combine the letter of the city government with the
information in *Meie Kirik* correctly?

Synod member (Signature)
Secretary (Signature)

From the Tallinn city government
24 March 1924, Nr. 3596   To the Estonian Orthodox Synod

In reply to your letter from 4 March 1924, no. 553/3510 [sic], the Tallinn city government
announces that the opening ceremony of the schoolhouse in *Raua* Street did not include
any religious acts or blessings, but only a speech by Pastor Mohrfeldt and the choir singing. How the newspapers, including *Meie Kirik* describe it, is their decision, since the city
government cannot force them to do anything.

Mayor (Signature)
Secretary (Signature)

---

119 Take note of and compare this to the second letter of the municipality [Original footnote
and emphasis].

We do not know what [the editor of *Meie Kirik*] thinks about this matter, but it would have been very interesting to hear his opinion: who is wrong, *Meie Kirik* or the city government?
The Orthodox Estonians should read these lines and ponder them in their hearts.[120]

Such disputes repeatedly occurred, although the practice of joint blessings seems to have worked most of the time.[121] However, this practice apparently embarrassed the Lutheran Estonians, and in some cases, they tried to circumvent it. In a description of the annual report of the Viljandi priory, the Lutheran journal claimed that "it is unfortunate that we have to celebrate blessing services jointly with another confession, just as in Russian times. This can only diminish the virtue of the service."[122] The Orthodox journal commented:

We do not know if this is still part of the report or the description of it, but in any case, the gist is clear. We would not have believed in this kind of intolerance anymore, but unfortunately, it persists.[...] Lately, at the preparations to some memorial site blessing ceremony somebody said that it would not be necessary to call 'a Russian priest' when the 'state religion' can do the work. The second-rank citizens replied 'did only your fire hit the enemy and ours not?!'
We also ask this of our intolerant fellow pastor and his friends, who cannot stand joint blessings. Or do they think Estonia has become so strong that the support from one fifth of the population is no longer necessary and the 'Russian-believers' can be dismissed? In any case, even if that is the train of thought, it is not very tactical to publicly express it. And strengthening intolerance and destroying the national feeling of justice with such sharp remarks is definitely an un-evangelical attitude.[123]

When the Orthodox portion of the joint service was positively mentioned by the secular press, this was quickly picked up in the journal, but only after an introduction contextualising this positive mention as something very unusual.[124]

The theme of arrogance reappears in the discourse in the repeated complaints that the Lutherans are unable to call the Orthodox by their true name.

---

120 "Mõned pudemed Eesti avaliku elu radadelt" [Some notes from Estonian public life] in *UE*, 4/6-7, 1924, p. 10-11. Another interesting fact about this story is that it did not end there. The Tallinn city government had to admit, three months later, that the schoolhouse had been built without the necessary safety precautions and could collapse any moment. The Orthodox journal exclaimed with glee: "And now we publicly admit our fault. The city government was right after all! For: if a house is not built by Jehova, its constructors run into problems...", "Tallinna uue koolimaja pühitsemise üle" [On the blessing of the new schoolhouse in Tallinn] in *UE*, 4/9, 1924, p. 8.
121 Sõtsov, 2009, p. 70-71.
122 "Eesti kirikuelu 1929. aastal" [Estonian church life in 1929] in *Eesti Kirik*, 7/28, 1930, p. 222.
123 "Teised lehed" [Other journals] in *UE*, 10/7, 1930, p. 8. See also Konstantin Kokla, "Kirikliku elu vaatlemisel" [Looking at church life] in *UE*, 10/9-10, 1930, p. 7-8; "Ajakirjanduse keskel" [Among the newspapers] in *UjE₂*, 1/3, 1933, p. 6.
124 "Haruldus Hiiumaalt" [A rarity from Hiiumaa] in *UjE₂*, 6/10, 1938, p. 159-160.

These complaints range from ironic comments that "our culture will, someday, arrive at a point where people know each other's names"[125] or "'Greek Catholic' (our quotation marks, for the rest of Estonia has used 'apostolic Orthodox' for more than ten years)"[126] to complete analyses of the Lutheran opinion. For example, the liberal Lutheran theologian Theodor Tallmeister claimed in 1930 that the name 'Apostolic Orthodoxy' was a slap in the face for Lutheranism:

> 'Strange people live on that farm (i.e. in the Estonian Orthodox Church). They take a name that is a slap in the face for all others and then demand that we use it sincerely and without quotation marks. If we could call your faith 'correct,'[127] we would have to convert at once, and if we could call it 'apostolic,' it would not be long before we knocked at your door.'[128]

The Orthodox journal defensively commented

> The author Th. T. wants us to take the name 'Greek Catholic,' for 'apostolic' is not legitimate; in the apostolic writings, there is nothing about incense burning or holy vestments.
> Unfortunately, this wish comes too late. When we chose for ourselves a name in free Estonia in 1919, a large faction of the Lutheran clergy wanted, and still want, to force the name 'Russian faith' on us and keep the much more agreeable-sounding 'Estonian faith' to themselves. We did not like the Russian name, because it contains a plain lie: the Russians have not invented any faith for themselves or for us. The name 'Greek Catholic' was also unsuitable, for it was completely foreign to the Estonian mind, moreover, it only appeared after Rome had left the Christian foundations. [...]
> The names 'apostolic' and 'correct' are more than 1600 years old and a 'slap in the face' only for those who suffer from self-aggrandisement. According to this logic, also Jesus hit the disciples with a slap in the face when he called Simon 'Peter' – 'rock.'[129]

---

125 "Mõndasugust" [This and that] in *UE*, 4/9, 1924, p. 8.
126 "Teised lehed" [Other journals] in *UE*, 10/7, 1930, p. 7. See also Anton Laar, "Eesti apostliku-õigeusu ja Rooma-katoliku kiriku ühinemisest" [On the union between the Estonian Orthodox and Roman Catholic Churches] in *UE*, 10/9-10, 1930, p. 13.
127 Orthographically, the Estonian word for 'Orthodoxy' is equal to 'the correct faith.'
128 Quoted in Konstantin Kokla, "Kirikliku elu vaatlemisel" [Looking at church life] in *UE*, 10/9-10, 1930, p. 7.
129 Konstantin Kokla, "Kirikliku elu vaatlemisel" [Looking at church life] in *UE*, 10/9-10, 1930, p. 7. A similar discussion took place in Latvia, but under completely different auspices, when Ludvigs Adamovičs, a Lutheran theologian and Minister of Education, published an article in the largest Riga daily called 'Eastern Orthodox or Greek Catholic?' In his explanation, Adamovičs very soberly emphasised that the 'Greek Catholic Church' was a different church altogether, and that there was no offense in calling oneself 'Orthodox.' After all, the Roman Catholic Church called itself 'Catholic' and the Lutherans 'Evangelical.' Ludvigs Adamovičs, "Austrumu pareizticīgie jeb grieķu katoli?" [Eastern Orthodox or Greek Catholic?] in *JZ*, 25/294, 1935, 28.12, p. 8. See also sch.,

Finally, especially with the new official journal *Elutõde* (Truth of Life) from 1936, this theme developed into mutual accusations. *Eesti Kirik* (the Lutheran journal) accused *Elutõde* of publishing intolerant articles about Lutheranism and *Elutõde* replied, accusing *Eesti Kirik* of voicing these accusations in a tone unworthy of fellow Christians.[130] A variation on this theme was the observation by an author O. K. that "friendship with Lutherans is not trustworthy."[131] Although the theme did not continue to dominate the pages of the Orthodox journals after 1936, a lead article from 1939 complains that the situation had not really changed. The Lutherans continued to accuse the Orthodox Church groundlessly.[132]

The final theme in relation to the Lutheran Church appeared whenever the Orthodox publicists felt that the Lutherans were spreading incorrect information about Orthodoxy. For example, this was the case with the conversion statistics they published:

> Regarding the annual report of the Lutheran bishop, which claimed that 500 Estonians had converted from Orthodoxy to Lutheranism in 1929, whereas only 23 had converted the other direction, we expressed our doubts at the correctness of these numbers, for there were 31 chrismations in the Tartu County alone. The Lutheran journal displays the same attitude in this matter as in the case of our name, saying: we do not believe you – on the basis of the very orderly bookkeeping of the Tallinn Holy Spirit congregation. We do believe both the Lutheran annual report as well as the bookkeeping qualities of Pastor Tallmeister. However, we express doubts as to whether the written word corresponds to reality. Otherwise, we would stand before a contemporary miracle, in that the total number of Orthodox Christians in Estonia is growing according to the census, while it is continuously shrinking in the Lutheran books.[133]

This theme of the Lutheran Church ignoring the Orthodox Church and spreading false information about it had been used since the consecration of Jakob Kukk as

---

"Austrumu pareizticīgie vaj grieķu-katoļi?" [Eastern Orthodox or Greek-Catholic?] in *TuD*, 12/2, 1936, p. 31.

130 M. Mäessa, "'Järvesalu naabrite' autori vastus J. Ora'le" [The answer of the author of 'Järvesalu naabrid' to J. Ora] in *ET*, 1/24-25, 1936, p. 8; Konstantin Kokla, "Huvitavat ajakirjandusest" [Interesting things from the press] in *UjE₂*, 4/8, 1936, p. 127-128; -nd., "'Eesti Kirik' salgab!" ['Eesti Kirik' hurts!] in *ET*, 1/33, 1936, p. 4-5.

131 O. K., "Sõprus luterlastega pole usutav" [Friendship with Lutherans is not trustworthy] in *ET*, 1/32, 1936, p. 7.

132 "Usk, takt ja vaimulikud" [Faith, common sense and the clergy] in *ET*, 4/15-16, 1939, p. 161.

133 Konstantin Kokla, "Kirikliku elu vaatlemisel" [Looking at church life] in *UE*, 10/9-10, 1930, p. 7. See also "Teised lehed" [Other journals] in *UE*, 10/7, 1930, p. 7; "Ajakirjanduse keskel" [Among the newspapers] in *UjE₂*, 1/6, 1933, p. 6; Konstantin Kokla, "Kirikute vahepiirilt Eestis" [On the boundary between the churches in Estonia] in *UjE₂*, 2/7, 1934, p. 115-117.

the first Estonian Lutheran bishop in 1921. Criticism of the consecration and its description in the press was symptomatic:

> The congratulation for the new bishop in the agenda mentioned above left a somehow alienated impression: 'Unite all faiths, all nations in our state and our country under the holy and light burden of Christ.' We also pray for 'unity in the faith' (not the impossible unity of faiths) in our churches, but we doubt that Jakob Kukk is the right person to unite the faiths in Estonia, at least not as long as Archbishop Aleksander is in office with a true apostolic mission. It remains a mystery to us, who the new Estonian bishop is supposed to 'unite under the holy and light burden of Christ;' there are practically no pagans in our country and there is not much talk about evangelical missions among the Jews.
> Moreover, it is a plain lie to call Kukk 'the first Estonian bishop,' which we would have taken to be a spelling error, if *Vaba Maa* had not reported the consecration under the heading 'the consecration of the first Estonian bishop.' The first Estonian Lutheran bishop would have been correct. For it remains a fact that the first Estonian bishop was Paul Kulbusch on 31 December 1917 and the second was Aleksander Paulus on 5 December 1920. –
> Although we may assume that both the author of the agenda and *Vaba Maa* forgot about this in their religious excitement, we involuntarily sense an intention, the purpose of which it is to keep everything that pertains to our faith as an Estonian faith under wraps.[134]

Anton Laar expanded on this suspicion of an intentional affront a month later, while emphasising how difficult and awkward it was to bring up this topic. The Lutheran journal *Meie Kirik* had replied to earlier Orthodox criticism of the consecration "in a really moralising manner," without any excuse or explanation. Laar, therefore, asked again:

> who are those pagans, who are not yet united under the light burden? [The editor] hints at an answer, when we remember how in 1920 he distributed the 'authentic Word of God,' i.e. an occupation-era brochure [...], in which a completely malformed 'Russian faith' was juxtaposed with the Protestant faith. *We* are supposed to be the people outside of the light burden of Christ![135]

The two accused Lutheran Pastors sent a letter to Laar, denying any involvement with the mentioned brochure. The latter ironically commented on this letter:

> We believe you, truly, that you really did not forbid the distribution of occupation-era brochures concerning the 'Russian faith.' And if you wish, we can even empa-

---

134 "Üks põhiõpetus Ev.-Lutheri kirikus" [A fundamental principle in the Lutheran Church] in *UE*, 1/5-6, 1921, p. 45-46.
135 "Meie vahekordadest" [Our relationship] in UE, 1/7, 1921, p. 49-51. This brochure from the First World War was also published in "Missugune vahe on Evangeeliumi ja Vene usu vahel?" [What is the difference between the Gospel's and the Russian faith?] in *Risti-rahva Pühhapäevaleht*, 44/27-29, 1918, p. 104, 108, 112.

thise with your 'grief' of not having had this 'honour': to distribute occupation-era 'literature' among the Estonians.[136]

This mudslinging at the Orthodox Church continued throughout the interwar period, but it peaked in 1936, when the Lutheran journals accused the Orthodox journals of deliberately provoking a conflict between the two churches. The Orthodox reaction was to return the accusations, claiming that the Estonian Lutheran Church acted with double standards; at an international Protestant conference in the Netherlands, the Lutheran pastor Eduard Steinwand had lectured about the tasks of the so-called 'Baltische Rußlandarbeit' (Baltic Aid for Russia). Steinwand had just become the leader of this loose association of mostly Baltic German pastors who had developed an interest in the Orthodox Church and characterised its tasks as "bringing the Gospel to the Orthodox Church, which is imbued with paganism and should be treated like any other unfaith."[137] This prompted an author with the pseudonym '-nd' to pen a polemical article regarding the Lutheran Church and its journal:

> We do not know on whose behalf Pastor Steinwand spoke, but we dare to assume that the discipline in the Lutheran Church is strong enough to make an official statement about the religious life of the entire nation at an international conference impossible without the prior consent of the consistory[138] chairman Dr. Rahamägi and the entire consistory.
>
> Nevertheless, we do not consider the story as tragic as we would have been justified to do. We have become used to a lot from the Lutherans over the last decades, and this story with Pastor Steinwand is nothing more than another one of the continuous disappointments in this regard. It is, however, boundlessly sad that by revealing the true character of the Lutheran home mission, Estonian religious life seems to have arrived at one of its most suspicious and blackest pages, whose logical consequences seem impossible to avoid.
>
> We still hope that the Orthodox Church remains loyal to the spirit of love and tolerance of its 'pagan' Gospel and will never refuse the once offered Lutheran helping hand, for somehow, we would like to hope that the true spirit of love and tolerance of the real Gospel will awaken also in the hearts of the participants and leaders of the Lutheran home mission. This, however, does not hinder us in raising our voice here, noting that not only is the Estonian Orthodox Church a *surrounded*, but even an *infiltrated*, castle. Every Orthodox Christian should keep this in mind – for purposes of self-defence. Therefore, – get in line![139]

---

136 Hugo Bernhard Rahamägi and Anton Laar, "Sissetulnud kirjad" [Incoming letters] in *UE*, 2/2, 1922, p. 8.

137 Quoted in -nd., "Järjekordne pettumus" [Repeated disappointment] in *ET*, 1/30, 1936, p. 5. See also Kahle, 1959, p. 236-271; Wittram, Heinrich, 2005, p. 448-459.

138 A consistory is the governing body of a Lutheran Church. Its chairman is usually the head bishop of the church.

139 -nd., "Järjekordne pettumus" [Repeated disappointment] in *ET*, 1/30, 1936, p. 6-7 (Emphasis in original).

'-nd' followed up this piece with other articles in the next issues, for "now that our church is *under attack*, it is high time to take leave of the former practice of quietly accepting the situation."[140] His militant language and harsh criticism did not pass unnoticed in the Lutheran press, but was just as harshly criticised in return.[141] This declaration of war by '-nd' was the starting signal of a long article series in the Orthodox journal, called 'Ajaloline tõde' (Historical truth), which is analysed in greater detail in chapter four.

3.2.3. Baltic Orthodoxy and Secular Society

The analysis of secular society by the Orthodox press focused on two main topics. First, there was the relationship between the church and the secular state. The perceived antagonism of the majority society to the Orthodox Church constituted a second topic, which was allowed frequent discussion. Alongside these issues, one should also mention the temperance movement, which the Orthodox Church intensively promoted in both Latvia and Estonia.[142] Another topic that merits mention is the internal mission, especially among the younger generations, which was usually presented in the journals as a neglected field.[143] In the

---

140 -nd., "Read koomale!" [Get in formation!] in *ET*, 1/31, 1936, p. 1 (Emphasis in original). See also -nd., "Ajaloline tõde ausse!" [Historical truth to the fore!] in *ET*, 1/32, 1936, p. 5-6; -nd., "'Eesti Kirik' salgab!" ['Eesti Kirik' hurts!] in *ET*, 1/33, 1936, p. 4-5; -nd., "Kiriku-mõtteid" [Church thoughts] in *ET*, 1/39, 1936, p. 4-5; -nd., "Selgituseks selgitajaile" [Explanation for the explainers] in *ET*, 1/45, 1936, p. 1-2. It has not been possible to identify the author of these articles. Toomas Schvak suggested that it might have been Deacon Joann Juhtund.

141 Jakob Aunver, "Eesti ap.-õigeusu suhtumisest Eesti ev.-luteriusu kirikule" [The relationship between the Estonian Orthodox and the Estonian Lutheran Churches] in *PL*, 31/344, 19.12.1936, p. 6. See also Nikolai Päts, "Vastuseks ja seletuseks" [Answer and explanation] in *ET*, 2/1, 1937, p. 7; Jakob Aunver, "Mõningaid tõsiasju ap.-õigeusu kiriku kohta" [Some facts about the Orthodox Church] in *Eesti Kirik*, 14/2, 14.01.1937, p. 1-3.

142 An indication of the importance of this movement in Latvia is that almost all important actors within the Latvian Orthodox Church were committee members of the Temperance Society. See V. J., "Latvijas pareizticības atturības biedrības gada sapulce" [The annual general meeting of the Latvian Orthodox Temperance Society] in *TuD*, 8/4, 1930, p. 62-63. Andrei Sõtsov mentions the temperance movement as one area where ecumenical co-operation was especially successful in Estonia. Sõtsov, 2009, p. 71-72.

143 Anton Laar, "Mõtted ja muljed sisemisjoni tööst" [Thoughts and impressions of the work of the internal mission] in *UE*, 4/8, 1924, p. 4-5; Kirils Zaics, "Kā ir ar misiju?" [What is with the mission?] in *TuD*, 7/10, 1929, p. 122-123; Konstantin Kokla, "Usuühtluse tunnused" [The features of Ecumenicity] in *UE*, 10/6, 1930, p. 5-6; Antonijs Pommers, "Jaunatnes kristīgie pulcini" [The meetings of young Christians] in *TuD*, 8/5, 1930, p. 70-72; "Sõnad ja teod" [Words and deeds] in *UE*, 12/7-8, 1932, p. 7-9; Nikolai Päts, "Noorus rahva tuleviku lootus" [The youth is the hope for the future of the nation] in *ET*, 1/8,

1930s, this topic often became criticism of the modern youth, who were perceived as lacking traditional values. This is especially the case with Nikolai Päts' editorials in the Estonian journal *Elutõde*.[144]

Turning to the relationship between the church and the state, many of the discussions have been mentioned in previous chapters. These relations were very different in the two nations. Whereas the Estonian Orthodox Church participated fully in the political life of the nation from the beginning of Estonian independence, the Latvian Church first had to struggle for recognition. Once this recognition was achieved in 1926, Archbishop Jānis and other Orthodox clergy continued to speak of the Orthodox Church as the step-child of the Latvian Republic. For example, in an article on the government's treatment of foreign state visitors, an unidentifiable author compared the Latvian head of state's visit to Finland with the Estonian head's visit to Riga:

> The Finns first of all took the visitor to church. Upon their return, the journalists wrote particularly and euphorically about the Finnish omnipresent religiosity (Zalts in *Brīvā Zemē*). I believe they did this (i.e. the journalists praising the Finns) not out of hypocrisy but with their full heart. [...]
>
> When the Estonian head of state visited us a year and a quarter ago, we did not take him to church. On the contrary: several churches were even closed to visitors. While he watched the parade at the Esplanade, the pavement on both sides of the street in front of our cathedral was lined with police officers, who stopped everybody wishing to enter. The Liturgy was held in an empty church.[145]

The article continued by listing how the Latvian state pursued anti-church policies, expropriating church property and using church buildings for secular purposes. The negative attitude towards ecclesiastic issues in Latvia even had repercussions in Estonia, when the formerly Orthodox Peter-and-Paul church in Riga, which had most recently housed the Estonian Lutheran parish of Riga, was expropriated in 1932. The Lutheran journals in Estonia published numerous arti-

---

1936, p. 1-2; Pēteris Gredzens, "Jaunatnes organisēšana draudzēs" [Organising the youth in the congregations] in *TuD*, 13/24, 1937, p. 375-376.

144 Pēteris Gredzens, "Ticība un dzīve" [Faith and life] in *TuD*, 13/15, 1937, p. 226; "Kirik ja kool" [Church and school] in *ET*, 2/15, 1937, p. 181; "Usuõpetus ja kool" [Religious instruction and the school] in *ET*, 2/16, 1937, p. 193-194; Nikolai Päts, "Kiriklikud sündmused seoses riigieluga" [Church events in connection with state life] in *ET*, 2/20, 1937, p. 241; Nikolai Päts, "Usuline kasvatus ja kool" [Religious upbringing and the school] in *ET*, 3/15-16, 1938, p. 169-170; Nikolai Päts, "Täit tähelepanu noorsoo usulisele kasvatusele!" [Full attention to the religious upringing of the youth!] in *ET*, 3/20, 1938, p. 233-234; E. Vendis, "Maniem draugiem" [To my friends] in *TuD*, 15/13, 1939, p. 194-195; Pēteris Gredzens, "Pareizticība, Vecā Deriba und jaunpaganisms" [Orthodoxy, the Old Testament and neopaganism] in *TuD*, 15/15, 1939, p. 226-229. See also chapter 2.3.3.

145 J. K--s., "Ko esam mācijušies no draugiem un kaimiņiem" [What we have learnt from our friends and neighbours] in *TuD*, 5/1, 1927, p. 13-15.

cles on this church, although they did not mention its Orthodox pre-history. The Orthodox journal repeatedly felt obliged to clarify the issue.[146]

Other occasions where the church-state relationship came into play in both countries were on the issue of religious instruction. The state was repeatedly accused of not following up its promises to guarantee Orthodox instruction when there were enough pupils and otherwise inter-confessional classes.[147] A real increase in articles on the church-state relationship appeared first in the mid-1930s, following the regime changes in both states. In Latvia, numerous propaganda articles by Edvards Dimiņš, head of the Department of Religious Affairs of the Ministry of the Interior flooded the press from 1934 on. In Estonia, the editorials of the journal *Elutõde*, founded in 1936, also published the same kind of propaganda. The kind of relationship promoted by this propaganda can be illustrated with the following quotation:

> A state with a religious population will be eternally strong and great. The strength and prominence of the state depends on the religious fervour of its population. Religion is that which guides the nation through everyday life and which gives even a small nation the strength to move mountains. Religion and especially Christianity, has become a characteristic of the Latvian nation. This is especially so because the Christian inner spirit matches the Latvian spirit. The deepest thoughts of Latvians have been born out of the spirit of Christianity, just as the clearest goals and most prominent achievements.[148]

Another example of this style of propaganda, this time from the viewpoint of the church, is the following excerpt from *Elutõde*:

> We are not only kept from entertaining an ideology of a masters' or state church through theological reflection and correct exegetics but equally from many vitriolic experiences in religious history: most of the ecclesiastic organisations that worked hand in hand with state powers have turned into anaemic and bland conglomerates. The faith and the church, according to the teachings of Jesus Christ, has nothing in common with worldly power and force. Faith is a matter of the heart and an element of spiritual life, and these two cannot be subordinated to human-led commands and programmes, for the faith and the church knows and preaches only the truth and God's commands. [...]
> One should not deduce from the above that the Estonian Orthodox Church opposes any kind of state power. No, – the church relates to any power with respect and loy-

---

146 Konstantin Kokla and Anton Laar, "Ajakirjanduse keskel" [Among the newspapers] in *UjE₂*, 1/1, 1933, p. 12; "Ajakirjanduse keskel" [Among the newspapers] in *UjE₂*, 1/3, 1933, p. 5-6.

147 A. K. no Lauberes, "Pareizticības stāvoklis Latvijā" [The situation of Orthodoxy in Latvia] in *TuD*, 10/3, 1934, p. 38-39; -nd., "Read koomale!" [Get in formation!] in *ET*, 1/31, 1936, p. 1; -nd., "Kirikumõtteid" [Church thoughts] in *ET*, 1/39, 1936, p. 4-5. See also chapters 2.2.4. and 2.3.3.

148 E. Dimiņš, "Latvijas 20 gadu pastāvēšanas svētkos" [The 20th anniversary of the Latvian existence] in *TuD*, 14/21, 1938, p. 322-324.

alty, as long as it recognises the basics of the ecumenical church and does not utilise weapons that make the human rationality cry out.[149]

This rhetoric suggests a church-state relationship where the state used the church for purposes of legitimisation but retained total control. The Orthodox Church thereby renounced any claim to worldly power and independence.[150] Opposition to this development was rigorously obstructed and criticism of the regime was minimised. When the Estonian regime liberalised and President Konstantin Päts founded a new national political party in 1937, *Elutöde* complained that its leadership was poorly chosen and deliberately ignored the Orthodox Church, acting as if the entire Estonian populace was Lutheran.[151] Such direct criticism of the state did not appear in Latvia.

Before concluding this chapter, the broad range of voices complaining about anti-Orthodox sentiments in the majority society must be analysed. In the Latvian case, these complaints are mostly attested by the polemical speeches and articles by Archbishop Jānis.[152] Jānis was not the only one to complain. Other Ortodox publicists, such as Archpriest Jānis Jansons, for example, also criticised the social majority. Jansons wrote a series of articles in 1925 titled 'Orthodoxy among the Latvians.' The series was a mixture of historical, theological, and sociological analysis of Latvian Orthodoxy, and Jansons repeatedly mentions these difficult times, when "the current moderns attempt to explain everything from a material point of view. Citing the Holy Scriptures' teaching on the beauty of creation is nowadays considered shameful, reactionary, and retrograde."[153] On the occasion of the demolition of the chapel in front of the Riga railway station in 1925, he wrote:

> I felt bad at heart and sad when I realised that an important part of Latvian society could not understand that this chapel was a Christian house of worship and not a monument to the former Tsarist regime. [...] Of the Latvian newspapers only *Latvijas Sargs* came out defending the chapel. The other Latvian newspapers either supported the demolition or remained diplomatically silent. What did Latvia gain through this demolition? [...] I think this is barbarism. It is vandalism. The spirit of the time, the spirit of Antichrist![154]

---

149 R., "Kirik ei tunnusta vägivalda ega sundust!" [The church does not sanction violence or force!] in *ET*, 2/12, 1937, p. 145-146.

150 See also Runce, 2008, p. 200.

151 -t., "Eesti ap.-õigeusu Kirik ja 'Isamaaliit'" [The Estonian Orthodox Church and the 'Isamaaliit' party] in *ET*, 2/18, 1937, p. 217-218.

152 See also chapter 2.2.6.

153 Jānis Jansons, "Pareizticība pie Latviešiem" [Orthodoxy among the Latvians] in *TuD*, 3/4, 1925, p. 10-15.

154 Jānis Jansons, "Pareizticība pie Latviešiem" [Orthodoxy among the Latvians] in *TuD*, 3/8, 1925, p. 13-16.

A month later, Jansons complained that "never has popular hate been as strong as currently."[155] He explained his argument in theological language, referring to Biblical passages that describe persecution and hatred. Jansons was reprimanded for his negative outlook and accused of being an "ultra-conservative 'canonic,' unsuited to the current progressive era of Latvian society."[156] Archbishop Jānis was also accused of greatly exaggerating the threat to Latvian Orthodoxy by 'an Orthodox Latvian,' writing in 1926 for a secular newspaper.[157] A third voice, the future Metropolitan Augustīns Pētersons, also joined in, criticising societal antagonism to Orthodoxy. In the Orthodox journal, Pētersons critically reviewed a pretentious article from 1930 on 'Russian Orthodoxy struggling with Latvian Lutheranism' by Pēteris Kalniņš:[158]

> I cannot help but allude to the words of the Apostle Peter, about the false prophets appearing in the midst of the Christian congregation. P. Kalniņš, judging by this article, is also one of these, for he is a 'former' Orthodox. Such 'former' authors are highly hostile, since they have, as it were, the foundations of truth. His basic assumptions are correct, I admit, but his arbitrarily drawn implications are wrong.[159]

There followed more than four pages of corrective commentary, claiming that Kalniņš not only had misjudged the historical role of Orthodoxy in Latvia, but also abused the linguistic and theological arguments for Orthodoxy. An example of these linguistic arguments claims that the Latvian word for 'God' was different from the Russian 'God,' which originated from the ancient Hebrew word: "Truly, the Orthodox believe in the same God as Moses and the other Hebrew speakers in the Old Testament, but I am convinced that also the faithful Lutherans believe in that same God."[160]

This negative outlook among the Orthodox apparently changed in the 1930s. P. Kaltiņš, for example, who later wrote so positively about the authoritarian regime, wrote as early as January 1934:

> That same state, which persecuted us and displayed such hatred towards us now helps maintain our theological seminary, provides us with financial support, just as the other confessions, depending on the number of members. [...] In addition to this, our neighbours of other faiths look at us differently than in the persecution era. If

---

155 Jānis Jansons, "Pareizticība pie Latviešiem" [Orthodoxy among the Latvians] in *TuD*, 3/9, 1925, p. 5-10.

156 Jānis Jansons, "Vai Pareizticība pie Latviešiem var palikt par nacionalu ticību?" [Can Orthodoxy among the Latvians remain a national faith?] in *TuD*, 4/5, 1926, p. 12-13.

157 Pareizticīgais latvietis, "Vai pareizticīgo baznīca Latvijā ir apdraudēta?" [Is the Orthodox Church in Latvia threatened?] in *Latvijas Sargs*, 8/195, 02.09.1926, p. 1.

158 Kalniņš, Pēteris, 1930.

159 Augustīns Pētersons, "Vai pareizticība ir krieviska un luterticība latviska?" [Is Orthodoxy Russian and Lutheranism Latvian?] in *TuD*, 8/12, 1930, p. 178.

160 Augustīns Pētersons, "Vai pareizticība ir krieviska un luterticība latviska?" [Is Orthodoxy Russian and Lutheranism Latvian?] in *TuD*, 8/12, 1930, p. 180.

there were many weak souls then, leaving the Orthodox Church to convert to
Lutheranism or even completely leave the Christian family, then this development is
now considered finished and survived. [...] We are Latvians, and we have an unalienable right to call ourselves children of Latvia, loving and protecting our mother
and even giving our life for her in case of emergency.[161]

Although this positive assessment of the current situation in Latvia was relativised two issues later, the Latvian discourse suggests a relatively peaceful situation. I have not found any complaints about social antagonism in the published
discourse of the 1930s.

Estonia was a very different case. The Orthodox journals repeatedly complained about anti-Orthodox reports in the secular press and anti-Orthodox sentiments in society at large. These complaints either reported anti-Orthodox mentions in the secular press or personal experiences of societal antagonism. As
early as April 1917, at the Tallinn gathering,[162] the Orthodox Estonians had
passed a resolution to "consider the scattered pogrom-like calls: 'Russian
believers expelled from the country!' as remainders of a medieval fanati-
cism."[163] Reporting on this gathering in the secular newspaper *Postimees*, the
editors added a footnote to this resolution, doubting that these calls had really
been heard.[164]

Jaan Lattik, a Lutheran pastor, expressed doubts in a critical article that the
decisions of the Tallinn gathering could really make him look at the Orthodox
Church positively. The Orthodox publicist Anton Laar replied to this article a
couple of days later under the title 'Unexpected Spleen Venting.' Here, Laar
harshly criticises Lattik for using his deceased mother as a shield while attacking
the Orthodox Church listing historical wrong-doings:

If you like, I could offer an even longer register of sins committed in the name of the
Orthodox Church, after which many priests no longer appear in such a good light.
[...] But you yourself correctly demanded that 'it is necessary to remove the bad and
black memories from the Estonian soul...' That was exactly what we were trying to
do, gathering in Tallinn and trying to bury the old hatchet finally in order to achieve
lasting religious peace, which, as you say, is currently so important for the building
of a common Estonian home. You are wrong in thinking that we simply juggle with
optimistic promises. We know very well that the Estonians take a man by his words
and a cow by her horns. [...]
It is very sad that you seem to judge us all through the painful memories of a single
priest. [...] If you still stick to criticising the unlucky sentence: 'Russian believers
expulsed from the country!' you should at least recognise that this is not 'our own

161 P. Kaltiņš, "Pareizticības pašreizējais stāvoklis Latvijā" [The current situation of the
    Orthodox Church in Latvia] in *TuD*, 10/1, 1934, p. 6-7.
162 See chapter 2.2.1.
163 Laar, 1917, p. 8.
164 Anton Laar, "Eesti õigeusuliste tegelaste üleüldine nõupidamine Tallinnas" [The general
    advisory meeting of the Estonian Orthodox actors] in *PM*, 61/81, 13.041917, p. 3.

shadow' but based on real occurrences, which we decided resolutely to counter. And you obviously exaggerate, when talking about 'the Lutherans straying around in medieval blindness.' We talked only about *scattered* calls, which we do not expect even you to begin defending. [...]

But let us finish! I tell you openly: we are not interested in settling old scores, where sometimes, maybe, the priests are to blame and sometimes, maybe, the pastors. [...] We are profoundly convinced that the Estonian people can correctly value our work and your work on its own and that we do not need to discuss this in length.[165]

This reply did not stop Lattik from replying in a similar vein, continuing to attack Laar as a representative of the oppressive Russian Empire.[166] Laar wanted to reply under the heading 'To the Militant Pastor Lattik' but changed his mind, arguing that

the purpose of a discussion is to clarify an issue and one's standpoints. When the discussion turns into 'fighting,' as pastor Lattik publicly acknowledges in his last introduction, then there is reason to doubt the value of the discussion. And finally, if the *Postimees* editorial office even happily sends my letters to the 'militant' party for pre-censorship, thereby clearly revealing the editorial standpoint, then I hold further discussions to be fundamentally impossible.[167]

Such long drawn-out exchanges of articles did not appear any more in the Estonian press. After an 1923 article in *Postimees* decried the Orthodox Church as still foreign to the Estonian spiritual life, Laar sent a commentary to the editors, claiming that much had been done since 1917 and that fundamental changes should always be approached carefully.[168] In his journal *Uus Elu*, he later complained that "the bias of *Postimees* did not allow my comments to be published without adding a distorting preface."[169] This preface warned the readers not to expect too much from the representatives of the Orthodox Church, for "they do not seem to be in a hurry concerning the *new spirit*. On the contrary, this kind of story makes us ask how much of the new spirit they have understood?!"[170] Laar continued by noting that the voices accusing the Orthodox Church of remaining too Russian were complemented by voices from inside the church which claimed that it was turning too far away from its roots.

165 Anton Laar, "Ootamata sapikarika" [Unexpected spleen venting] in *PM*, 61/94, 28.04. 1917, p. 1. See also chapter 2.2.1.
166 Jaan Lattik, "Vastuseks preestri herra A. Laar'ile" [Answer to the priest Mr. A. Laar] in *PM*, 61/99, 04.05.1917, p. 1.
167 Letter from A. Laar to the editors of *Postimees*, 08.05.1917, in *Eesti Ajaloo Arhiiv* [Estonian Historical Archives], f. 1655, n. 3, s. 380.
168 Anton Laar, "Vana vaim ja Eesti ap. Kirik" [The old spirit and the Estonian Apostolical Church] in *PM*, 67/33, 04.02.1923, p. 5. The original article was: -n [Jaan Tõnisson], "Vana Vaim" [The old spirit] in *PM*, 67/22, 24.01.1923, p. 1.
169 Anton Laar, "Vana vaim" [Old spirit] in *UE*, 3/2, 1923, p. 5-6.
170 Anton Laar, "Vana vaim ja Eesti ap. Kirik" [The old spirit and the Estonian Apostolical Church] in *PM*, 67/33, 04.02.1923, p. 5 (Emphasis in original).

Other Orthodox Christians also accused the secular press of antagonism. 'Saarepoeg,'[171] for example, reviews the Saaremaa press, for "while the continental press oppresses the Orthodox Church indirectly and quietly – this cannot be said about the Saaremaa press, which does so without any cover."[172] T. Lepik complained about the negative portrayal of Orthodoxy in Estonian novels.[173] Another author commented on a newspaper article marvelling at 'a parish with six churches.' This was in the most Orthodox region of Estonia (except Petserimaa), where there were five Orthodox churches within the boundaries of one Lutheran parish:

> The Lutheran parishes do not – thank God – present any official, administrative, or judicial regional entities, within which the churches of other confessions can be counted. Every confession has its own parish boundaries, and let those boundaries remain within a single confession. Even if the Lutheran Church wishes to count itself as the only church in Estonia, (this opinion is currently being cultivated at all levels [...]) then it seems too much when the newspapers themselves, apart from the pastors-journalists, also seem to want to spread this opinion.[174]

Regarding the anti-Orthodox press reports, a special mention must be given to the issue of the Aleksander Nevskij Cathedral in Tallinn. This large cathedral, clearly visible in the Tallinn skyline, right in front of the Estonian parliament building, was built on this prominent spot on the order of the Estonian governor S. P. Šakhovskoj during the heyday of Russification. Since its completion in 1900, it had been a thorn in the eye of the Baltic Germans and the Estonians, who saw it as a monument to the Russian Empire. In the face of this sentiment, Archbishop Aleksander and the Orthodox Synod deemed it necessary to write an open letter in 1922 "on the occasion of *Vaba Maa*'s warfare against the 'Russian huts with images of God.'"[175] In this letter, they mentioned the cathedral, whose destruction

> only those may support, who are not positively inclined towards Estonia as a cultural and democratic republic. It is clear how the fact that the official voice of one of our biggest political parties publicly calls for war against the churches and chapels influences our foreign relations. On the other hand, we cannot let the extreme intolerance this warfare shows towards Orthodoxy pass unnoticed. People still talk about Russian oppression, which is supposed to hide in these chapels and the cathedral. We ask publicly: How can these buildings and this confession have been more oppres-

---

171 This is the vernacular expression for somebody from the island Saaremaa. See chapter 6.1. for a map.
172 Saarepoeg, "Saaremaa ajakirjandus ja ap.-õigeusk" [The Saaremaa press and Orthodoxy] in *UE*, 3/3, 1923, p. 2-3.
173 T. Lepik, "Ap.-õigeusu asjust" [On Orthodoxy] in *UjE₂*, 5/6, 1937, p. 90-91.
174 Apostlik, "Kihelkond 6 kirikuga" [A parish with 6 churches] in *ET*, 1/19, 1936, p. 5-6.
175 *Vaba Maa* was the newspaper of the Estonian Labour Party, and the most sensationalist of the Estonian newspapers.

sive than similar German churches together with the confession they brought? [...]
Estonia does not yet have any of its own churches in the sense of the word: they all
belong either to the German or Russian faith. [...]
We do not support the Russian orientation, but we need to face the truth that even
the Bolshevik Russians have not yet touched the Lutheran churches or collected
money for their destruction.[176]

However, no Estonian newspapers published the open letter, which prompted
Anton Laar to exclaim that

anyway, we now know what to expect: you Orthodox minority with all your stuff is
hurting our majority religious feeling and therefore we ask you in the name of freedom and tolerance: down! Be quiet and go home! [...] We Orthodox Estonians will
never subordinate ourselves to the Germanism that is entering Estonia as a proud
victor through doors and windows, claiming to be 'Western culture.'[177]

Vaba Maa acknowledged this protest but dismissed it as yet another inconse-
quence from the 'Orthodox camp.' From the point of view of *Vaba Maa*, "it
never occurred to us to attack one or the other confession, we are only talking
about the removal of the signs of the Russian oppression and Tsarist demonstration of power."[178]

For the six following years, there was quiet regarding the Aleksander
Nevskij Cathedral but 1928 was a critical year. One year after the forceful transfer of the nearby Lutheran Cathedral from a Baltic German parish to the Estonian episcopal seat,[179] the political gaze passed to the Orthodox Cathedral. In
October 1928, four members of the Estonian parliament presented a private bill
stipulating that the cathedral should be pulled down.[180] The ensuing discussions
have been analysed in detail by the Finnish church historian Mikko Ketola, who
concludes that although the bill did not succeed, it functioned as a kind of
'national therapy,' enhancing the loyalty of the Orthodox Estonians to the state
and legitimising the Estonian Orthodox Church in the eyes of the authorities.[181]
Considering the discussions in the Orthodox press both before and after 1928,

176 Eesti Ap.-usu kiriku Ülempiiskop ja Sinod, "Avalik kiri 'Vaba Maa' sõjakäigu puhul
    'vene jumalkujude-putkate' vastu" [A public letter on the occasion of *Vaba Maa*'s war-
    fare against the 'Russian huts with images of God'] in *UE*, 2/2, 1922, p. 3-4. There had
    been calls to demolish it as early as 1921, after reports on the cathedral question in Riga
    had reached Estonia. See chapter 2.2.5.; Lääne, 2009, p. 148-149.
177 "Ajalehtede keskel" [Among the newspapers] in *UE*, 2/2, 1922, p. 4-5. Another protest
    letter by Laar was not printed either. Anton Laar, "Kas meelega või kogemata" [On pur-
    pose or unconsciously?] in *UE*, 2/2, 1922, p. 7.
178 "Kirik. 'Uus Elu'" [Church. 'Uus Elu'] in *VM*, 5/67, 21.03.1922, p. 5. See also "Ajaleht-
    ede keskel" [Among the newspapers] in *UE*, 2/3, 1922, p. 3-4.
179 See Ketola, 2000a, p. 177-212.
180 Ketola, 1996, p. 119; Fülberth, 2005, p. 113-115; Lääne, 2009, p. 150.
181 Ketola, 1996, p. 151-152. See also Fülberth, 2005, p. 110-128; Lääne, 2009, p. 150-156.

this conclusion can be doubted, although 1928 certainly represented an important point in the development for some Estonians. In the Orthodox journal, a special issue was devoted to the question of the cathedral.[182] This issue contained an overview of the cathedral's history as well as various statements in its defence. These included opinions from influential members of the Lutheran Church and Orthodox priests. They all emphasised that nothing is gained from demolishing the cathedral and such a move would only exacerbate the tensions between the Orthodox minority and the state.

Although the 1928 bill was a critical point in the debate about the Aleksander Nevskij Cathedral, it did not end there, as Ketola's conclusion might suggest. Commenting on plans to demolish an Orthodox chapel in Narva two years later, Anton Laar noted with resignation that

> It is not difficult to recognise that the drive to demolish churches and chapels origi-
> nates primarily in anti-religious circles. [...] Our short-sighted Lutherans do not
> seem to realise that and think that they serve the Estonian nation by sacrificing an
> Orthodox chapel or two... Even the demolishment of the Tallinn Cathedral would
> not have failed if the demolishers in their first flush of victory had not expressed the
> wish to 'also remove the Jaani church from the Freedom Square.' That made an
> impression! It is high time for the Christian confessions, whose foundations are the
> same, to come closer – start co-operating. The danger is nearer than many believe.[183]

The question reappeared in 1936, when the Orthodox journal reported that a Tallinn newspaper had asked a number of prominent Estonians about their opinion on demolishing the Aleksander Nevskij Cathedral. The author, signing with '–ht.–', complains that out of the six persons asked, four "seem to tend towards supporting a demolishment."[184] In order to end these discussions, the Synod decided to force the Russian parish using the cathedral to hand it over to the Metropolitan, making it an episcopal seat. This transfer, which had been on the agenda since 1922, happened peacefully later in 1936, when the congregation of the cathedral switched buildings with an Estonian parish in Tallinn. The transfer was reported positively by the secular press and the Orthodox journals.[185]

---

182 *UE*, 8/10, 1928.
183 Editor's remarks to Konstantin Kokla, "Veel üks 'lammutamine'" [Another 'destruction'] in *UE*, 10/8, 1930, p. 6-7. See also Fülberth, 2005, p. 148-182 for more on the discussions surrounding the Jaani church.
184 -ht.-, "Kas jälle katedraali lammutamine?" [Once more the demolishment of the Cathedral?] in *ET*, 1/30, 1936, p. 1. The Cathedral had also been briefly mentioned in 1932, at
   the heyday of the 'Monastery War.' Qestor, "Kas Vene kodanike huvid?" [Is this in the
   interest of the Russian population?] in *PL*, 27/24, 25.01.1932, p. 8.
185 "Katedraal metropoliidi esinduskirikuks" [The Cathedral becomes the representative
   church of the Metropolitan] in *VM*, 19/270, 25.11.1936, p. 5; "Katedraali saatus otsustatud" [The fate of the Cathedral decided] in *ET*, 1/41, 1936, p. 5; "Переход русскаго

Under the leadership of Archpriest Nikolai Päts, the new tenants Estonianised the cathedral, fundamentally renovating it, and removing the church Slavonic psalms adorning it. According to Konstantin Kokla, the cathedral in its
new shape "is literally besieged by the foreign tourists visiting Tallinn."[186] However, antagonism between the Orthodox and the majority persisted. The Estonian
journalist and art critic Rasmus Kangro-Pool and others repeatedly and publicly
argued for a demolishment of the cathedral, on the grounds that it did not fit
Estonian culture and national pride and polluted the beauty of the capital.[187]
Orthodox replies emphasised that Orthodox churches are no more monuments to
Russian oppression than the Lutheran buildings are monuments to Baltic
German oppression: "I think there would be very little left of Tallinn if we
would demand demolishment of all buildings once housing oppressive powers."[188] They also argued that Orthodoxy brought the Estonians many benefits,
of which more will be said in the next chapter.

Before turning to the historiographic discourse, I will turn briefly to the personal accounts of Orthodox Estonians who experienced this antagonism firsthand. These accounts report numerous cases of intolerance, diligently listed by
an anonymous author in the Orthodox journal in 1931:

> For example, applicants for the Bergmann monetary aid for the needy are not asked
> about their confession, but the 'Russian believers' still have a separate queue! A
> Lutheran magister [i.e. with an academic degree], who you would think was not
> stupid, is amazed to hear that the members of the 'Russian faith' on the islands are
> not Russians, but Estonians. On the election of a well known Estonian 'Russian
> faith' priest to a new teacher's post, people grumble: 'do we really have no suitable

---

таллинскаго Александро-Невскаго прихода в Симеоновскую церковь" [The transfer
of the Russian Aleksander Nevskij parish to the Simeonov church] in *PS*, 6/11, 1936, p.
156-160.

186 Konstantin Kokla, "Eesti ap.-õigeusu Kiriku katedraal" [The Estonian Orthodox Cathedral] in *UjE₂*, 6/9, 1938, p. 140-141. See also "Toompea katedraalist kõrvaldatakse venekeelsed salmid" [Russian psalms are removed from the Toompea Cathedral] in *PL*,
34/126, 10.05.1939, p. 3; "Kahe tähtsa mehe seisukohad" [The positions of two important men] in *UjE₂*, 6/12, 1938, p. 178.

187 J. T., "Rasmus Kangro-Pool peab katedraali lammutamist rahvuslikuks auasjaks" [Rasmus Kangro-Pool holds that the destruction of the Cathedral is an issue of national
honour] in *ET*, 3/1, 1938, p. 2; Nikolai Päts, "Toompea Katedraal ja rahvustunne" [The
Toompea Cathedral and national feelings] in *ET*, 3/3, 1938, p. 25-26; "Katedraal Kalevi
kalmul jälle komistuskiviks..." [The Cathedral on Kalev's tomb again the bone of contention...] in *Esmaspäev*, 18/24, 17.06.1939, p. 4; Konstantin Kokla, "Segast juttu"
[Nebulous talk] in *UjE₂*, 7/6, 1939, p. 93-94; "Tallinna Toompea katedraalist" [The
Cathedral on the Tallinn *Toompea*] in *UjE₂*, 7/8, 1939, p. 125; "Millise pinnapealsusega..." [With what superficiality...] in *ET*, 4/11, 1939, p. 124-125.

188 M. Mäessa, "Kas venestuse kantsiks või Eesti piiskopi esinduskirikuks?" [Fort of Russification or representative church of the Estonian bishop?] in *ET*, 3/3, 1938, p. 28.

teachers anymore but have to resort to a Russian *papp*?'[189] The same grumble is heard when somebody of the 'Russian faith' wins a scholarship at the university. [...] Religious instruction for Orthodox children has been permitted but under the star of impossibility. Forced catechisation in the 'state faith' has already been mentioned.[190]

Almost every issue of the Orthodox journals contained a passing mention of the negative connotations associated with the 'Russian faith,' which remained the common word for Orthodoxy. Several manifestos also appeared against the use of this name, proclaiming that "even if you search with a magnifying glass, there is no Russian faith nor Russian churches in Estonia, nor anywhere else, for that matter."[191] Finally, the story of a young priest, who wanted clarification after the Lutheran pastor had buried an Orthodox child whose mother had died giving birth, will close this chapter:

> After all, the priest himself had baptised the child some weeks ago, and its father had said: 'the mother died giving birth, I have to bring it to the orphanage. But before I do that, I will baptise it into the Orthodox Church, for that is where we want to live and die. Elsewhere our souls will not be taken care of!'
> The young priest went to the orphanage to clarify the issue. He was received by a chubby lady with glasses, the deputy director. 'I ask for clarification. How could this happen, when there are enough Orthodox priests in the area?' – 'What's the difference, who buries, the Lutheran pastor or the Russian priest? In the face of God, we are all the same.' – 'Excuse me, this is a public institution and you just called me a Russian priest, thereby transgressing the law. The law knows no Russian faith, only apostolic Orthodoxy.' – 'The people still call it the Russian faith and the Russian *papp*.' – 'Only your kind of people...' The lady went red. 'Get out!!!'
> The young priest asked for advice from an older colleague: what to do? Act like they do? The older one consoled him: Jesus did not imitate his enemies but protested: If I speak the truth, then testify to it, but why hit me![192]

---

189 Another word for priest with negative connotations.
190 "Ususallimatusest Eestis" [Religious intolerance in Estonia] in *UE*, 11/11, 1931, p. 3-4.
191 Nikolai Kokla, "Eestis ei ole ei veneusku ega vene kirikuid" [There is neither a Russian faith nor Russian churches in Estonia] in *UjE₂*, 4/12, 1936, p. 187-189; Nigul Hindov, "Huvitavat usuelust ajakirjanduse kaudu" [Interesting news of the religious life from the press] in *UjE₂*, 2/9, 1934, p. 156-157.
192 "Vene...papp...välja!..." [The Russian...*papp*...out!...] in *UjE₂*, 6/13, 1938, p. 208. The reference in the last sentence is to Jesus and the high priest (Jn, 18:23) but does not completely correspond to the Bible text.

4. Orthodox Baltic Historiography

What I identified as the third challenge of modernity profoundly changed the dominant view of history and historical identity. It was not enough to be somebody, but one needed to justify this identity based on historical developments and narratives. Whereas historians in the eighteenth century generally analysed the past as past, the nineteenth century saw a rise in historiographic narratives which regarded the past as a stage preceding the present. These historical narratives, which were constructed by historians, media, and politicians, played an important role in the consolidation of each national society. The national elites desired a national history to describe a trajectory of progress, and the modern regime of historicity provided the nation with a future *telos*.[1] This was the case in many states of Eastern Europe, including Estonia and Latvia, where the interwar period was the first experience of national independence.

On a more concrete level, as the Czech historian Miroslav Hroch has noted, "a tension between the uncritical or ideologised myth on the one hand and the critical and, as far as it was possible, the exact product of scholarly research on the other" arose in each modern historiography.[2] The case of the Baltic Provinces of the Russian Empire and later the Baltic States of Estonia and Latvia provide ample proof of this tension. In the time before 1940, this region experienced three different hegemonic historiographic traditions, each with a different view of the past, present, and future of the Baltic region and each nurturing specific myths and paradigms. These were the Baltic German account, the Imperial Russian view, and finally the national historiography of Estonians and Latvians. In the first chapter of this part, I consider these three historiographic traditions and the way they analysed the historical role of the Orthodox Church in the region. A following chapter is then devoted to the popular historiography of the interwar years and how it was perceived and challenged by Orthodox Estonians and Latvians.

4.1. The Hegemonic Historiographic Narratives of the Baltic Region

Krijn Thijs argues that each particular historiographic text tends to follow a master narrative, which "defines a more or less loose set of narrative elements [...] which function as a main framework for concrete stories of (part of) the

---

1   See Berger and Lorenz, 2008, p. 12-14.
2   Hroch, 1999, p. 99.

national past."[3] This loose framework, centred on certain key actors, enemies, and events, "enables a broad range of possible versions of history to exist alongside each other."[4] In this chapter, I briefly analyse the three master narratives, according to this definition, that developed in the area of interwar Estonia and Latvia from the nineteenth century until 1940. The first section attempts an overview of these three historiographic traditions, whereas the second section considers their understanding of the Orthodox Church's role in the region before independence. The professional historiography of interwar Estonia and Latvia on the role of the Orthodox Church is then dealt with by the third section.

4.1.1. The Historiographies of the Baltic Provinces

Prior to the twentieth century, there was no Estonian or Latvian history, only Baltic history, written by either the Baltic Germans or the Russians. In both cases, this history tended to overemphasise the positive role played by either the Baltic Germans or the Russian Empire. In the case of the Baltic Germans, there was a centuries-old tradition to draw from, dating from the Chronicles of Henry of Livonia in the twelfth century.[5] Therefore, the rise of modern historiography among the Baltic Germans around the mid-nineteenth century did not have to start from scratch. Until 1918, this modern Baltic German historiography had a very high scholarly output on a variety of topics.[6] However, this historiographic activity was limited to particular events and periods, partly because of increasingly strong censorship during Russification.

Nonetheless, Baltic Germans always had the option of having their non-approved works published in Germany, which many historians did. Among these, we should first mention Carl Schirren, the "grandfather of Baltic historical research."[7] Schirren was a good example of the tension between the production of scholarly history and the creation of popular myths. Within the history of the Baltic Provinces, he was most interested in the gradual downgrading of the rights and privileges the Baltic German nobility had been granted at the peace of Nystad in 1721.[8] After publishing a polemical reply to a manifesto calling for more Russian influence in the Baltic Provinces by the Russian publicist Jurij

---

3   Thijs, 2008, p. 72.
4   Thijs, 2008, p. 72.
5   See the contributions in von Rauch, 1986. See also Kala, Tiina, 1998.
6   See Garleff, 1986.
7   Garleff, 1986, p. 243.
8   Neander, 1986, p. 180-182; Haltzel 1977.

Samarin in 1869, he lost his position at the University of Dorpat (Tartu) and was exiled to Germany, where he continued his political and historiographic work.[9]

Schirren was not the only scholar engaged in countering Russian ambitions. Several Baltic Germans had replied to Samarin's polemic. The self-conception of the Baltic Germans, including the historians among them, increasingly saw the Baltic Provinces as something essentially German, and Russian influence as something to keep at bay.[10] As the German historian Michael Garleff contends, many Baltic German historians and historical publicists since Schirren "conformed to the new type of historian '*cum* ira et studio' [*with* anger and fondness] appearing in Germany, which would have damaging consequences, especially concerning the occasionally aggressive view of the historical role of Russia among Baltic Germans."[11] The highly developed historical consciousness of the Baltic German population absorbed this academic discourse, perpetuating the myth of the inalienable privileges of the Germans in the Baltic Provinces.

Russian historiography during the nineteenth century pursued an entirely different approach. Without a traditional narrative to rely on, the starting signal for the Russian Baltic historiography was given by the above-mentioned Jurij Samarin. He was an ardent Slavophile who harshly criticised the privileges granted Baltic Germans in 'our Russian borderlands.'[12] The theme of Russian Baltic historiography, as formulated by Evgraf V. Češichin, one of its main proponents, was that "there can be no place in Russia other than Russia and there can be no patriotism apart from the Russian one."[13] For Samarin, Češichin, and others, the Baltic Provinces were natural parts of the Russian Empire. The time from the German crusades of the twelfth century was a historical anomaly, which luckily Peter the Great had begun to remedy in the early eighteenth century. The modern tenor of this historiographical discourse is evident when "Češichin remarks that the time has now come to remove the consequences of this anomalous development."[14] In this discourse, historiography was the justification of Imperial political activity directed against the Baltic Germans.

The Estonian historian Tiit Rosenberg contends that "Russian Baltic his-toriography was considerably more voluminous and comprehensive than is generally admitted."[15] This misconception is primarily due to the public controversy of the 1860s between Baltic Germans like Carl Schirren and

---

9   Wittram, Reinhard, 1973, p. 164-182; Haltzel, 1981, p. 126-133.
10   Haltzel, 1981, p. 132-133, 143-144; Garleff, 1986, p. 254-255, 270-271. See also Garve, 1978, p. 193-208 for this development within the Lutheran Church.
11   Garleff, 1986, p. 271 (Emphasis in original).
12   Haltzel, 1981, p. 126-133; Thaden, 1986; Samarin, 1996 [1867]; Rosenberg, 2005, p. 78.
13   Quoted in Rosenberg, 2005, p. 79.
14   Rosenberg, 2005, p. 83. See also Brüggemann, 2006, p. 405-406.
15   Rosenberg, 2005, p. 108.

Russians like Jurij Samarin, which overshadowed other narratives. Nonetheless, even admitting to the occasional exception, the historiography of the nineteenth century largely centred on the role of the Russian and Baltic German communities and their relationship with each other. Still in 1869, there was mutual agreement between the two great powers that

> the Latvians [and Estonians] only have two options, either to become German and Protestant or Russian and members of the Greek Church. They cannot stand alone and their constant reluctance to accept the old German or the new Russian influences are not helping them in the long run. They are already half Germanised, with only the language left.[16]

In later years, the Estonian and Latvian peasant population was also touched upon by historians but often only as pawns serving one or the other of the two great powers. In the words of the German historian Anna Veronika Wendland, the "hegemonic narratives were thus 'master'-narratives in the literal sense of the term: narratives governed by the perspective of the rulers within the social hierarchy of Eastern Europe, that is, the landed gentry and the Imperial bureaucracy."[17]

Towards the end of the nineteenth century, with the rise of the national movements and the national consciousness of the Estonians and Latvians, a third counter-narrative appeared, taking similar forms in its Estonian and Latvian guise. These alternatives to the 'master' narratives remained marginal and rather unprofessional until the First World War.[18] In the newly independent Latvian and Estonian states, the new indigenous elites founded a number of institutions devoted to national history in the sense of a history of the Estonian and Latvian peoples, not of the various hegemonic structures in the Baltic region.[19] A real professionalisation of Estonian and Latvian national history only occurred in the 1930s, when the first academic historians of the independence period started to publish their research.[20]

According to Wendland, the emerging populist national history

> carried out a negative transfer from neighbouring historiographies, referring to established hegemonic narratives *ex negativo*. As far as formal aspects were concerned, they all used the very narrative structures of dominant historiographies as a blueprint for the respective national counter-projects. They all attempted to estab-

---

16   Samarin, 1996, p. xi-xii, 260.
17   Wendland, 2008, p. 408.
18   Kivimäe and Kivimäe, 1987, p. 277-279; Plakans, 1999, p. 293-295; Kukk, 2005, p. 20-31; Wendland, 2008, p. 412, 427.
19   Johansons, 1987; Wendland, 2003, p. 217-218; Kukk, 2005, p. 56-62; Wendland, 2008, p. 427.
20   Kivimäe and Kivimäe, 1987; Feldmanis, 1995; Helme, 1995; Plakans, 1999, p. 299-303.

lish a differing perspective on the very same historical individuals, structures and events.[21]

However, it is important to note that the dominant historiographic narrative, which was used to frame the new national historiography, was generally the Baltic German one. It is telling that the Imperial Russian historiography of the Baltic Provinces is not even mentioned in many historiographic surveys.[22] This historiographic focus was facilitated by the fact that Baltic Germans remained important figures in Estonian and Latvian society after independence while there were few influential Russians left.

The main focus of the new national historiographies was the history of the Estonians and Latvians, who had been 'forgotten' by the two other histo-riographies. In 1930, the Estonian Academic Historical Society concluded that "these historians have not paid enough attention to the historical past of the Estonian people, tending to underestimate the role of the Estonians (and Latvi-ans) in the Baltic historical past and excessively glorifying the role of the German element."[23] The new historiographies were primarily devoted to ques-tions of agrarian and cultural history and the 'national awakening,' showing the "path of the Estonian people from a passive historical object without a history to an active subject, capable of maintaining its own nation state."[24]

In the 1930s, the rise of the authoritarian regimes further strengthened this nationalistic focus of academic history. This was especially the case in Latvia, where Kārlis Ulmanis looked at history "as a constituent part of political ideol-ogy and its most efficient weapon" on his way to a Latvian Latvia.[25] However, in Estonia, academic history also received a "close-fitting ideological corset" towards the end of the 1930s.[26] While the Latvian historian Inesis Feldmanis assesses this development positively, because of the increased financial and political support for academic history, the Estonian Rein Helme notes the nega-tive aspects of limits on innovation and academic freedom. Both aspects proba-

---

21   Wendland, 2008, p. 414.
22   Helme, 1995; Hackmann, 2005; Kukk, 2005. Sirje and Jüri Kivimäe mention the Russian historiography in passing but later talk only about opposition to the Baltic German narra-tives. Kivimäe and Kivimäe, 1987, p. 278. Andrejs Plakans mentions the Russian-lan-guage historiography but claims that it "did not feature prominently [...] though Russian-language primary sources were used extensively." Plakans, 1999, p. 304. Tiit Rosenberg argues that the impact of Russian historiography on both the Baltic German and national Baltic historiographies is still largely unexplored. Rosenberg, 2005, p.108.
23   Quoted in Kivimäe and Kivimäe, 1987, p. 279.
24   Hans Kruus, quoted in Kivimäe and Kivimäe, 1987, p. 279. See also Hackmann, 2005; Hackmann, 2010.
25   Feldmanis, 1995, p. 134. See also chapter 2.3.3. for more on the Baltic authoritarian regimes.
26   Helme, 1995, p. 145-146.

bly played a role in both cases, although the impression is that the boom of Estonian academic historiography was over by 1937, while Latvian history writing remained in its prime.[27]

Dealing with the nineteenth century, both Estonian and Latvian historiography was primarily directed against the Baltic Germans and only secondarily concerned with the Russian Imperial administration.[28] When the latter was mentioned, it was mainly as a mediator between Baltic Germans and the indigenous population. Moreover, there was a tendency to ascribe the role of the internal enemy to the Baltic Germans while the Russians were the external enemy. In other words, the Russian Imperial administration was situated outside of the frame of action, whereas the Baltic German nobility, which was either carrying out or trying to circumvent the Russian orders, sought their own benefit at the expense of the local peasant population.[29] In the beginning, Baltic German historians had been the arch-enemy of the national historians because they had arguably misunderstood Baltic history. By the 1930s, however, "the treatment Baltic German historians received [...], while dismissive, was far less verbally insulting than the treatment accorded to the 'bourgeois nationalist' historians [after 1945]."[30]

Again, the differences between the Latvian and the Estonian historiographies pertained more to degree than to content. Latvian national historiography of the late 1930s was far more anti-German than its Estonian counterpart, where the integration of Baltic German historiographic heritage was more successful.[31] Kārlis Ulmanis wanted a Latvia where everything – including historical truth – was based on Latvianness. This led to the establishment of numerous historically dubious paradigms, such as the existence of cities and political units in Latvia before the German crusades or the Latvianness of the first Baltic chronicler, Henry of Livonia. Alternative narratives were forbidden and the remaining Baltic German historians had to publish critical articles in foreign journals, mainly in Germany.[32]

---

27 Andrejs Plakans also mentions this later boom in Latvia, whereas Sirje and Jüri Kivimäe mention the flattening out of Estonian academic history after 1936. Kivimäe and Kivimäe, 1987, p. 289; Plakans, 1999, p. 297-299. See also Wendland, 2003, p. 235.
28 Plakans, 1999, p. 296-297; Laur, 2007, p. 301-302; Wendland, 2008, p. 414-415.
29 Laur, 2007, p. 303.
30 Plakans, 1999, p. 303.
31 von zur Mühlen, 1986, p. 340; Feldmanis, 1995, p. 137-138; Wendland, 2003, p. 219-221.
32 von Hehn, 1986, p. 389-394.

4.1.2. The Baltic Historiographies and the Orthodox Church

The assessment of the role of the Orthodox Church in the Baltic Provinces was one of the most controversial issues in the two dominant nineteenth century historiographies. For the Baltic German historians, the history of the Baltic region started with the crusades of the twelfth century and the subsequent dominance of the Roman Catholic Church on the Baltic shores. Archaeological investigations were primarily concerned with proving that the original inhabitants of the area had been Germanic people.[33] The Orthodox Church was, therefore, seen as an altogether foreign element in the Baltic area. Its sudden arrival in the midst of the Baltic German realm in the 1840s came as a surprise, and historians and commentators attributed it to the agitation of Russian Orthodox clergy.[34] The mass conversions had occurred because "Bishop Filaret and the lower clergy subordinated to him had exploited the hardships of the local peasant population."[35] They had done this by spreading rumours of free land for converts.

However, not only the clergy were to blame, but also the Tsar himself, since he had 'forced through' new statutes for the Lutheran Church of Russia in 1832 and installed an Orthodox vicar bishop in Riga in 1836. Baltic German historiography connected both of these acts with the conversion movement a decade later, although there was no such direct link. Also the subsequent history of the Orthodox Church was depicted in a similar vein, i.e. as continuous attacks on the Lutheran Church. This military rhetoric can be illustrated with reference to some of the more polemic treatments of the topic.

Friedrich Waldorff, for example, wrote in 1891 an article titled, 'The Lutheran Church in its Battle with Panslavism and 'Orthodoxy,'' placing Orthodoxy in inverted commas to emphasise his disagreement to the etymology of the word.[36] In this work, Waldorff complained about the Russification measures following the general audit of Senator N. A. Manasein in 1882 and 1883.[37]

---

33 Lenz, 1986, p. 227-228.
34 Kruus, 1930, p. 12, 29-34. This topic remained vivid for a long time. See for example Stephany, 1931, p. 21-28; von Schrenck, 1933, p. 61-66; Kroeger, 1956. Many historians still instinctively mention the pivotal role of the Orthodox clergy, although this role has been convincingly relativised. See Kruus, 1930, p. 307-311; Gavrilin, 1988; Ryan, 2008, p. 201-205. See also chapter 2.1.1.
35 Kroeger, 1956, p. 186.
36 Waldorff, 1891. See also Rebane, 1933, p. 80-81 and chapter 2.1.2.
37 Senator N. A. Manasein travelled around the Baltic Provinces for sixteen months, talking with people from all social strata. His reports to the Imperial administration included general remarks about the political situation and recommendations on how to make these provinces conform to the rest of Russia. This general audit ('ревизия') was very anti-German and is often perceived as the starting point of Russification. See Thaden, 1969.

These measures were overtly pro-Orthodox and constituted a direct attack on Baltic German culture and the Lutheran Church. After the revolutionary upheavals in 1905, Astav von Transehe complemented this narrative with the remark that the Russification measures aimed at strengthening the Orthodox Church were the main factor in the rise of atheist and socialist thought among the Estonians and Latvians.[38]

This negative rhetoric did not change with the Estonian and Latvian independence, as Maximilan Stephany's 'Conversion and Reconversion in Livland' from 1931 shows. The introductory remarks clarify the author's opinions: "From 1845 on, the Russian State brutally, with brutal means, attacked the legitimate position of the church of Livland."[39] Stephany elucidates the hopeless position of the Lutheran pastors in the 1880s, when "the Greek clergy literally lay in ambush [...] in order to find a reason to prosecute the pastors."[40] Erich von Schrenck's 1928 lectures in church history propagate a similar view, albeit less pronounced.[41]

Russian historiography also adopted a relatively monolithic view of the role of Orthodoxy in the Baltic provinces. The main features of this view was that Orthodox Christianity was the first form of Christianity brought to the Baltic shores through peaceful missionary activity in the tenth and eleventh centuries. The militant Catholic crusaders had swept away the peacefully preaching Orthodox missionaries from the twelfth century onwards. Roman Catholic and Lutheran Christianity had only survived in the area because of the powerful position of the Baltic Germans, which the Estonians and Latvians had finally dared to defy in the 1840s, *returning* to Orthodoxy *en masse*. The task now was to further this emancipation from the Baltic German clutch, so that the Estonians and Latvians could become true Russians.[42] This view was closely aligned to the dictum of Count Uvarov, which became the dominant ideological doctrine of the Russian Empire in 1833: *Orthodoxy, autocracy, national character* (Pravoslavie, samoderžavie, narodnost'). In this triad of the most Russian of characteristics, Orthodox Christianity ranked first. It was through Orthodox Christianity that true Russianness should be achieved.

The rhetoric of this narrative was completely different, focusing on the 'oppressive' and 'arrogant' Baltic Germans who used unfair practices to maintain their power over the peasants. The first large scale occurrence of this rhetoric, interspersed with references to the Russian character of the Baltic region and the necessity to abolish the special status of the Baltic Provinces, was in the

---

38 von Transehe, 1907, p. 43-45, 178-180, 381-383.
39 Stephany, 1931, p. 3-4.
40 Stephany, 1931, p. 51.
41 von Schrenck, 1933, p. 61-66, 97-104, 132-138.
42 Kruus, 1930, p. 12-28; Brüggemann, 2006, p. 401, 405; Ryan, 2008, p. 302-326.

writings of Jurij Samarin.[43] The first volume of his *Okrajny Rossii* (Russian Borderlands) from 1867 discussed the conversion movement in polemical terms:

> When the conversion movement took hold in Livland, he alone [the Tsar] understood that this was no artificial agitation, no accidental flare, but the historical and spontaneous movement of an entire people towards Russia, a movement born out of unsatisfied spiritual needs and simultaneously out of deep animosity towards the stagnation of the agrarian situation at that time. Regardless of all the slander and attempts to intimidate the government by governor general Baron Pahlen, the Tsar did *not* put the movement to a halt. [...]
>
> Only one circumstance was forgotten, namely that the conversion of the peasantry was threatening to erode the German-Lutheran colony, and that nobody in the higher administration remained neutral. There was a secret agreement among all pastors, manor lords, police officers, administration clerks and judges that was impossible to paralyse. [...] Only the governor general in his castle [i.e. Pahlen's successor, the Russian-friendly E. Golovin] could remain neutral, relying on three or four Russian officials, but otherwise encircled by intrigues, without hands, ears or eyes and always having to expect a scheme against him to be hatched out in Petersburg.[44]

The later accounts by Russian historians are less polemical in nature, but basically stick to the narrative that among the peasants, Orthodox Christianity was hindered from unfettered development by the Baltic German Lutherans.[45] A special group of these 'Russian' historians of Baltic Orthodoxy were ethnic Estonian and Latvian Orthodox theologians. Of these, the Estonians Jüri Truusman, Aleksander Värat, and Nikolai Leismann especially ought to be mentioned.[46] These three all argued that Orthodox Christianity was close to the Estonian mentality, whereas Lutheranism would always remain a German faith. With the upheavals of 1917, the three went very different ways. Aleksander Värat, editor of the Estonian-language Orthodox journal of the Riga Eparchy, was evacuated to St. Petersburg, where he became involved in the 'Living Church' movement in the 1920s.[47] Jüri Truusman retired from his post as Imperial censor in 1908 and did not involve himself in society life anymore. In democratic Estonia, he moved to the Petseri Monastery, where he lived in seclusion for another

---

43   See Haltzel, 1981, p. 127-129; Samarin, 1996, p. v-ix.

44   Samarin, 1996 [1867], p. 56.

45   Kryžanovskij, 1884; von Bröndsted, 1888 [a German account based on a Russian one]. See also Rosenberg, 2005, p. 100-101.

46   Rosenberg, 2005, p. 101-106. Also the Latvian Orthodox priest Jānis Līcis (1830-1905), whose polemical autobiography was published by Samarin as the story of 'Indrik Straumit' could be counted in this group. Samarin, 1869b. This work was published in Latvian after Līcis' death as Straumīte, 1906. For more on this text and its career, see Infant'ev, 2001.

47   See also chapter 2.2.1.

decade.[48] Only Nikolai Leismann continued his involvement in the church and societal life, even becoming Bishop of Petseri in 1933.[49]

After Tsar Nikolai II's Manifesto of Tolerance in 1905, the discourse changed, with the rise of Latvian and Estonian national historiographies. With freedom of conscience, the discourse on religious affiliation was freed from its bureaucratic implications, albeit not from censorship.[50] Some Estonian and Latvian Lutherans, possibly inspired by the views of their Baltic German pastors, branded the Orthodox Christians as separatists and accused them of being Russifiers and destroyers of national unity.[51] The discussions in Latvia during the lead-up to the First World War on creating a 'national faith' that was neither German nor Russian have already been mentioned. Aleksander Värat, the editor of the Estonian-language journal, had but one comment on these discussions:

> Before the nationalists, raised in the Lutheran faith, begin to reform religion after their own ideas, they ought to become seriously acquainted with Orthodoxy. We believe that, if they wish to be just, they will find that ecumenical Orthodoxy and its institutions satisfies all the needs of the Estonian and the Latvian nations, just as it has satisfied the spiritual needs of thousands of Estonians and Latvians for several decades already.[52]

This statement suggests that in the early twentieth century, Orthodoxy was still not seen as an alternative to Lutheranism and that the Baltic German myth of the Baltic shores as an eminently Lutheran area was stronger than the Russian attempts to redefine it as Orthodox. This obviously put Orthodox Latvians and

---

48 Lõuna, Anneli, 2002, p. 109-117.
49 See chapter 2.2.1. and 2.3.1.
50 Rimestad, 2007, p. 57-58. The academic work by the later Estonian Lutheran Bishop Johan Kõpp on the conversion movement of the 1840s from 1905 ought to be mentioned, as it did not display the tendencies described in the following, but remained rather objective and impartial. Kruus, 1930, p. 34-35; Rosenberg, 2000, p. 48-49.
51 "Kādu ticību Latviešiem pienāktos saukt par 'savu'?" [Which faith can the Latvian call 'his own'?] in *PLV*, 6/1, 1907, p. 3-11; J. A., "Pareizticība un latvieši" [Orthodoxy and the Latvians] in *PLV*, 7/17, 1908, p. 1-2; "Rahvuslaste märatsemine" [The rage of the nationalists] in *UjE₁*, 6/10, 1909, p. 109-111; 6/11, 1909, p. 121-125; "Head ja halba" [Good and bad] in *UjE₁*, 6/45, 1909, p. 521-523; *Kas õigeusk*, 1911; -???-, "Grāmatas un laikraksti" [Books and Periodicals] in *PLV*, 11/50-51, 1912, p. 190-191; NB, "Latviešu laikraksti par ticību" [The Latvian press on religion] in *PLV*, 13/14, 1914, p. 214-219; 13/15, 1914, p. 225-227.
52 "Mis kõnelevad teised ajalehed" [What other newspapers write about] in *UjE₁*, 8/32, 1911, p. 380-381. See also -???-, "Luteraņu mācitāji atzīst savu bankrotu" [The Lutheran Pastors admit their bankruptcy] in *PLV*, 13/42, 1914, p. 661-66; Kr. Lappuķe, "Luterisma pārkrievošana un nacionālā religija" [Russification of Lutheranism and the national religion] in *PLV*, 13/51, 1914, p. 802-805; "Par tautisko ticību" [On the national faith] in *PLV*, 16/3-4, 1917, p. 20-24; Kahle, 1959, p. 239.

Estonians in a difficult position, since they had to justify their historical identity against both the Baltic Germans and the Lutheran Latvians and Estonians. During the First World War and immediately after it, this justification seems to have borne fruit, if only within a limited scope. In Estonia, the murder of Bishop Platon (Kulbusch) together with Baltic German Lutheran pastors by the retreating Bolsheviks in January 1919 created a common ordeal for the two churches, on the basis of which they instituted common ceremonies.[53] In Latvia, attempts to create a national Latvian faith resulted in joint activities with Orthodox and Lutheran clergy in 1919-1921, but this did not continue after the arrival of Archbishop Jānis.[54]

4.1.3. Interwar Professional Historiography on the Orthodox Church

Professional historical scholarship on the Orthodox Church in Estonia and Latvia during the interwar period was carried out by a handful of people primarily around 1930. The above-mentioned Orthodox Archpriest Nikolai Leismann, sensing that "there is apparently an interest in the topic [of Orthodox Christianity in Estonia], but the local sources are not very yielding," published a bibliographical article of Russian-language sources and historical treatments of Baltic Orthodoxy in 1929.[55] In this article, he divided the nineteenth century literature on Baltic Orthodoxy in three groups: objective historical treatments, polemical accounts, and primary source material:

> As the largest, most serious and most important source for [the conversion movement], we should consider Jüri Samarin's 'Okrajny Rossii.' Samarin, in his day known as a defender of the peasants, after having played a significant role in the abolition of serfdom in Russia, could not remain quiet seeing the sad situation of the Baltic peasants. [...] Although Samarin's work is interspersed with polemics, it provides the reader with a rich fund of materials, which are otherwise difficult to find.[56]

It is difficult to assess the impact of Leismann's call to use Samarin as an authoritative source, since only one publication devoted specifically to the 1840s appeared in the period before 1940. Hans Kruus, one of the most productive

---

53 Sõtsov, 2009, p. 70.
54 "Iz L.U. Teoloģijas fakultātes pareizticīgo nodaļas vēstures" [From the history of the Latvian University Orthodox section of the Faculty of Theology] in *TuD*, 16/7, 1940, p. 108-109; Bušueva, 1993, p. 59-60. See also chapter 2.2.5.
55 Leismann, 1929, p. 129.
56 Leismann, 1929, p. 132-133. See also Thaden, 1986, who asserts that Samarin was one of the best available sources to Western scholars during the Cold War.

interwar Estonian historians and an active politician on the left wrote his doctoral dissertation in 1930 on this movement because he considered it the first important grassroots movement among Estonians since the thirteenth century:

> It has been touched upon by numerous authors relatively at length, so that authorita-tive Baltic German historians deemed the existing treatments exhaustive. In reality, however, we lack a historical account that would treat the problem with the desired impartiality and objectivity, taking all available sources and data into account in order to reconstruct the movement.[57]

The result was an objective historical reconstruction of the movement "in largely materialist terms."[58] According to Kruus, the conversion movement accompanying the peasant unrest arose "not because of external factors or inter-nal rational and logical argumentation. Rather, the psychological disposition of the people triggered certain external associations that were carried on and devel-oped through mass auto-suggestion."[59] Kruus, thus, considered the rumours about material benefits for converts the primary cause of the spread of the movement. Doing this, he leaned towards the Baltic German interpretation, which insisted that rumours had been a decisive factor, whereas the Russian accounts hardly mentioned the rumours at all.[60] The topic of Orthodox clergy agitation and religious propaganda was also emphasised.[61]

Analysing the consequences of the conversion wave, Kruus repeated the positions of some of his Baltic German and Estonian predecessors:[62] The posi-tive consequences of the movement lay mainly in its impact on the Lutheran Church, which was forced to rethink its position and teachings. The negative consequences consisted of the movement's effect on the Livland countryside: "A foreign body emerged in the political and religious organism of Livland, which grew and developed, leaving a heritage that is still there."[63] The Estonian people were, according to Kruus, divided in two without underlying reasons, facilitating the later Imperial Russification policy. Nonetheless, Konstantin Kokla published a rather sympathetic review of this dissertation in the Estonian

---

57   Kruus, 1930, p. 1, 411-412. The pages 410-449 are the German summary, where direct translations of the most important statements of the study can be found. See also Kivimäe and Kivimäe, 1987, p. 282; Kivimäe and Kivimäe, 1995; Hackmann, 2005, p. 128-129; Ryan, 2008, p. 19-22.

58   Ryan, 2008, p. 19.

59   Kruus, 1930, p. 407, 449.

60   Ryan, 2008, p. 316-321.

61   Kruus, 1930, p. 307-312, 444. For a relativisation of this claim, see Gavrilin, 1988; Ryan, 2008, p. 186-227.

62   Kruus, 1930, p. 409, 449.

63   Kruus, 1930, p. 449 [Only in the German summary].

Orthodox journal, while claiming that an even more positive picture of the movement could have been given.[64]

In 1927, Kruus had edited and published the diary of the Baltic German pastor Heinrich Georg von Jannau from 1845-1846. In his introduction to this work, his inclination towards the Baltic German interpretation of the conversion movement is even clearer. After describing the installation of an Orthodox vicar bishop in Riga, the introduction of Estonian- and Latvian-classes in the Pskov Orthodox Seminary, and the translation of Orthodox catechism and prayer book, Kruus noted, in the style of his Baltic German predecessors:

> By 1845, when the peasant unrest began anew, the preparations to successfully spread Orthodox Christianity had come quite far. But a local obstacle still had to be removed – the governor general Baron von Pahlen, whose administration resolutely had stopped all religious propaganda of the Orthodox Church among the peasants.[65]

Kruus again turned to the question of Orthodox Church history in Estonia in an article from 1936. Here, he pointed to the lack of an objective treatment of the so-called re-conversion movement of the 1860s, when a number of Orthodox converts expressed the wish to return to the Lutheran Church.[66] Following his earlier logic, that the original conversion movement was induced by clergy agitation and a mass psychosis, Kruus presented examples from local archives, demonstrating that the re-conversions were not spontaneous acts by desperate peasants but most likely inspired by the local Lutheran pastors.[67] However, to my knowledge, nobody responded to this call for academic research.

The most interesting observation concerning Hans Kruus and Nikolai Leismann is that, concerning what they claimed to be the available secondary sources, they seemed to live in different worlds. Leismann maintained that German Lutheran accounts were spread across a number of journals and that they were relatively few.[68] Kruus on the other hand claimed that Baltic German accounts were numerous, and that the Russian accounts all seemed to repeat Samarin, whose work he dismissed as pure journalism without much historical value.[69] This discrepancy can only be explained by reference to the biographies

---

64 Konstantin Kokla, "Mis ajas eestlasi usuvahetusele?" [What drove the Estonians to conversion?] in *UE*, 11/7, 1931, p. 2-4. See also chapter 4.2.2.

65 Kruus, 1927b, p. xi.

66 Kruus, 1936, p. 180-181. There are, to my knowledge, currently only three extensive objective studies of the aftermath of the conversion movement available. Of them, Garve, 1978 and Gavrilin, 1999 are incomplete, as they focus on German and Russian source material respectively. Ryan, 2008 has an outsider's perspective, focusing on the Estonian-language archive material.

67 Kruus, 1936, p. 182-184.

68 Leismann, 1929, p. 134.

69 Kruus, 1930, p. 19-28, 413-414.

of the two authors. Kruus was an Estonian socialist, from a culturally Lutheran family and with a doctoral degree from the national Estonian University of Tartu. Leismann was an Estonian Orthodox priest with higher education from the Saint Petersburg Theological Academy. The different academic biographies of these two led them to emphasise completely different bodies of available sources.

A third professional historian of Baltic Orthodoxy was Antonijs Pommers, the younger brother of Archbishop Jānis of Riga by fourteen years. He received his higher education from the University of Warsaw. Pommers published his most famous work, 'Orthodoxy in Latvia,' in 1929-1931.[70] This work sketched the history of Orthodox Christianity on Latvian territory from the earliest beginnings until the present, using a variety of source materials. It kept to the Russian historiography as outlined by Samarin, always depicting Orthodoxy as progressive and suited to the Latvians. This was the case already in the twelfth century, when "the Byzantine culture was much more developed than the Roman culture."[71] However, the Catholic missionaries had come with the sword and swept away the peaceful Orthodox missionaries. In the following 600 years, Orthodoxy was eradicated from the Baltic lands, although the Catholic and later Lutheran confessions were only formally instituted among the Latvians.

In the fashion of traditional Orthodox Church history, Pommers arranged the developments from the nineteenth century onwards according to the periods of the different bishops of Riga. The achievements of each were lauded as better than the predecessor's. The conversion movement was "not at all motivated by worldly desires but only by the wish to attain peace at heart."[72] The opening of the Riga Orthodox School and Seminary was described as a chance for which the Latvians had waited 600 years. Moreover, according to Pommers, this was the starting point of the Latvian and Estonian national movements. In Pommers' view, the low numbers of Orthodox re-converts after 1905 showed that "Orthodoxy was, is, and will always remain with the people and for the people, in spite of the changed and changing historical circumstances."[73] Finally, the situation of the Latvian Orthodox Church since 1917 was depicted as a history of persecution and mistreatment, until Archbishop Jānis was elected to the *Saeima* and achieved legal and political recognition for the Orthodox Church of Latvia.[74]

---

70 First printed over 16 issues of *Ticība un Dzīve*, then published parallel in Latvian and Russian as Pommers, 1931a and Pommers, 1931b. Since this work was also published in the more accessible Russian language, it remained the basis for most subsequent non-Latvian accounts of the Latvian Orthodox Church.
71 Pommers, 1931a, p. 4.
72 Pommers, 1931a, p. 30.
73 Pommers, 1931a, p. 74.
74 See also chapters 2.2.5 and 2.2.6.

Pommers' book, although written by a professional historian, can, in many ways, be considered a work of popular history. It only occasionally referred to sources, and the language was not especially objective. I have not been able to find any interwar discussions among historians on Pommers' book, which suggests that it was not widely acknowledged by the Latvian academic community. Pommers' 'habilitācija' thesis,[75] printed as a thirteen-page article in the journal of the Orthodox department of the Latvian University of Riga in 1940, was more scholarly. It was devoted to the installation of an Orthodox vicar bishop in Riga in 1836. Here, Pommers began with a survey of the Baltic German interpretations of this act, which had presumed that

> 1) Tsar Nikolai I in the 1830s wished to start Russifying the inhabitants of the Baltic Provinces, 2) his main tool in this respect was the Orthodox Church, which is why he decided to install an episcopal see in Riga in 1836. 3) Bishop Irinarch, following the idea of his superiors, with the help of his clergy, set rumours about 'warm land' for converts in circulation. 4) The Orthodox priests abused the situation, writing fake pleas for the parishioners, who knew no Russian and 5) the bishop sent agitator priests into the countryside.[76]

Unfortunately, according to Pommers, the vast majority of Latvian historians had uncritically accepted this version of events, without taking into account the Russian narrative and the Russian documents. In these original Russian documents, there was almost no mention at all of local peasants or dealings with Lutherans. For Pommers, it was therefore clear that

> from the official documents, it is impossible to say what the Russian authorities, i.e. Tsar Nikolai I and the members of the Most Holy Synod, wanted to achieve. If there were any secret and 'jesuitic' aims among the Russian politics regarding the Baltic Lutherans, the Baltic Germans' compatriots in the highest administration of the Russian Empire would easily have found out.[77]

In the following, Pommers cited a Russian official, dispatched from Petersburg to investigate the peasant unrest of 1845 at length. This official concluded that the wish to convert was a sincere religious wish, since the Lutheran Church of the Baltic Germans could not satisfy the spiritual needs of the peasantry. Moreover, he claimed that "the entire alarm and worry among the Baltic Germans was caused by their fear of drawing nearer to the Russians."[78] Pommers concluded the article by maintaining that there was no evidence of Orthodox

---

75 In order to have a teaching position at the Latvian University of Riga, the applicant needed to have completed his 'habilitācija,' similar to the German *Habilitation*. Pommers was designated as lecturer of Orthodox Church history in the summer of 1939.
76 Pommers, 1940, p. 100.
77 Pommers, 1940, p. 106.
78 Pommers, 1940, p. 109.

agitation, and it was the Germans who had spread rumours, fearing concerted action on the side of the Orthodox Church that would lead to the loss of their 'well-earned' privileges.[79] However, since this article appeared in 1940, there was no time for any published discussion in the Latvian historical community before the Second World War.

The last professional account to be mentioned is the master's thesis of Leida Rebane at the Estonian University of Tartu from 1932. This was the only historical master's thesis in interwar Estonia devoted to nineteenth century Estonian history.[80] A shortened version of the thesis on the beginning of the conversion movement of the 1880s in the Estland Province was published across three issues of *Ajalooline ajakiri* (Historical journal). Rebane analysed the 1880s movement primarily because "previous treatments have not been interested in the problems of the actors of this movement, but have simply used the movement as an arena of mutual accusations."[81] Both the Germans and the Russians tended to view this movement as a direct continuation of the conversions of the 1840s, simply relocated a bit further north.[82] In the following analysis, Rebane depicted the movement in amazing detail, concluding that conversion had been a more concrete way of expressing an Estonian national identity than supporting some project in far-away Tallinn or Tartu.[83] However, this article also did not receive any attention in the published discourse.

4.2. The Orthodox Church in Popular Historiography

By popular historiography, I mean the way certain events and developments were presented in the public discourse by non-historians. There is obviously a more or less intensive interplay between professional and popular historiography. This interplay is most easily detectable in published history schoolbooks, where professional historians provide the young generations with a view of history. Along with these sources, there are treatments by hobby historians on various occasions and the published accounts of events from recent history in the recollections of more or less active participants. Finally, the way an event or its participants are described in works of fiction also belongs to popular historiography. All four of these types provide insights into the image of Orthodox

---

79 Pommers, 1940, p. 111. This was a common topic among the Russian accounts of the movement. See Ryan, 2008, p. 319-320.
80 Kivimäe and Kivimäe, 1986, p. 281.
81 Rebane, 1933, p. 79.
82 Rebane, 1933, p. 79-82. The author acknowledges that the Russian side of the argument had been a bit more objective, referring to the works of Truusman, Värat and Leismann.
83 Rebane, 1933, p. 84. The author starts with the conclusion and in the end of the article brings an outlook at the consequences.

Christianity in the popular historiography of Estonia and Latvia in the interwar years. These are necessarily only limited insights, for it is impossible to grasp popular historiography in full.

This chapter consists of two sections. The first section considers everything which was written about the Orthodox Church history in the secular sources and the criticism thereof in the Orthodox journals. The section begins with the accounts treating the earliest times and closes with accounts of the most recent history. The second section turns to the historiographic contributions of the Orthodox journals. These include first, pure narratives intended to provide the readers with historical knowledge. From the mid-1930s onwards, the tone of the journals became more aggressive, and several series of active criticism of contemporary historiography were published. These articles claimed that professional historiography did not treat the Orthodox Church positively enough and that those positive analyses that existed were not adequately considered in popular historiography. If one believes some of the more polemical accounts in the journals, Orthodox Latvians and especially Estonians constantly had to fight an endless battle with the Lutheran majority society for their historical identity.

4.2.1. Popular Historiography on the Orthodox Church

Just as in Baltic German historiography, the history that Estonians and Latvians learned in school began with the Catholic missionaries and crusaders of the twelfth century, with references to some previous Russian influences as well. In 1939, an author signing as 'Apostolicus' characterised the schoolbook historiography as follows:

> So far in Estonia, we have been taught that Christianity arrived on the Baltic shores at the end of the twelfth century and that it was brought here by German Roman Catholic missionaries. Every school child will tell you that from this moment onwards, the crusaders, led by the Bishop of Riga, would spread Catholicism in the area of the Estonian and Latvian Republics with fire and sword; that this confession was replaced in the sixteenth century by Lutheranism and then, finally, in the 1840s, there was a conversion movement to Orthodoxy. This movement occurred only because of the hope to get land. That is what the schoolbooks say and that is how also the rest of the people are being told both orally and in written form. [...][84]

The problem had apparently also existed in Latvia during the 1920s, as an article from 1937 in the Latvian journal noted. This article maintained that until Antonijs Pommers' book appeared in 1931,

---

84   Apostolicus, "Ristiusu tulek Baltimaale" [The arrival of Christianity to the Baltics] in *ET*, 4/8, 1939, p. 87.

the schools only taught that Christianity was brought to Latvia from the West and by the crusaders, who forced it upon the Latvians with fire and sword, with lies and deceit. Until then, the Latvians had been pagans, who venerated the forces of nature and other divinities. However, recent scholarship shows that the Latvians were no 'pagans,' but had been culturally and religiously civilised, not only having contact with Christian peoples before the advent of the Germans, but even being partly Christianised, through Orthodox missionaries.[85]

The author continued to praise the recent research of the professors Francis Balodis and Augusts Tentelis into early Latvian history, which showed that the Latvians were quite mighty before the arrival of the crusaders.[86] The author ended with praise for *Vadoṇis* (the Leader, Kārlis Ulmanis), who had finally made the Latvians free in a religious sense. That in these early times, Orthodoxy as such was not negatively connoted can be seen in a critical review of three Estonian historical novels, taking place in medieval times and touching upon Orthodox Christianity. The author mentions that two of the works are "unbiased, even sympathetic, towards Orthodoxy in their descriptions" whereas the last one makes the error of conflating Orthodoxy with Catholicism, when it talks about castrated monks from Byzantium singing the higher voices in the choir.[87]

The conversion episode of the 1840s was given much more attention than the medieval era. A survey of the most important schoolbooks of Estonia and Latvia in the interwar period reveals that a slightly modified version of the Baltic German view dominated, although the Latvian accounts seem less tainted than the Estonian ones. In the influential Latvian history book by Frīdis Zālītis from 1921, for example, the conversion movement was explained as follows:

> A majority of the Baltic German historians explain the conversions with Orthodox clergy agitation. Obviously, such a large popular movement cannot be explained that easily, and in order to understand the movement, we need to take the contemporary situation of the peasants into account.[88]

A survey of the economic and religious circumstances on the Livland country-side follows, before the appeal of the Orthodox Church to improve both of these aspects is explained. Then, the movement itself is described, followed by the opposition of the Lutheran Baltic Germans to it.[89] This rather positive image was also presented in the 'Latvian History' for secondary schools by Antonijs Pommers, published in 1930. Pommers analysed the conversion movement from

---

85   J. Baumanis, "Pareizticība Latvijā" [Orthodoxy in Latvia] in *TuD*, 13/2, 1937, p. 18-19. See also Kalniņš, Pēteris, 1930, p. 172-173. Kalniņš here attempted to deconstruct Samarin's evidence to medieval Orthodoxy in the Baltic region.
86   These two professors were both active in the re-writing of Latvian history during the Ulmanis-regime. See chapters 2.3.3 and 4.1.1.
87   T. Lepik, "Ap.-õigeusu asjust" [On Orthodox matters] in *UjE₂*, 5/6, 1937, p. 90-91.
88   Zālītis, 1921, p. 184-185.
89   Zālītis, 1921, p. 185-189.

the point of view of the Orthodox Church, depicting the Baltic German authorities as obstacles in the free development of the Latvian nation.[90] The eighth edition of the 'Latvian History' for secondary schools by Frīdis Zālītis from 1937 also follows the same scheme: There were three reasons for the conversion movement; first, religious dissatisfaction, second, the unpalatable economic situation and third, the wish to emancipate from the Baltic Germans.[91]

In the most influential Estonian school history book, written by Hans Kruus in 1927, the latter's reliance on the Baltic German historiography becomes evident. According to this schoolbook, Bishop Irinarch in 1841 "continued to receive the peasants with the aim of increasing the number of Orthodox in his Eparchy."[92] In the following years, the Orthodox Church was "preparing" for large scale conversions and the change of governor general Pahlen in 1845 was a sign of the "changing Livland-policy of the Russian Imperial administration. [...] Bishop Filaret now went about actively spreading Orthodoxy among the Livland peasants [and] the Orthodox converts, once they saw that their hopes of worldly benefits were not fulfilled and that their Lutheran neighbours were making fun of them, were filled with disappointment about the step they had taken."[93]

While the Latvian schoolchildren were taught that the conversion movement was the first active demonstration of Latvian peasants, the Estonians were taught that the movement was the result of a massive mistake. The reason for this difference is best explained by the biographies of the three authors. Whereas both Zālītis and Pommers were born on the countryside and both in villages where the conversion movement of the 1840s had been especially strong,[94] Kruus was the son of a factory worker in Tartu.[95] For the two Latvian historians, peasant hardships were probably more tangible than for Kruus, who would also have had less experience with religious issues in general.

Criticism of these standard schoolbooks was voiced in the Estonian Orthodox journal *Elutõde* in 1939, with the author comparing the preference for the

---

90   Pommers, 1930, p. 242-249.

91   Zālītis, 1937, p. 219-221.

92   Kruus, 1927a, p. 105. That the schoolbooks had not been better before 1927 becomes clear in "Eesti ap.-kiriku 75 aasta juubeli puhul" [On the occasion of the 75th anniversary of the Estonian Orthodox Church] in *UE*, 1/5-6, 1921, p. 33-34.

93   Kruus, 1927a, p. 112-115. See also H.S., "Ääremärkused Vene usu pealesurumise esimestest aastatest" [Notes on the first years of forced conversions to the Russian faith] in *Kirjandus - kunst - teadus,* 1/17, 06.06.1921, 06.06, p. 131-133.

94   I have not been able to ascertain the confessional affiliation of Frīdis Zālītis, but the Orthodoxy of Pommers cannot be doubted.

95   Kivimäe and Kivimäe, 1995, p. 156.

Lutheran Church in these books to advertisement campaigns for some product.[96] This kind of criticism cannot be found in the Latvian case. However, criticism of the treatment of the Orthodox Church in historiography was commonplace in both cases, including criticism of the professional historiographic accounts described above. Upon the publication of Hans Kruus' doctoral dissertation on the 1840s conversion movement, Konstantin Kokla welcomed it, since it dispelled the myth that "Orthodoxy and its arrival was the result of a mass fraud."[97] However, he noted that Kruus did not go far enough and claimed that in addition to the social and political aspects of the conversions, there was a religious one. For one, the Catholic and Lutheran confessions had both truly been 'master's churches,' without making serious efforts to bring the Christian message to the people. Conversion was thus, according to Kokla, the natural way for the peasants to express their political desires. Moreover, if material benefits had been their only aim, Orthodoxy would not have remained a viable option until the present, according to Kokla.[98]

However, as Kokla also noted, the "majority of the Estonian public opinion has joined the German Lutheran standpoint: the Estonian left Lutheranism as a result of Orthodox clergy agitation and misleading promises of 'soul land.'"[99] This view did not change markedly throughout the 1930s, although the emphasis shifted more to the political and economic injustices of the time.[100] Latvian soci-

---

96 "Eesti ap.-õigeusk ja standardõpikud" [Estonian Orthodoxy and standard schoolbooks] in *ET*, 4/13-14, 1939, p. 145.

97 Konstantin Kokla, "Mis ajas eestlasi usuvahetusele?" [What drove the Estonians to conversion?] in *UE*, 11/7, 1931, p. 3.

98 Konstantin Kokla, "Mis ajas eestlasi usuvahetusele?" [What drove the Estonians to conversion?] in *UE*, 11/7, 1931, p. 3.

99 Konstantin Kokla, "Mis ajas eestlasi usuvahetusele?" [What drove the Estonians to conversion?] in *UE*, 11/7, 1931, p. 2. See also H. S., "Ääremärkused Vene usu pealesurumise esimestest aastatest" [Notes on the first years of forced conversions to the Russian faith] in *Kirjandus – kunst – teadus*, 1/17, 06.06.1921, p. 131-133. This second article was commented on in [Anton Laar], "Lühike ülevaade Eesti ap.-õigeusu elukäigust 75 a. jooksul" [Short overview of 75 years of Estonian Orthodox life] in *UE*, 1/5-6, 1921, p. 35.

100 "Miks toimus meil üleminek vene usku" [Why was there a mass conversion to the Russian faith] in *PL*, 30/38, 07.02.1935, p. 3; Konstantin Kokla, "Huvitavat usuelust kirjanduses" [Interesting facts about religious life in the press] in *UjE₂*, 3/2, 1935, p. 25-26; Konstantin Kokla, "'Veneusk' Eesti uues ajaloos – 'imena'" [The 'Russian Faith' in recent Estonian history as 'a wonder'] in *UjE₂*, 5/9, 1937, p. 131-132; K., "'Hingemaast' mille pärast usk vahetati" [The 'soul land' for which they converted] in *UjE₂*, 7/6, 1939, p. 92; Apostolicus, "Ristiusu tulek Baltimaale" [The arrival of Christianity to the Baltics] in *ET*, 4/8, 1939, p. 87-88; J. Tõnissoo, 1951. In the first official biography of Konstantin Päts, whose grandfather had been among the Orthodox converts, the conversions are described politically and economically. There is no mention of any religious aspects. Einbund, 1934, p. 17-19.

ety seems less biased in its treatment of the conversion movement, as I noted above. However, there were also cases in Latvia, where the conversions and their aftermath did not appear in a positive light.[101]

The same difference between the two nations is also detectable in their treatments of Russification. In spite of significant agreements among the three above mentioned schoolbook authors as to the structure, order, and content of the chapter on Russification in their history books, the two Latvian accounts devote more space to the deteriorating relationship between Germans and Latvians and describe the Russification measures more objectively.[102] Kruus, on the other hand, repeatedly refers to the 'mean' measures initiated by the Imperial government and its 'unfair' practices in the religious realm.[103] He even included a section on the situation of the Orthodox Church in Estonia in the second half of the nineteenth century, describing it as "extremely lacking outer and inner qualities" while its members lived under despicable social and economic conditions.[104]

In the public discourse on the Russification period, there are two themes that dominate the discourse. These are first the discussions surrounding the Aleksander Nevskij Cathedral in Tallinn and other Orthodox houses of worship and second the appreciation or condemnation of the societal role of the Riga Orthodox Seminary. The public condemnation of Orthodox Church buildings as monuments of Russian oppression, especially in Estonia, has already been mentioned.[105] According to an account in an Estonian newspaper, "the cathedral has been repeatedly under criticism, for we have not yet managed to forget the politics of the former governor [count Šakhovskoj, 1885-1894], which the cathedral especially brings vividly to mind."[106] Russification was seen primarily as a negative era in Baltic history, both in Estonia and in Latvia. This negative connotation was then projected onto everything with Russifying potential,

---

101 Kalniņš, Pēteris, 1930; Augustīns Pētersons, "Vai pareizticība ir krieviska un luterticība latviska?" [Is Orthodoxy Russian and Lutheranism Latvian?] in *TuD*, 8/12, 1930, p. 178-183; Pēteris Gredzens, "Noklusētais ienaidnieks" [The silent enemy] in *TuD*, 15/17, 1939, p. 261-263.

102 Pommers, 1930, p. 296-301; Zālītis, 1937, p. 275-279.

103 Kruus, 1928, p. 78-96.

104 Kruus, 1927a, p. 170.

105 See chapter 3.2.3.

106 "Katedraal Kalevi kalmul jälle komistuskiviks..." [The cathedral on Kalev's tomb again the bone of contention...] in *Esmaspäev*, 18/24, 17.06.1939, p. 4. The article was written on the occasion of the death of count Šakhovskoj's widow. See also M. M., [M. Mäessa] "Kas venestuse kantsiks või Eesti piiskopi esinduskirikuks?" [Fort of Russification or representative Church of the Estonian bishop?] in *ET*, 3/3, 1938, p. 28.

including the Riga Orthodox Seminary and the Orthodox clergy.[107] An interesting viewpoint concerning the role of the Seminary is found in Pāvils Gruzna's
autobiographical novel 'Bursaki,'[108] published in 1928, which depicts life in the
Seminary. According to one critic,

> the most interesting point is the New Year's sermon on page 232, in which the pro-
> tagonist not only issues an open invitation to atheism and calls the Saviour a liar, but
> even promotes anarchy and the rejection of basic legal principles. The 'teacher'
> Rasa openly invites the listeners to steal, rob, kill, commit adultery. He wants to turn
> everybody into pigs, not accepting any chains, any boundaries...[109]

The novel, harshly criticised by the Lutheran and Orthodox press alike, nevertheless became quite popular in Latvia.[110] An attempt of the Valmiera Lutheran
clerical conference to add this novel to the official list of undesirable literature
failed, because

> 1) The novel does not have enough impact to put it on the list of obscene literature;
> in the novel, there are *several unconventional passages* (emphasis mine, A.Š.), but
> considering the work's tendency and spirit on the whole, it becomes clear, that the
> aim of the author was not obscenity in order to captivate the reader, 2) the novel is
> not at all puerile, but the author informs the reader about life in the Russian theo-
> logical seminary and the psychology inherent in this life, bringing it in connection
> with the developments going on in Latvian society at the time.[111]

Even the intervention by the Lutheran Church did not help the Orthodox Church
in its quest to redress its perceived historical role.

---

107 A. Goba, "Kristiešu Mācitaji un Latvieši tautiskie centieni" [The Christian clergy and the
Latvian national consciousness] in *Labietis*, 3, 1933, p. 33-39; "Huvitavad read
'venestamisest'" [Interesting lines on 'Russification'] in *UjE₂*, 7/5, 1939, p. 77-78;
Pēteris Gredzens, "Noklusētais ienaidnieks" [The silent enemy] in *TuD*, 15/17, 1939, p.
261-263; K. K., [Konstantin Kokla] "Kas eesti preestrid ignoreerisid eesti rahvast?" [Did
the Estonian priests ignore the Estonians?] in *UjE₂*, 8/2, 1940, p. 29-30.

108 The nickname for students of the Riga Orthodox Seminary. Gruzna had himself studied
many years at the Seminary. The novel had previously appeared as a feuilleton in 1914.
See Vāvere, 1992, p. 20.

109 Kirils Zaics, "Mūsu rakstniecības ēnas puses" [The dark side of our literature] in *TuD*,
7/2, 1929, p. 24.

110 Ančaugs., "Lubu literaturas plūdi" [The flood of trash literature] in *TuD*, 6/5, 1928, p.
77-80; Jānis Jansons, "Pareizticība pie latviešiem" [Orthodoxy among the Latvians] in
TuD, 6/6, 1928, p. 83-85; Kirils Zaics, "Mūsu rakstniecības ēnas puses" [The dark side of
our literature] in *TuD*, 7/2, 1929, p. 23-26; Bursaks, "Ko sludina P. Gruzna savā romanā
'Bursaki'" [What P. Gruzna showed in his novel 'Bursaki'] in *TuD*, 14/6, 1938, p. 90-91;
Vāvere, 1992, p. 21-26.

111 Kirils Zaics, "Mūsu rakstniecības ēnas puses" [The dark side of our literature] in *TuD*,
7/2, 1929, p. 24-25. This is the reproduction of an article from a Lutheran newspaper by
Pastor A. Šaurums.

After Russification and the Manifesto of Tolerance of 1905, the religious question had been conclusively subordinated to secular life and was no longer seen to play an important role in history. Thus, there was not much in the published discourse about the role of the Orthodox Church in more recent history. For example, the Estonian historian Eduard Laaman, characterised as "the most productive and best informed author concerning the actual developments and sociology of power in Estonia," hardly ever turned to religious issues.[112] In his biographies of the (Orthodox) politicians Jaan Poska and Konstantin Päts, Laaman perpetuated the old clichés maintaining that "the converts hoped to get 'soul land', better working conditions, and tax alleviations"[113] and that the Riga Orthodox Seminary "was instituted to facilitate the Russification of the Baltic Provinces."[114] Interestingly, the biographies of Konstantin Päts usually mention that his grandfather had converted and that he himself had studied at the Riga Orthodox Seminary. However, once their narrative arrives at his entrance to the Pärnu Secondary School in 1892, all mentions of Orthodox Christianity disappear.[115]

A case of popular historiography on the most recent history of the Orthodox Church was a novel by the German author Edzard Schaper, which appeared in 1936. In this novel, Schaper follows a Russian Orthodox priest in a small Estonian town through the early period of independence.[116] While the novel was universally hailed as bringing an authentic light on the latest developments of Orthodoxy in Estonia, the author did not get all the facts right.[117] He repeatedly refers to the Holy Synod, which "was holy, infallible in its decisions, its executive originated with God and no appeal was possible..."[118] In the Estonian case, as I have argued, the Russian parishes did not accord the Estonian Synod such a high authority and communication with the Petersburg Synod was impossible. Another description of the contemporary situation claims that

> the holy Orthodox Church in this country has split into two parties, as apparently is the case in other countries, and this split runs right through the Holy Synod. On one side, there was the Russian clergy, faithfully seeking to sustain and survive the

---

112 Quote from Karjahärm and Sirk, 2001, p. 324. See also Arens, 1973.
113 Laaman, 1998 [1935], p. 11.
114 Laaman, 1949 [1940], p. 11.
115 Tupits, 1934; Laaman, 1949 [1940].
116 Schaper, 1953 [1935]. Importantly, Schaper was not a Baltic German, but he had chosen Estonia as his home only in 1932.
117 "Saksa romaan Eesti ainestikul" [A German novel on Estonian matters] in *Kunst ja Kirjandus* 4/45, 10.11.1935, p. 180; Evald J. Voitk, "Saksa sulg kirjeldab eesti elu" [A German pen describing Estonian life] in *Rahvaleht*, 17/15, 18.01.1939, p. 10; Garleff, 1996.
118 Schaper, 1953, p. 78.

severity of the times. On the other, in the majority, there was the clergy of the nation now dominating the state. And while the church lay weak and bleeding after several years of war and revolution, only gradually regaining its faithful, a number of foreign sects, as well as the Roman Catholic Church, had entered the scene. Now certainly, none of the Russian priests asserted any claim to a privileged position in the new state, as they were used to in earlier times; on the contrary, they wanted to confidently suffer God's ordeals and remain steadfast in the faith of the fathers; only, they painfully heard the voice of those who once had been deviously converted. Tired of martyrdom and stimulated by the benevolence of the secular authorities – who would rather see Western Catholicism than the faith of their former oppressors that was directed towards the East, for the state turned now towards the West – this stronger part of the ecclesiastic authorities had turned to the mighty Roman Catholic Church for support. [...] Byzantium was to acknowledge the papal primacy. In return for this price, the church would be allowed to sap generously from the Roman might and feel elevated from its misery. And the majority of the priests were willing to renounce their religion in return for this pleasure, since it had never really become *their* faith; it had not been born among them and painfully developed into *their* church.[119]

In this description, Schaper follows the bias of many Baltic German commentators, identifying Orthodoxy with Russianness, not bothering to investigate the internal discourses of Estonian Orthodoxy. Exactly the same bias is detectable in the sociological-political account of Helmut Risch.[120] Nevertheless, neither Schaper's novel nor Risch's article were mentioned in the Estonian Orthodox journals.

In the Latvian case, there were no such novels. Moreover, the accounts of the Latvian Orthodox Church that appeared in western languages were openly pro-Orthodox. An article exchange in the London-based *Church Times*, mostly concerning recent history, was initiated by the letter of protest from the Latvian Synod on Archbishop Jānis' living conditions in 1924. The introduction to the publication of the letter sweepingly declared that

the state machines [in the new states along Russia's western border] have been used with the greatest skill to eliminate everything Russian that could be eliminated. [...] The natural expression of this policy is the use of the law for the pacific crushing the Orthodox Church out of existence in all five successor states. [sic, ...]
There seems some ground for the Orthodox complaint that the Bolshevik persecution of their church in Russia is distinguished from the Latvian only by violence.[121]

The unofficial Latvian ambassador to London, Georgs Bisenieks, did not want to let this bad press pass unnoticed, explaining the official Latvian view on the

---

119 Schaper, 1953, p. 175-176. Another novel by Schaper, written after the Second World War, turns back to the subject of the Catholicism in Estonia. It also touches on the Orthodox Church, but only tangentially. Schaper 1963.
120 Risch, 1937.
121 "An Archbishop in a Cellar" in *Church Times*, 19.09.1924, p. 315-316.

history of Orthodoxy in Latvia. His reply exaggerated the most blatant Baltic German clichés about promises of land, claimed that the total Russian population in Latvia was only 3%, and that the government played no part in the persecution of the Orthodox Church.[122] The article exchange continued for three more issues, with the last word given to the Orthodox representative in the Latvian *Saeima*, A. S. Bočagov, who accused Bisenieks of ignorance.[123] A short article on the Orthodox Church in Latvia by Walter Schubart from 1940 is equally pro-Orthodox, mainly because its main source was the 1931 book by Antonijs Pommers.[124]

4.2.2. Popular Historiography by the Orthodox Church

The historiographic accounts in the Orthodox journals of Estonia and Latvia were primarily directed at the faithful, in order to make them better understand their own history. Antonijs Pommers' sixteen issue series (1929-1931), mentioned above, was the most comprehensive historiographic account published in the Orthodox journals.[125] A commentary, written by Juris Kreics, who primarily added archaeological and folkloristic evidence to Pommers' discussion of the medieval period, accompanied it in six of the issues. According to Kreics, "the Russians were more interested in bringing the Gospel to the Latvians, for they continued to come to the Latvians with schools and books, with the Cross and the Bible, even in the face of the Germans' mission by fire and sword."[126] Also the previously mentioned article by 'Apostolicus' emphasised the veracity of the Russian mission as opposed to the politically motivated German crusaders. Moreover, 'Apostolicus' provided an explanation for the Baltic Germans' attempts to hush up the pre-crusade existence of Orthodox Christianity in the Baltics:

> Why the Baltic German historians did not know anything, or rather did not want to know anything about Orthodoxy in early Baltic history might seem quite obvious to us. As the only justifying (!?) reason for why the German crusaders under the lead-

---

122 G. W. Bisseneek [Bisenieks], "The Orthodox in Latvia" in *Church Times*, 03.10.1924, p. 368. The Latvian 1930 census counted 10.6% Russians, and it is unlikely that their percentage should have tripled in six years.

123 A. Bochogoff [Bočagov], "The Orthodox in Latvia" in *Church Times*, 05.12.1924, p. 641-642.

124 Schubart, 1940.

125 See chapter 4.1.3. The view of history propagated by Archbishop Jānis in his *Saeima* speeches has already been mentioned. See chapter 2.2.7.

126 Juris Kreics, "Piezīmes pie raksta 'Pareizticība Latvijā'" [Commentary to the article 'Orthodoxy in Latvia'] in *TuD*, 8/6, 1930, p. 93.

ership of the Bishop of Riga descended upon our country, they always claimed that they were bringing Christianity to us wild pagans, who had never heard of the Saviour Jesus Christ and that the arrival of the crusaders and their activity here, even if it was bloody, was only in order to defend the Christians from the pagans. [...] If we now allow the idea that there was Orthodox Christianity in the Baltic region long before the arrival of the German Catholics, then the entire historical perspective collapses together with the fairy tale of the Germans as the bringers of Christian culture. For almost a century, at least for several decades, the practical authorities in our lands – the Baltic Germans – have tried to foster a hate against everything Russian, especially Orthodox Christianity, which, according to them, was the Russian faith, as if it was some object the Russians had invented. This fostering has produced fruits, and even nowadays, in sovereign Estonia, the young historian, still dependent on his teachers and books, writes down and accepts this fairy tale of the Baltic nobility, as if Orthodox Christianity arrived to our lands for the first time in the 1840s and managed to spread solely because of stupid peasants hoping for land.[127]

The author calls on Estonian historians to "keep in mind the Latin saying: 'Introite, et hinc dii sunt' [sic] (Enter, for there are Gods here too)" and to stop ignoring the Orthodox Church.[128] The series of articles by 'Apostolicus', which began as a furious review of a new textbook of Estonian church history by Olaf Sild from 1938 for "students of theology, pastors and teachers of religion, as well as the intelligentsia and the most knowledgeable of the congregation members,"[129] continued in four more issues, presenting evidence from Russian chronicles to claim that Orthodoxy was widely spread in the Estonian and Latvian lands when the German crusaders first arrived at the end of the twelfth century. Both Kreics, in Latvia, and 'Apostolicus,' in Estonia, emphasised the importance of the eastern regions of the state (Latgale and Petserimaa) in these early times, attempting to enhance the esteem of these 'backward' regions in the eyes of the nation, at least among the Orthodox. It is difficult to ascertain whether this had any effect, as I have not found an acknowledgment of either series of articles anywhere outside of Orthodox circles.

Most of the historiographic sketches given in the Orthodox journals appeared at the approach of some kind of anniversary. The first of these accounts during the independence period was Anton Laar's comments on the

---

127 Apostolicus, "Ristiusu tulek Baltimaale" [The arrival of Christianity to the Baltics] in *ET*, 4/8, 1939, p. 88.

128 Apostolicus, "Ristiusu tulek Baltimaale" [The arrival of Christianity to the Baltics] in *ET*, 4/8, 1939, p. 87. This phrase, traditionally attributed to Heraclitus, correctly reads 'Introite, nam et hic dii sunt'.

129 Sild, 1995 [1938], p. 1.

75th anniversary of the Orthodox Church in Estonia in 1921.[130] Laar was motivated by a state of affairs in which the great great majority of the Estonians

> do not have difficulties finding the words to make a fool or a devil out of Orthodoxy
> [...] even publicly and from the pulpits. [...] Our Estonian primary and secondary
> school history books are written with such a strong bias (obviously, in favour of the
> 'only correct' faith and against the hated Russian faith) that even an impartial edu-
> cation specialist felt the need to protest. [...] Even stranger still is the attitude of
> some Lutheran pastors, who see in apostolic Orthodoxy some half-pagan sect. [...]
> But the main criticism is obviously nationalism, where our guilt is most strong:
> apparently, we are Russifiers. Obviously, the critics cleverly leave out two facts: 1)
> how many Estonians actually have been Russified through Orthodoxy and 2) how
> many of the most important Estonian politicians and academics, some of whom have
> entered the national hall of fame, actually have been Orthodox. [...]
> But let these sorrowful lines be enough for this time. We just want to show how
> absolutely necessary it is, in order for our faith to be understood correctly, that we
> gather historical data and spread it among the population and put the matter to the
> court of academic judgement. – We would not dream of hiding the dark pages of our
> history; on the contrary, it is from them that we can learn. But it would be just as
> unthinkable to let the genuine benefits Orthodoxy has brought our history be hushed
> up, which we will never accept. We will find ways to redress this imbalance![131]

The following short historical overview of the preceding 75 years pursued this
narrative, which reappeared in various forms throughout the interwar period.[132]
Laar divided the history of the Orthodox Church in Estonia into five periods: the
era of suffering (1846-1868), the era of organisation (1868-1888), the Russification attempts (1888-1895), the last Russian period (1895-1917), and the independence period (1917-1921). The first period was a difficult time, when the
Lutherans, under the leadership of the Baltic German nobility, had "pulled out
all the stops to impede the conversion movement and to undo the conversions

---

130 [Anton Laar], "Eesti ap.-kiriku 75 aasta juubeli puhul" [On the occasion of the 75th anniversary of the Estonian Orthodox Church] in *UE*, 1/5-6, 1921, p. 33-34; [Anton Laar],
"Lühike ülevaade Eesti ap.-õigeusu elukäigust 75 a. jooksul" [Short overview of 75 years
of Estonian Orthodox life] in *UE*, 1/5-6, 1921, p. 34-37; 1/7, 1921, p. 51; 1/8, 1921, p.
58-60; 1/9, 1921, p. 66-67. It is difficult to ascertain what exactly Laar considers to be
the starting point but he probably meant the establishment of the first Estonian-speaking
congregation in 1846.

131 [Anton Laar], "Eesti ap.-kiriku 75 aasta juubeli puhul" [On the occasion of the 75th anniversary of the Estonian Orthodox Church] in *UE*, 1/5-6, 1921, p. 33-34.

132 See *inter alia* Redakcija, "Vēsturisks atskats" [Historical sketch] in *TuD*, 7/8-9, 1929, p.
97-108; P. Balodis, "Latvijas pareizticīgās Baznīcas arķibīskapijas 85 gadi" [85 years of
the Latvian Orthodox Archbishopric] in *TuD*, 11/5, 1935, p. 67-69; Pēteris Gredzens,
"No vikariāta līdz mitropolijai" [From a vicariate to a metropolitanate] in *TuD*, 12/5,
1936, p. 67; Pēteris Gredzens, "Rīgas biskapu katedras 100 gadu jubileja" [The centenary
of the Riga bishop's seat] in *TuD*, 12/11, 1936, p. 168-169; 12/12, 1936, p. 184.

that had already taken place."[133] Moreover, the congregations were weak and lacked buildings, priests, and schools. During the second period, which started with the appointment of P. Albedinskij as governor general of Riga, "our church received the foundations which it still has today," i.e. churches were built, priests were named, and they were offered a state salary, all the while pursuing various activities in the Estonian national movement.[134] The following period of Russification was consciously not called an 'era' but 'attempts,' for Laar wanted to distance himself from the Baltic German periodisation. It was initiated by Bishop Arsenij (1887-1897),

> who proclaimed that there will be no more Estonian-language liturgies forty years from now. The faithful will all know enough Church Slavonic by then. And truly, some idiocies happened, and quite quickly. The former good relationship with the people was destroyed. [...] The relationship with the Lutheran Church became militant. [...] In the Riga Seminary, all instruments were restringed with chords of Russianness, which, however, did not really have influence. On the contrary, it brought forth an even stronger Estonian movement, which organised a secret library, established Estonian periodicals and societies. [...] In a nutshell, everything that had been gradually and quietly built up in the preceding period for the good of the faith was sacrificed for political Panslavism. As a result, unfortunately, the rather positive attitude of the majority of the people, regardless of the faith, towards Orthodoxy, especially her schools, cooled down. The best alumni from the Orthodox Seminary turned to secular careers – a development that became universal towards the end of this sad time.[135]

The last Russian period was, according to Laar, characterised by inconsequent Tsarist authority and great difficulties for the Orthodox Church, especially concerning its schools. The bright spot in this period was the proclamation of freedom of conscience in 1905. The First World War dealt another blow to the church, since several members of the clergy realised that the church would not be able to hold them and moved on to other professions. Laar managed to give this a positive spin, since it freed the church from some financial constraints once it was on its own.[136] Laar's introduction to the most recent period (since 1917) began with a review of the first attempts to establish an ethnic Estonian bishop in the 1880s. It then moved on to list all who had an impact on the Esto-

---

133 [Anton Laar], "Lühike ülevaade Eesti ap.-õigeusu elukäigust 75 a. jooksul" [Short overview of 75 years of Estonian Orthodox life] in *UE*, 1/5-6, 1921, p. 35.

134 [Anton Laar], "Lühike ülevaade Eesti ap.-õigeusu elukäigust 75 a. jooksul" [Short overview of 75 years of Estonian Orthodox life] in *UE*, 1/5-6, 1921, p. 36-37. The payment of a state salary for priests was unusual in the rest of Russia, but the special conditions of Orthodoxy in the Baltic Provinces justified their introduction. See Rimskij, 1998, p. 38.

135 [Anton Laar], "Lühike ülevaade Eesti ap.-õigeusu elukäigust 75 a. jooksul" [Short overview of 75 years of Estonian Orthodox life] in *UE*, 1/5-6, 1921, p. 37.

136 [Anton Laar], "Lühike ülevaade Eesti ap.-õigeusu elukäigust 75 a. jooksul" [Short overview of 75 years of Estonian Orthodox life] in *UE*, 1/7, 1921, p. 51.

nianisation of Orthodoxy during the Russian period, especially the composers of church music.[137] The last instalment of the 'short overview' concerned the memorandum of the Orthodox Estonians from Tallinn and its aftermath in Tartu during 1916.[138] Unlike the rest of the narrative, Laar wrote this part primarily from memory and partly in the present tense, probably in order to better captivate his readers. Strangely, the series did not continue, although Laar had made many promises as to what he would say in later instalments.

On the occasion of the Constantinople *tomos* of autonomy from 1923, which Laar understood as an acknoweldgement of complete independence, he wrote a long article elaborating on the developments following the First World War.[139] A number of other articles and series followed. These included Orthodox accounts of local history, often compiled from memories, and comments on non-Orthodox historical accounts.[140] In the years 1937-1939, the Latvian Orthodox journal published a long series by a pseudonymous author ('Testis') on the various Bishops of Riga during the past 100 years. From Archbishop Agafangel (1897-1910) through the period of the communist rule in Latvia, the author

---

137 [Anton Laar], "Lühike ülevaade Eesti ap.-õigeusu elukäigust 75 a. jooksul" [Short overview of 75 years of Estonian Orthodox life] in *UE*, 1/8, 1921, p. 58-60. See also Engelhardt, 2005, p. 108-153; chapter 3.1.2.

138 [Anton Laar], "Lühike ülevaade Eesti ap.-õigeusu elukäigust 75 a. jooksul" [Short overview of 75 years of Estonian Orthodox life] in *UE*, 1/9, 1921, p. 66-67. See also chapter 2.2.1.

139 Anton Laar, "Ülevaade Eesti ap-õigeusu kiriku elukäigust – Eesti abipiiskopist kuni iseseisvuseni" [Overview of the life of the Estonian Orthodox Church – from the Estonian vicar bishop to independence] in *UE*, 3/7-8, 1923, p. 5-8. These developments and their description in Laar's article were extensively discussed in chapter 2.2.1. and 2.2.2.

140 See *inter alia*: Jānis Lapiķens, "Pareizticīga baznīca. (Atbilde Pāvilam Gruznam)" [The Orthodox Church – an answer to Pāvils Gruzna] in *TuD*, 1/5, 1923, p. 5-11; J. Picalcelm, "Atmiņas no bērnības līdz tagadnei" [Memories from childhood until today] in *TuD*, 6/6, 1928, p. 88-90; N. R. [Nikolai Raag], "Eesti ja läti keel Pihkva vaimulikus seminaris" [Estonian and Latvian in the Pskov Orthodox Seminary] in *UE*, 8/11, 1928, p. 3-4; Purviņš, 1929; Aug. K., "Mälestisi ap.-õigeusu tulekust Hiiumaale" [Memories of the arrival of Orthodoxy to Hiiumaa] in *UE*, 11/9, 10, 1931, p. 6-7, 5-7; Konstantin Kokla, "Meie kirikukoolide saatus" [The fate of our parish schools] in *UjE₂*, 2/11, 1934, p. 179-180; Vambola Hiiesalu, "Sugemeid 1840. aastate usuliikumisest Põides" [Notes on the conversion movement of the 1840s in Põide] in *ET*, 1/34, 1936, p. 4-5; "Dāvids Balodis un 1845. g. kustiba" [Davids Balodis and the movement of 1845] in *TuD*, 13/7, 1937, p. 98-100; Nikolai Leismann, "Ajalooline õiendis õigeusu kirjanduse tsensuuri kohta Riia piiskopkonnas" [Historical correction on the censorship of Orthodox literature in the Riga Eparchy] in *ET*, 3/5, 1938, p. 52-53; K., "Suurest 'ärkamisest' Läänemaal ja Vormsi saarel" [On the big 'awakening' in the West County and the Vormsi island] in *UjE₂*, 6/13, 1938, p. 204-206.

wrote primarily about his own memories.[141] In 1939 three different series describing memories from the Riga Orthodox Seminary appeared in the journal.[142] One of these, written by the same 'Testis,' began with an introduction lamenting the lack of independent historical scholarship on the Seminary:

> The 'bursaki' could find a good example in the Latvian former riflemen, who have turned to the huge task of collecting all their historical material and memories in an anthology, as long as there are still riflemen alive. The 'bursaki' should do the same, for they are still alive in various generations, in Latvia and in Estonia. Each of them might offer valuable details for the coming history of Latvian and Estonian Orthodoxy and its activities.[143]

This 'coming history' never came, probably because of the Second World War. However, the gist of this history became clear in eleventh instalment of the series, when 'Testis' emphasised that the strict regime of the typical Russian seminary had never been introduced in Riga:

> Even in my time in the Latvian Society, there was talk that all the Latvian and Estonian youngsters at the Seminary would be Russified and forget their original nation. That this never became true can be seen from the activities of the Seminary alumni in Estonian and Latvian society, but more about that some other time.
> First, it is difficult to Russify a healthy nation, as the Latvians and Estonians were at that time. What would a poor Latvian or Estonian peasant's son do without education? The German manor lords did not care about organising education for the Latvians and Estonians and fostering their intelligence, which could have compromised their rule and become dangerous. The only way for the poorest peasant sons to be educated was through the Riga Orthodox School and Seminary.
> At the Orthodox School, nobody worried about 'the most worthy' youngsters, as the Germans did, but simply about youngsters. Therefore, those that proceeded to the Seminary were those same youngsters from the School, as conscientious Estonians and Latvians, who from the beginning officially attended classes in Estonian and Latvian. That was how our bishops cared. Even the ethnic Russian youngsters had to choose one of these languages, Estonian or Latvian.[144]

Moreover, 'Testis' maintained that the Riga Orthodox School and Seminary was the first education institution where Latvians and Estonians came to know each other as Latvians and Estonians, laying the foundations for the intensive political co-operation and international friendship since the First World War. He could even tell many stories about this friendship from his later career, when simple

---

141 I have not been able to identify the author behind the pseudonym 'Testis.' His articles appeared in almost all issues of *TuD* from 13/8, 1937 to 16/3, 1940.

142 These were first, the memories of Archpriest Jānis Svemps, then those of 'Testis' before 'Testis' wrote down his memories of the murdered Archbishop Jānis, whom he had known from his years in the Seminary.

143 Testis, "Garigā Skolā" [At the Seminar] in *TuD*, 15/10, 1939, p. 152.

144 Testis, "Garigā Skolā XI" [At the Orthodox Seminary] in *TuD*, 16/1, p. 9.

Estonians had trusted him – a Latvian – much more than they would ever trust any Russian.[145]

One of the early series of articles was 'Orthodoxy among the Latvians,' begun by Archpriest Jānis Jansons in 1925. At several occasions in this series, Jansons related pieces of historical fiction about the early days of Latvian Orthodoxy.[146] It is difficult to ascertain whether these stories were pure fiction or had a basis in truth, but this kind of historical fiction was also popular in Estonia and remained so in later years. Here, we should especially mention the feuilleton story 'The Neighbours at Järvesalu' by M. Mäessa[147] from 1936, which was published in the Estonian Orthodox journal *Elutõde* (Truth of Life). Mäessa told the story of a Lutheran pastor and an Orthodox priest during the uprisings of 1905. The publication of this story was one of the occasions when the Orthodox journal was acknowledged in the Estonian Lutheran Church. J. Ora, in the Lutheran journal *Eesti Kirik* (Estonian Church), commented on the new Orthodox journal, which had been launched the same year. He accused it of launching unprovoked attacks on the Lutheran Church and its clergy. Special criticism was reserved for 'The Neighbours at Järvesalu.'

> This feuilleton, with bitter-sweet sentimentality repeats the worn out fairy tale of the German-minded Lutheran pastor of the Russian era and the popular and nationalistic Orthodox priest-hero. On this religio-national background, spiced up with the kisses and embraces of the priest's lovesick daughter, a fictional story is narrated, which in this form definitely is inappropriate for a Christian journal.[148]

Mäessa replied rather ironically in *Elutõde*, asking whether such an article as Ora's was appropriate for a Christian journal and countering that

> if you can prove to me that all Lutheran pastors were always great nationalists and friends of the Estonian nation, then I am willing to edit my fictional story according to your taste. [...] Maybe you, for reasons unknown to me, hold that innocent kissing is immoral and that love is an act of marriage which should not be mentioned in public. [...] Regarding your criticism of having used too much 'bitter-sweet sentimentality,' I am unfortunately not really impressed until I get to know your aesthetic

---

145 Testis, "Garigā Skolā XI" [At the Orthodox Seminary] in *TuD*, 16/1, p. 9-10. See also Vana seminarist, "Mõned mälestused Riia vaim. Seminarist" [Some memories from the Riga Orthodox Seminary] in *UE*, 8/12, 1928, p. 4-8; Paavel, 1934.

146 Jānis Jansons, "Pareizticība pie Latviešiem" [Orthodoxy among the Latvians] in *TuD*, 3/2, 1925, p. 10-15; 3/4, 1925, p. 10-15; 3/7, 1925, p. 3-7; 3/8, 1925, p. 13-16; 3/9, 1925, p. 5-10. See also Jānis Jansons, "Atmiņas par Kārzdabu" [Memories from Kārzdaba] in *TuD*, 3/11-12, 1925, p. 6-10; Jansons, 1940.

147 I have not been able to find out who hides behind this pseudonym, so I will treat it as a normal name.

148 J. Ora, "Elutõde kõverpeegel" [*Elutõde*, the distorting mirror] in *Eesti Kirik*, 13/27, 02.07.1936, p. 5.

knowledge and taste. Looking at the style of your article, however, I do not think it is worth arguing with you about taste.[149]

From an early stage, the new Estonian Orthodox journal *Elutõde* was more direct in its criticism than the earlier journals. Following the above article by Mäessa, another article arguing for a re-appraisal of the Russification period,[150] and a polemical exchange of articles with the Lutheran journal, *Elutõde* began a series of articles titled 'Ajalooline Tõde' (Historical Truth), which continued for almost three years with a total of forty-five instalments. The starting point was a call by an author using the pseudonym '-nd' to 'bring historical truth to the fore!' because "our representatives in positions of power quietly accept the large scale historical revision going on, letting the positive aspects of the arrival of the Orthodox Church be taken away from her."[151] Over the next three years, the unidentifiable author[152] harshly criticised the dominant historiography regarding the role of Orthodox Christianity in Estonian history. An interesting aspect of this historiographic account is that it did not order its narrative chronologically, but thematically, using each instalment to deconstruct an argument of the existing historiography. This suggests that the author was not interested in just re-writing history, but to provide the readers with counter-arguments for historical discussions.

The first eighteen instalments of the series read primarily as frustrated venting on the conclusions Hans Kruus had drawn in his doctoral dissertation, such as the economic character of the conversion movement and its consequences. According to the author, Kruus had simply accepted a Baltic German historiographic fallacy by arguing that the arrival of Orthodox Christianity among the Baltic peasants destroyed the unity of the peasantry and the Lutheran Church. The pietistic Herrnhut brotherhoods[153] had played a much more impor-

---

149 M. Mäessa, "'Järvesalu naabrite' autori vastus J. Ora'le" [The answer of the author of 'The Neighbours at Järvesalu' to J. Ora] in *ET*, 1/24-25, 1936, p. 8.

150 Interestingly written by a history teacher belonging to the Estonian neo-pagan union: Järvo Tandre-Stokeby, "Ajaloo revisjon" [Historical revision] in *ET*, 1/22-23, 1936, p. 3-4; 1/24-25, 1936, p. 3.

151 -nd, "Ajalooline tõde ausse!" [Historical Truth to the fore!] in *ET*, 1/32, 1936, p. 5-6. A similar appeal to collect and publish historical material appeared in the Latvian journal: Ant. K., "Vāksim materialus mūsu draudžu vēsturei" [We will gather material of the history of our congregations] in *TuD*, 13/6, 1937, p. 91-92. Another call was disguised as something for the schoolchildren to do in the summer holidays: –m–, "Kāds uzdevums mūsu skolu jaunatnei" [A task for our school youth] in *TuD*, 15/11, 1939, p. 166.

152 The series was never signed, not even with a pseudonym. It might have been one of the two main protagonists in the run-up to the series, '-nd' or M. Mäessa, neither of which I have been able to identify. Another possibility is the author with the pseudonym 'Apostolicus' mentioned above.

153 These brotherhoods appeared in the eighteenth century and quickly spread over all Baltic Provinces. In most villages, there was a Herrnhut prayer house, where several peasants,

tant role undermining the monopoly of the Lutheran Church, and the Lutheran clergy's anti-Orthodox agitation was more to blame for the division of the peasantry than the Orthodox Church.[154] Moreover, the argument that the Orthodox peasantry became a supporting pillar for the later Russification attempts was dismissed as a fairy tale. The Baltic Germans, creating this narrative, had not wanted to accept at any price that their own anti-Russian outlook was the reason for the fierce official politics of Russification. Nor would they accept that the Orthodox Church freed the peasantry from the Lutheran 'slave holders' rather than preparing the way for Russification.[155] Four articles followed on the beneficial relationship between Orthodoxy and the national 'awakening,'[156] whereas the next eleven instalments deconstructed the accusation that the Orthodox were active Russifiers. Instead, the so-called 'clerical wing' of the Estonian national movement was blamed for having caused Russification. There might have been Russifiers among the Orthodox, but Russifiers had also existed among the Lutherans.[157]

The last twelve instalments of the series proposed a new historiography of the period of Russification, as the existing ones only "list historical facts and actors; categorise and evaluate them only on the basis of biased negative *a priori* criteria, conflated with a kind of sentimentality and an experience of pain and remorse."[158] Instead, 'Historical Truth' would not tell the story of Russification with hindsight, blaming Baltic factors, but as it really happened, in the context of world politics. This context included the ambivalent relationship between the Russians and the Germans and the unclear role of Tsar Aleksander III in this relationship.[159] Moreover, the author questioned the designation 'Russification' for the period from Aleksander III (1881-1917), arguing that Russification had existed before. He therefore proposed to call this period 'true Russification.' He also challenged the dominant view that Aleksander III was 'weaker than the Baltic nobility' because the Russification measures had stalled by 1890. Instead, he claimed that, by the 1880s, the Estonian people had become strong enough to

---

usually the most intelligent ones, gathered to pray without the parish priest and other theological authorities. The brotherhoods were repeatedly outlawed as detrimental to the social cohesion of the provinces, but continued to exist as underground networks. See Hope, 1998; Talonen, 2001.

154 "Ajalooline tõde" [Historical Truth] in *ET*, 1/42-2/6, 1936-1937.
155 "Ajalooline tõde" [Historical Truth] in *ET*, 2/8-2/14, 1937.
156 "Ajalooline tõde" [Historical Truth] in *ET*, 2/15-2/18, 1937. See also Aleksander Värat, "Koguduste uuendamine XIII. Õigeusk, kui Eestirahva enesemääramise tegur" [Renewal of the congregations XIII. Orthodoxy as an actor in the Estonian national consciousness] in *UjE₁* 14/40-44, 1917, p. 349-352.
157 "Ajalooline tõde" [Historical Truth] in *ET*, 2/19-3/5, 1937-1938.
158 "Ajalooline tõde" [Historical Truth] in *ET*, 3/13, 1938, p. 152.
159 "Ajalooline tõde" [Historical Truth] in *ET*, 3/13-3/20, 1938.

refuse the Russification measures of the Tsar.[160] Unfortunately, this conclusion is only hinted at in the final instalment before the series stopped abruptly, leaving the detailed explanation of this argument unfinished.

The series demonstrates a profound understanding of Baltic history during the nineteenth century and a gifted systematising mind putting various sources together to form a consistent criticism of the historiography dominating in society. However, this highly elaborated and extensive narrative – which was probably planned as a book – only received two mentions outside of the journal *Elutõde*, neither of which added anything of value. First, Andrejs Jansons published translations of the first three instalments of the series in the Latvian Orthodox journal *Ticība un Dzīve*.[161] More importantly, the Lutheran journal *Eesti Kirik* critically reviewed the first five instalments in a January 1937 editorial. The editorial dismissed the historiography of *Elutõde* with reference to the 'respected historian' Professor Hans Kruus and retold the traditional Lutheran view of the conversion movement in short, concluding that "we get the impression that that farm [the Orthodox Church] does not want to take account of the truth but to form it so that it seems to benefit the Orthodox Church."[162]

Another attempt to reach the Lutheran Church was in an article published in *Elutõde* in 1939 titled 'Now is the last chance to dissolve the past's inheritance!' Here, the author, signing as 'an Estonian,' called upon the Lutheran Church to reassess its claim that the Estonian soul was Lutheran by nature, especially in connection with the departure of the remaining ethnic German pastors following Hitler's call.[163] He continued to argue that Lutheranism never actually became part of the Estonians' soul, for the gap between the pastors and the congregation always remained too large, even during independence:

> It is possible to ask: why these hateful words? Well, in order for the church men to understand once and for all that we need to dissolve the inheritances of the past and build a new Estonian church, a real national creation. We do not care whether the Estonian hears the true Word of God from a Lutheran pastor or an Orthodox priest, but we wish the Word of God to be preached in an Estonian spirit by true People of God, not some 'mercenaries' speaking with sweet tongues while at the same time poisoning the Estonian soul, bringing up people, who blackmail their own nation and then flee like wolves at night...[164]

---

160 "Ajalooline tõde" [Historical Truth] in *ET*, 3/21-4/2, 1938-1939.
161 A. Jansons, "Vēsturiskā patiesība" [Historical Truth] in *TuD*, 13/9, 1937, p. 137-138; 13/10, 1937, p. 153-154..
162 Jakob Aunver, "Mõningaid tõsiasju ap.-õigeusu kiriku kohta" [Some facts about the Orthodox Church] in *Eesti Kirik*, 14/2, 14.01.1937, p. 1-3.
163 Eestlane, "Viimne aeg likvideerida mineviku pärandused" [Now is the last chance to dissolve the past's inheritance!] in *ET*, 4/20, 1939, p. 213-214. See also chapter 2.3.4.
164 Eestlane, "Viimne aeg likvideerida mineviku pärandused" [Now is the last chance to dissolve the past's inheritance!] in *ET*, 4/20, 1939, p. 214.

The editor of the Lutheran journal had offered very similar advice to the Orthodox Church some years earlier, to "let the past be history and start living in the present."[165] The two churches had talked past each other. The call by 'an Estonian' was not acknowledged at all in the Lutheran journal, probably because of the priority of organisational questions in connection with the Lutheran episcopal elections and the replacement of the departed German pastors.[166]

In closing this chapter, I want to dwell on a special exchange of articles in 1940 between the two Estonian Orthodox journals on this 'need for the past.' That no such discussion had occurred in the Latvian case can be seen as symptomatic of the less polemical and more theological Latvian approach to Orthodoxy, but might also be explained by the monopoly position of the Latvian Orthodox journal and the stricter censorship in Ulmanis' Latvia. The discussion in Estonia was initiated by an already cited review of the Estonian Orthodox calendar for 1940 in *Elutõde* by the young nationalist Eugen Tamm.[167] His criticism was that there was too much 'Russianness' in the calendar, starting with the martyrology, which included 'unsuitable' Russian national heroes, such as Aleksander Nevskij, and ending with a criticism of the transcription of Greek names. Instead of 'Basileios,' for example, the calendar included 'Vassiili,' a phonetic approximation of the Russian pronunciation of the name.

A long reply by Archpriest Konstantin Gustavson, the calendar's editor, followed, in which he justified his decisions on the basis that everybody cannot be satisfied and that he had tried to take as many factors into account as possible.[168] The afore mentioned M. Mäessa commented on Gustavson's reply under the heading 'Away with the past!,' doubting Gustavson's loyalty to the Estonian Church. In order to understand Mäessa's arguments, the article deserves to be quoted in length:

> I dare to claim here that K. Gustavson is wrong to argue with E. Tamm about this issue, especially when looking at it from a standpoint of Estonianness. First, there is no organic link between the Estonian Orthodox Church and the former Russian state church, apart from the fact that many of our clergymen received their education in Russia and were consecrated in the jurisdiction of the Russian Church [...]
> If we follow Gustavson's logic further, then a large section of our army leadership, which once declared their loyalty to the Russian Tsar, would have to respect and celebrate old Russian traditions and also the last Tsar, for also in his life, there was 'neighbourly love and religious activity across national boundaries.' It ought to be

165 Jakob Aunver, "Vastuseks naabrile" [An answer to the neighbour] in *Eesti Kirik*, 13/38, 17.09.1936, p. 3.

166 For the Lutheran 'crisis year' of 1939, see Ketola, 2000b.

167 Eugen Tamm, "Märkmeid 1940 a. kalendri kohta" [Notes on the calendar of 1940] in *ET*, 5/5, 1940, p. 59-60. See also chapter 3.1.1.

168 Konstantin Gustavson, "Vastuseks kalendri arvustusele" [Answer to the calendar review] in *ET*, 5/7, 1940, p. 77-79. See also chapter 3.1.1.

clear that Gustavson's argument, in this case, is rather shaky. Especially those who acknowledge, as Gustavson no doubt does, that the Russian Orthodox Church was an indivisible part of the Russian Empire and that its leadership was the roughest centre of Russification [...].

The argument that our head of the church received the episcopal consecration from the Moscow Patriarch is another example of Gustavson's unfortunate defence strategy. We only need to remember the struggles the Estonian-minded clergy fought for the patriarchal recognition of our own autonomous Eparchy and the 'Walk to Canossa' to Moscow, from which P. Sepp brought the Estonian Orthodox Church an approval.[169] There is no doubt – the Russian Orthodox Church would never have given the Estonian Church autonomy if the situation had not been as chaotic as it was.

Second, Archpriest Gustavson should also know why the Estonian Church switched to the jurisdiction of Constantinople. This was not an accidental move, but a direct attempt to free ourselves from the Russian Church, which was so hostile to us. When an Estonian author (he happened to be Orthodox) visited Paris two years ago, he met with the Russian exile hierarchs and asked: 'how do you relate to the Orthodox Church of Estonia?'

The answer he received was that 'this kind of church does not exist for the united Russian Church!' And if we call to mind the former archpriest Aristov of the Tallinn Cathedral[170] and the Finnish Orthodox civil war with Archbishop Serafim concerning the Finnicisation of the Orthodox Church, then the picture is clear. At least to those that are Estonians and nationalists, not some cautious compromise-seekers.

Personally, from a Christian viewpoint, I think that creating a schism with another church is certainly not a noble act. However, it is therefore not automatically necessary always and everywhere to emphasise that the Estonian Church was formerly an indivisible part of the Russian Church (actually, the Estonian Church did not exist yet, then!), that we lived in the Russian Empire, received Russian education etc. One eventually becomes just as sick of that as of the rant about the '700 years of slavery' or 'our tiny Estonia.' An individual, an organisation, a nation, a state wanting to survive and achieve something cannot stay in the bosom of the past. Past is only past, but the present is where we must work for the future. [...] If we want to speak about the past, then it begins with the day that the Estonian men established the independent Estonian Orthodox Church. [...] It is not the task of the calendar to be a 'monument' to the state that held our nation in slavery or to the church masters that denied the minority nations autonomous activities or service in the mother tongue.[171]

As this article makes clear, a radical nationalist group was forming among the Estonian Orthodox activists. In striving to lose the stigma of being a 'Russian' faith, this group would not accept any compromises regarding the Russian past. Reacting to this comment by Mäessa, Archpriest Gustavson 'fled' to the other, more moderate Estonian Orthodox journal *Usk ja Elu* (Faith and Life), edited by

---

169 See chapter 2.2.2.

170 See chapter 2.2.3.

171 M. Mäessa, "Lahti minevikust!" [Away with the past!] in *ET*, 5/8, 1940, p. 88-89.

Konstantin Kokla, where he published a long reply.[172] This reply began with a polemic, arguing that Mäessa applied inconsistent logic and greatly exaggerated both Tamm's criticism and Gustavson's justification. Moreover, he emphasised that "the Estonian Orthodox Church has not the faintest reason to be ashamed of its distant or recent past."[173] Mäessa's criticism was, according to Gustavson, addressed in the wrong direction. The slave-holders were hardly the Russian Empire, for one, and leaving out all the saints who were national heroes would leave the calendar empty. Gustavson even had counsel for Mäessa:

> Psychoanalysis teaches that these calls [such as 'away with the past!'] are screams of pain from the subconscious. Some unpleasant event of the past can seethe for a long time in the subconscious and suddenly erupt. To avoid repetition and heal various uncomfortable mental sufferings, there is but one cure, according to psychoanalysis: the individual must find the reason of the suffering himself, and then tell somebody trustworthy about it and together agree on a remedy. The Apostolic Church calls this confession.[174]

M. Mäessa's short answer appeared in the very last issue of *Elutöde*, where he emphasised that Gustavson had not effected a change of mind but only strengthened him in his views: "the time, when people still believed that the Russian Church, subordinated to the Russian Empire, pursued Estonian-friendly aims, is long past."[175] The discussion had not ended, although it could not continue. The radically changed circumstances of the following years stifled all public discussion on the relationship between Estonianness/Latvianness, Russianness, and Orthodox Christianity. Instead, questions turned to the more fundamental issue of how to survive under the atheistic communist regime, which allowed only purely religious content to be published, if any at all.

---

172 Konstantin Gustavson, "Kas on Eesti Apostlik-õigeusu Kirikul vaja lahti ütelda oma minevikust?" [Does the Estonian Orthodox Church need to get away from its past?] in *UjE₂*, 8/6, 1940, p. 82, 94-96. Kokla had already commented on the polemics in the other journal, emphasising that the past cannot be dismissed that easily and calling Mäessa's argumentation ill-conceived: Konstantin Kokla, "Minevikuvajadus" [The need for a past] in *UjE₂*, 8/5, 1940, p. 68-69; Konstantin Kokla, "Lahti minevikust!" [Away with the past!] in *UjE₂*, 8/5, 1940, p. 77.

173 Konstantin Gustavson, "Kas on Eesti Apostlik-õigeusu Kirikul vaja lahti ütelda oma minevikust?" [Does the Estonian Orthodox Church need to get away from its past?] in *UjE₂*, 8/6, 1940, p. 95.

174 Konstantin Gustavson, "Kas on Eesti Apostlik-õigeusu Kirikul vaja lahti ütelda oma minevikust?" [Does the Estonian Orthodox Church need to get away from its past?] in *UjE₂*, 8/6, 1940, p. 96.

175 M. Mäessa, "M. Mäessa vastus Ülempr. K. Gustavsonile" [M. Mäessa's answer to Archpr. K. Gustavson] in *ET*, 5/11-12, 1940, p. 129.

5. Concluding Remarks

Modernity, as I defined it in the first part of this book, posed several challenges to the worldwide Orthodox Church following the First World War. The most formidable challenge arose in the Soviet Union, where the militantly atheist state attempted to suppress all manifestations of religion and replace them with rituals and celebrations to the socialist ideal. Arguably, the Orthodox Church was persecuted more severely than smaller religious groups in Russia, since it had been a pillar of the autocratic regime and, thus, should be eradicated as an obstacle to human progress.[1] Just as in most states with an Orthodox majority population, the challenges of modernity had appeared in the Russian Empire prior to the First World War and only intensified during the interwar period. Only in the new nation states on the western fringe of the Russian Empire, from Finland in the north to Poland in the south, however, did these challenges arise in a more or less liberal environment and in a predominantly non-Orthodox context. Among these, Estonia and Latvia are special cases, since the Orthodox minority in these two states did not belong exclusively to an ethnic minority, as in Poland and Lithuania, nor were they concentrated in specific Orthodox regions, as in Finland. In Estonia and Latvia, the Orthodox minority were forced to reply to the challenges as a *religious minority* without a clear territorial base.[2]

The challenges primarily appeared in three interconnected forms. First, the organisation of the modern Estonian and Latvian states challenged a church that had hitherto received its directions from the Most Holy Synod in St. Petersburg. The state authorities did not readily accept that a foreign body could regulate the internal affairs of the Estonian and Latvian Orthodox Churches, especially not one that was situated in the potentially hostile Soviet Union. The restoration of canonical leadership in the Russian Orthodox Church, through the 1917 Moscow *sobor* and the election of Patriarch Tikhon (Bellavin), did not help the perception of the Orthodox Church. Next to this external aspect, there was the question of the Russian minority population in the two states, which was regarded with suspicion by the secular authorities as potentially disloyal citizens. Authorities in the Orthodox Church, especially in the Estonian case, adopted this suspicion and sought to limit the influence of the Russian wing.

The second challenge of modernity was the need for a consistent Estonian and Latvian Orthodox identity. Internally, this meant adapting Orthodox theo-

---

1 Kolarz, 1962, 37-38; Pospielovsky, 1984, p. 40-41.
2 Petserimaa cannot be counted as the base of Estonian Orthodoxy, since it was considered backward and undeveloped. Of the important actors in interwar Estonian Orthodoxy, none came from Petserimaa, except the infamous Bishop Joann (Bulin). See chapter 2.3.1.

logical and liturgical elements to the purported Latvian or Estonian 'national spirit.' Externally, the challenge was to counter the repeated arguments from the Lutheran majority, claiming that Orthodox Christianity did not conform to this national spirit and would never be able to. The final form of the challenge of modernity encompassed the whole of Estonian and Latvian historiography. Instead of continuing the 'History of Power' of the Baltic Germans, and to a lesser extent the Russian Empire, the new political circumstances called forth a new view of Estonian and Latvian history, in which the protagonists were not foreign rulers but the Estonians and Latvians themselves. The young historians of the two states masterfully tackled this challenge, although Orthodox Christians criticised them for not finishing the task. The history of Orthodox Christianity in Estonia and Latvia was, according to the Orthodox, still portrayed in a distorted fashion.

Each of these challenges encompassed an internal and an external dimension, having practically the same aim in each case. Externally, the Orthodox Church was challenged to redefine itself in order to adapt to changing political circumstances and to be recognised as a legitimate and influential actor in the young nation states. The internal challenge, closely connected with the external one, consisted in inculcating this redefined self-consciousness among members so as not to lose them. This internal, pedagogic challenge was the main task of the Orthodox journals.

This study has presented an insight into the rhetorical strategies and discursive positions of some influential interwar Orthodox Estonians and Latvians, namely those that publicly claimed to represent the Orthodox Church in the two young nation states. Even if this is only a small section of either Orthodox community, it represents the best available approximation to the atmosphere in the church as a whole. Within such small communities, encompassing less than 200,000 people, even archives cannot contain better overviews, for much communication would have occurred face-to-face and, thus, left no trace in the archives. Those who participated in the mainstream published discourse had to represent a dominant view, possess influential connections, or demonstrate highly sophisticated rhetorical skills.

The upheavals of the First World War and the ensuing struggles for independence brought about a shift in the social hierarchies of both Estonia and Latvia. In society at large, the heretofore dominant Baltic Germans suddenly lost most of their influence and power, and the Russian administrators also had to leave the stage. In turning the previous hierarchy upside-down, the new leaders of the two societies created a new 'normality' and expected all societal institutions to follow suit. The Orthodox Church was not excepted. However, in each of the two cases it reacted somewhat differently. In Estonia, where the Russians had been seen as especially distant due to the location of the bishop and administration in Riga, the switch to Estonian leadership happened quickly. Less than two months after the February Revolution of 1917 installed a quasi-liberal order in the Russian Empire, preparations for an Estonian Eparchy of the Orthodox Church began. Originally designed to encompass all Estonians throughout the Russian Empire, these aspirations were soon redirected towards a territorial Eparchy. However, the idea of an independent Eparchy exclusively for ethnic Estonians was repeatedly voiced well into the 1930s.

In the Latvian case, the Russians could not be 'externalised' from the church, since most societal life was concentrated in the cosmopolitan and multi-ethnic capital Riga, which had housed the administration of the Riga Eparchy. After the evacuation of the administration in 1915 and the devastating years of war, it took some time until Riga gradually regained its former grandeur. The redesign of Latvian Orthodoxy, therefore, started in the countryside. Unfortunately, this discursive context has not survived. When the discussions reached Riga in 1920, the ethnic Latvian Ascension parish wanted to take on a directing role in the reconstruction of the local Orthodox Church but was overruled by the Russian parishes. According Jānis Dāvis, the main protagonist of creating an ethnic Latvian Orthodox Church, this was because the Russians were more rhetorically gifted and could convince the countryside parishes to remain Russian in spirit. It is difficult to assess this claim, as the arrival of Archbishop Jānis (Pommers) in 1921 stifled all separatism in the Orthodox Church of Latvia. Jānis was able to channel all attention from the question of internal ethnic organisation to an external enemy, first the hostile government and later the 'communists' of the Social Democratic Party. His uncompromising attitude and wide-ranging political activity made it impossible for the secular authorities to ignore the Orthodox Church.

The Orthodox Churches in Estonia and Latvia emerged after the tumultuous upheavals of 1914-1921 as two practically independent churches. Both claimed that their canonical ties to Moscow were a mere theoretical connection and that their members were loyal citizens of their respective nation state. In the Latvian case, Archbishop Jānis' rhetoric was so successful and so domineering that it is difficult to discern any critical discourse concerning ecclesiastic organisation in the 1920s. Jānis considered the canonical and structural questions done with, and most further discussion on structural question was drowned in the all-encompassing opposition to communists and atheists. The Estonians, on the other hand, lacked a powerful figure to present a unified Estonian Orthodox Church to the government. The 'Estonian' and 'Russian' factions retained their disparate spheres of influence, and ultimately, the leadership of the Estonian Church decided to go one step further and sever the canonical tie to Moscow completely. In 1923, Archbishop Aleksander (Paulus) travelled to Constantinople and the Estonian Orthodox Church was granted autonomy under the jurisdiction of the Ecumenical Patriarch.[3] Although this did not silence the 'Russian' faction, it supported the 'Estonian' faction in its struggle for legitimacy.

In the Latvian Orthodox Church, the question of organising the church on firm foundations that were both canonical and acceptable to the secular authorities returned after Jānis' mysterious death in 1934. Due to changes in both Latvian and Soviet politics over the previous fifteen years, it was entirely inconceivable to ask the Patriarch of Moscow to install a successor, and after long drawn-out discussions, a transfer to the jurisdiction of Constantinople was also effected here. Close monitoring of the process by the secular authorities and their clear interest in the outcome seriously hampered the freedom of the decision-making process. Arguably, this atmosphere also prevailed in Estonia during the quasi-authoritarian Päts-regime. The new statutes and the staffing decisions of both churches during the latter half of the 1930s did not occur in a liberal, democratic context. There was virtually no criticism of or debate on structural decisions, until the advent of Soviet authorities put criticism of Ulmanis and Päts on the agenda. By then, however, publishing activity was too weak to provide a conclusive picture, and the political atmosphere was even less liberal than before.

Nevertheless, all these attempts to adapt the Orthodox Church to the political structures of the new nation state and satisfy the secular authorities did not engender a change of the perception of the Orthodox by the Lutherans in the majority. Orthodox Estonians and Latvians continued to be seen as second-order citizens: less educated, less intellectual, and less nationally minded. This perception colours the published non-Orthodox accounts and is especially attested to in the Orthodox complaints about their treatment by society. While it may be difficult to ascertain how many of these complaints were mere rhetoric, the overall perception of the Orthodox Church in society was certainly negative. The origin of this perception becomes clear when the discussion of historiography is considered. The Baltic Germans, previously the undisputed masters of the Baltic Provinces of the Russian Empire, could not come to grips with the Orthodox element intervening in *their* provinces from the mid-nineteenth century onwards. In their eyes, conversion away from the right path of Lutheranism could not be based on rational thinking, and Estonian and Latvian converts must, therefore, have been less developed and more easily misled than the others. Until 1917, the Baltic Germans propagated the myth of

---

3   This is the interpretation of the Moscow Patriarchate. The Patriarchate of Constantinople argues that the insecure situation of the Orthodox Church in the Soviet Union in the early 1920s was the triggering factor for the switch to Constantinople. Both factors were assuredly important. However, the wish to emancipate from Russian tutelage may have been more of an unreflected reaction to the contextual changes than a formulated argument. The developments in Finland and in the Soviet Union then triggered the decision to join the Finnish delegation to Constantinople. See also chapters 2.2.2. and 2.2.8.

backward Orthodox faithful to such an extent that it entered the Estonian and Latvian discourse of nation-building as an undisputed fact. Even the relatively high number of influential Orthodox politicians in Estonia could not turn around this perception.

A second problem with which the Orthodox Estonians and Latvians had to contend, was the perception of Orthodoxy as the 'Russian faith' and the Orthodox faithful as 'Russian believers.' The Orthodox publicists countered these 'accusations' in three ways. First, they made a theological argument that Orthodox Christianity existed long before the Russians were Christianised and had nothing to do with Russia as such. The only connection to Russia was that Orthodoxy had, incidentally, arrived to the Baltic shores *via* Russia. This was the main argument of Archbishop Jānis, who refused to agree that the Orthodox Church was a remnant of Russian power, as many Latvian politicians claimed. The second rhetorical strategy was sociological and historical; if Orthodoxy was the 'Russian faith,' then Lutheranism should be called the 'German faith.' Furthermore, this 'German faith' had been much less friendly and beneficial to the Estonians and Latvians than the 'Russian faith.' The third strategy was to attempt to denigrate the users of the designation 'Russian faith' as stupid and ignorant. The Estonian Orthodox journals, in particular, repeatedly brought articles which concluded, somewhat ironically, that the Lutherans might learn the real name of the Orthodox Church at some point. The Latvian Minister of Education under Ulmanis, the Lutheran Professor of Theology Ludvigs Adamovičs, seemed to affirm this point in 1935, when he published an article on the correct name of the Orthodox Church.[4]

The Latvian Orthodox Church seemed to receive a small boost of popular support after the death of Archbishop Jānis and the transfer to the jurisdiction of the Patriarchate of Constantinople, although the strict censorship of the time makes the veracity of this claim difficult to ascertain. Official relations between secular authorities and the church certainly intensified in both Latvia and Estonia during the quasi-authoritarian period. In both states, however, the emphasis of the presidents was on 'the church' and 'Christianity' in general terms, without confessional specification. Thus, both the Lutheran and the Orthodox (and the Roman Catholic) Church could feel included, although the Lutheran Church might have felt (or even been) exclusively addressed. Nonetheless, the external perception of Orthodox Christianity as a 'foreign' faith continued throughout the interwar period, and there are offshoots of this perception in Estonia and Latvia surviving till today.

---

4   Ludvigs Adamovičs, "Austrumu pareizticīgie jeb grieķu katoli?" [Eastern Orthodox or Greek Catholics?] in *JZ*, 25/294, 28.12.1935, p. 8. However, this article does not mention the designation 'Russian faith.'

The success of the internal challenge – strengthening the identification of the Estonian and Latvian faithful as Orthodox Christians – is much more difficult to assess. There were numerous attempts to adapt Orthodox theological and liturgical elements to the mainstream of national consciousness in the new nation states. In most cases, this meant borrowing from Lutheran practice. These adaptations often proceeded in an unorganised fashion on the periphery, and the published debate centred on whether such 'innovations' had gone too far. For the 'Russian' faction in the Estonian Orthodox Church, they certainly had, but even among Estonian and Latvian clergy, they were sometimes eyed suspiciously. However, with the possible exception of the case of musical style, the available sources only allow limited insight into the actual changes and often only when they had gone too far. The occurrence of modernisations is undeniable, but it is impossible to assess their exact scope and magnitude. The success of the internal Orthodox historiographic discourse is even less conclusive, as it was very seldom referred to by anyone other than those who disseminated it.

A general conclusion must emphasise that both churches tackled the challenges of modernity in modern ways. Unlike the Old Believers on the shores of Lake Peipsi, who had retreated from the public sphere as early as the eighteenth century[5] and the Russian minority, which was divided among many splinter groups, some of dubious character,[6] the Orthodox Church in both Estonia and Latvia managed to present a legitimate, united organisation that participated in political and societal life as an equal partner. The arguments published by Estonian and Latvian Orthodox actors display a modern character, based on rational argument and equal exchange. While the Latvians were united around the politically active and powerful Archbishop Jānis, the Estonians had to rely on their collective strengths and ethnic identity, losing the 'Russian' faction in the process, so to speak. This difference between the two churches is of prime importance for assessing their later developments. The Estonian publicists were more radical than their Latvian counterparts and remained so until the Second World War, as exemplified in the discussions on the need for the past in 1940. The more radical Latvian Orthodox voices were overruled and redirected towards an external enemy. The Latvian jurisdictional transfer of 1935/1936 was not the result of a majority decision within the church, but pressure from the secular authorities, who wanted a more pliable leadership in the Orthodox Church.

However, the modernity of church activities should not be exaggerated. The Orthodox journals of interwar Estonia and Latvia were not modern in the sense that they were produced by full-time journalists and commercialised.[7] Rather,

---

5   See Ammann, 1936; Ponomareva, 2006.
6   Isakov, 2001, p. 62-98.
7   See Requate, 1999, p. 16-17.

they were a secondary activity of the editor-priests, often seen as a financial burden. The Estonian journal *Elutõde* from 1936 was a step in the modern direction, but all the other journals were primarily personal forums for the editor-priests. This was especially clear with Anton Laar in Estonia and Kirils Zaics in Latvia. Whether the opinions published in their journals really reflected all standpoints within their respective Orthodox community is very difficult to verify.

That the church attempted to present an appearance of modernity to the surrounding world remains beyond doubt. All of Estonian and Latvian society embraced modernity in this way, and the Orthodox Church was no different. It did not, however, manage to change the way it was perceived in the majority society. The hypothetical question remains of what would have happened if it had rejected modernity. This was the case only in the Lithuanian Orthodox Church, which retained all links with the Moscow Patriarchate and did not directly undergo any renewal.[8] However, in Lithuania, the Orthodox Church was the church of the Russian minority, and therefore represented a parallel society without many points of contact with the majority Lithuanian Catholic society. In regard to its relations with secular authorities, the Lithuanian Orthodox Church also had to adapt to modernity, adopting (modern) statutes and adjusting some untenable traditions to the new political atmosphere. In Latvia and Estonia, on the other hand, modernity entered all areas and levels of ecclesiastic life, with the possible exception of the most die-hard representatives of the 'Russian' faction in Estonia.

The Second World War and the following forty-six years of Soviet occupation destroyed many of the achievements in Latvian and Estonian Orthodox Christianity. However, the Estonian and Latvian interwar experience remains one of the bright spots in the history of Orthodox Christianity and modernity.

---

8   See Laukaitytė, 2003, p. 87-94; Marcinkevičius and Kaubrys, 2003, p. 46-81.

6. Appendixes

6.1. Maps

6.1.1. Map of the Baltic Provinces in 1888.

Source: Wittram, 1973, Appendix VI

6.1.2. Map of Estonia and Latvia, 1920-1940.

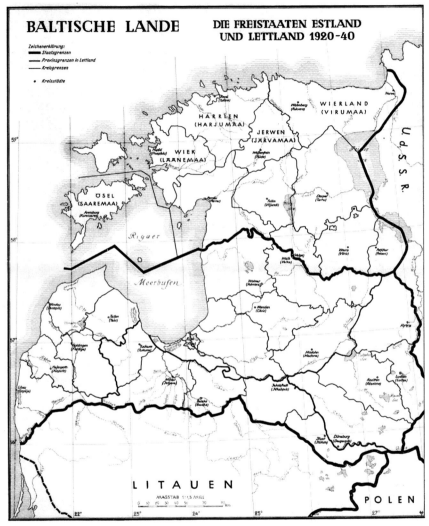

Source: Wittram, 1973, Appendix VII

6.2. Timeline

	General	Estonia	Latvia	Chapter
1914	Start of First World War			
1915			Evacuation of Riga	2.2.1. and 2.2.5.
1916		The 200th anniversary of the Tallinn Transfiguration church		2.2.1.
1917	February Revolution			
		Apr.: 'Tallinn gathering'		2.2.1.
		May: Riga Eparchy Congress, Tartu		2.2.1.
		Aug.: Riga Eparchy Assembly, Tartu		2.2.1.
	Sep.: Riga occupied by German Army			
	Sep.: Moscow *sobor*			
		Dec.: Consecration of Bishop Platon of Tallinn		2.2.1., 2.2.2. and 2.2.5.
1918	Feb.: German occupation of Estonia			
	Nov.: End of First World War – beginning of struggle for independence			
1919		Jan.: Bolshevik murder of Archbishop Platon		2.2.2.
		Mar.: First Estonian *täiskogu*		2.2.2.
1920	Feb.: Peace treaties with the Soviet Union			
			Feb.: First Latvian ecclesiastic *saeima*	2.2.5.
		May: Patriarch Tikhon establishes the autonomous Tallinn Eparchy		2.2.2.

	General	Estonia	Latvia	Chapter
1920			Aug.: Second, state-sponsored Latvian ecclesiastic *saeima*	2.2.5.
		Sep.: Second Estonian *täiskogu*		2.2.2.
		Dec.: Consecration of Bishop Aleksander of Tallinn		2.2.2.
1921			Jul.: Archbishop Jānis arrives to Riga with autonomy from Patriarch Tikhon	2.2.6.
1922		Jun.: Third Estonian *täiskogu*		2.2.2.
1923		Jun.-Jul.: Archbishop Aleksander of Tallinn travels to Constantinople and receives a *tomos* of autonomy from the Ecumenical Patriarch		2.2.2.
			Oct.-Nov.: Third Latvian ecclesiastic *saeima*, consolidating Archbishop Jānis' hold on the church	2.2.6. and 6.3.
1924		Sep.: Fourth Estonian *täiskogu*, finalising independence		2.2.2.
1925			Oct.: Archbishop Jānis elected to the *Saeima*	2.2.7.

	General	Estonia	Latvia	Chapter
1926		Jul.: Orthodox Church legally registered		2.2.4.
			Oct.: Orthodox Church legally registered	2.2.7.
1929	Stock market crash and ensuing global economic depression			
1930		Nov.-Dec.: Struggle over the Petseri Monastery 'Monastery War' I		2.3.1.
1932		Jun.-Aug.: *Täiskogu* overrules the 'Russian' faction 'Monastery War' II		2.3.1.
1934		Jan.: Ex-Bishop Joann travels to Constantinople to complain		2.3.1.
	Konstantin Päts in Estonia (Mar.) and Kārlis Ulmanis in Latvia (May) stage *coups d'état*			2.3.3.
			Oct.: Archbishop Jānis is murdered	2.3.2.
1935		Jun.: New statutes		2.3.3.
1936			Mar.: Consecration of Metropolitan Augustīns of Riga and All Latvia	2.3.2.
			Mar.: Archpriest Kirils Zaics acquitted of embezzlement charges	2.3.2.

	General	Estonia	Latvia	Chapter
1936			Jul.: Last ecclesiastic *saeima*, passing new statutes	2.3.3.
1937		Jul.: Last *täiskogu*, finally electing a Bishop of Narva		2.3.3.
		Aug.: First joint bishops' Synod in Finland		2.3.3.
1938		Aug.: Second and last joint bishops' Synod in Petseri		2.3.3.
1940	Jun.: Soviet takeover of both Estonia and Latvia, bringing the discourse to a sudden halt			2.3.4.

6.3. Archbishop Jānis' Speech at the Ecclesiastic Saeima, 30.10.1923

1   The work of the Archbishop stands in close and direct co-operation with
2   the work of the Synod, which you will hear about shortly.[1] The work of
3   the Archbishop is an indivisible part of the Synod's activities. A report
4   about the Synod's work is, therefore, to a certain extent also a report
5   about the activity of its chairman. But only to a certain extent. The over-
6   view of the Synod's activities does not include those activities of the
7   Archbishop which he carried out himself in the past years. From that
8   overview, the ideas providing the foundation of my personal as well as
9   our collective work might not come fully into focus. I, standing before
10 you as your Archbishop and the most humble servant of the nation, must
11 therefore steal your attention for some moments, in order to say that
12 which will not be said in the coming reports. I consider this extremely
13 necessary because our grudgers and enemies have spun a thick net of lies
14 around us.
15   Reports about three meetings of the Latvian Orthodox Church that
16 unanimously wanted to see me as head of the Latvian Orthodox Church
17 reached me through the representative of the Latvian government in
18 Moscow. It is obvious that I regarded this threefold unanimous election
19 by my people as a great honour and serving the Latvian Orthodox
20 Church as a holy task. However, at the same time, there were other
21 Russian Eparchies that relentlessly called on me to take on their leader-
22 ship. I'll mention only the Metropolitanate of Caucasus and the Eparchy
23 of Tver here. Also my clerical links with the Eparchy of Penza, where
24 your call reached me, had developed quite nicely and my spiritual guid-
25 ance there was considered indispensable by the leadership of the Russian
26 Orthodox Church. These authorities simply did not allow me to accept
27 the first invitation. Later, when the authorities gave in to the repeated
28 pleas of the Latvian Synod and agreed to let me go, the faithful, with
29 whom I had lived through many indescribable moments in Penza, kept
30 me there. Once accepted, my travel permit was withdrawn. In order to
31 clarify the situation, I was personally invited to Moscow, where tempta-
32 tions were awaiting me. I was told that my native country was poor, that

---

1   This is my own translation of the Latvian version available in Kalniņš I, 1993, p. 22-26.
See also chapter 2.2.6. for more on this speech. There are two words for 'Archbishop' in
Latvian: *Arhibīskaps* and *Virsgans*. The former is based on the Greek original while the
latter is a loan translation, meaning 'head shepherd.' In this speech, Jānis always talks
about himself as 'head shepherd' while all other prelates are *bīskaps* or *arhibīskaps*. In
the translation, I have tried to do this distinction by translating *Virsgans* as Archbishop
with a capital A.

33   it was smaller than a single priory in Tver, that there would be no possi-
34   bilities for a career in Latvia, and that there were irreconcilable compli-
35   cations there, etc. My decision is known to you. Hastily passing the
36   Eparchy of Penza on to my successor, I accepted working for my native
37   church without hesitation.
38   I must admit that there immediately followed some material loss.
39   Due to Soviet laws, I had to leave most of my library and my other
40   belongings in Penza and getting them back is now impossible. However,
41   I decided to sacrifice this in the Christian hope that it would be rewarded
42   by my beloved people, who had offered me such a lovely childhood and
43   youth. My first action for the native land and the Latvian Orthodox
44   Church was to organise the independence of the church. In an
45   independent state and within a sovereign people, the church must also be
46   independent. It was not easy to succeed, for I was alone. There were
47   opponents of Latvian ecclesiastic independence in the Russian Orthodox
48   Church and among Russian citizens, and that is understandable. I spent
49   two hard months in Moscow until on 6 (19) July, I had ploughed through
50   all the canons and convinced the highest authorities of the Russian
51   Orthodox Church of the necessity of independence for the Latvian
52   Orthodox Church and received from them, with Patriarch Tikhon's
53   signature, a document that grants the Latvian Orthodox Church
54   unquestionable and unalienable canonical independence. The content of
55   this document is well known to you all. Not in order to boast, but
56   because of the vilifying attacks of those who accuse me of being an
57   enemy of Latvian independence, I can report that this independence of
58   the Latvian Orthodox Church is the result of God's help and my own
59   hard work, personal strengths, efforts, and means, of my own personal
60   initiative, expressively done out of patriotic love for the Fatherland and
61   its lovely, sincere people. I can add that this work was done while many
62   of my opponents were still agents of the red commission, cursing and
63   vilifying 'white' Latvia and putting nationalists to death in the name of
64   internationality. I can add that some of my opponents still, consciously
65   or without their knowledge, are paying 'comrade fees' for red events. I
66   add this so that you know who are my enemies and what kind of wind
67   blows in their sails and shapes their opinions.
68   I will provide you with some documentary examples from our
69   neighbouring churches, in order to shed light on the importance of my
70   work so far.   You will have read newspapers, in which the massive
71   complications the independence question brought to one of our neigh-
72   bouring Orthodox Churches were described. Fighting about this
73   question, several bishops were imprisoned, one Metropolitan was
74   murdered and the people and the clergy were so divided that decades

75   will pass before the wounds are healed. [2] Many esteemed delegates were
76   sent to Moscow and to Constantinople. I possess a document, which
77   shows that the state budget provided this Orthodox Church several
78   billions.[3] And after all this, the local Metropolitan received a document
79   from the Patriarch of Constantinople which said: 'I wish you good luck
80   ruling your Metropolia within the bounds set out by my brother in Christ
81   Patriarch Tikhon.' Thus, after massive efforts, complications, bloodshed,
82   and billions of tax money spent, the church received a document, whose
83   value is nil. According to the latest news, the bishops of this church
84   decided at a council in September to forget everything done so far and
85   begin anew, turning again to the Patriarch of Moscow. Another Ortho-
86   dox Church sent a delegation with church and state representatives and
87   costly gifts to the Patriarch in order to look for ecclesiastic independ-
88   ence...[4] The matter ended with a document from Constantinople in
89   Greek, listing thirty paragraphs. Great celebrations of autocephaly were
90   organised and autocephaly was proclaimed. But then, when the docu-
91   ment was translated from Greek, it turned out to say nothing about auto-
92   cephaly: 'We also underline the autonomy you have been given from
93   Patriarch Tikhon of Moscow ..., but you definitely must fulfil the
94   following obligations...,' listing six strict limitations to this autonomy.
95   Thus, with expensive delegations and gifts, they received limitations.
96   The struggle for inner peace, for independence, was lost also in this
97   church. A third expensive delegation looking for ecclesiastic independ-
98   ence has not achieved anything yet.[5]
99   In our case, not a single public santim[6] has been spent, not one of our
100   state functionaries was pressed, but still I have a document in my hands
101   guaranteeing the Latvian Orthodox Church unquestionable and unalien-
102   able independence. I say unquestionable and unalienable, for a document
103   of independence can be legally given to us only from the church on
104   which we were earlier dependent, i.e. the Russian Orthodox Church, and
105   she gave it to me. Both earlier examples and the holy canons – III, 8; IV,
106   17; VI, 25 – show that turning to other patriarchs in this question, even
107   the Ecumenical Patriarch, is an illegal act. And still many do not under-
108   stand us when we give this advice. Stealing and robbing will always be

2   This and what follows, is a selective reading of the recent history of the Orthodox
    Church of Poland. One year after this speech, the Polish Orthodox Church received
    autocephaly from the Ecumenical Patriarch. See Papierzyńska-Turek, 2005.
3   There is no mention what kind of billions.
4   This is a mixture of Estonia and Finland.
5   This might be Belarus or Ukraine, which at that time were still struggling against
    becoming part of the Soviet Union.
6   The smallest value Latvian coin.

109 better than the legal path for the degenerated communist soul. This was
110 my first work for the good of Latvia and the Latvian Orthodox Church.
111   Everything that was connected with my arrival to Latvia, I organised
112 using my own, personal means.
113   My life and work in Latvia stands before you and the entire society. I
114 live and work openly and clearly, as a person who has nothing to hide
115 and need not hide. All my life and work is based on one thought and one
116 wish: to serve my dear people and its independent church and country
117 with all my power, with a never exhausted willingness to sacrifice
118 everything to Church and Fatherland, even myself.
119   My first and most holy task, as is every other clergyman's too, is to
120 praise God and proclaim his word. Conscious of my ministry, I realise
121 that this task requires my complete conscience. Organising an episcopal
122 liturgy is not an easy task in current circumstances. Especially if taking
123 into account that I am not allowed to organise a congregation in my
124 cathedral. This house of God, in which I have served and prayed, and
125 lived, for the last two years, was completely destroyed when I arrived.
126 There was only one priest and one deacon there. God's word was only
127 proclaimed on Sundays and holy days. Organising a high liturgy was
128 complicated because of the lack of participants, means, vestments, and
129 other items. This huge room had to be heated and illuminated. A choir
130 had to be organised. That's the kind of circumstances I have had to work
131 in. So far, I have managed indefatigably and without grief. All expensive
132 bishops' items, I have organised with my personal means and powers. I
133 am, so to speak, doing social work with my own work tools. I have not
134 taken a dime[7] from either state or church. I have done all the organisa-
135 tion of high liturgies myself, which was not easy. Nevertheless, there
136 have been many high liturgies. Even without a congregation, enough
137 means have been collected, and thanks to God, continue to come in.
138 Now, I can even think about tomorrow without fear. Now there are even
139 services in the cathedral every day, morning and evening. Next to char-
140 ity, which has taken a lot of time, means and power, no small time has
141 been spent celebrating the Liturgy. In these two and a quarter years,
142 there have been about two hundred days of celebration. According to
143 Orthodox tradition, celebrations not only happen on the saint's day, but
144 on the eve as well. Therefore, I have personally celebrated more than
145 four hundred liturgies.
146   In this time, I have written and given more than two hundred and
147 fifty sermons. If I take only these liturgies and sermon-writing into
148 account, I have had more than 2000 working hours. I have visited more

---

7   A 'Groschen'

149 than a hundred parishes, to which must be added the travel there and
150 back.
151   I have participated in almost all Synod committee meetings, which
152 lasted at least three hours each.
153   I have participated as chairman in all plenary Synod meetings.
154   I participated in the All-Latvian clergy gathering in June as chairman
155 and as contributor. In the run-up to this ecclesiastic saeima, I participated
156 in the preparations, agreeing to hold the most responsible speeches. Not
157 one important ecclesiastic question has been solved without my personal
158 active co-operation. The question of a revision committee, about the
159 legal commission, press section, property protection unit, etc., have been
160 solved and carried out by myself personally. And then there is the
161 question of theological education....
162   As head of the Latvian Orthodox Church, I have participated in the
163 work of the Swedish Red Cross committee to help needy Orthodox
164 members. More than a thousand have been helped.
165   As head of the Latvian Orthodox Church, I have participated in the
166 work of the American Red Cross committee. More than a thousand
167 needy Orthodox have been helped.
168   I have visited schools in and out of Riga to look after the religious
169 instruction there.
170   I personally organised a new edition of the Holy Scriptures, giving
171 the needy more than thousand New Testaments.
172   I have personally established contact with all neighbouring Orthodox
173 churches, in order to be able to paint a picture of the situation in the
174 Orthodox World.
175   As an independent journalist, I work for Ticība un Dzīve as well as
176 several other Latvian and foreign newspapers.
177   I have personally appeared before and approached Latvian state
178 authorities as much as possible, in order to receive a better standing for
179 the Latvian Orthodox Church.
180   I have remained in contact with several persons from different
181 foreign confessions.
182   I have personally carried out all work of the episcopal admini-
183 stration.
184   To finish, I have received a number of supplicants turning to me
185 with all kinds of questions.
186   If all the above said is converted into working hours, then it becomes
187 obvious that the entire day of a bishop consists of working hours and that
188 his working day cannot be limited to eight hours a day.
189   It is important to bear in mind in what circumstances all this work
190 happened. One esteemed foreigner, visiting my apartment, exclaimed:

191   "Believe me; in my country every prisoner has better accommodation
192   than you, the head of the Latvian Orthodox Church!" What kind of
193   apartment that is, you'll see from the Synod act, to be published in
194   *Ticība un Dzīve*, or by visiting it yourself. Please also take into account
195   that I personally had to maintain this pit myself ..., that my labour peace
196   was disturbed by the 'red barons' with their attacks, with their speeches
197   and articles, interpreting my thoughts and work and even my person,
198   hoping, thereby, to come to political fame or simply being envious. Peo-
199   ple with an unfaltering consciousness are always suspect to these people.
200   Everybody who does not participate in their gang or clique becomes an
201   untrustworthy and dangerous person. They called me an enemy of
202   Latvian freedom and independence, although I was but a fighter for the
203   independence of the Latvian Orthodox Church. I, a clergyman and
204   nothing but a clergyman, working only for the Word of God and not
205   belonging to any political party, not looking for promotion, they consider
206   me the leader of some political movement. I would sit in my under-
207   ground mansion and wait for a destructive revolution.
208   A loyal, unselfish citizen's work and his abstinent life cannot be
209   understood by them. They cannot or will not understand that I live in the
210   dark, mouldy cellar and do not ask for an apartment either from the state
211   or the church only because I can see thousands of tax payers who still
212   live in shanties and improvised dwellings. They cannot, or will not,
213   understand that I work day and night under the most uncomfortable
214   conditions, walk around in lumps and do not receive anything from the
215   state budget or the church only because I can see ten thousands of my
216   compatriot Latvians – tax payers – who work in even worse
217   circumstances, walking barefoot, without any coats, fighting utmost
218   famine and poverty. They cannot and will not understand that if they had
219   lived through the past difficult years, being just as unselfish and self-
220   humiliating as Archbishop Jānis of Riga and All Latvia instead of
221   building up immense wealth and posh houses with the Latvian
222   taxpayer's money, then the sun of Latvian national grandeur would long
223   since have risen, our compatriots would no longer live in shanties and
224   improvised dwellings, and each Latvian would have a home, clothes and
225   food.
226   In the eyes of these dishonest opinion leaders of the nation, our
227   churches and chapels appear too Russian. They need to be damaged;
228   they must be demolished as Tsarist remnants, bearing witness to Russian
229   unfairness and terror. These people cannot tell the Byzantine style from
230   the Russian one; even the Orthodox churches that were built in Greece
231   and Palestine would be Russian to them. On the other hand, they cannot
232   and will not see that one specific Tsarist remnant is propagated in the

233 entire Latvian territory, from one end to the other, propagated in exactly
234 the old Tsarist form and with the old Tsarist content. We are talking
235 about the so-called liquor monopoly. This Tsarist remnant is
236 hypocritically accepted by those who despise everything Russian. Why
237 is that so?
238 They do not and will not understand that the tens of thousands of
239 Russians who are encountered with such hatred are also our full brothers
240 in the faith and full citizens of Latvia. It would be much better not only
241 for the church, but also for the country if they learn to respect and love
242 the Latvian people without any hatred. It is important to teach them that
243 Latvia is not a stepmother to them, but a real mother. We should not
244 forget that these despised Russians, who live in the border regions of
245 Latvia, will be the first to meet the Latvian enemy and the first to defend
246 the Latvian border posts. I consider it my responsibility, not only as
247 Archbishop of a Christian Church, but also as a Latvian citizen, to ensure
248 that these Russians identify not only with the church but also with the
249 Latvian state. And in this I have shown successes. Under my leadership,
250 we in the Latvian Orthodox Church have not had any complications or
251 misunderstandings with the Russians. None of the Russians in my care
252 have said or done anything that can damage the Latvian Orthodox
253 Church. And not only the Latvian Orthodox Church, but also the Latvian
254 State. That is not only my observation. His Excellency, the Minister of
255 the Interior told me on 24 October that he knew no negative facts about
256 the Orthodox Russians either.
257 Through all this, I have always retained my Christian humility,
258 patience, and boundless love of liberty and goodwill, respect and love
259 towards everything Latvian. I have not taken a single step that might
260 damage my dear Mother Latvia. My first activities were for the good of
261 Latvia – the independence of the Latvian Orthodox Church. My further
262 steps were also taken with a deep love for the Fatherland. I strongly
263 object to any attempts to achieve anything with means contrary to the
264 Latvian interests. Many of you know that such temptations have been
265 tried in the past and that we would have had all the means to put pressure
266 on the government on behalf of me and my institution.
267 This – my life and work and tactics of resistance – is a symbol for
268 my supporters nearby and far off. In other words, it symbolises the life,
269 work, and resistance of the entire Latvian Orthodox Church. My vest-
270 ments and my in every sense uncomfortable apartment in the cellar per-
271 fectly describe the situation in which the life of the Orthodox Church is
272 lived in Latvia: extreme poverty, such poverty which you can find only
273 in the first years of early Christian history, hatred and envy on all sides,
274 vilification and torture. There is no shelter, no defence. Even the bright

275   windows, which earlier enlightened our life in the cellar and in our
276   schools are now closed off to us. Even the few possessions we had were
277   taken away from us, either by way of law or simply taken. Also what is
278   currently in our hands is threatened. Our situation cannot be described
279   only as a state of persecution; it is an especially degenerated form of
280   torture. Our Christian love for peace is not only failing to appease the
281   hearts of our persecutors, but make them even more eager to destroy us.
282   We can compare it to the torture of the first Christians, for the greater
283   our Christian patience, the eviller the methods of torture. We patiently
284   await the expropriation of our property... The tormentors turn now to our
285   sanctuaries, to our monasteries, to our churches, some to be given to our
286   most hated enemies, others to be demolished, some to be sold in auc-
287   tions, others to be turned into secular institutions, etc. If we retain our
288   Christian patience and peacefulness, then we are threatened: we have not
289   yet reached the peak, we will turn your highest sanctuary, the ruling
290   Archbishop's cathedral, into a museum ... It quite seems that they expect
291   some kind of outcry from us, on the basis of which they can turn against
292   our church with full force...

293   Dear fellow campaigners and brothers in Christ, in this difficult
294   situation, when we can still expect the worst, I consider it my
295   responsibility to make you remain moderate and careful, for the times
296   are difficult and capricious; gather all your strength that you may remain
297   patient and goodhearted about all that has happened and all that will
298   come. Calm down in the holy love and faith, strengthen one another, and
299   let the hope in God's truth never allow such actions as we in our
300   thoughts nurture in relation to our tormenters. Fill your hearts and minds
301   with the conviction that it is not the sovereign nation in whose name the
302   terror is done that is at fault, believe that the Latvian sovereign nation in
303   its entirety nurtures goodwill towards you, that it is not responsible for
304   these excesses just as the Russian nation is not responsible for everything
305   done in its name. We are all sons of the working people, we truly know
306   the people, and we know we can say that the Russian nation is
307   experiencing its brutally hard times. They are caught in a similar
308   situation to us. Therefore, let's join our hands, the suffering with the suf-
309   fering in deep love and hope that God's truth lets the sun rise and
310   together with the entire people, we will rise with the sun from the dark,
311   musty cellar, the shanties and improvised dwellings. If we peacefully get
312   along with the people now, then we will also get along with them on
313   sunny days and the day of national abundance will also be our day of
314   abundance.

315   Therefore, together with the sovereign Latvian people we pray to
316   God that he spread out power and hope to his patient and peaceful

317　Christian flock; that as in the past centuries, so now, peace will gain hold
318　in the difficult phases of life. Therefore, in deep love and bereft of
319　hypocrisy in our relations with the Latvian sovereign nation and together
320　with it let us also in the future use all our spiritual and peaceful powers
321　to strengthen the national peace and wealth and let it be enlightened by
322　God's truth and love and let all Latvian citizens live together without
323　schism for many, many years.

6.4. Brief Biographies of the Main Actors[1]

Abbreviations:

EAOC	Estonian Apostolic Orthodox Church (from 1923)
EE	Estonian
LAOC	Latvian Autonomous Orthodox Church (from 1936)
LV	Latvian
MP	Moscow Patriarchate
PTA	St. Petersburg Theological Academy
ROCOR	Russian Orthodox Church Outside Russia
ROS	Riga Orthodox Seminary
RU	Russian
UT	University of Tartu (Dorpat, Юрьев)

Agapov, Boris (Агапов, Борис Е., 1884-?, RU)
St. Petersburg lawyer. Drafted to the Russian Baltic Front in 1915. Stranded in Tallinn when the Russian Navy was disbanded in 1917. Became active in the Russian minority. Head of the Clerical Council of the Russian Parishes of the Estonian Orthodox Church (CCRP). Disappeared from Estonia in 1924.

Aleksander (Paulus) (1872-1953, EE) Metropolitan of Tallinn and All Estonia
Finished ROS in 1894. Consecrated Bishop of Tallinn in 1920. Travelled to Constantinople in 1923, where the Patriarch named him Metropolitan of the EAOC. Member of the Estonian parliament (1929-1932). Summoned to Moscow in 1940 to publicly repent of the schism of the EAOC. Denied repentance during the following German occupation (1941-1944) and fled to Germany before the second Soviet occupation. Led the EAOC in Exile until his death in Stockholm, Sweden.

Aleksandrs (Vītols) (born Adams, 1876-1942, LV)
Finished ROS. Worked as teacher and priest in the Latvian countryside. Consecrated Bishop of Jersika in 1938. Charged with administration of the Latvian Orthodox parishes by Metr. Sergij (Voskresenskij, MP Exarch of Estonia and Latvia) in 1942, but died unexpectedly later that year.

1　The following biographies have been compiled using a variety of sources, especially Unāms, 1975; Raudsepp, 1998a, p. 94-150; Sõtšov, 2004, p. 164-205; Sidjakov I-III, 2008-2011. Moreover, internet databases, especially at http://www.kirmus.ee and http://www.eleison.lv have also been helpful.

Augustīns (Pētersons) (1873-1955, LV) Metropolitan of Riga and All Latvia
Finished ROS in 1895. Schoolteacher and priest. Evacuated to Novgorod in 1917. Returned to Latvia in 1921 and worked as priest and teacher in Daugavpils. Elected and consecrated bishop of the LAOC in 1936. Summoned to Moscow in 1940 to publicly repent of the schism of the LAOC. Denied repentance during the following German occupation (1941-1944). Fled to Germany before the second Soviet occupation and attempted to lead an exile church until his death.

Bogojavlenskij, Ioann (Богоявленский, Иоанн, 1879-1949, RU)
Finished PTA in 1915 and arrived in Estonia in 1919. Archpriest at the Aleksander Nevskij Cathedral of Tallinn (1919-1936) and a member of the Estonian Synod (1924-1939). Editor of the Russian-language Orthodox journal in Estonia (1931-1940). Subordinated himself to the MP in 1942. Consecrated as Bishop Isidor of Tallinn and All Estonia in 1947. Brother of Metropolitan Elevferij of Vilnius and All Lithuania (1868-1940).

Dāvis, Jānis (1867-1959, LV)
Latvian Orthodox nationalist and teacher, active in the temperance movement. Chairman of the Parish Council of the Ascension church in Riga from 1917. Argued for an autocephalous Latvian Orthodox Church. Member of the Latvian Synod 1923-1926, but thereafter no longer active in the church, except in the temperance movement.

Evsevij (Grozdov) (Евсевий (Гроздов), 1866-1929, RU) Bishop of Pskov
Fled Pskov in 1919 to Estonia. Named Archbishop of Narva (in the EAOC) in 1925.

Germanos (Strenopoulos) (1872-1951) Metropolitan of Thyateira (London)
Named Exarch of Central and Western Europe by Patriarch **Meletios IV (Metaxakis)** in 1922. Responsible for the EAOC and the Orthodox Church of Finland from 1923 and active in the transfer of the LAOC to the Patriarchate of Constantinople in 1935-1936.

Gredzens, Pēteris (1887-1942, LV)
Finished ROS in 1908. Archpriest of Talsi in Latvia and provost of the Jelgava priory (1921-1941). Editor of the Latvian-language Orthodox journal from 1934. Deported by Soviet Authorities in 1941.

Gruzna, Pāvils (1878-1950, LV)
Latvian writer. Expelled from the ROS in 1898 as a freethinker. Wrote 'Bursaki' (The Seminarians) and 'Jaunā Strāva' (The Modern Current). Fled to Germany before the second Soviet occupation.

Hermann (Aav) (1878-1961, EE) Archbishop of Karjala and All Finland
Finished ROS in 1900. Served as parish priest. Consecrated Bishop of Sortavala during the official visit to Constantinople in 1923. Pushed the acting Bishop of Helsinki and All Finland, **Serafim (Lukjanov)** out of office with the help of the Finnish government. Involved in a canonical dispute with the MP after the Second World War, which the Finnish Orthodox Church won.

Ioann (Smirnov) (Иоанн (Смирнов) 1844-1919, RU) Archbishop of Riga
Last Russian Archbishop of Riga (1910-1918). Evacuated to Tartu in 1915. Left for the Moscow *sobor* in 1917 and transferred to his native Rjazan'.

Jānis (Pommers) (1876-1934, LV) Archbishop of Riga and All Latvia
Finished ROS in 1897. Studied in Kiev, where he became a monk. Consecrated Bishop of Sluck in 1912, became Archbishop of Penza in 1918. Became Archbishop of Riga after three calls from Latvia in 1921. Active member of the Latvian parliament until his death. Canonised by the ROCOR in 1981 and by the MP in 2001. Brother of **Antonijs Pommers**.

Jansons, Andrejs (1871-1948, LV)
Finished ROS in 1894. Served in several Latvian parishes along the border with Estonia. Only identifiable Orthodox clergyman able to speak both Latvian and Estonian. Occasionally published translations of Estonian articles in the Latvian Orthodox journal. Brother of **Jānis Jansons**.

Jansons, Jānis (1878-1954, LV)
Finished ROS in 1900. Continued his studies at PTA. Returned to Latvia, but was evacuated in 1915. Returned in 1920. Director of the reopened ROS (1926-1936). Candidate to succeed Archbishop Jānis. Entertained a Moscow-friendly orientation. Therefore, pushed out of influential positions. Head of the new Orthodox Department in the Theological Faculty of the Latvian University (1936-1940). Happily subordinated himself to the MP in 1940 and continued as provost of Riga. Brother of **Andrejs Jansons**.

Jēkabs (Karps) (1865-1943, LV) Bishop of Jelgava
Finished ROS in 1887. Teacher, priest, and provost. Consecrated Bishop of Jelgava in 1936. Subordinated himself to the MP in 1940.

Joann (Bulin) (born Nikolai, 1893-1941, EE) Bishop of Petseri
Ethnic *Setu*. Finished ROS in 1915. Continued his studies at PTA. Interrupted by war involvement. Became a monk in 1918 and Bishop of Petseri in 1926. Member of the Estonian parliament (1929-1934). Named Bishop of Narva in 1932 but refused the post, travelling to Constantinople to complain. Stayed in Yugoslavia as part of the ROCOR hierarchy. Returned to Estonia as an icon painter in 1938. Arrested and executed by Soviet authorities in 1941.

Kaelas, Aleksander (1880-1920, EE)
Finished ROS in 1901. Continued his studies at the Moscow Theological Academy and Moscow University. Became a professor at the Moscow University, later evacuated to Irkutsk, where he died.

Kokla, Konstantin (1878-1946, EE)
Estonian Orthodox teacher and sacristan from the island Hiiumaa in the Estland Province. Passed an external clergy exam in 1911 and consecrated a priest. Contributor to the Estonian Orthodox journals. Revived the pre-First World War-journal in 1933 after **Anton Laar** had passed away. Tartu provost (1926-1944).

Kreics, Juris (1870-1962, LV)
Latvian Orthodox teacher, linguist, and historian from the Latgale region. Retired from 1927.

Laar, Anton (1885-1933, EE)
Finished the ROS in 1903. Studied at UT. Teacher, priest, and active member of the Estonian Constituent Assembly. Founded a very national-minded Estonian Orthodox journal in 1918. Functioned as the voice of Estonian Orthodoxy.

Martinson, Vassili (1874-1955, EE)
Finished ROS in 1896. Continued his studies at PTA. Teacher, inspector, and director of the St. Petersburg Orthodox Seminary (1900-1918). Professor of Theology at the University of Tartu in 1923 with his own chair in 1931. Emigrated to USA during the Second World War.

Meletios IV (Metaxakis) (1871-1935) Patriarch of Constantinople
Named Metropolitan of Athens 1918. Ousted from office in 1920. Emigrated to USA. Elected Patriarch of Constantinople in 1921, under somewhat chaotic circumstances. Expelled from Constantinople for Greek nationalism by the Turkish authorities in 1923, a day after receiving the Finnish-Estonian delegation and granting the two churches autonomy under Constantinople's jurisdiction. Withdrew temporarily to Mount Athos. Patriarch of Alexandria from 1926 until his death.

Nikolai (Leismann) (1862-1947, EE) Bishop of Petseri
Finished ROS in 1883. Continued his studies at PTA. Head censor of Estonian-language publications in Riga 1896-1914. Member of the Estonian Synod (1924-1926, 1933-1940) and various other important functions in the EAOC. Consecrated bishop in 1933. Retired in 1940.

Päts, Konstantin (1874-1956, EE)
Left ROS in 1892. Studied at UT. Active politician in Estonia. Served repeatedly as State Elder. From 1934 the authoritarian President of Estonia. Arrested in 1940 and interned in Russia until his death. Brother of **Nikolai Päts**.

Päts, Nikolai (1871-1940, EE)
Finished ROS in 1894. Influential priest in Tallinn. Chairman of the Estonian Synod from 1920 until his death. Brother of **Konstantin Päts**.

Pavel (Dmitrovskij) (Дмитровский, Павел, 1872-1946, RU) Bishop of Narva
Came to Estonia in 1919 and stayed as priest of the Narva Cathedral (1919-1937). Consecrated bishop in 1937. Subordinated himself to the MP in 1941. Named Archbishop of Tallinn and All Estonia in 1945.

Platon (Kulbusch) (born Paul, 1869-1919, EE) Bishop of Tallinn and All Estonia
Finished ROS in 1890. Continued his studies at PTA. Provost for the Estonian parishes in St. Petersburg. Consecrated Bishop of Tallinn on the final day of 1917. Arrested and executed by retreating Bolshevik forces. Canonised by the MP and the Patriarchate of Constantinople (separately) in 2000.

Pommers, Antonijs (1890-1944, LV)
Finished ROS. Studied at the University of Warsaw. Returned to Latvia as a history teacher and schoolbook writer. Member of the Latvian Synod. Arrested and executed by Soviet authorities. Brother of Archbishop **Jānis (Pommers)**.

Poska, Jaan (1866-1920, EE)
Finished ROS in 1887. Studied at UT. Lawyer in Tallinn. First chairman of the united Estonian province of the Russian Empire in 1917. Represented Estonia at the Versailles Peace Negotiations, but survived the Peace Treaty with Russia only by one month.

Serafim (Lukjanov) (Серафим (Лукянов) 1879-1959, RU) Archbishop of Helsinki and All Finland
Last Russian Bishop of Helsinki. Ousted from power by the Finnish government in 1923, following the consecration of **Hermann (Aav)** as Bishop of Sortavala against his will. Moved to the Konevitsa Monastery. Emigrated to Paris in 1926. Subordinated himself to the ROCOR. Rejoined the MP in 1945. Named Exarch for Western Europe. Returned to the Soviet Union in 1954.

Tikhon (Bellavin) (Тихон (Беллавин) 1865-1925, RU) Patriarch of Moscow and All Russia
First Patriarch of Moscow since 1700. Elected at the Moscow *sobor* in 1917. Led the Russian Orthodox Church through the difficult early years of the Soviet Union, challenged from the (Red) 'Living Church' Movement and the (White) ROCOR. Diplomatically managed to retain the trust of the Russian Orthodox community. Imprisoned by Soviet authorities (1922-1923). Died a natural death.

Truusmann, Jüri (1856-1930, EE)

Finished ROS in 1879. Continued his studies at PTA. Official censor of Estonian-language publications in Tallinn (1885-1908). Never acclimated to independent Estonia and retired completely from societal life.

Ulmanis, Kārlis (1877-1942, LV)

Studied in Germany and USA. Active politican in Latvia. Served repeatedly as Prime Minister. After a *coup d'état* in 1934, he was authoritarian Latvian leader until the Soviet occupation. Arrested by Soviet authorities in 1941 and died in internment.

Värat, Aleksander (1858-1931, EE)

Finished ROS in 1881. Priest of the Estonian parish in Riga (1906-1916). Proponent of Russification. Editor of the first Estonian-language Orthodox journal (1908-1917). Evacuated to Russia in 1915. Not allowed to return to Estonia. Joined the 'Living Church' Movement.

Zaics, Kirils (1869-1948, LV)

Finished ROS in 1891. Priest in the Latvian parishes in Latgale. Delegate of the Eparchy of Polock-Vitebsk at the Moscow *sobor*, where he participated actively on questions of liturgical reform. Returned to Riga. Co-editor of both the Latvian and Russian-language Orthodox journals in 1923. Gradually took over the journals and reacted to the Synod decision to stop funding them by closing the Latvian one and turning the Russian one into an international journal for Orthodox internal mission. Charged with embezzlement and slander in 1933. Acquitted in 1936. Rejected any involvement in the LAOC. Returned to ecclesiastic life in 1940, leading the 'Pskov Mission' to re-Christianise the Russians in the areas under German occupation. Convicted to twelve years of labour camp in 1945.

7. Bibliography

7.1. Archival Sources

Letter from A. Laar to the editors of *Postimees*, 08.05.1917, *Eesti Ajaloo Arhiiv* [Estonian Historical Archives], f. 1655, n. 3, s. 380.

"Täiskogu protokollid", *Eesti Ajaloo Arhiiv* [Estonian Historical Archives], f. 1655, n. 3, s. 6.

Setälä, E. N., 1923, "Selontekona matkastani Konstantinopoliin...", Official report from the journey to Constantinople to the Finnish Ministry of the Interior, *Suomen Ulkoasianministeriön Arkisto* [Archives of the Finnish Foreign Ministry], 44, J.

7.2. Periodicals

The following list includes all the periodicals that are cited in the footnotes of this book, including the abbreviated ones. It also gives a brief characterisation of the periodicals. The abbreviations EE (Estonian), LV (Latvian) and RU (Russian) indicate the language of the periodical.

Aamun Koitto [Dawn]
  Official journal of the Finnish Orthodox Church (Joensuu, 1897 – today)

Baltijas Vēstnesis [The Baltic Messenger, LV]
  Latvian daily newspaper (Rīga, 1868-1920)

Brivā Zēme [The Free Land, LV]
  Latvian daily newspaper of the Agrarian Union (Rīga, 1919-1940)

Eesti Kirik [The Estonian Church, EE]
  Weekly journal of the Estonian Lutheran Church (Tallinn, 1923-1940)

ET   *Elutõde* [Truth of Life, EE]
  Official journal of the Estonian Orthodox Church (Petseri, 1936-1940)

Esmaspäev [Monday, EE]
  Monday Edition of *VM* (Tallinn, 1922-1940)

JZ   *Jaunākas Ziņas* [Latest News, LV]
  The largest Latvian daily newspaper (Rīga, 1911-1940)

Kaja [The Echo, EE]
  Estonian daily newspaper of the People's Party (Tallinn, 1919-1935)

Kirjandus – kunst – teadus [Literature – art – science, EE]
   Art supplement of *PL* (Tallinn, 1921-1922)

Krusta Ēna [The shadow of the cross, LV]
   Orthodox quarterly journal, which only appeared for two issues (Rīga, 1920)

Kunst ja Kirjandus [Art and Literature, EE]
   Art supplement of *PL* (Tallinn, 1932-1940)

Labietis [The Good One, LV]
   Bi-monthly journal of the Latvian neo-pagan union (Rīga, 1933-1940)

Latgolas Wōrds [The Word from Latgale, LV]
   Latvian daily newspaper from the predominantly Catholic Latgale region in the Latgale dialect (Rēzekne, 1919-1940)

Latvijas Kareivis [The Latvian Soldier, LV]
   Latvian daily newspaper of the Army (Rīga, 1920-1940]

Latvijas Sargs [The Latvian Guardsman, LV]
   Latvian weekly newspaper (Rīga, 1919-1934)

PL   *Päevaleht* [Paper of the Day, EE]
   The largest Estonian daily newspaper (Tallinn, 1905-1940)

PLV *Pareizticīgo Latviešu Vēstnesis* [The Orthodox Latvian Messenger, LV]
   Official Latvian-language journal for the Riga Eparchy (Tukums, 1906-1917)

Pēdēja Brīdi [Last Moment, LV]
   Latvian daily newspaper (Rīga, 1927-1936)

Petseri Uudised [Petseri News, EE]
   Estonian daily newspaper from Petserimaa (Petseri, 1932-1937)

PM   *Postimees* [Postman, EE]
   Estonian daily newspaper (Tartu, 1886-1944), including *Postimees* (hommikuväljaanne) [Morning issue]

PS   *Православный Собеседник* [Orthodox Messenger, RU]
   Russian-language Orthodox journal published in Estonia (Tallinn, 1931-1940)

Rahvaleht [The People's Paper, EE]
   Estonian daily newspaper (Tallinn, 1923, 1940)

Revaler Bote, Russland-Beilage
   Weekly supplement to the last German-language daily newspaper in Estonia (Tallinn, 1919-1930)

Riigi Teataja [The State's Messenger, EE]
   Official journal of the Estonian State (Tallinn, 1918-1940)

Ristirahva Pühhapäevaleht [The Sunday Paper for the Christians, EE]
Weekly Lutheran newspaper (Tallinn, 1875-1919)

Rīts [Morning, LV]
Latvian daily newspaper (Rīga, 1934-1940)

Saeimas Stenogrammas [The Saeima Protocols, LV]
The published protocols of the parliamentary debates.

Seg Сегодня [Today, RU]
One of the largest Russian-language daily newspapers outside the Soviet Union appearing twice daily (Rīga, 1919-1940)

Svētdienas Rīts [Sunday Morning, LV]
Weekly journal of the Latvian Lutheran Church (Rīga, 1920-1940)

Tallinna Teataja [The Tallinn Messenger, EE]
Estonian daily newspaper (Tallinn, 1910-1922)

TuD *Ticība un Dzīve* [Faith and Life, LV]
Official journal of the Latvian Orthodox Church (Rīga, 1923-1932; Talsi, 1934-1940)

UjE₁ *Usk ja Elu* [Faith and Life, EE]
Official Estonian-language journal of the Riga Eparchy (Rīga, 1908-1917)

UjE₂ *Usk ja Elu* [Faith and Life, EE]
Journal for Orthodox Estonians (Tartu, 1933-1940)

Uus Eesti [New Estonia, EE]
Estonian daily newspaper (Tallinn, 1935-1940)

UE *Uus Elu* [New Life, EE]
Official journal of the Estonian Orthodox Church (Tartu, 1919-1932)

VM *Vaba Maa* [Free Country, EE]
Estonian daily newspaper of the Labour Party (Tallinn, 1918-1938)

Valdības Vēstnesis [The State's Messenger, LV]
Official daily newspaper of the Latvian State (Rīga, 1919-1940)

ViŽ Вера и Жизнь (Faith and Life, RU)
Official journal of the Latvian Orthodox Church in Russian (Rīga, 1923-1940)

Жизнь [Life, RU]
Estonian daily newspaper in Russian, published by the *VM* publishing house (Tallinn, 1922)

Последния Известия [Latest Bulletin, RU]
Estonian daily newspaper in Russian (Tallinn, 1920-1927)

Трудовая Мысль [TheWorking Thought, RU]
Latvian Newspaper in Russian (Daugavpils, 1928-1934)

7.3. Unpublished Sources

Brandt, Gerhard, 1959, *Der estländische Gouverneur Fürst Šachowskoj und die behördlichen Maßnahmen zur Russifizierung Estlands (1881-1894)*, unpublished PhD Dissertation, Universität Göttingen.

Bühmann, Henning, 2008, *Die Rezeption der "baltischen Märtyrer" von 1919 im deutschbaltischen und deutschen Protestantismus bis zum Zweiten Weltkrieg*, unpublished Master's thesis, Tübingen.

Engelhardt, Jeffers, 2005, *Singing in "Transition": Musical Practices and Ideologies of Renewal in the Orthodox Church of Estonia*, unpublished PhD Dissertation, Chicago, IL.

Hatlie, Mark R., 2009a, *Riga at War 1914-1919*, unpublished PhD Dissertation, Tübingen.

Hindov, Nigul, 1929, *Esimene Eesti ap.-õigeusu piiskopp-usukannataja Platon: tema elu ja tegevus* [The first Estonian Orthodox Bishop-Martyr Platon: his life and activity], unpublished paper, Tartu.

Kala, Martin, 2007, *L'Église orthodoxe en Estonie: approche canonique et du droit civil ecclésiastique Européen*, unpublished PhD Dissertation, University of Paris XI.

Klaas, Urmas, 1998, *Õigeusu kirik Lõuna-Eestis 1848-1917: halduskorraldus ja preesterkond* [The Orthodox Church in South Estonia: Organisation and Clergy], unpublished Master's thesis, Tartu.

Kukk, Kristi, 2005, *Rahvuse arengu peegeldumine ajalookäsitlustes Eesti näitel* [The development of the nation in the mirror of historiography – the Estonian case], unpublished Master's thesis, Tartu.

Lõuna, Anneli, 2002, *Jüri Truusmann ja teised õigeusklikud Eesti haritlased Tallinnas 19. sajandi teisel poolel – 20. sajandi algul* [Jüri Truusman and other Orthodox Estonian intellectuals in Tallinn around the turn of the 20th century], unpublished Master's thesis, Tartu.

Papathomas, Grigorios D., 2004, *Autocéphalie et Nation*, unpublished course compendium, Institut Saint-Serge, Paris.

Rimestad, Sebastian, 2007, *Orthodox Christianity in Estonia as a Factor in the Emergence of the Estonian National Consciousness*, unpublished Master's thesis, Erfurt.

Rohtmets, Priit, 2006, *Eesti Evangeeliumi Luteri Usu Kiriku välissuhted aastatel 1919-1940* [The external relations of the Estonian Lutheran Church, 1919-1940], unpublished Master's thesis, Tartu.

Runce, Inese, 2008, *Valsts un Baznīcas attiecības Latvijā: 1906.-1940. gads* [The State-Church relations in Latvia: 1906-1940], unpublished PhD Dissertation, Rīga.

Ryan, Daniel C., 2008, *The Tsar's Faith: Conversion, Religious Politics, and Peasant Protest in Imperial Russia's Baltic Periphery, 1845-1870s*, unpublished PhD Dissertation, University of California, LA.

7.4. Published Sources

Adler, Philip, 1979, "Nation and Nationalism among the Serbs of Hungary 1790-1870", in *East European Quarterly*, 13/3, p. 271-285.

Afanasiev, Nicholas N., 1967 [1936], "The Canons of the Church: Changeable or Unchangeable?", in *St. Vladimir's Seminary Quarterly*, 11/2, p. 54-68.

Aleksij, 1999 = Алексий II, Патриарх Московской и Всея Русь, 1999, *Православие в Эстонии* [The Orthodox in Estonia], ЦНЦ Православная энциклопедия, Москва.

Aleksov, Bojan, 2006, *Religious dissent between the modern and the national*, Harrassowitz, Wiesbaden.

Alenius, Kari, 1999, "Petserimaa ja Narvataguse integreerimine Eestiga ning idaalade maine Eesti avalikkuses 1920-1925" [The Integration of Petseri Province and the Region beyond the Narva into Estonia and Image of the Eastern Regions in the Estonian Public, 1920-1925], in *Akadeemia*, 11/11(128), p. 2301-2322.

Alexeev, Wassilij, 1957, "Le drame de l'exarque Serge Voskresenskij et l'élection du patriarche de Moscou à la lumière des documents confidentiels allemands", in *Irénikon*, 30, p. 189-202.

Alexeev, Wassilij, 1974, "The Orthodox Church under German Occupation: An Unpublished Memorandum by the Exarch of the Baltic Area, Metropolitan Sergii", in *Eastern Churches Review*, 4/2, p. 131-161.

Alexeev, Wassilij and Theofanis G. Stavrou, 1976, *The Great Revivial – The Russian Church Under German Occupation*, Burgess, Minneapolis, MN.

Ammann, Albert Maria, 1936, "Bei den Altgläubigen am Peipus-See", in *Stimmen der Zeit*, 131, p. 185-192.

Anderson, Benedict, 1998 [1983], *Imagined Communities – Reflections on the Origin and Spread of Nationalism*, 2nd revised ed., Verso, London and New York.

Andresen, Lembit, 1995, *Eesti kooli ajalugu* [History of the Estonian School], Avita, Tallinn.

Apine, Ilga, 1996, "Multikulturālisma tradīcijas Latgalē" [The traditions of multiculturalism in Latgale], in Josifs Šteimanis (ed.), *Latgale un Daugavpils: vēsture un kultūra* [Latgale and Daugavpils: history and culture], Multinacionālas kultūras centrs, Daugavpils, p. 7-21.

Apostlik õigeusk, 1951 = *Apostlik õigeusk 100 aastat Eestis* [100 Years of Apostolic Orthodoxy in Estonia], Vetlanda Trykkeriet, Vetlanda.

Arens, Olavi, 1973, "Eduard Laaman as a Historian", in Arvids Ziedonis, Jr., William L. Winter, and Mardi Valgemäe (eds.), *Baltic History*, AABS, Columbus, OH, p. 217-226.

Avvakumov, Georgij, 2006, "Die Fragen des Ritus als Streit- und Kontroversgegenstand. Zur Typologie der Kulturkonflikte zwischen dem lateinischen Westen und dem byzantinisch-slavischen Osten im Mittelalter und in der Neuzeit", in Rainer Bendel (ed.), *Kirchen- und Kulturgeschichtsschreibung in Nordost- und Ostmitteleuropa*, LIT Verlag, Berlin, p. 191-233.

Avvakumov, Georgij, 2007, "Metropolit Andrej Septyckyj und die Problematik der christlichen Einheit in Rußland. Zum geschichtlichen Hintergrund und Inhalt des Briefwechsels zwischen Andrej Septyckyj und Antonij Chrapovickij, 1903-1908", in Hans-Christian Maner and Norbert Spannenberger (eds.), *Konfessionelle Identität und Nationsbildung: die griechisch-katholischen Kirchen in Ostmittel- und Südosteuropa im 19. und 20. Jahrhundert*, Steiner, Stuttgart, p. 51-63.

Baberowski, Jörg, 2007, "Dictatorships of Unambiguity: Cultural Transfer from Europe to Russia and the Soviet Union, 1861-1953", in Manfred Hildermeier (ed.), *Historical Concepts between Eastern and Western Europe*, Berghahn Books, New York and Oxford, p. 59-72.

Badcock, Sarah, 2005, "Autocracy in Crisis: Nicholas the Last", in Ian D. Thatcher (ed.), *Late Imperial Russia – Problems and Prospects*, Manchester University Press, Manchester, p. 9-27.

Balašov, 2001 = Балашов, Николай, 2001, *На пути к литургическому возрождению* [On the road towards liturgical renewal], Круглый стол по религиозному образованию и диаконии, Москва.

Balevics, Zigmunds, 1964, *Baznīca un valsts buržuaziskajā Latvijā* [Church and state in bourgeois Latvia], Latv. Valsts Izd., Rīga.

Balevics, Zigmunds, 1987, *Pareizticīgo baznīca Latvijā* [The Orthodox Church in Latvia], Avots, Rīga.

Balevics and Kadiķis, 1962 = Балевиц, З. and А. Кадикис, 1962, *Православное духовенство в Латвии 1920-1940* [The Orthodox clergy in Latvia 1920-1940], Латв. гос. изд., Rīga.

Bauman, Zygmunt, 1993, "Modernity", in Peter Beilharz (ed.), 2001, *The Bauman Reader*, Blackwell, Malden, MA, p. 163-172.

Bensch, Rochus Johannes, 2003, *Neuere baltische Kirchenrechtsgeschichte*, Bautz, Nordhausen.

Benwell, Bethan and Elizabeth Stokoe, 2006, *Discourse and Identity*, Edinburgh University Press, Edinburgh.

Benz, Ernst, 1952, *Die Ostkirche im Lichte der protestantischen Geschichtsschreibung von der Reformation bis zur Gegenwart*, Alber, Freiburg.

Benz, Ernst, 1998, "Zwischen konfessioneller, regionaler und nationaler Identi-tät. Die Katholiken in Lettgallen und Lettland im 19. und 20. Jahrhun-dert", in *Nordostarchiv*, 7/2, p. 443-495.

Berg, Eiki and Hill Kulu, 1996, "Peipsivenelased, Rahvus- ja regionaalpoliiti-lised realiteedid" [The Peipsi Russians, Realities of National and Regional Politics], in *Akadeemia*, 8/6(87), p. 1164-1183.

Berger, Stefan and Chris Lorenz, 2008, "Introduction: National History Writing in Europe in a Global Age", in Stefan Berger and Chris Lorenz (eds.), *The Contested Nation – Ethnicity, Class, Religion and Gender in National Histories*, Palgrave Macmillan, Houndmills, Basingstoke, p. 1-23.

Bicilli, 1923 = Бицилли, Пётр М., 1923, "Католичества и римская церковь" [Catholicism and the Church of Rome], in Пётр М. Бицилли (ed.), *Россия и Латинство* [Russia and 'Latindom'], Berlin, p. 40-80.

Blaschke, Olaf, 2000, "Das 19. Jahrhundert: Ein Zweites Konfessionelles Zeit-alter?", in *Geschichte und Gesellschaft*, 26/1, p. 38-75.

Bleiere, Daina, Ilgvars Butulis, Inesis Feldmanis, Aivars Stranga, and Antonijs Zunda, 2008 [2005], *Geschichte Lettlands – 20. Jahrhundert*, Jumava, Rīga.

von Bröndsted, M., 1888, *Die russische Kirche in Livland unter Nikolaus I*, Georg F. Nagel, Berlin.

Bruce, Steve, 2002, *God is dead: Secularization in the West*, Blackwell, Oxford.

Brüggemann, Karsten, 2005, "Kontinuität in der Revolution: Der russische Blick auf das Baltikum während der 'Zeit der Wirren' 1917-1920 am Beispiel der weißen Bewegung", in Olaf Mertelsmann (ed.), *Estland und Russland – Aspekte der Beziehungen zweier Länder*, Verlag Dr. Kovač, Hamburg, p. 127-156.

Brüggemann, Karsten, 2006, "Das Baltikum im russischen Blick: Rußland und sein Anspruch auf die baltischen Staaten in der Perspektive des 19. Jahr-hunderts" in Jörg Hackmann and Robert Schweitzer (eds.), *Nordost-europa als Geschichtsregion*, Schmidt-Römhild, Lübeck, p. 392-411.

Bryner, Erich, 1996, *Die Ostkirchen vom 18. bis zum 20. Jahrhundert*, Evangeli-sche Verlagsanstalt, Leipzig.

Buss, Andreas E., 2003, *The Russian-Orthodox Tradition and Modernity*, Brill, Leiden.

Bušueva, 1993 = Бушуева, И., 1993, "История прихода Рижского Кафе-дрального Собора во имя рождества христова в 1915-1920-х годах" [The history of the Riga Cathedral Parish of the Mother of God, 1915-1920], in Александр В. Гаврилин (ed.), *Православие в Латвии: исторические очерки, том I* [The Orthodox in Latvia: Historical Studies, Vol. I], Filokalija, Rīga, p. 43-64.

Butulis, Ilgvars, 2001, "Autoritäre Ideologie und Praxis des Ulmanis-Regimes in Lettland 1934-1940", in Erwin Oberländer (ed.), *Autoritäre Regime in Ostmittel- und Südosteuropa 1919-1944*, Ferdinand Schöningh, Paderborn et al., p. 249-298.

Cavarnos, Constantine, 1992 [1971], *Orthodox Tradition and Modernism*, Center for Traditionalist Orthodox Studies, Etna, CA.

Cherney, Alexander, 1985, *The Latvian Orthodox Church*, Stylite Press, Welshpool.

Coriden, James A., 2000, *Canon Law as Ministry*, Paulist Press, New York/ Mahwah, N.J.

Cox, Lloyd, 2007, "Socialism", in George Ritzer (ed.), *The Blackwell Encyclopedia of Sociology*, Vol. 9, Blackwell, Malden, MA, p. 4549-4554.

Crols, Dirk, 2005, "Old and new minorities on the international chessboard", in David J. Smith (ed.), *The Baltic States and their Region – New Europe or Old?*, Rodopi, Amsterdam and New York, p. 185-209.

Crone, Patricia, 2003, *Pre-Industrial Societies – Anatomy of the Pre-Modern World*, 2nd ed., Oneworld Publications, Oxford.

Cunningham, James W., 1981, *A Vanquished Hope – The Movement for Church Renewal in Russia, 1905-1906*, St. Vladimir's Seminary Press, Crestwood, NY.

Delanty, Gerard, 2007, "Modernity", in George Ritzer (ed.), *The Blackwell Encyclopedia of Sociology*, Vol. 6, Blackwell, Malden, MA, p. 3068-3071.

Destivelle, Hyacinthe, 2006, *Le concile de Moscou (1917-1918)*, Cerf, Paris.

Dolbilov and Staliūnas, 2005 = Михаил Долбилов and Дариус Сталиунас, 2005, "'Обратная уния': Проект к присоединения католиков к православной церкви в Российской Империи (1865-1866 годы)" ['Reverse union': The project of uniting the Catholics with the Orthodox Church in the Russian Empire (1865-1866)], in *Славяноведение*, 14/5, p. 3-34.

Edge, Peter W., 2000, *Religion and Law – An Introduction*, Ashgate, Aldershot.

Einbund, Karl, 1934, "Pätsi elu" [Päts' life], in Karl Tupits (ed.), *K. Päts: Tema elu ja töö, kaaseglaste mälestus* [K. Päts: His Life and Work, Memories of Contemporaries], Ühiselu, Tallinn.

Eklof, Ben, John Bushnell, and Larissa Zakharova, 1994, *Russia's Great Reforms, 1855-1881*, Indiana University Press, Bloomington, IN.

Emhardt, William C. (ed.), 1929, *Religion in Soviet Russia*, Morehouse Publishing, Milwaukee, WI.

Engelstein, Laura, 2009, *Slavophile Empire: Imperial Russia's Illiberal Path*, Cornell University Press, Ithaca et al.

Fedorov, 2003 = Фёдоров, В. А., 2003, *Русская Православная Церковь и государства – Синодальная период, 1700-1917* [The Russian Orthodox Church and the State – The synodal period, 1700-1917], Русская панорама, Москва.

Feldmanis, Inesis, 1995, "Die lettische Historiographie", in Michael Garleff (ed.), *Zwischen Konfrontation und Kompromiss – Oldenburger Symposium: "Interethnische Beziehungen in Ostmitteleuropa als historiographisches Problem der 1930er/1940er Jahre"*, R. Oldenbourg, München, p. 133-138.

Feldmanis, Inesis, 2001, "Umgestaltungsprozesse im Rahmen des Ulmanis-Regimes in Lettland 1934-1940", in Erwin Oberländer (ed.), *Autoritäre Regime in Ostmittel- und Südosteuropa 1919-1944*, Ferdinand Schöningh, Paderborn et al., p. 215-248.

Finartijs, P., 1976, "Archibīskapa Jāņa Pommera 100 gadu dzimšanas atcerei" [The centenary of the birth of Archbishop Jānis Pommers], in *Universitas*, 37, p. 71-72.

Firsov, 2002 = Фирсов, Сергей, 2002, *Русская Церковь накануне перемен (конец 1890-х – 1918 гг.)* [The Russian Church at the Eve of Change (End of 1890s – 1918)], Круглый стол по религиозному образованию и диаконии, Москва.

Florovsky, Georges, 1979 [1937], *Ways of Russian Theology*, ed. by Richard S. Haugh, Transl. by Robert L. Nichols, Nordland Publishing Company, Belmont, MA.

Freeze, Gregory L., 1983, *The Parish Clergy in Nineteenth-Century Russia – Crisis, Reform, Counter-Reform*, Princeton University Press, Princeton, NJ.

Freeze, Gregory L., 2004, "Lutheranism in Russia: Critical Reassessment", in Hans Medick and Peer Schmidt (eds.), *Luther zwischen den Kulturen*, Vandenhoeck & Ruprecht, Göttingen, p. 297-317.

Fridolin, E., 1953, *Apostlik-Õigeusk Eestis* [Apostolic Orthodoxy in Estonia], Jumala Abiga, Los Angeles.

Frilander, Timo, 1995, "Valtiovalta, venäläiset ja kalenterikysymys 1917-1923" [The State, the Russians and the Calendar Question 1917-1923], in *Ortodoksia*, 44, p. 56-84.

Frilander, Timo, 1997, "Ajanlaskukysymys ja Suomen kansallistuva ortodoksinen kirkko 1923-1927" [The Calendar Question and the Nationalising Orthodox Church of Finland 1923-1927], in *Ortodoksia*, 46, p. 80-103.

Fülberth, Andreas, 2005, *Tallinn – Riga – Kaunas. Ihr Ausbau zu modernen Hauptstädten 1920-1940*, Böhlau Verlag, Köln et al..

Garleff, Michael, 1986, "Geschichtsschreibung der Neuzeit in den baltischen Provinzen, 1870-1918", in Georg von Rauch (ed.), 1986, *Geschichte der deutschbaltischen Geschichtsschreibung*, Böhlau Verlag, Köln et al., p. 233-271.

Garleff, Michael, 1996, "Erlebte und gedeutete Geschichte im Werk Edzard Schapers", in Frank-Lothar Kroll (ed.), *Wort und Dichtung als Zufluchtstätte in schwerer Zeit*, Gebr. Mann, Berlin, p. 123-133.

Garleff, Michael, 2001, *Die baltischen Länder*, Friedrich Pustet, Regensburg.

Garve, Horst, 1978, *Konfession und Nationalität – Ein Beitrag zum Verhältnis von Kirche und Gesellschaft in Livland im 19. Jahrhundert*, J. G. Herder-Institut, Marburg(Lahn).

Gavrilin, 1984 = Гаврилин, Александр В., 1984, "Некоторые вопросы крестьянского движения за переход в православие в 1841 году в Прибалтике в интерпретации апологетов православия" [Some questions on the peasant conversion movement to Orthodoxy in 1841 in the interpretation of the Orthodox apologetics], in *Latvijas agrārās vēstures jautājumi – Вопросы аграрной истории Латвии* [Questions of the agrarian history of Latvia], Latvijas Universitāte, Rīga, p. 126-144.

Gavrilin, 1988 = Гаврилин, Александр В., 1988, "Роль православного духовенства в переходе латышских и эстонских крестьян в православие в 1845-1849 гг." [The Role of the Orthodox Clergy in the Conversions of Latvian and Estonian Peasants, 1845-1848], in *Latvijas PSR Zinātņu Akadēmijas Vestis*, 11(496), p. 40-51.

Gavrilin, 1999 = Гаврилин, Александр В., 1999, *Очерки истории Рижской епархиию 19 век* [Historical Sketches of the Riga Eparchy - 19th Century], Filokalija, Rīga.

Gavrilin, 2006 = Гаврилин, Александр В., 2006, "Архиерейское управление на рубеже XIX-XX столетий: Его Преосвященство епископ Рижский и Митавский Агафангел (Преображенский)" [Episcopal governing at the turn of the 19th and 20th centuries: Bishop Agafangel of Riga and Mitava], in *Россия и Балтия – Человек в истории* [Russia and Baltia – Man in history], Наука, Москва, p. 117-133.

Gavriļins, Aleksandrs, 2008, "Padomju varas attieksme pret Latvijas Pareizticīgo Baznīcu 1940.-1941. gadā" [The Soviet authorities' attitude to the Latvian Orthodox Church 1940-1941], in *Latvijas Vēsture*, 2(70), p. 38-48.

Gavrilin, 2009 = Гаврилин, Александр В., 2009, *Под покровом Тихвинской иконы – Архипастырский путь Иоанна (Гарклавса)* [Under the cover of the Tikhvin icon – the pastoral path of Ioann (Garklavs)], Алаборг, Тихвин, СПб.

Gavrilin, Alexander and Baiba Pazāne, 2009, "L'Église orthodoxe au XXe siècle dans les pays baltes : Estonie, Lettonie et Lithuanie", in Christine Chaillot (ed.), *L'Église orthodoxe en Europe orientale au XXe siècle*, Cerf, Paris, p. 215-228.

Gellner, Ernest, 1983, *Nations and Nationalism*, Basil Blackwell, Oxford.

George, Jim, 1994, *Discourses of Global Politics: A Critical (Re)Introduction to International Relations*, Lynne Rienner, Boulder, CO.

Gherasim, Alexandru Gabriel, 2007, "Droits et statuts dans l'Église orthodoxe", in *Révue de droit canonique*, 57/1, p. 19-28.

Giesen, Bernhard, 1999, "Codes kollektiver Identität", in Werner Gephart and Hans Waldenfels (eds.), *Religion und Identität*, Suhrkamp, Frankfurt/Main, p. 13-43.

Golikov and Škarovskij, 2002 = Голиков, Андрей and Михаил Шкаровский, 2002, "Протоиерей Кирилл Зайц" [Archpriest Kirils Zaics], in *Санкт-Петербургские епархиальные ведомости*, 26-27, available at http://www.mitropolia-spb.ru/eparhialnie-smi/eparchialnie_vedomosti/26-27/txt/zaic.php [last accessed 15.03.2012].

Grichin, Kadi, 2003, "Riiklik poliitika Petserimaa usuelu korraldamises 1920.-1930. Aastatel" [State policy concerning the organisation of religious life in Petserimaa in the 1920s and 1930s], in *Õpetatud Eesti Seltsi aastaraamat, 2000-2001* [Yearbook of the Learned Estonian Society, 2000-2001], ÕES, Tartu, p. 167-182.

Gubonin, 1994 = Губонин, М. Е. (ed.), 1994, *Акты святейшего Тихона, Патриарха Московского и всея России* [The acts of the most holy Tikhon, Patriarch of Moscow and all Russia], Издательство Православного Свято-Тихоновского Богословского Института, Москва.

Hackmann, Jörg, 2005, "'Historians as Nation-builders'. Historiographie und Nation in Estland von Hans Kruus bis Mart Laar", in Markus Krzoska and Hans-Christian Maner (eds.), *Beruf und Berufung – Geschichtswissenschaft und Nationsbildung in Ostmittel- und Südosteuropa im 19. und 20. Jahrhundert*, LIT Verlag, Münster, p. 125-142.

Hackmann, Jörg, 2010, "Narrating the Building of a Small Nation: Divergence and Convergence in the Historiography of Estonian 'National Awakening', 1868-2005", in Stefan Berger and Chris Lorenz (eds.), *Nationalizing the Past – Historians as Nation Builders in Modern Europe*, Palgrave Macmillan, Houndmills, Basingstoke, p. 170-191.

Haltzel, Michael H., 1977, *Der Abbau der deutschen ständischen Selbstverwaltung in den Ostseeprovinzen Rußlands 1855-1905*, J. G. Herder-Institut, Marburg(Lahn).

Haltzel, Michael H., 1981, "The Baltic Germans", in Edward C. Thaden (ed.), *Russification in the Baltic Provinces and Finland, 1855-1914*, Princeton University Press, Princeton, NJ, p. 111-204.

von Harleß, Adolf, 1887, *Geschichtsbilder aus der lutherischen Kirche Livlands vom Jahre 1845 an*, Duncker und Humblot, Leipzig.

von Harnack, Adolf, 1901, *Das Wesen des Christentums*, Evangelische Verlagsanstalt, Berlin.

Hatlie, Mark R., 2005, "Crisis and Mass Conversion: Russian Orthodox Missions in Livonia 1841-1917", in István Keul (ed.), *Religion, Ethnie, Nation und die Aushandlung von Identität(en): regionale Religionsgeschichte in Ostmittel- und Südosteuropa*, Frank & Timme, Berlin, p. 115-145.

Hatlie, Mark R., 2009b, "Riga und der Erste Weltkrieg: Eine Exkursion", in *Nordostarchiv*, 27, p. 13-33.

von Hehn, Jürgen, 1984, *Die Umsiedlung der baltischen Deutschen – das letzte Kapitel baltisch-deutscher Geschichte*, J. G. Herder-Institut, Marburg (Lahn).

von Hehn, Jürgen, 1986, "Die deutschbaltische Geschichtsschreibung 1918-1939/45 in Lettland", in Georg von Rauch (ed.), 1986, *Geschichte der deutschbaltischen Geschichtsschreibung*, Böhlau Verlag, Köln et al., p. 371-398.

Heikkilä, Pauli, 2008, "The Pros and Cons of Paneurope – Estonian discussion on European unification in the interwar period", in *Acta Historica Tallinnensis*, 13, p. 68-91.

Heiler, Friedrich, 1971, *Die Ostkirchen*, Ernst Reinhard, München/Basel.

Helme, Rein, 1995, "Die estnische Historiographie", in Michael Garleff (ed.), *Zwischen Konfrontation und Kompromiss – Oldenburger Symposium: "Interethnische Beziehungen in Ostmitteleuropa als historiographisches Problem der 1930er/1940er Jahre"*, R. Oldenbourg, München, p. 139-154.

Heyer, Friedrich, 1958, "Die umgesiedelte Ikone – Eine Studie über die orthodoxe Kirche in Finnland", in *Kirche im Osten*, 1, p. 95-108.

Hiden, John, 2004, *Defender of Minorities – Paul Schiemann, 1876-1944*, Hurst & Company, London.

Hiden, John and Patrick Salmon, 1994, *The Baltic Nations and Europe. Estonia, Latvia and Lithuania in the Twentieth Century*, Longman, London and New York.

Hildermeier, Manfred, 2000, "Rußland oder Wie weit kam die Zivilgesellschaft?", in Manfred Hildermeier, Jürgen Kocka, and Christoph Conrad (eds.), *Europäische Zivilgesellschaft in Ost und West*, Campus Verlag, Frankfurt/Main, New York, p. 113-148.

von Hirschhausen, Ulrike, 2006, *Die Grenzen der Gemeinsamkeit. Deutsche, Letten, Russen und Juden in Riga 1860-1914*, Vandenhoeck & Ruprecht, Göttingen.

Hirvoja, Toomas and Merike Pau (eds.), 2002, *Õigeusu hingekarjased Eestimaal* [Orthodox Shepherds in Estonia], Püha Issidori Õigeusu Kirjastusselts, Tallinn.

Hitchins, Keith, 1992, "Historiography of the Countries of Eastern Europe: Romania", in *The American Historical Review*, 97/4, p. 1064-1083.

Hope, Nicholas, 1998, "Die Herrnhuter in Livland und Estland im 19. Jahrhundert", in Reinhard Staats and Siret Rutiku (eds.), *Estland, Lettland und westliches Christentum*, Wittig, Kiel, p. 133-152.

Hotz, Robert, SJ, 1979, "Die orthodoxe Kirche Finnlands auf dem Weg zur Unabhängigkeit", in *Der christliche Osten*, 34, p. 132-134.

Hroch, Miroslav, 1999, "Historical belles-lettres as a vehicle of the image of national history", in Michael Branch (ed.), *National History and Identity*, Finnish Literature Society, Helsinki, p. 97-108.

Infant'ev, 2001 = Б. Инфантьев, "Янис Лицис, его 'записки православного латыша' и 'летопись Адеркашской церкви'" [Jānis Līcis, his 'Writings of an Orthodox Latvian' and 'Chronicle of the Aderkasis Church'], in Александр В. Гаврилин (ed.), *Православие в Латвии: исторические очерки, том III* [The Orthodox in Latvia: Historical Studies, Vol. III], Filokalija, Rīga, p. 56-62.

Isakov, 2001 = Исаков, Сергей Г. (ed.), 2001, *Русское национальное меньшинство в Эстонской Республике (1918-1940)* [The Russian national minority in the Estonian Republic (1918-1940)], Kripta, Tartu and St. Petersburg.

Istina, 2004 = "Le plaidoyer de l'Église orthodoxe d'Estonia pour la défense de son autonomie face au Patriarcat de Moscou", in *Istina*, 49/1, p. 3-105.

Jääts, Indrek, 1998, "Setude etnilise identiteedi ajalugu" [The History of the Ethnic Identity of the *Setu*], in *Akadeemia*, 10/6(111), p. 1127-1153; 10/7(112), p. 1520-1546.

von Jannau, Heinrich Georg, 1927, *Die Anfänge der Konversion zur griechisch-orthodoxen Kirche in Südestland i. J. 1845-46*, ed. by Hans Kruus, K/Ü 'Loodus', Tartu.

Jansons, Jānis, 1940, "Kristus Latvijā un pie latviešiem" [Christ in Latvia and among the Latvians], in *Latvijas Pareizticīgais Teoloģijas Vēstnesis*, 2/1(2), p. 136-141.

Jensen, Anne, 1986, *Die Zukunft der Orthodoxie – Konzilspläne und Kirchenstrukturen*, Benziger Verlag, Zürich/Einsiedeln/Köln.

Jockwig, Franz, 1971, *Der Weg der Laien auf das Landeskonzil der Russischen Orthodoxen Kirche – Moskau 1917/18*, Augustinus-Verlag, Würzburg.

Johansons, Andrejs, 1987, "Die Lettländische Universität in Riga 1919-1940. Unter besonderer Berücksichtigung der philologisch-philosophischen Fächer", in Gert von Pistohlkors, Toivo U. Raun, and Paul Kaegbein (eds.), *Die Universitäten Dorpat/Tartu, Riga und Wilna/Vilnius 1579-1979*, Böhlau Verlag, Köln et al., p. 255-262.

John, Metropolitan of Finland, 1988, "The Finnish Orthodox Church", in Pedro Ramet (ed.), *Eastern Christianity and Politics in the Twentieth Century*, Duke University Press, Durham and London, p. 267-285.

Juhkam, Martin (ed.), 1961, *Eesti Apostlik Ortodoksne Kirik Eksiilis 1944-1960* [The Estonian Apostolic Orthodox Church in Exile 1944-1960], Culture Fund of the Estonian Apostolic Orthodox Church, Stockholm.

Jung, Matthias, 2006, "Diskurshistorische Analyse – eine linguistische Perspektive", in Reiner Keller, Andreas Hirseland, Werner Schneider and Willy Viehöver (eds.), *Handbuch Sozialwissenschaftliche Diskursanalyse, Band I: Theorien und Methoden*, Verlag für Sozialwissenschaften, Wiesbaden.

K voprosu, 1933 = *К вопросу о положении Православной Церкви в Эстонии* [To the Question of the Situation of the Orthodox Church in Estonia], Tallinn.

Kahle, Wilhelm, 1959, *Die Begegnung des baltischen Protestantismus mit der russisch-orthodoxen Kirche*, E. J. Brill, Leiden and Köln.

Kala, Tiina, 1998, "Old Livonia (c. 1200-1500) and Christianization", in Reinhard Staats and Siret Rutiku (eds.), *Estland, Lettland und westliches Christentum*, Wittig, Kiel, p. 57-74.

Kaljukosk, August (ed.), 1994, *Eesti apostliku-õigeusu kiriku päevastik, 1995*, Akadeemia Trükk, Tallinn.

Kalniņš I, 1993 = Kalniņš, Jānis (ed.), 1993, *Rīgas un visas Latvijas Arhibīskaps Jānis (Pommers) – Svētrunas, raksti un uzstāšanās, I* [The Archbishop of Riga and all Latvia Jānis (Pommers) – Preachings, articles and appearances, I], Labvēsts, Rīga.

Kalniņš II, 1993 = Kalniņš, Jānis (ed.), 1993, *Rīgas un visas Latvijas Arhibīskaps Jānis (Pommers) – Svētrunas, raksti un uzstāšanās, II* [The Archbishop of Riga and all Latvia Jānis (Pommers) – Preachings, articles and appearances, II], Labvēsts, Rīga.

Kalniņš, Jānis, 2001, *Svētais Rīgas Jānis* [Holy Jānis of Riga], Jumava, Rīga.

Kalniņš, Jānis, 2005a, *Mans ceļš pie Dieva* [My Road to God], 2nd ed., Rīga.

Kalniņš, Jānis, 2005b, "Pārdomas par grāmatu 'Metropolīts Augustīns Pētersons'" [Thoughts on the Book 'Metropolīts Augustīns Pētersons'], in *Latvijas Vēsture*, 2005/4(60), p. 113-116.

Kalniņš, Jānis, 2007, *Latvijas Pareizticīgā Baznīca – Vēstures komentārs* [The Latvian Orthodox Church – a historical commentary], San Estera, Rīga.

Kalniņš, Pēteris, 1930, "Krieviskās pareizticības cīņa ar luteriski latvisko" [The Fight of Russian Orthodoxy with Latvian Lutheranism], in *Izglītības Ministrijas Mēnešraksts*, 11/9, p. 172-189.

Karjahärm, Toomas (ed.), 1997, *Venestamine Eestis 1880-1917 – Dokumente ja materjale* [Russification in Estonia 1880-1917 – Documents and Materials], Tallinn.

Karjahärm, Toomas, 1998a, *Ida ja Lääne Vahel* [Between East and West], Eesti Entsüklopeediakirjastus, Tallinn.

Karjahärm, Toomas, 1998b, "Konfession und Nationalismus in Estland zu Beginn des 20. Jahrhunderts", in *Nordostarchiv*, 7/2, p. 533-553.

Karjahärm, Toomas and Väino Sirk, 2001, *Vaim ja võim – Eesti haritlaskond 1917-1940* [Power and Spirit – the Estonian Intelligentsia 1917-1940], Argo, Tallinn.

Kas õigeusk, 1911 = *Kas õigeusk lõhub Eesti rahvusliku ühistunnet?* [Does Orthodoxy divide Estonian national unity?], Otto Ramisch, Rīga.

Katerelos, Kyrillos, 2003, "Der Panorthodoxe Kongress von Konstantinopel im Jahre 1923", in Hartmut Zapp, Andreas Weiß, and Stefan Korta (eds.), *Ius canonicum in oriente et occidente: Festschrift für Carl Gerold Fürst zum 70. Geburtstag*, Peter Lang, Frankfurt/Main, p. 197-238.

Kehl, Medard, 2007, "Ekklesiologie", in *Lexikon für Theologie und Kirche*, Vol. 3, Herder, Freiburg, p. 568-573.

Keller, Reiner, Andreas Hirseland, Werner Schneider, and Willy Viehöver (eds.), 2006, *Handbuch Sozialwissenschaftliche Diskursanalyse, Band I: Theorien und Methoden*, Verlag für Sozialwissenschaften, Wiesbaden.

Kennedy, James C., 2008, "Religion, Nation and European Representations of the Past", in Stefan Berger and Chris Lorenz (eds.), *The Contested Nation – Ethnicity, Class, Religion and Gender in National Histories*, Palgrave Macmillan, Houndmills, Basingstoke, p. 104-134.

Ketola, Mikko, 1996, "Tallinnan ortodoksisen katedraalin purkuhanke vuonna 1928 – uskonnollista sortoa vai 'kansallista terapiaa'?" [The Plans to Tear Down the Tallinn Orthodox Cathedral in 1928 – Religious Oppression or 'National Therapy'?], in *Ortodoksia*, 45, p. 115-158.

Ketola, Mikko, 2000a, *The nationality question in the Estonian Evangelical Lutheran Church, 1918-1939*, Suomen Kirkkohistoriallinen Seura, Helsinki.

Ketola, Mikko, 2000b, "Eesti Evangeliumi Luteriusu Kirik 1939: Kriisiaasta" [The Estonian Lutheran Church in 1939: A year of crisis], in Riho Altnurme (ed.), 2000, *Johan Kõpp 125*, Tartu Ülikooli Kirjastus, Tartu, p. 71-85.

Kitromilides, Paschalis M., 1989, "'Imagined communities' and the origins of the national question in the Balkans", *European History Quarterly*, 19/2, p. 149-192; reprinted in Paschalis M. Kitromilides, 1994, *Enlightenment, Nationalism, Orthodoxy*, Variorum, Aldershot, Hampshire, text XI.

Kitromilides, Paschalis M., 2006, "The legacy of the French Revolution: Orthodoxy and nationalism", in Michael Angold (ed.), *The Cambridge History of Christianity*, Vol. 5, Cambridge University Press, Cambridge, p. 229-249.

Kitsikis, Dimitri, 1994, "Les anciens calendaristes depuis 1923 et la montée de l'intégrisme en Grèce", in *Cahiers d'études sur la Méditerranée orientale et le monde turco-iranien*, 17, p. 17-51.

Kiverik, Indrek, 2005, "Der politische Kampf um das Bildungswesen der Esten im 19. Jahrhundert", in Detlef Kühn (ed.), *Schulwesen im Baltikum*, Verlag Carl-Schirren-Ges., Lüneburg, p. 51-66.

Kivimäe, Sirje and Jüri Kivimäe, 1987, "Estnische Geschichtsforschung an der Universität Tartu 1920-1940. Ziele und Ergebnisse", in Gert von Pistohlkors, Toivo U. Raun, and Paul Kaegbein (eds.), *Die Universitäten Dorpat/Tartu, Riga und Wilna/Vilnius 1579-1979*, Böhlau Verlag, Köln et al., p. 277-292.

Kivimäe, Jüri and Sirje Kivimäe, 1995, "Hans Kruus und die deutsch-estnische Kontroverse", in Michael Garleff (ed.), *Zwischen Konfrontation und Kompromiss – Oldenburger Symposium: "Interethnische Beziehungen in Ostmitteleuropa als historiographisches Problem der 1930er/1940er Jahre"*, R. Oldenbourg, München, p. 155-170.

Klinke, Lambert, 2000a, *Erzbischof Eduard Profittlich und die katholische Kirche in Estland 1930-1942*, Gerhard Hess, Ulm.

Klinke, Lambert, 2000b, "Katoliku Kirik Eestis – 1918-1998" [The Catholic Church in Estonia – 1918-1998], in *Akadeemia*, 12/4, p. 862-881.

Klueting, Harm, 2007, "Confessionalization", in *Religion Past and Present, Vol. 3*, Brill, Leiden/Boston, p. 391-392.

Knöbl, Wolfgang, 2001, *Spielräume der Modernisierung – Das Ende der Eindeutigkeit*, Velbrück, Weilerswist.

Kocka, Jürgen, 2007, "Civil Society in Nineteenth-Century Europe: Comparison and Beyond", in Manfred Hildermeier (ed.), *Historical Concepts between Eastern and Western Europe*, Berghahn Books, New York and Oxford, p. 85-100.

Kolarz, Walter, 1962, *Religion in the Soviet Union*, Macmillan & Co. Ltd., London.

Kostjuk, Konstantin, 2005, *Der Begriff des Politischen in der russisch-orthodoxen Tradition*, Ferdinand Schöningh, Paderborn et al..

Koukkunen, Heikki, 1982, *Tuiskua ja tyventä – Suomen ortodoksisen kirkko 1918-1978* [Whirling and Grinding – the Orthodox Church of Finland 1918-1978], Valamon luostari, Heinävesi.

Kroeger, Gert, 1956, "Die evangelisch-lutherische Landeskirche und das griechisch-orthodoxe Staatskirchentum in den Ostseeprovinzen 1840–1918", in Reinhard Wittram (ed.), *Baltische Kirchengeschichte*, Vandenhoeck & Ruprecht, Göttingen, p. 177-206.

Kruus, Hans, 1927a, *Eesti ajalugu kõige uuemal ajal, I – Eesti rahvusliku ärkamiseni* [Estonian History of the Most Recent Times, I – until the Estonian National Awakening], K/Ü 'Loodus', Tartu.

Kruus, Hans, 1927b, "Der Beginn des Übertritts des südestnischen Landbevölkerung zur griechisch-orthodoxen Kirche i. J. 1845", editor's introduction to Heinrich Georg von Jannau, 1927, *Die Anfänge der Konversion zur griechisch-orthodoxen Kirche in Südestland i. J. 1845-46*, ed. by Hans Kruus, K/Ü 'Loodus', Tartu.

Kruus, Hans, 1928, *Eesti ajalugu kõige uuemal ajal, II* [Estonian History of the Most Recent Times, II], K/Ü 'Loodus', Tartu.

Kruus, Hans, 1936, "Liivimaa õigeusuliste talupoegade rekonversiooni-liikumine 1860-ndail aastail uurimisülesandena" [The reconversion movement of the 1860s as a research topic], in *Ajalooline Ajakiri*, 15/3-4, p. 180-184.

Kruus, Hans, 1930, *Talurahva käärimine Lõuna-Eestis XIX sajandi 40-ndail aastail* [The peasant unrest of the 40s of the nineteenth century in South Estonia], EKS Kirjastus, Tartu.

Kryžanovskij, 1884 = Крыжановский, Евфимий Михаилович, 1884, *Остзейскій вопросъ и Православіе* [The Baltic question and the Orthodox], СПб.

Krzoska, Markus and Hans-Christian Maner, 2005, "Einleitung" in Markus Krzoska and Hans-Christian Maner (eds.), *Beruf und Berufung – Geschichtswissenschaft und Nationsbildung in Ostmittel- und Südosteuropa im 19. und 20. Jahrhundert*, LIT Verlag, Münster, p. 7-17.

Kūla, Andris, 2007, "Metropolīts Sergijs un Pareizticīgo baznīca nacistu okupētajā Latvijā (1941-1944)" [Metropolitan Sergey and the Orthodox Church in Nazi-occupied Latvia], in *Latvijas Vēsture 20. gadsimta 40.-90. gados* [Latvian History from the 1940s to the 1990s], Latvijas Vēstures Institūts, Rīga, p. 172-215.

Kulis, 1993 = Кулис, А. [Andris Kūla], 1993, "К вопросу об автокефалии латвийской православной церкви в 30-х годах XX века" [The question of Autocephaly in the Latvian Orthodox Church in the 1930s], in Александр В. Гаврилин (ed.), *Православие в Латвии: исторические очерки, том I* [The Orthodox in Latvia: Historical Studies, Vol. I], Filokalija, Rīga.

Kumyš, 1999 = Кумыш, Владислав, 1999, *Жизнеописание священномученика Платона, епископ Ревельского* [Biography of the Holy Martyr Platon, Bishop of Tallinn], Журнал "Нева", СПб.

Laaman, Eduard, 1949 [1940], *Konstantin Päts: poliitika- ja riigimees* [Konstantin Päts: a man of politics and state], Vaba Eesti kirjastus, Stockholm.

Laaman, Eduard, 1998 [1935], *Jaan Poska – Eesti riigitegelase elukäik* [Jaan Poska – the career of an Estonian statesman], 3rd ed., Eesti Kirjanduse Selts, Tartu.

Lääne, Margus, 2009, "Aleksander Nevski katedraali lugu" [The Aleksander Nevskij Cathedral story], in *Tuna*, 12/2, p. 148-156.

Laar, Anton, 1917, *Eesti õigeusuliste tegelaste üleüldine nõupidamine Tallinnas, 6. ja 7. aprill, 1917* [The General Consultation of Estonian Orthodox Actors in Tallinn, 6 and 7 April 1917], K. Sööt & G. Roht, Tartu.

Laatsi, Theophil, 1966, "Die estnische orthodoxe Kirche in der Heimat und im Exil", in *Acta Baltica*, 6, p. 63-73.

Larikka, Arhm. Andreas, 2004, "Põhjamaade kirik: Soome ja Baltimaade õige-
    usu kirikute koostöö maailmasõdade vahelisel perioodil" [The Northern
    Churches: Interwar Co-Operation between the Finnish and Baltic
    Orthodox Churches], in *Usk ja Elu*, 34/1, p. 4-7.
Latvijas Pareizticīgā baznīca, 2009 = *Latvijas Pareizticīgā baznīca. 1988.-2008.
    gads.* [The Latvian Orthodox Church 1988-2008], Latvijas Pareizticīgas
    Baznīcas Sinodes Izdevums, Rīga.
Laukaitytė, Regina, 2003, *Stačiatikių Bažnyčia Lietuvoje XX amžiuje* [The
    Orthodox Church in Lithuania in the 20th century], Lietuvos istorijos
    institutas, Vilnius.
Lauluraamat, 2003 = *Apostlik-õigeusu lauluraamat* [Orthodox Hymnal], EAÕK
    Kirjastustoimkond, Tallinn.
Laur, Mati, 2007, "Die Russenzeit und das Petersburger Imperium in der estni-
    schen Geschichtsschreibung seit 1918", in Frank Hadler and Matthias
    Mesenhöller (eds.), *Vergangene Größe und Ohnmacht in Ostmittel-
    europa: Repräsentationen imperialer Erfahrung in der Historiographie
    seit 1918*, Akademische Verlagsanstalt, p. 301-309.
Leerssen, Joop, 2008, "Nation and Ethnicity", in Stefan Berger and Chris
    Lorenz (eds.), *The Contested Nation – Ethnicity, Class, Religion and
    Gender in National Histories*, Palgrave Macmillan, Houndmills, Basing-
    stoke, p. 75-103.
Lehmann, Hartmut, 2002, "Die Säkularisierung der Religion und die Sakralisie-
    rung der Nation im 20. Jahrhundert: Varianten einer komplementären
    Relation", in Hans-Christian Maner and Martin Schulze Wessel (eds.),
    Religion und Nationalstaat zwischen den Weltkriegen – 1918-1939, Franz
    Steiner, Stuttgart, p. 13-27.
Leismann, Nikolai, 1929, "Kirjandus ap.-õigeusu ajaloo kohta Baltimaal" [Lite-
    rature concerning the history of Orthodoxy in the Baltic Countries], in
    Usuteadusline Ajakiri, 3/3-4, p. 129-134.
Lenz, Wilhelm, 1986, "'Alt-Livland' in der deutschbaltischen Geschichts-
    schreibung 1870-1918", in Georg von Rauch (ed.), 1986, *Geschichte der
    deutschbaltischen Geschichtsschreibung*, Böhlau Verlag, Köln et al., p.
    203-232.
Lorenz, Chris, 2008, "Representations of Identity: Ethnicity, Race, Class, Gen-
    der and Religion. An Introduction to Conceptual History" in Stefan Ber-
    ger and Chris Lorenz (eds.), *The Contested Nation – Ethnicity, Class,
    Religion and Gender in National Histories*, Palgrave Macmillan, Hound-
    mills, Basingstoke, p. 24-59.
Lõuna, Kalle, 1999, "Usuküsimus Petserimaal 1920.-30. aastatel ja *kloostri-
    sõda*" [The religious question in Petserimaa in the 1920s and 1930s and
    the *Monastery War*], in *Ajaloline Ajakiri*, 3-4(106-107), p. 57-69.

Lõuna, Kalle, 2003, *Petserimaa integreerimine Eesti Vabariigi 1920-1940* [The integration of Petserimaa into the Estonian Republic 1920-1940], Eesti Entsüklopeediakirjastus, Tallinn.

Lukaševičs, Valentins, 1996, "Latgaliešu vēstures lappuses" [Pages from the history of the Latgalians], in Josifs Šteimanis (ed.), *Latgale un Daugavpils: vēsture un kultūra* [Latgale and Daugavpils: history and culture], Multinacionālas kultūras centrs, Daugavpils, p. 22-26.

Makrides, Vasilios N., 2005, "Orthodox Christianity, Rationalization, Modernization: A Reassessment", in Victor Roudometof, Alexander Agadjanian and Jerry Pankhurst (eds.), *Eastern Orthodoxy in a Global Age – Tradition Faces the Twenty-first Century*, Altamira Press, Walnut Creek et al, p. 179-208.

Makrides, Vasilios N., 2011, "Orthodoxes Christentum und Moderne – Inkompatibilität oder langfristige Anpassung?", in *Una Sancta*, 66/1, p. 15-30.

Manchester, Laurie, 2008, *Holy Fathers, Secular Sons: Clergy, Intelligentsia and the Modern Self in Revolutionary Russia*, Northern Illinois University Press, DeKalb.

Marcinkevičius, Andrius and Saulius Kaubrys, 2003, *Lietuvos Stačiatikių Bažnyčia 1918-1940 m.* [Die orthodoxe Kirche in Litauen 1918-1940], VAGA, Vilnius.

Martinson, Vassili (ed.), 1931, *Idamaa õigeusu ja anglikaani kiriku ühinemisest* [The unification of the Eastern Orthodox and the Anglican Churches], M. Hermann, Tartu.

Maximos of Sardes, 1980 [1972], *Das ökumenische Patriarchat in der orthodoxen Kirche*, 1st German ed., Herder, Freiburg.

Mazower, Mark, 1997, "Minorities and the League of Nations in Interwar Europe", in *Daedalus*, 126/2, p. 47-63.

Memorandum, 1932 = *Меморандум митрополиту Александру* [Memorandum to Metropolitan Aleksander], Põhja-Eesti Trükk, Tallinn.

Meyendorff, John, 1984, *Marriage: An Orthodox perspective*, St. Vladimir's Seminary Press, Crestwood, NY.

Meyendorff, John, 1996 [1960], *The Orthodox Church – Its Past and Its Role in the World Today*, 4th rev. ed., St. Vladimir's Seminary Press, Crestwood, NY.

Millas, Hercules, 2008, "History Writing among the Greeks and Turks: Imagining the Self and the Other", in Stefan Berger and Chris Lorenz (eds.), *The Contested Nation – Ethnicity, Class, Religion and Gender in National Histories*, Palgrave Macmillan, Houndmills, Basingstoke, p. 490-511.

Mironowicz, Antoni, 2005, *Kościół prawosławny na ziemiach polskich w XIX i XX wieku* [The Orthodox Church in the Polish lands in the 19th and 20th centuries], Wydawnictwo Uniwersytetu w Białymstoku, Białystok.

Mironowicz, Antoni, Urszula Pawluczuk, and Piotr Chomik (eds.), 2005, *Autokefalie Kościoła prawosławnego w Polsce* [The Autocephaly of the Polish Orthodox Church], Wydawnictwo Uniwersytetu w Białymstoku, Białystok.

Mojzeš, Marcel, 2005, *Il movimento liturgico nelle chiese bizantine: analisi di alcune tendenze di riforma nel XX secolo* [The Liturgical Movement in the Byzantine Church: an analysis of some tendencies of reform in the twentieth century], CLV, Ed. Liturgiche, Roma.

von zur Mühlen, Heinz, 1986, "Die deutschbaltische Geschichtsschreibung 1918 -1939/45 in Estland", in Georg von Rauch (ed.), 1986, *Geschichte der deutschbaltischen Geschichtsschreibung*, Böhlau Verlag, Köln et al., p. 339-369.

Neander, Irene, 1986, "Carl Schirren als Historiker", in Georg von Rauch (ed.), 1986, *Geschichte der deutschbaltischen Geschichtsschreibung*, Böhlau Verlag, Köln et al., p. 175-202.

Neo-Sil'vestr, 1971 = Нео-Сильвестр [Генрих Гроссен], 1971, *На буреломе* [At Windbreaks], Поссев, Frankfurt/Main.

Nokelainen, Mika, 2010, *Vähemistövaltiokirkon synty* [The Birth of a Minority State Church], Suomen Kirkkohistoriallinen Seura, Helsinki.

Nyssen, Wilhelm, Hans-Joachim Schulz, and Paul Wiertz (eds.), 1984, *Handbuch der Ostkirchenkunde, Band 1*, Patmos Verlag, Düsseldorf.

Oberländer, Erwin, 2001, "Die Präsidialdiktaturen in Ostmitteleuropa – 'Gelenkte Demokratie'?", in Erwin Oberländer (ed.), *Autoritäre Regime in Ostmittel- und Südosteuropa 1919-1944*, Ferdinand Schöningh, Paderborn et al., p. 3-17.

Oboznyj, 2008 = Обозный, Константин Петрович, 2008, *История Псковской православной миссии: 1941-1944 гг.* [The History of the Pskov Orthodox Mission: 1941-1944], Крутицкое Патриаршее Подворье Общество Любителей Церковной Истории, Москва.

Ohme, Heinz, 2007, *Das Ökumenische Patriarchat von Konstantinopel und die türkische Religionspolitik*, Universität Erfurt, Erfurt.

Ozoliņš, K., 1997, "Положение Латвийской Православной Церкви в 20-е годы XX века" [The situation of the Latvian Orthodox Church in the 1920s], in Александр В. Гаврилин (ed.), *Православие в Латвии: исторические очерки, том II* [The Orthodox in Latvia: Historical Studies, Vol. II], Filokalija, Rīga, p. 13-29.

Paavel, Joann, 1934, "Õppeaastad Riia vaimulikus seminaris" [The Education Years in the Riga Orthodox Seminary], in Karl Tupits (ed.), *K. Päts: Tema elu ja töö, kaasaeglaste mälestus* [K. Päts: His Life and Work, Memories of Contemporaries], Ühiselu, Tallinn, p. 27-33.

Pajur, Ago, 2001, "Die 'Legitimierung' der Diktatur des Präsidenten Päts und die öffentliche Meinung in Estland", in Erwin Oberländer (ed.), *Autoritäre Regime in Ostmittel- und Südosteuropa 1919-1944*, Ferdinand Schöningh, Paderborn et al., p. 163-213.

Pajur, Ago, 2009, "Der Ausbruch des Landeswehrkriegs. Die estnische Perspektive", in Mati Laur and Karsten Brüggemann (ed.), *Forschungen zur baltischen Geschichte, Band 4*, p. 145-169.

Papathomas, Grigorios D. and Matthias H. Palli (eds.), 2002, *The Autonomous Orthodox Church of Estonia*, Éditions Épektasis, Katérini.

Papierzyńska-Turek, Mirosława, 1989, *Między tradycją a rzeczywistością. Państwo wobec prawosławia 1918–1939* [Between Tradition and Reality. The State and Orthodoxy 1918-1939], Państwowe Wydawnictwo Naukowe, Warszawa.

Papierzyńska-Turek, Mirosława, 2005, "Historyczne uwarunkowania ogłoszenia autokefalii Kościoła prawosławnego w Polsce w 1925 r." [The historical circumstances leading to the autocephaly of the Polish Orthodox Church in 1925], in Antoni Mironowicz, Urszula Pawluczuk, and Piotr Chomik (eds.), *Autokefalie Kościoła prawosławnego w Polsce* [The Autocephaly of the Polish Orthodox Church], Wydawnictwo Uniwersytetu w Białymstoku, Białystok, p. 151-164.

Parming, Tönu, 1981, "The Pattern of Participation of the Estonian Communist Party in National Politics, 1918-1940", in *The Slavonic and East European Review*, 59/3, p. 397-412.

Patsavos, Lewis, 1975, *The Canonical Tradition of the Orthodox Church*, available at http://www.goarch.org/ourfaith/ourfaith7071 [last accessed 15.03.2012].

Pazāne, 2008 = Пазане, Баиба, 2008, "Клир латышских православных приходов в Видземе в 20-30-е годы XX века" [The clergy of the Latvian Orthodox parishes of Vidzeme in the 1920s and 1930s], in Александр В. Гаврилин (ed.), *Православие в Латвии: исторические очерки, том VII* [The Orthodox in Latvia: Historical Studies, Vol. VII], Filokalija, Rīga, p. 33-62.

Pispala, Elisa, 1978, "Suomen ortodoksisen Kirkkon itsenäistyminen" [The Finnish Orthodox Church becoming independent], in *Ortodoksia*, 27, p. 69-79.

Plaat, Jaanus, 2001, *Usuliikumised, kirikud ja vabakogudused Lääne- ja Hiiumaal* [Religious Movements, Churches and Free Congregations in Lääne- and Hiiumaa], Eesti Rahva Muuseumi Sari, Tartu.

Plakans, Andrejs, 1995, *The Latvians – A Short History*, Hoover Institution Press, Stanford, CA.

318　　　　　　　　　　　　　Bibliography

Plakans, Andrejs, 1999, "Looking Backward: the Eighteenth and Nineteenth Centuries in Inter-War Latvian Historiography", in *Journal of Baltic Studies*, 30/4, p. 293-306.

Plank, Peter, 2007, "Der Ökumenische Patriarch Meletios IV. (1921-1923) und die orthodoxe Diaspora", in *Orthodoxes Forum*, 21, p. 251-269.

Plasseraud, Yves, 2003, *Les États Baltiques – les sociétés gigognes*, Armeline, Crozon.

Pljuchanov, 1993 = Плюханов, Борис В., 1993, *Р.С.Х.Д. в Латвии и Естонии* [The RSKhD in Latvia and Estonia], YMCA-Press, Paris.

Polunov, 1996 = Полунов, Александр Юрьевич, 1996, *Под властью обер-прокурора: Государство и церковь в эпоху Александра III* [Under the Power of the Oberprocuror: State and Church in the Epoch of Aleksander III], Серия "Первая Монография", Москва.

Pommers, Antonijs, 1930, *Latvijas vēsture – Vidusskolas kurss* [Latvian History – for secondary schools], Valters un Rapa, Rīga.

Pommers, Antonijs, 1931a, *Pareizticība Latvijā – Vēstures apcerējumi* [Orthodoxy in Latvia – historical sketches], Autora izdevums, Rīga.

Pommers, Antonijs, 1931b, *Православие в Латвии – исторические очерки* [The Orthodox in Latvia – historical sketches], изд. автора, Rīga.

Pommers, Antonijs, 1940, "Pareizticība biskapa katedras nodibināšana Rīgā 1836. gadā" [The Establishment of an Orthodox Episcopal See in Riga in 1836], in *Latvijas Pareizticīgais Teoloģijas Vēstnesis*, 2/1(2), p. 99-111.

Ponomareva, Galina, 2006, *Eesti vanausulised – väike kirikuloo teatmik = Староверы Эстонии = The Old Believers of Estonia*, Eesti Vanausuliste Kultuuri- ja Arendusühing, Tartu.

Poska, Jüri, 1968, *The Martyrdom of Bishop Platon*, Culture Fond of the Estonian Apostolic Orthodox Church, Stockholm.

Pospielovsky, Dmitry, 1984, *The Russian Orthodox Church under the Soviet Regime 1917-1982. Volume I*, St. Vladimir's Seminary Press, Crestwood, NY.

Požidaev, 2004 = (Пожидаев), Игумен Феофан, 2004, *Священномученик Иоанн, Архиепископ Рижский* [The Holy Martyr Ioann, Archbishop of Riga], Riga.

Pravoslavie, 1911 = *Православие и Лютеранство в Прибалтийском крае по новейшим данным русской периодической печати* [The most recent facts about the Orthodox and Lutheranism in the Baltic Provinces in the Russian periodical press], Государственная Типография, СПб.

Pravoslavie, 2010 = *Православие в Эстонии, I и II* [The Orthodox in Estonia, I and II], ЦНЦ Православная энциклопедия, Москва.

Prekup, 1998 = Прекуп, Игорь, 1998, *Православие в Эстонии* [The Orthodox in Estonia], Trükis, Tartu.

Purmonen, Veikko, 1984, *Orthodoxy in Finland – Past and Present*, Orthodox Clergy Association, Kuopio.

Purmonen, Veikko, 1986, *Arkkipiispa Hermanin elämä – Ortodoksisen kirkon vaiheita Virossa ja Suomessa* [The Life of Archbishop Hermann – The Orthodox Church between Estonia and Finland], Ortodoksisten Pappien Liitto, Pieksämäki.

Purviņš, Kārlis, 1929, *Pirmās pareizticīgo Latviešu draudzes vēsture* [The History of the First Latvian Orthodox Congregation], Rīgas debessbraukšanas draudzes izdevums, Rīga.

Raag, Nikolai, 1938, "Petserimaa kogudused" [The parishes of Petserimaa], in *Usuteadusline Ajakiri*, 10/1, p. 24-35.

Raivo, Petri J., 1997, "The limits of tolerance: the Orthodox milieu as an element in the Finnish cultural landscape, 1917-1939", in *Journal of Historical Geography*, 23/3, p. 327-339.

Ramet, Pedro (ed.), 1988, *Eastern Christianity and Politics in the Twentieth Century*, Duke University Press, Durham and London.

von Rauch, Georg, 1977, *Geschichte der baltischen Staaten*, 2nd revised ed., dtv, München.

von Rauch, Georg (ed.), 1986, *Geschichte der deutschbaltischen Geschichtsschreibung*, Böhlau Verlag, Köln et al.

Raudkepp, L., 1934, "K. Päts usu ja kiriku kaitsjana." [K. Päts as defender of faith and church], in Karl Tupits (ed.), *K. Päts: Tema elu ja töö, kaasaeglaste mälestus* [K. Päts: His life and work, memories of contemporaries], Ühiselu, Tallinn, p. 365-368.

Raudsepp, Anu, 1998a, *Riia Vaimulik Seminar 1846-1918* [The Orthodox Seminary of Riga 1846-1918], Eesti Kirjandusmuuseum, Tartu.

Raudsepp, Anu, 1998b, "Das Rigaer Geistliche Seminar (1846-1918)", in *Nordostarchiv*, 7/2, p. 497-532.

Raun, Toivo U., 1991, "The Petseri Region of the Republic of Estonia", in *Jahrbücher für die Geschichte Osteuropas*, 39/4, p. 514-532.

Raun, Toivo U., 2001 [1987], *Estonia and the Estonians* [Studies of Nationalities], 2nd updated ed., Hoover Institution Press, Stanford, CA.

Raun, Toivo U. and Andrejs Plakans, 1990, "The Estonian and Latvian National Movements: an Assessment of Miroslav Hroch's Model", in *Journal of Baltic Studies*, 21, p. 131-144.

Rebane, Leida, 1932, "Osav üleskutse vene-õigeusu propageerimiseks 1882. a." [A cunning call to propagate Russian Orthodoxy from 1882], in *Ajalooline Ajakiri*, 11/4, p. 222-228.

Rebane, Leida, 1933, "Usuvahetuslik liikumine Läänemaal aa. 1883-1885" [The conversion movement in Läänemaa (West County) 1883-1885], in *Ajalooline Ajakiri*, 12/2, p. 79-93; 12/3, p. 129-147; 12/4, p. 195-206.

Reckwitz, Andreas, 2008, "Moderne. Der Kampf um die Öffnung und Schlie-ßung von Kontingenten", in Stephan Moebius and Andreas Reckwitz (eds.), *Poststrukturalistische Sozialwissenschaften*, Suhrkamp, Frankfurt/Main, p. 226-244.

Requate, Jörg, 1999, "Öffentlichkeit und Medien als Gegenstand historischer Analyse", in *Geschichte und Gesellschaft*, 25/1, p. 5-32.

Riikonen, Juha, 2007, *Kirkko politiikan syleilyssä – Suomen ortodoksisen arkki-piispakunnan ja Moskovan patriarkaatin välinen kanoninen erimielisyys, 1945-1957* [Church in the Embrace of Politics – The Canonical Controversy between the Finnish Orthodox Church and the Moscow Patriarchate, 1945-1957], University of Joensuu publications in Theology, Joensuu.

Rimestad, Sebastian, 2009, "Co-Operation and Mutual Perceptions Amongst the Orthodox Churches in the Baltic Region (1917-1940)", in Kari Alenius, Anita Honkala and, Sinikka Wunsch (eds.), *Itämeren itälaidalla II* [On the Eastern edge of the Baltic Sea II], Societas Historica Finlandiae Septentrionalis, Rovaniemi, p. 137-143.

Rimestad, Sebastian, 2011, "Die Russische Orthodox Kirche in den Ostseeprovinzen und in den Nordwestprovinzen im Vergleich", in Markus Krzoska (ed.), *Zwischen Glaube und Nation?*, Martin Meidenbauer, München, p. 71-85.

Rimestad, Sebastian, forthcoming (2013a), "The two Orthodox Churches of Estonia", in Alfons Bruening and Sebastian Rimestad (eds.), *Orthodox Christianity in Europe – Borders Constructed and Deconstructed*, Peeters, Leuven.

Rimestad, Sebastian, forthcoming (2013b), "Orthodox Churches in Estonia", in Lucian Leustean (ed.), *Eastern Christianity and Politics in the Twenty-First Century*, Routledge, Abingdon/Oxon.

Rimskij, 1998 = Римский, С. В., 1998, "Конфессиональная политика России в Западном крае и Прибалтике XIX столетия" [Russian Confessional Politics in the Western and Baltic Provinces in the 19th Century], in *Вопросы Истории*, 3, p. 25-45.

Ringvee, Ringo, 2008, "State, Religion and the Legal Framework in Estonia", in *Religion, State & Society*, 36/2, p. 181-196.

Risch, Helmut, 1937, "Die estnische apostolisch-rechtgläubige Kirche", in *Kyrios*, 2, p. 113-142.

Rosenberg, Tiit, 2000, "Johann Kõpp ajaloolasena" [Johan Kõpp as historian], in Riho Altnurme (ed.), *Johan Kõpp 125*, Tartu Ülikooli Kirjastus, Tartu, p. 43-57.

Rosenberg, Tiit, 2005, "Die russische baltische Historiographie in der zweiten Hälfte des 19. und zu Beginn des 20. Jahrhunderts", in Olaf Mertelsmann (ed.), *Estland und Russland – Aspekte der Beziehungen zweier Länder*, Verlag Dr. Kovač, Hamburg, p. 77-108.

Runciman, Steven, 1968, *The Great Church in Captivity*, Cambridge University Press, Cambridge.

Saard, Riho, 2007a, "Eestlane ja luterlus" [The Estonian and Lutheranism], in *Akadeemia*, 19/6, p. 1238-1268; 19/7, p. 1424-1451.

Saard, Riho, 2007b, "Eestlane luterluse ja õigeusu vahel" [The Estonian between Lutheranism and Orthodoxy], in *Usk ja Elu*, 37/4, p. 117-134.

Saard, Riho, 2008, "Eesti Apostlik-Õigeusu Kiriku algusaastad" [The first years of the Estonian Apostolic Orthodox Church], in *Akadeemia*, 20/7, p. 1543-1582.

Samarin, 1869 = Самарин, Юрий Ф., 1869, *Окрайны России – сер. 1, вып. 2* [The Russian Borderlands – Vol. 1, No. 2], B. Behr, Berlin.

Samarin, Jurij, 1996, *Das russisch-baltische Küstenland im gegenwärtigen Augenblick* [Reprint of the Leipzig 1869-edition, translated by Julius Eckardt], ed. by Frank Kämpfer and Lothar Maier, LIT Verlag, Münster.

Sanders, Thomas, 1999, "Introduction: 'A Most Narrow Present'", in Thomas Sanders (ed.), *Historiography of Imperial Russia: the Profession and Writing of History in a Multinational State*, Sharpe, Armonk, NY, p. 3-14.

Schabert, D. Oskar, 1932, *Die Dorpatschen Märtyrer der orthodoxen Kirche vom Jahr 1919*, Verlag O. Schabert, Riga.

Schaper, Edzard, 1953 [1935], *Die sterbende Kirche*, Fischer, Frankfurt/Main.

Schaper, Edzard, 1963, *Der Aufruhr des Gerechten*, Jakob Hegner, Köln.

Scheidegger, Gabriele, 1999, *Endzeit – Russland am Ende des 17. Jahrhunderts*, Peter Lang, Bern.

Schmemann, Alexander, 1992 [1963], *Historical Road of Eastern Orthodoxy*, 2nd revised ed., St. Vladimir's Seminary Press, Crestwood, NY.

von Schrenck, Erich, 1933, *Baltische Kirchengeschichte der Neuzeit*, Ernst Plate, Riga [Reprint 1988, Harro von Hirschheydt, Hannover].

Schubart, Walter, 1940, "Die orthodoxe Kirche des Ostens in Lettland. 1919-1939", in *Kyrios*, 4, p. 151-155.

Schulz, Günter, 1995, *Das Landeskonzil der Orthodoxen Kirche in Rußland 1917/18 – ein unbekanntes Reformpotential*, Vandenhoeck & Ruprecht, Göttingen.

Schulz, Günter, Gisela-A. Schröder, and Timm C. Richter, 2005, *Bolschewistische Herrschaft und Orthodoxe Kirche in Rußland – Das Landeskonzil 1917/1918*, LIT Verlag, Münster.

Seligman, Adam B., 2000, *Modernity's Wager – Authority, the Self and Transcendence*, Princeton University Press, Princeton, NJ.

Setälä, U.V.J., 1962, "Viron apostolisen oikeauskoisen kirkon syntyvaiheita" [The birth moment of the Estonian Orthodox Church], in *Ortodoksia*, 13, p. 50-77.

Setälä, U.V.J., 1966, *Kansallisen ortodoksisen kirkkokunnan perustamiskysymys Suomen politiikassa, 1917-1925* [The Question of the Establishment of a National Orthodox Community in Finnish Politics, 1917-1925], Söderström, Helsinki.

Setälä, U.V.J., 1972, "Põhjala kirik – Kalevipoja sild 1919-1922" [The Northern Church – The *Kalevipoeg* bridge 1919-1922], in *Usk ja Elu*, 3-4, p. 6-12.

Sidjakov I, 2008 = Сидяков, Юрий Львович (ed.), 2008, *Из архива св. священномученика архиепископа Рижского и Латвийского Иоанна (Поммера) – Письма и другие документы, I* [From the Archive of Holy Martyr Ioann (Pommer), Archbishop of Riga and Latvia – Letters and other documents, I], Rīga.

Sidjakov II, 2010 = Сидяков, Юрий Львович (ed.), 2010, *Из архива св. священномученика архиепископа Рижского и Латвийского Иоанна (Поммера) – Письма и другие документы, II* [From the Archive of Holy Martyr Ioann (Pommer), Archbishop of Riga and Latvia – Letters and other documents, II], Rīga.

Sidjakov III, 2011 = Сидяков, Юрий Львович (ed.), 2011, *Из архива св. священномученика архиепископа Рижского и Латвийского Иоанна (Поммера) – Письма и другие документы, III* [From the Archive of Holy Martyr Ioann (Pommer), Archbishop of Riga and Latvia – Letters and other documents, III], Rīga.

Sild, Olaf, 1938, "Eesti kirikulugu vanimast ajast olevikuni" [Estonian church history from ancient times until today], in Vello Salu (ed.), 1995, *Lühike Eesti Kirikulugu* [Short Estonian Church History], Tartu.

Simon, Gerhard, 1969, *Konstantin Petrović Pobedonoscev und die Kirchenpolitik des Heiligen Sinod 1880-1905*, Vandenhoeck & Ruprecht, Göttingen.

Slesarev, 2009 = Слесарев, А. В., 2009, *Старостильный раскол в истории православной церкви (1924-2008)* [The Calendarist Schism in the History of the Orthodox Church (1924-2008)], Крутицкое Патриаршее Под-ворье Общество Любителей Церковной Истории, Москва.

Smirnoff, Eugene, 1908, *A Short Account of the Historical Development and Present Position of Russian Orthodox Missions*, Rivingtons, London.

Smith, Anthony D., 1998, *Nationalism and Modernism*, Routledge, London and New York.

Smith, David J., 2005, "Non-territorial cultural autonomy as a Baltic contribution to Europe between the wars", in David J. Smith (ed.), *The Baltic States and their Region – New Europe or Old?*, Rodopi, Amsterdam and New York, p. 211-226.

Smolitsch, Igor, 1964, *Geschichte der Russischen Kirche 1700-1917*, Brill, Leiden.

Sohm, Rudolph, 1892, *Kirchenrecht I: die geschichtlichen Grundlagen*, Duncker und Humblot, Leipzig.

Sõtšov, Andrei, 2002, "Achievement of and Fight for Independence of the Orthodox Church of Estonia in 1940-1945", in Grigorios D. Papathomas and Matthias H. Palli (eds.), *The Autonomous Orthodox Church of Estonia*, Éditions Épektasis, Katérini, p. 285-305.

Sõtšov, Andrei, 2004, *Eesti õigeusu piiskopkond Stalini ajal aastail 1945-1953* [The Estonian Orthodox Eparchy during the Stalin years, 1945-1953], TÜ Kirjastus, Tallinn.

Sõtšov, Andrei, 2009, "Ecumenical Relations of the Orthodox Church", in Riho Altnurme (ed.), *History of Estonian Ecumenism*, Eesti Kirikute Nõukogu, Tartu and Tallinn, p. 62-82.

Staab, Nicolai, 2011, *Rumänische Kultur, Orthodoxie und der Westen*, Peter Lang, Frankfurt/Main et al.

Stamatopoulos, Dimitrios, 2006, "From Millets to Minorities in the 19th-Century Ottoman Empire: an Ambiguous Modernization", in S. G. Ellis, G. Hálfadanarson and A. K. Isaacs (eds.), *Citizenship in Historical Perspective*, Pisa University Press, Pisa, p. 253-273.

Stamatopoulos, Dimitrios, 2004, "The 'Return' of Religious and Historiographic Discourse: Church and Civil Society in Southeastern Europe (19th-20th centuries)", in *Journal for the Study of Religions & Ideologies*, 8, p. 64-75.

Stamoolis, James J., 1986, *Eastern Orthodox Mission Theology Today*, Orbis Books, Maryknoll, NY.

Starcs, P., 1954, "Latvijas pareizticīgo baznīca ārpus dzimtenes" [The Latvian Orthodox Church outside of the Fatherland], in H. Tichovsks (ed.), *Latviešu trimdas desmit gadi* [Ten Years of Latvian Exile], Astra Apgāds, Toronto, p. 47-49.

Stephany, Maximilian, 1931, *Konversion und Rekonversion in Livland*, G. Löffler, Riga.

Stokes, Gail, 1979, "Church and Class in early Balkan Nationalism", in *East European Quarterly*, 13/3, p. 259-270.

Straumīte, Indriķis, 1906, *Pareizticīgā latvieša Indriķa Straumīša raksti (1840.-1845.)* [The Writings of the Orthodox Latvian Indriķis Straumīte (1840-1845)], ed. by A. Kanger, Rīga.

Strods, Heinrihs, 1984, "Baltijas zemnieki un pareizticība (1841. g.-1864. g.)" [The Baltic peasants and Orthodoxy (1841-1864)], in *Latvijas agrārās vēstures jautājumi – Вопросы аграрной истории Латвии* [Questions of the agrarian history of Latvia], Latvijas Universitāte, Rīga, p. 79-125.

Strods, Heinrihs, 2005, *Metropolīts Augustīns Pētersons – Dzīve und darbs, 1873-1955* [Metropolitan Augustīns Pētersons – Life and Work, 1873-1955], AV Fonds, Riga.

Strods, Heinrihs, 2008, "Latvijas Pareizticīgā Baznīca. Vēstures komentārs" [The Latvian Orthodox Church. A historical commentary], in *Diena*, 02.04.2008, available at http://www.diena.lv/lat/izklaide/literatura/recenzijas/latvijas_pareizticiigaa_bazniica_veestures_komentaars [last accessed 15.03.2012].

Sugar, Peter F., 1996, "Nationalism and Religion in the Balkans since the Nineteenth Century", in *The Donald W. Treadgold Papers*, 8, p. 7-50; reprinted in Peter F. Sugar, 1999, *East European Nationalism, Politics and Religion*, Variorum, Aldershot, Hampshire, Text IX.

Sundhaussen, Holm, 2003, "Der Balkan: Ein Plädoyer für Differenz", in *Geschichte und Gesellschaft*, 29/4, p. 608-624.

Suttner, Ernst Christoph, 1997, "Die orthodoxe Kirche und das Aufkommen der Nationalstaaten in Südosteuropa", in Ernst Christoph Suttner (ed.), *Kirche und Nationen I*, Augustinus-Verlag, Würzburg, p. 235-248.

Suttner, Ernst Christoph, 1999, *Die Christenheit aus Ost und West auf der Suche nach dem sichtbaren Ausdruck für Ihre Einheit*, Augustinus-Verlag, Würzburg.

Suur, A., 1940, "Kinnisvarade kinnistamine ja 'kloostrisõda' Petserimaal" [The land registration and the 'Monastery War' in Petserimaa] in *Loodushoid ja Turism*, 2/2, p. 82-84.

Šejkin, 1997 = Шейкин, Геннадий, 1997, *Полоцкая епархия* [The Eparchy of Polotsk], Белорусское Православное Братство трех виленских мучеников, Минск.

Škarovskij, Michail V., 2005, "Orthodoxe estnische Gemeinden in Nordwestrussland im 19. und 20. Jahrhundert", in Olaf Mertelsmann (ed.), *Estland und Russland – Aspekte der Beziehungen zweier Länder*, Verlag Dr. Kovač, Hamburg, p. 213-228.

Šor, 2008 = Шор, Татьяна, 2008, "Крестный путь епископа Иоанна Печерского (Булина, 1893–1941)" [The way of the cross of Bishop Ioann of Petseri (Bulin, 1893-1941)], in *Альманах № XV*, available at http://www.humanitatis.info/15%20almanax/15%20scor.htm [last accessed 15.03.2012].

Talonen, Jouko, 2001, "Herrnhut and the Baltic Countries from 1730 to the Present: Cultural Perspectives", in Riho Altnurme (ed.), *Estnische Kirchengeschichte im vorigen Jahrtausend*, Wittig, Kiel, p. 98-108.

Talonen, Jouko, 2008, *Latvian kansallisen teologian synty* [The Birth of Latvian National Theology], Societas Historica Finlandiae Septentrionalis, Rovaniemi.

Thaden, Edward C., 1969, "N. A. Manaseins Senatorenrevision in Livland und Kurland während der Zeit von 1882 bis 1883" in *Jahrbücher für die Geschichte Osteuropas*, 17/1, p. 45-58.

Thaden, Edward C. (ed.), 1981, *Russification in the Baltic Provinces and Finland, 1855-1914*, Princeton University Press, Princeton, NJ.

Thaden, Edward C., 1986, "Iurii Fedorovich Samarin and Baltic History", in *Journal of Baltic Studies*, 17/4, p. 321-328.

Thijs, Krijn, 2008, "The Metaphor of the Master: 'Narrative Hierarchy' in National Historical Cultures in Europe", in Stefan Berger and Chris Lorenz (eds.), *The Contested Nation – Ethnicity, Class, Religion and Gender in National Histories*, Palgrave Macmillan, Houndmills, Basingstoke, p. 60-74.

Timmermann, Heiner, 1998, "Nationalbewegungen und Nationalismus in Europa: Wurzeln und Entwicklungen", in Heiner Timmermann (ed.), *Entwicklung der Nationalbewegungen in Europe 1850-1914*, Duncker und Humblot, Berlin, p. 11-16.

Tõnissoo, J., 1951, "Apostlik õigeusk Eestis" [Apostolic Orthodoxy in Estonia], in *Apostlik õigeusk 100 aastat Eestis* [100 Years of Apostolic Orthodoxy in Estonia], Vetlanda Trykkeriet, Vetlanda, p. 17-20.

von Transehe, Astav, 1907, *Die lettische Revolution*, Georg Reimer, Berlin.

Treulieb, Eberhard, 1965, "Metropolit Sergij von Riga und die 'Orthodoxe Mission' in Pleskau", in *Kirche im Osten*, 8, p. 55-66.

Tschoerner, Helmut, 2005, *Kirchenordnungen und Statute der Evangelisch-Lutherischen Kirche in Rußland – von 1832 bis 1924*, Martin-Luther-Verlag, Erlangen.

Tuchtenhagen, Ralph, 1995, *Religion als minderer Status*, Peter Lang, Frankfurt/Main.

Tupits, Karl (ed.), 1934, *K. Päts: Tema elu ja töö, kaasaeglaste mälestus* [K. Päts: His life and work, memories of contemporaries], Ühiselu, Tallinn.

Turda, Marius, 2008, "National Historiographies in the Balkans, 1830-1989", in Stefan Berger and Chris Lorenz (eds.), *The Contested Nation – Ethnicity, Class, Religion and Gender in National Histories*, Palgrave Macmillan, Houndmills, Basingstoke, p. 463-489.

Unāms, Žanis, 1975 [1940], *Es viņu pazīstu* [I know him], 2nd ed., Raven Printing, Grand Haven, MI.

Ustav, Karl, 1914, "Õigeusulised eestlased Pihkva mail" [Orthodox Estonians in the Pskov lands], in Konstantin Kokla (ed.), *Eesti õigeusuliste kalender 1915 a.* [Calendar for Estonian Orthodox, 1915], p. 57-8.

Valk, Pille, 1997, *Ühest heledast laigust Eesti kooli ajaloos: Usuõpetus Eesti koolidel aastatel 1918-1940* [One Dark Spot in Estonian School History: Religious Education in Estonian Schools 1918-1940], Logos, Tallinn.

Vāvere, Vera, 1992, "Pāvils Gruzna un viņa romāni 'Bursaki' un 'Jaunā Strāva'" [Pāvils Gruzna and his novels 'Bursaki' and 'Jaunā Strāva'], in Pāvils Gruzna, *Bursaki – Jaunā Strāva* [The Seminarians – the Modern Current], "Zinātne", Riga, p. 5-30.

Viscuso, Patrick, 2006, *A Quest for Reform of the Orthodox Church – The 1923 Pan-Orthodox Congress*, InterOrthodox Press, Berkeley, CA.

de Vries, Wilhelm, 1980, "Entstehung und Entwicklung der autonomen Ostkirchen im ersten Jahrtausend", in *Kanon IV – Jahrbuch der Gesellschaft für das Recht der Ostkirchen*, Herder, Wien, p. 45-67.

Waldorff, Friedrich, 1891, *Die lutherische Kirche im Kampfe mit Panslawismus und ‚Orthodoxie'*, Chr. Belser, Stuttgart.

Waldron, Peter, 2005, "Late Imperial Constitutionalism" in Ian D. Thatcher (ed.), *Late Imperial Russia – Problems and Prospects*, Manchester University Press, Manchester, p. 28-43.

Walicki, Andrzej, 1992, *Legal Philosophies of Russian Liberalism*, University of Notre Dame Press, Notre Dame and London.

Weber, Max, 1919, "Wissenschaft als Beruf", in Max Weber, 1968, *Gesammelte Aufsätze zur Wissenschaftslehre*, J.C.B. Mohr, Tübingen, p. 582-613.

Weber, Renate, 1993, *Die Russische Orthodoxie im Aufbruch: Kirche, Gesellschaft und Staat im Spiegel der geistlichen Zeitschriften (1860-1905)*, Hieronymos, München.

Weeks, Theodore R., 1996, "The 'End' of the Uniate Church in Russia: The *Vozsoedinenie* of 1875", in *Jahrbücher für die Geschichte Osteuropas*, 44, p. 28-40.

Weeks, Theodore R., 2001, "Between Rome and Tsargrad: The Uniate Church in Imperial Russia", in Robert P. Geraci and Michael Khodarkovsky (eds.), *Of Religion and Empire: Missions, Conversion, and Tolerance in Tsarist Russia*, Cornell University Press, Ithaca et al., p. 70-91.

Wendland, Anna Veronika, 2003, "Volksgeschichte im Baltikum? Historiographien zwischen nationaler Mobilisierung und wissenschaftlicher Innovation in Estland, Lettland und Litauen (1919-1939)", in Manfred Hettling (ed.), *Volksgeschichten im Europa der Zwischenkriegszeit*, Vandenhoeck & Ruprecht, Göttingen, p. 205-238.

Wendland, Anna Veronika, 2008, "The Russian Empire and its Western Borderlands: National Historiographies and Their 'Others' in Russia, the Baltics and Ukraine", in Stefan Berger and Chris Lorenz (eds.), *The Contested Nation – Ethnicity, Class, Religion and Gender in National Histories*, Palgrave Macmillan, Houndmills, Basingstoke, p. 405-441.

Werth, Paul W., 2007, "Arbiters of the Free Conscience: State, Religion, and the Problem of Confessional Transfer after 1905", in Mark D. Steinberg and Heather J. Coleman (eds.), *Sacred Stories: Religion and Spirituality in Modern Russia*, Indiana University Press, Bloomington, IN, p. 179-199.

Wittig, Andreas Michael, 1987, *Die orthodoxe Kirche in Griechenland*, Augustinus-Verlag, Würzburg.

Wittram, Heinrich, 1956, "Theologie und Kirche in den Ostseeprovinzen in der Auseinandersetzung mit der kritischen Theologie und den modernen Strömungen Deutschlands", in Reinhard Wittram (ed.), *Baltische Kirchengeschichte*, Vandenhoeck & Ruprecht, Göttingen, p. 220-243.

Wittram, Heinrich, 2005, "Eduard Steinwand (1890-1960). Weite und Tiefe religiöser Existenz in der Begegnung zwischen westlichem und östlichem Christentum", in Heinrich Wittram, 2011, *Einblicke in die baltische Kirchengeschichte*, cmz, Rheinbach, p. 439-464.

Wittram, Reinhard (ed.), 1956, *Baltische Kirchengeschichte*, Vandenhoeck & Ruprecht, Göttingen.

Wittram, Reinhard, 1973 [1954], *Baltische Geschichte*, 2nd revised ed., Wissenschaftliche Buchgesellschaft, Darmstadt.

Zālītis, Frīdis, 1921, *Latvijas vēsture skolam un pašmācībai* [Latvian History for Schools and Independent Learning], V. Olava Fondes Izdevums, Rīga.

Zālītis, Frīdis, 1937, *Latvijas vēsture vidusskolām* [Latvian History for Middle Schools], 8th ed., Valters un Rapa, Rīga.

Zariņš, Jānis, 1939, *Pareizticīgās baznīcas un tās mantas tiesiskais stāvoklis Latvijā* [The Orthodox Church Properties and their legal status in Latvia], Latvijas Pareizticīgas Baznīcas Sinodes Izdevums, Rīga.

Zellis, Kaspars, 2009, "Die Schlacht bei Cēsis, die Esten und das historische Bewusstsein der Letten", in Mati Laur and Karsten Brüggemann (eds.), *Forschungen zur baltischen Geschichte, Band 4*, p. 170-189.

Zernov, Nicolas, 2004 [1954], "The Eastern Churches and the Ecumenical Movement in the Twentieth Century", in Ruth Rouse and Stephen Charles Neill (eds.), *A History of the Ecumenical Movement – Volume 1 (1517-1948)*, World Council of Churches, Geneva, p. 643-674.

Žitie, 2008 = *Житие святаго священномученика Иоанна, Архиепископа Рижского* [The Life of the Holy Martyr Ioann, Archbishop of Riga], Издание Кафедральная собора Рождества Христова, Rīga.

Index of Places

In this index of places, the pages that are indicated with *italics* refer to mentions in the footnotes.

---

[*] Clerical Council of the Russian Parishes of the Estonian Orthodox Church

Index of Names

In this index of names, the pages that are indicated with *italics* refer to mentions in the footnotes. Those that are **bold** refer to the brief biographies in chapter 6.4.

Erfurter Studien zur Kulturgeschichte des Orthodoxen Christentums

Herausgegeben von Vasilios N. Makrides

Band 1 Vasilios N. Makrides (Hrsg.): Religion, Staat und Konfliktkonstellationen im orthodoxen Ost- und Südosteuropa. Vergleichende Perspektiven. 2005.

Band 2 Klaus Buchenau: Kämpfende Kirchen. Jugoslawiens religiöse Hypothek. 2006.

Band 3 Angelos Giannakopoulos: Tradition und Moderne in Griechenland. Konfliktfelder in Religion, Politik und Kultur. 2007.

Band 4 Kristina Stoeckl: Community after Totalitarianism. The Russian Orthodox Intellectual Tradition and the Philosophical Discourse of Political Modernity. 2008.

Band 5 Nicolai Staab: Rumänische Kultur, Orthodoxie und der Westen. Der Diskurs um die nationale Identität in Rumänien aus der Zwischenkriegszeit. 2011.

Band 6 Sebastian Rimestad: The Challenges of Modernity to the Orthodox Church in Estonia and Latvia (1917-1940). 2012

www.peterlang.de